THE WAR IN ITALY
1943–1944

DESPATCHES FROM THE FRONT

The Commanding Officers' Reports From the Field and At Sea.

THE WAR IN ITALY
1943–1944

Introduced and compiled by
Martin Mace and John Grehan
With additional research by
Sara Mitchell

Pen & Sword
MILITARY

First published in Great Britain in 2014 by
Pen & Sword Military
an imprint of
Pen & Sword Books Ltd
47 Church Street
Barnsley
South Yorkshire
S70 2AS

ISBN 978 1 78346 213 1

Printed and bound in England
By CPI Group (UK) Ltd, Croydon, CR0 4YY

Pen & Sword Books Ltd incorporates the Imprints of
Pen & Sword Aviation, Pen & Sword Family History,
Pen & Sword Maritime, Pen & Sword Military, Pen & Sword Discovery, Pen &
Sword Politics, Pen & Sword Atlas, Pen & Sword Archaeology, Wharncliffe Local
History, Wharncliffe True Crime, Wharncliffe Transport, Pen & Sword Select, Pen
& Sword Military Classics, Leo Cooper,
The Praetorian Press, Claymore Press, Remember When,
Seaforth Publishing and Frontline Publishing.

For a complete list of Pen & Sword titles please contact:
PEN & SWORD BOOKS LIMITED
47 Church Street, Barnsley, South Yorkshire, S70 2AS, England
E-mail: enquiries@pen-and-sword.co.uk

Website: www.pen-and-sword.co.uk

CONTENTS

INTRODUCTION

It had been decided at the Casablanca Conference in January 1943 that following the complete defeat of the Axis forces in North Africa, the invasion of Italy could be undertaken. The first step was to occupy Sicily and this operation forms the first despatch in this book. In the planning for the invasion of Sicily it was expected that the enemy forces on the island would amount to eight mobile divisions and five coastal defence divisions. The worry was that two of these might be German divisions and this led the Joint Planning Staff to warn that: "We are doubtful of the chances of success against a garrison which includes German formations."

The man given responsibility for the operation, Field Marshal Harold Alexander, thought that this was "too strongly expressed" and he insisted on pressing ahead. Interestingly, he was possibly more concerned that the Germans would be in charge of the defence of the island than of the number of troops they had there. German organisation and efficiency would improve the Italian forces chances of repelling the invaders.

The balance of forces was also roughly even. Equally, whilst the Allies would be able to choose the time and place of attack, the large number of troops that would be needed to overcome the enemy meant that the invading forces could not be landed together would have to be widely dispersed. It was also expected that the Italians would show a greater determination to defend their own soil than they had shown in the fighting in North Africa. Furthermore, Alexander points out, the assault upon Sicily was the first large-scale amphibious operation in the war against a defended coastline and facing opponents equipped with modern weapons. The recollections of what had happened at Gallipoli in 1915 must have weighed heavily on Alexander's mind.

The various, and changing, plans form a large part, around half, of the content of this first despatch. As Alexander points out, one of the most difficult tasks he faced was co-ordinating the forces for a simultaneous assault, as those forces were despatched from all over the southern and eastern shores of the Mediterranean as well as from the United Kingdom and United States.

The air operation was also on an unprecedented scale. The air attacks upon Sicily began almost as soon as the battle for Tunis had ended with raids upon the island's infrastructure and enemy installations. For the entire operation *Husky*, the total aircraft employed, including transports but excluding gliders, amounted to over four thousand, which came from 110 British and 132 American squadrons.

Though not every element of the operation was a great success, especially the airborne assault which was a marked failure, the capture of Sicily was achieved in just thirty-eight days

A highly detailed description of the naval element to the invasion of Sicily is included in Admiral Andrew Cunningham's despatch. This takes the form of a narrative provided by Vice-Admiral Bertram Ramsay, who was the commander of the Eastern Task Force.

Admiral Cunningham is also the author of a despatch concerning the Salerno landings. The reason why the Gulf of Salerno was chosen for the landing of the Allied forces which began on 9 August 1943 was its proximity to Naples, the port of which was considered essential as a base from which the rest of Italy could be subdued. Operation *Avalanche* came perilously close to failure with the Germans defending their positions with, as Cunningham described it, "a ferocity which we have now come to regard as normal."

The despatch dealing with the rest of the operations in Italy forms the bulk of this volume, amounting to almost 100,000 words and represents possibly the most detailed analysis of this important campaign ever published. It is complemented by Orders of Battle of both the Axis and Allied armies at different stages of the campaign.

The Italian theatre was never intended to be the main focus of operations for either the Allies or for the Germans. It was understood by both sides that the ultimate victory would be won on the Eastern and Western fronts. Italy was a sideshow with the objective of bringing to battle the maximum number of German troops thus preventing their deployment to the main theatres. This was also the principle objective of the Germans – to tie down large numbers of Allied troops thus reducing the numbers that could be sent against northern Europe in what everyone knew would be the decisive operation.

It was with this in mind that Alexander planned his moves. "At every minute of the campaign, therefore, I had to pose to myself the question, who was containing whom in Italy?" He wrote. "This was the vital question for the Germans also, and to them the answer can never have been satisfactory. In all, forty-five German divisions were employed in Italy, together with four Italian regular divisions, one Cossack division and miscellaneous formations of Czechs, Slovaks and Russians. The Allies employed in Italy a total of forty divisions of which eight were transferred to Western front in 1943 and ten in 1944 and followed by three diverted to the Balkans." Not all of these forces were employed at any one time, but throughout the fighting, the Axis forces employed generally exceeded those of the Allies.

The operations of the Allied forces could not just be of a holding nature. A real possibility was that if a large part of Italy could be occupied by the Allies, the Italians might be forced to capitulate. Though as Alexander stated, the Italian troops were not of the finest quality, they did perform important garrison duties throughout many Axis-occupied territories. In the summer of 1943 Italy still had seven divisions in Southern France, extending as far west as Marseilles, and no less than thirty-two in the Balkans, together with many non-divisional anti-aircraft and coast defence units in both theatres. If Italy withdrew from the war the loss of these garrisons would thrown a severe strain upon the Germans.

Fortunately, just before the invasion began in earnest, and far earlier than had been expected, the Italians surrendered, on 8 September. Alexander now only had to contend with the Germans.

There were, of course, two principle factors that assisted Alexander. Firstly, as the aggressor, he was in many instances able to chose the time and place of his offensive operations, though the nature of the terrain and the location of the major population centres limited his choices. Many of the key objectives were also obvious to both sides, making surprise impossible.

The second factor was, as Alexander, put it 'psychological'. Once the Italians had surrendered, there was nothing to be gained by attempting to hold the entire country. The obvious line of defence for the Germans was the Apennines, where indeed they built the fortifications known as the 'Gothic Line'. With relatively few troops these defences could have been held against frontal assault indefinitely. The Allies would not have wasted lives attacking such formidable positions and the Italian theatre of operations would have drifted into stalemate.

But, what Alexander called Hitler's "well-known reluctance, exhibited both previously and subsequently, to yield any ground without a fight," meant that the Germans were forced to commit troops to hold territory that otherwise would have been abandoned.

Alexander's conclusion is a fitting one also for this brief introduction. "It was the Germans therefore, who were contained in Italy and not the Allies; the Italian campaign drained their strength more than ours. The reasons why the Germans decided to fight in Italy rather than withdraw to the Alps I have already discussed; they were not, or at least the more important were not, military reasons but political. Perhaps the future German historian, if he is as eager as his predecessors have always been to extol the virtues of Prussian military science, will admit the folly of protracted resistance in Italy and, throwing the blame on a megalomaniac Fuehrer, will seek consolation by pointing to the bravery and stubbornness in defence of the German soldier. He will be justified in so doing; but a still finer theme will be that of the historian who describes how that stubborn defence and the barrier of so many mountains and rivers were triumphantly overcome by the Allies."

*

The objective of this book is to reproduce the despatches of Alexander and Cunningham exactly as they first appeared to the general public some seventy years ago. They have not been modified or edited in any way and are therefore the original and unique words of the commanding officers as they saw things at the time. The only change is the manner in which the footnotes are presented, in that they are shown at the end of each despatch rather than at the bottom of the relevant page as they appear in the original despatch. Any grammatical or spelling errors have been left uncorrected to retain the authenticity of the documents.

List of Illustrations

9   A photograph of a 240mm howitzer of 'B' Battery, 697th Field Artillery Battalion, US Fifth Army, taken just before it fires into German-held territory around Monte Cassino, Italy, on 30 January 1944.

10   German vehicles destroyed during an Allied air attack north of Cassino, Italy, in 1944. The halftrack artillery tractor carries the identification plate WH1028 348. (US National Archives)

11   Bombs lie on an Allied airfield in Italy ready to be loaded into RAF Consolidated B-24 Liberators during January 1944. (US National Archives)

12   The aftermath of one of the most successful German attacks on Allied shipping of the Second World War. During the raid on Bari Harbour on 2 December 1943, 105 Junkers Ju 88s of *Luftflotte 2*, achieving complete surprise, bombed shipping and personnel operating in support of the Allied campaign in Italy, sinking twenty-seven cargo and transport ships and a schooner in Bari harbour. (The James Luto Collection)

13   Another view of the devastation at Bari during the *Luftwaffe* attack on 2 December 1943. Not for nothing has the raid been called, with some justification, "The Second Pearl Harbor". One of the merchant vessels destroyed – the U.S. Liberty Ship *John Harvey* – had been carrying a quantity of mustard gas bombs which exploded with devastating consequences. (The James Luto Collection)

14   British gunners are pictured preparing to fire on enemy positions during the fighting in and around the Serchio Valley in late 1944. The Allied intention was to dislodge German troops from a number of well-defended, but important, positions. (Historic Military Press)

15   A Consolidated B-24 Liberator of No.205 Group flies over the target area during a daylight attack on the port of Monfalcone, Italy. Smoke from exploding bombs can be seen rising from the shipbuilding and repair yards and other installations in the harbour.

16   US troops in action during the Battle of Garfagnana, 26–28 December 1944. Known to the Germans as Operation *Unternehmen Wintergewitter* ("Winter Storm") and nicknamed the "Christmas Offensive", this was an Axis offensive on the western sector of the Gothic Line in the north Tuscan Apennines, near Massa and Lucca. (US National Archives)

1

VISCOUNT ALEXANDER'S DESPATCH ON THE CONQUEST OF SICILY

10 JULY TO 17 AUGUST 1943

The War Office, February, 1948

THE CONQUEST OF SICILY FROM IOTH JULY, 1943 TO I7TH AUGUST, I943

The following Despatch was submitted to the Secretary of State for War on 9th October, 1946, by HIS EXCELLENCY FIELD-MARSHAL THE VISCOUNT ALEXANDER OF TUNIS, K.G., G.C.B., G.C.M.G., C.S.I., D.S.O., M.C., former General Officer Commanding-in-Chief, Fifteenth Army Group.

The Decision.

At the Casablanca conference in mid-January, I943, it was decided by the Prime Minister and President Roosevelt, assisted by the Combined Chiefs of Staff, that after Africa had been finally cleared of the enemy the island of Sicily should be assaulted and captured as a base for operations against Southern Europe and to open the Mediterranean to the shipping of the United Nations. I attended the conference and was designated the Commander-in-Chief of the group of Armies entrusted with the operation. As I was also appointed to an identical rôle in command of the operations then proceeding in Tunisia, in which I was soon involved in the day to day conduct of an intricate and difficult battle situation, it was not possible for me to take direct control immediately of the planning of the operations. A tentative outline plan had already been produced by the Joint Planning Staff in London, supplemented at Casablanca, and this was given, as a basis on which to work, to the nucleus of my future Headquarters, known for security purposes as "Force 141," which assembled at Bouzarea, near Algiers, on 12th February, 1943. This planning staff was headed by Major-General C.H. Gairdner, as Chief of General Staff.[1] The operation was given the code name HUSKY.

Although provision had thus been early made for the planning of the operation it was none the less surrounded with great difficulties. The prerequisite that the whole of the North African coastline should be cleared of the enemy meant that the battle in Tunisia took first priority and, until that was concluded, it would be impossible to know what resources would be available for the invasion of Sicily. The question of the date to be aimed at was also affected. It was calculated at Casablanca that the Tunisian campaign would be completed by 1st May and the target date for Sicily was provisionally fixed at the favourable moon period in July. The Combined Chiefs of Staff subsequently directed that an attempt should be made to advance this date to the corresponding period in June. This proved impossible, owing to the need for adequate training for the assaulting divisions and the preparation of the necessary administrative basis for the operation, and on 15th April the Combined Chiefs of Staff agreed that 10th July should be the target date.

Elements of the Problem.

The problems to which the main attention could be directed in the early stages of planning were those presented by geography and logistics and the probable scale of enemy resistance. The island of Sicily has been compared to "a jagged arrowhead with the broken point to the west." The total area is about ten thousand square miles, the greatest measurement from east to west is one hundred and fifty miles and the length of the coastline is about six hundred miles. In the north-eastern corner Cape Peloro is separated from the peninsula of Calabria by the Straits of Messina, only two miles at their narrowest. Cape Passero, the south-eastern corner, scene of a British naval victory in 1718, is about fifty-five miles due north of the island of Malta and about four hundred miles from Benghazi. At the western end of the island Cape Boeo (also known as Cape Lilibeo) is about ninety miles to the northeast of Cape Bon in Tunisia. In the straits between Tunisia and Sicily lies Pantelleria which the Italians claimed to have transformed into a fortress of a strength to rival Malta.

The greater part of Sicily is mountainous with many peaks over three thousand feet. The most extensive plain lies south and west of Catania, dominated by the conical peak of Etna. All round the coast, however, except for a short stretch on the north coast, there is a narrow strip of low-lying country through which runs the main road encircling the island. The coastline is divided into a series of wide-sweeping bights, separated from each other by more or less prominent capes. Over ninety stretches of beach were enumerated by the planning staff, ranging from less than a hundreds yards to many miles in length, usually of sand but sometimes of shingle; offshore gradients were in most cases rather shallow. These beaches generally admit direct access into the narrow coastal strip. The main ports, in order of importance, are Messina in the north-east, Palermo in the north-west, Catania and Syracuse on the east coast; none of these is a first class port and their daily clearance capacity was reckoned, after making due allowance for possible damage from air bombardment and demolitions, at four to five thousand tons per day for Messina, two thousand five hundred for Palermo, one thousand eight hundred for Catania and one thousand for Syracuse. Minor ports, all reckoned as having a capacity of about six hundred tons per day, are Augusta on the east coast (mainly a naval base with a good protected anchorage), Licata and Porto Empedocle on the south coast and Trapani on the west coast.

There were nineteen known airfields in Sicily when planning started, a figure which was subsequently raised by new construction to over thirty at the time of the attack. They fell into three main groups, in the east, south-east and west of the island. The first two were mutually self-supporting but could neither afford fighter cover to the western group nor be themselves covered from there. All were situated within some fifteen miles of the coast. Most important for the German Air Force was the eastern group, Catania-Gerbini; there were important supply and operational organisations here and the capture of the area would probably mean that the German Air Force could no longer operate effectively in Sicily. If we could bring these airfields into operation we could cover the Straits of Messina, only sixty-five miles away, and the German Air Force would be driven back on Naples and Brindisi, both about two hundred miles away, for the three small airfields in the toe of Italy were only suitable for use as advanced landing grounds.

It was more difficult to calculate the probable strength of the enemy defending forces. The greater part of these were known to be Italian and in January there were in the island three regular infantry divisions and five "coastal" divisions. The latter were composed of lower quality troops than the ordinary divisions, had a lower scale of equipment and were almost entirely non-mobile. Their task was to man the coastal defences and to form a covering screen to break the first impact of an assault and allow time for the intervention of the "field" divisions. The major interest centred on the latter. It was reasonable to expect that the Italians would wish to increase the garrison of so important and so obviously threatened a portion of their metropolitan territory and, to be on the safe side, we calculated that by July the garrison would probably have risen to a total of eight mobile divisions, excluding the coastal divisions. It would be easy to reinforce, for communications were excellent, the train ferries at Messina could move up to forty thousand men in twenty-four hours or, in the same period, seven thousand five hundred men and seven hundred and fifty vehicles.

We were naturally particularly interested in the prospects of reinforcement by German troops. There were already in Sicily extensive German Air Force establishments, which included detachments for the ground defence of airfields as well as anti-aircraft gunners and the normal Air Force service troops, and there was also a fluctuating number of German troops at various points, particularly in the west, representing units in transit in Tunisia. Perhaps, when resistance ceased in Tunisia, it might be found that the Germans had been able to evacuate sufficient troops to Sicily to make a considerable difference to the strength of the island garrison. In any event it was likely that Germany would consider it necessary to reinforce the Italians and it was calculated that two out of the eight divisions expected as the strength of the garrison might be German. The Joint Planning Staff, in their original report, felt it necessary to state, "We are doubtful of the chances of success against a garrison which includes German formations." This seemed to me to be too strongly expressed, but all the commanders concerned agreed that if the Italians should be reinforced with substantial, well-equipped German forces before the attack the chances of success would be considerably reduced, not only because of the superior fighting quality of the Germans but because, if the German proportion of the garrison approached parity with the Italian, they would certainly demand a share, probably the predominant share, in the direction of the operations.

The First Plan.

When the headquarters of Force I4I was set up in Bouzarea on I2th February, I943, the basis on which the staff were in the first instance to work was the plan drawn up for the Casablanca conference. This was accepted by me as a preliminary and tentative basis of planning, though I realised, from such attention as I had been able to give it, that it would undoubtedly need modification when I should be free to give my mind wholly to it. Certain elements were bound to remain constant. It was clear, as laid down in the plan, that for many reasons the operation would have to be a joint Anglo-American undertaking. Each nation would provide a task force of Army size commanded respectively by General Montgomery[2] and General Patton.[3] Naval and Air forces would be also jointly provided and commanded by Admiral Sir Andrew Cunningham [4] and Air Chief Marshal Tedder.[5] The British assault force would be mounted mainly from the Middle East Command and the United States force from North Africa.

The strategic conception of the operation was influenced very largely by administrative considerations. It was still an essential element of the doctrine of amphibious warfare that sufficient major ports must be captured within a very short time of the initial landings to maintain all the forces required for the attainment of the objectives; beach maintenance could only be relied on as a very temporary measure. The experiences of operation TORCH, the North African landing, though difficult to interpret in view of the special circumstances of that operation, were held to confirm this view. This meant that attention was at once directed to the three major ports of Messina, Catania and Palermo. Messina was clearly out of the question as an immediate objective. It was strongly defended, difficult of access and well out of range of air cover that had to be provided from Tunisia and Malta. An assault on Catania could be given air cover, though the port itself was at the extreme end of our range, and successful exploitation would give us control of the main group of enemy airfields in the island, from which it would be possible to provide cover over the Straits of Messina, our final objective. On the other hand it was calculated that the port could only maintain four divisions in the first month and six divisions subsequently, and this would be insufficient for the reduction of the whole island. Palermo would give us sufficient maintenance facilities provided the enemy allowed us time enough to build up to the strength required. The disadvantages of an assault in that area were that it left the enemy in possession of Catania and Messina through which to reinforce, and the eastern and south-eastern groups of airfields, while exploitation towards Messina, our final objective, would be difficult.

The plan therefore proposed a simultaneous assault in the west and south-east. On D-day the Eastern Task Force (British) was to land at four points, Avola, Pachino, Pozzallo and Gela, with forces totalling three infantry divisions, four parachute and two tank battalions. The tasks of the force were to capture the ports of Syracuse and Augusta and the airfields at Pachino, Comiso and Ponte Olivo. At the same time an American force of one infantry division and a tank battalion from the Western Task Force (United States) was to land at Sciacca and Marinella in the south-western corner of the island to capture the airfields, in particular the large airfield at Castelvetrano, in order to be able to provide air cover over the landings in the Palermo area. On D plus 2 the main American landings would be made in the Palermo area, from the Gulf of Castellammare to Cape Zaffarano, east of the port, in a total strength of two infantry divisions and two tank battalions. The tasks of this force were to capture Palermo and cut off the enemy in the west of the island by linking up with the force at Castelvetrano. On D plus 3 the Eastern Task Force was to make another landing, with one infantry division, plus a brigade group, and an airborne division, in the Catania area, to capture the port and the Gerbini group of airfields. A reserve division was allotted to each

Task Force, to follow up into Catania and Palermo, when secured, and by D plus 7 it was hoped that sufficient forces would be ashore to deal with any forces which could be brought against them.

Modification of the First Plan.

The month of February and the early days of March were the most critical periods in Tunisia, where I assumed command on 19th February, and it was impossible for me to give the plans for Sicily any detailed attention. I did, however, suggest certain modifications to General Gairdner when he saw me at the end of February, for the consideration of his planning staff. These were directed to eliminate certain unsatisfactory points, in the original London plan; to ensure, for instance, that divisions were employed as such and not split up unnecessarily, to provide a Force Reserve and to ensure a more concentrated use of our airborne forces to neutralise the beach defences by cancelling a proposed operation against communications in Calabria. I also considered at this time concentrating the efforts of both Task Forces against the south-eastern corner of the island. This was a proposal to which I was later to return but on first consideration it was rejected on the ground that port facilities in this area would be insufficient to support our whole force, and it still seemed essential to ensure the early capture of Palermo. To overrun the island if defended by a garrison of eight enemy divisions, which was the current Intelligence estimate of the probable enemy strength, would require at least ten divisions and I was informed that only with the use of both Palermo and Catania could we be sure of maintaining that number.

It would be unnecessary to describe in detail the many conferences at which the strategy of the attack was thrashed out until they resulted in the adoption of the final plan. Nor need I emphasise again the difficulties involved; I myself and my two future Army commanders were engaged actively in the field and even when a conference would have been physically possible the hazards of air communications in the uncertain weather of a North African spring often meant that we could not meet. The staff at Bouzarea were short-handed and many of the heads of branches, still fully employed at my Eighteenth Army Group Headquarters, were unable to take over as yet or divert their attention from the Tunisian battle. All that was possible was to work out loading tables, training schedules and all such matters which must of necessity be taken in hand long before the date of the assault, while preserving complete flexibility of mind about the objectives which might eventually be selected for the assault. Flexibility was, indeed, the keynote of the whole planning period and every proposed solution was examined on its own merits. It is for this reason that it is difficult to show in detail how the final plan grew to completion but it will be useful to consider the main aspects that presented themselves and sketch the way in which they contributed to the ultimate solution.

The air situation received my first attention. From our bases in Malta and Tunisia we could give air cover over the southern half of Sicily south of a line running from Trapani to Catania; both these two places, however, were near to the limit of effective air action. The plan provided for an early attack on all three groups of airfields, but at the cost of a loss of concentration. The Eastern Task Force, in particular, would be dispersed in assaults all along the coast between Catania and Gela. This raised serious doubts as to whether it would be strong enough at the crucial point, the landing at Avola; it was vital that there should be no risk of failure here, for the whole enterprise depended on seizing the ports of Syracuse and Augusta, and if possible Catania, very soon after landing. The plan entrusted this task to one division and one brigade, only a third of the total force, and it was apparently impossible to increase this except by abandoning one of the other landings. The obvious solution was to divert the division which it was intended to land at Gela, and this was suggested by General Montgomery. On the other hand Air Chief Marshal Tedder pointed out that Ponte Olivo, the airfield centre inland from Gela, had been developed into a first class air base and unless it were captured for our use our air forces would labour under an intolerable situation. Admiral Cunningham agreed, from the naval point of view, that the risk of allowing the enemy air forces to operate from the south-eastern group of airfields would be unacceptable.

This was a serious dilemma since both the arguments for strengthening the east coast assault and for the early capture of the airfields inland from Gela were overwhelmingly strong. My first solution was to transfer to the Avola assault the division assigned to Gela and entrust the latter assault to an American division, transferred from the landings at Sciacca – Marinella, which would therefore have to be cancelled. It was not a satisfactory solution, for I was unwilling to put an isolated American division under command of Eighth Army, but it seemed the best available. Air cover for the assault on Palermo would now have to be given from the south-eastern group of airfields, when captured, and this would cause some delay. I recommended this change of plan to General Eisenhower on 19th March and at a conference on 20th March he agreed to it. My staff continued, however, to explore the possibility of mounting another British division and by 6th April it had been found possible to provide one from Middle East which would stage at Malta. I therefore, in the new plan which was presented on 6th April, restored the American assault at Sciacca – Marinella, added an armoured brigade to the Avola landing and still left the Eastern Task Force with a reserve division which could either be used for the landings south of Catania, as originally planned, or, as now seemed more likely, put in to support the main landings on the south-eastern coast. The western, American, assaults were put back a little, the Sciacca – Marinella landing to D plus 2 and Palermo to D plus 5 or later.

So far changes which had been adopted had represented only modifications of the plan as prepared by the Joint Planning Staff in London but as the time for a final decision approached I began to consider more and more the dangers presented by the dispersal of our forces. It was particularly difficult to estimate the likely scale of enemy resistance, and even our calculations of the fighting value of enemy troops seemed possibly subject to error. General Montgomery shared the same views. In a signal to me on 24th April he said: "Planning so far has been based on the assumption that the opposition will be slight and that Sicily will be captured relatively easily.[6] Never was there a greater error. The Germans and also the Italians are fighting desperately now in Tunisia and will do so in Sicily." Indeed it was only natural to expect that the Italians would show some reasonable spirit in defence of their own soil for they were at that time, to our surprise, stubbornly resisting the Eighth Army attack on the Enfidaville positions. The estimate on which we were working, as already stated, assumed an enemy garrison of two German and six Italian mobile divisions and five Italian coastal divisions, against which we were bringing a force of just over ten divisions with two more in reserve. From the point of view of numbers, therefore, we had no actual superiority and such advantages as we enjoyed – the initiative to attack where we chose, command of sea and air, and a certain superiority in equipment, at least over the Italians – would be diminished by dispersion. Moreover, it must be remembered when considering the frame of mind in which we set out on this expedition that this was the first large-scale amphibious operation in the war against a defended coastline and opponents equipped with modern weapons. I am not belittling in any way the landings of 8th November, 1942, but the description I have given above could not be applied to the resistance met on that occasion and we could not expect the fighting in Sicily to cease as quickly as it had done in Algeria and Morocco. No care was too great to ensure that our first landing in Europe should be successful beyond doubt.

With the end of the fighting in Africa the enemy picture had become clearer. One extra Italian mobile division had been added to the garrison and the German forces in the island were reckoned as the equivalent of one division; but none of the forces in Africa had escaped and any further reinforcement must come from the mainland of Italy, from Germany and from enemy-occupied countries. There was still time, and excellent communications, to admit of such a reinforcement. The whole question of comparative strengths was due for discussion at a new conference on 27th April in Algiers.

The conference was eventually called, after some mishaps, on 29th April and attention was at once directed to proposals for strengthening the assault in the south-east. General Leese[7] represented Eighth Army's point of view. He argued that the Army was, on the present plan, divided into two halves which were too widely separated to be able to support each other and possibly too weak for either to be able to achieve their respective objects. He therefore proposed that both Corps should assault the east coast, one in the area of Avola and the other on either side of the Pachino peninsula (Cape Passero); this would give a firm base for the conquest of the island. Admiral Cunningham did not approve of the suggested change. Apart from his conviction, on general grounds, that in amphibious operations the landings should be dispersed, he considered it essential to secure the use of the south-eastern airfields in order to give protection to ships lying off the beaches. Air Chief Marshal Tedder also entered strong objections from the air point of view. The Eighth Army plan would leave thirteen landing grounds in enemy hands, and this was far too many for effective neutralisation by air action. He considered that it was vital to success to capture these airfields for our own use at the earliest possible opportunity and gave as his formal opinion that unless this could be guaranteed he would be opposed to the whole operation. I was therefore faced with a complete contradiction of opinion between the Army view, represented by General Leese, and the views of the Commander-in-Chief, Mediterranean and the Air Commander-in-Chief. On the existing plan it was impossible to reconcile these conflicting points of view.

I therefore decided to recast the whole plan. I took the decision on 3rd May, based on a conference on 2nd May which I had been prevented from attending by impossible flying weather, to cancel the American assault in the west and transfer the whole weight of Seventh Army to the south-east of the island, on the immediate left of Eighth Army. I decided, in fact, to take a risk on the administrative side rather than the operational risk of dispersion of effort. This was contrary to what had hitherto been regarded as one of the fundamental principles of the operation: that we must capture Palermo at the earliest possible opportunity if we were to have a hope of maintaining sufficient forces for the reduction of the island. On my new plan the only ports we should be certain of capturing in the first stage would be Syracuse and Augusta, the latter more a naval anchorage than a port, and possibly Catania; the whole of Seventh Army would have to depend on beach maintenance except for such help as it might get from the small port of Licata which, as already stated, was only rated at a capacity of six hundred tons a day.[8] The risk was therefore grave, but there were two factors which brightened the prospect. The first was that there was a reasonable probability of suitable weather in July for beach maintenance. The second was the coming of the DUKW. I need not describe these ingenious amphibious vehicles, which are now familiar to everyone, but it is interesting to note, in view of the great part they later played, that I had never seen one up to that time. General Miller[9], my Major General, Administration, had received advance reports and had ordered large quantities from the United States on 22nd March. When they arrived it was discovered that the claims made for them were fully justified by their performance. It is not too much to say, indeed, that the DUKW revolutionised the problem of beach maintenance. Nevertheless I arranged that Eighth Army should meet the commitment of providing a thousand tons per day through Syracuse for Seventh Army from D plus I4 to supplement their maintenance over the beaches until they could capture and bring into use the port of Palermo.

In changing my plan in this way to obtain concentration of force I was proceeding on sound strategic lines but there was one consideration which gave me some concern and which I should like to mention here. As I have said, I had decided to take a calculated administrative risk for operational reasons; but this risk was unevenly divided and almost the whole would fall on the Seventh Army. In other ways also it might well seem that the American troops were being given the tougher and less spectacular tasks: their beaches were more exposed than Eighth Army's and on some there were awkward sand bars, they would have only one small port for maintenance and Eighth Army would have the glory of capturing the more obviously attractive objectives of Syracuse, Catania and Messina, names which would bulk larger in press headlines than Gela or Licata or the obscure townships of central Sicily. Both I and my staff felt that this division of tasks might possibly, on these understandable grounds, cause some feeling of resentment. I knew, from the Tunisian campaign, General Patton's punctilious and scrupulous sense of duty and that there was no possibility of his questioning any orders he might receive from me, but in the case of so difficult and important an operation and since it might appear that an American Commander was being required to scrap the results of difficult and tedious planning and undertake a heavier burden than he had expected at the order of a British superior, I felt a natural anxiety about American reactions. I wish to place on record here that General Patton at once fell in with my new plan, the military advantages of which were as clear to him as to me, and neither he nor anyone in Seventh Army raised any form of objection. It is an impressive example of the spirit of complete loyalty and inter-Allied co-operation which inspired all operations with which I was associated in the Mediterranean theatre.

The Final Plan

The new plan was approved by the Combined Chiefs of Staff on I2th May, the day before that on which German resistance in Tunisia came to an end. I accordingly issued on I9th May my Operation Instruction No. I. This laid down the principles on which the plan of operations was based and the tasks of the two Armies. At the risk of some repetition of facts already given it will serve a useful purpose to set out the main lines of this instruction.

"An operation is to be prepared to seize and hold the island of Sicily as a base for future operations . . . The intention of the Allied Commander-in-Chief is to seize and hold the island by operations in five phases

    "Phase I.

Preparatory measures by Naval and Air forces to neutralize enemy naval efforts and to gain air supremacy.

"*Phase* 2.
Pre-dawn seaborne assaults, assisted by airborne landings with the object of seizing airfields and the ports of Syracuse and Licata.

"*Phase* 3.
The establishment of a firm base from which to conduct operations for the capture of the ports of Augusta and Catania, and the Gerbini group of airfields.

"*Phase* 4.
The capture of the ports and airfields outlined in Phase 3.

"*Phase* 5.
The reduction of the island."

The naval, ground and air commanders were nominated as follows: Eastern Task Force, Vice-Admiral B.H. Ramsay; Western Task Force, Vice-Admiral H.K. Hewitt; Seventh Army, Lieutenant-General George S. Patton Junior, Eighth Army, General Sir Bernard Montgomery, North-west African Tactical Air Forces, Air Marshal Sir Arthur Conmgham, Seventh Army Air Force, Colonel Lawrence P. Hickey, U.S.A.A.F., Eighth Army (Desert Air Force), Air Vice Marshal H. Broadhurst.

The Army tasks were defined as follows:

(a) *Eighth Army.*
  (i)   The assault between Syracuse and Pozzallo, supported by such parachute troops as could be lifted in one third of the available transport aircraft.
  (ii) Capture of the port of Syracuse and the airfield at Pachino.
  (iii) Establish itself on the general line Syracuse – Pozzallo – Ragusa and gain touch with Seventh Army.
  (iv) The rapid capture of the ports of Augusta and Catania and the Gerbini group of airfields.

(b) *Seventh Army.*
  (i)   The assault between Cape Scaramia and Licata, supported by such parachute troops as could be lifted in two thirds of the available transport aircraft.
  (ii) Capture of the port of Licata and the airfields of Ponte Olivo, Biscari and Comiso.
  (iii) Establish itself so as to gain contact with Eighth Army at Ragusa and protect the airfields and port in (ii) above.
  (iv) Subsequently to prevent enemy reserves moving eastwards against the left flank of Eighth Army.

Future tasks for the Armies were only sketched out at this stage but I indicated that my intention for the first phase was to establish the group of Armies across the south-eastern corner of the island on a line from Catania to Licata with a view to final operations for the reduction of the island. It was not practicable to plan further ahead for the present but I was clear in my own mind how I wanted to develop operations after the firm base had been established. The next thing to do was to split the island in half, and the first stage would be to seize and hold the irregular rectangle of roads in the centre round Caltanissetta and Enna. This would by itself seriously hamper all enemy east-west communications. From there I should be able to press on to Nicosia, which would leave only the north coast road open to the enemy, and then to the coast near San Stefano. I could probably only maintain a small force at San Stefano but if it could hold firm the interruption of communications would be complete.

On 2Ist May my headquarters issued Operation Instruction No 2 which gave fuller details of the forces to be used and the conduct of operations in the first two phases, the Preparatory Measures and the Assault. Eighth Army were allotted two Corps Headquarters, six infantry divisions, one infantry brigade and one airborne division.[10] Seventh Army had one Corps Headquarters, four infantry divisions, one armoured division and one airborne division. [11] One infantry division in each Army was designated as reserve, not to be used without reference to me, and a further infantry division of those allotted to Eighth Army was designated as a reinforcing division, only to be moved from North Africa if need should arise. In the event it was not needed and became available, therefore, for the landings at Salerno.

Eighth Army's plan called for a simultaneous assault by both Corps. On the right I3 Corps was to land on a three brigade front, with 5 Division right and the 50th left, over the beaches from Cape Murro di Porco, south of Syracuse, to just south of Noto. Commandos were to land on Cape Murro di Porco to capture the coast defence guns there and a brigade of I Airborne Division was to be landed in gliders to capture the bridge over the River Anapo south of Syracuse, and also, by a landing in the western suburbs, to assist in the capture of the town. 5 Division, when ashore, was to move north and capture Syracuse and Augusta while 50 Division secured Avola and protected the left flank. Subsequently the Corps was to move north and capture Catania, being relieved in its original area by 30 Corps. 30 Corps was to assault on the left of I3 Corps with 23I Infantry Brigade on the right at Marzamemi, on the east of the peninsula of Cape Passero, 5I Division, four battalions up, astride the tip of the peninsula and I Canadian Division, two brigades up, on the west side. A Special Service Brigade of two Royal Marine Commandos was to land on the Canadians left. The first task of the Corps was to seize the airfield at Pachino, which had been ploughed up by the enemy, and restore its serviceability at the earliest possible moment. It was then to seize the line of the road from Noto to Ispica (also known as Spaccaforno) and thereafter relieve 50 Division of I3 Corps at Avola. In the second phase the Corps' objective was the high ground in the area Palazzolo – Ragusa, and at the latter place the Canadians were to make contact with the Americans.

Seventh Army's assaults were divided between two forces, II Corps on the right and 3 Infantry Division, reinforced, on the left. II Corps consisted of 45 Infantry Division on the right and I Infantry Division, less one Regimental Combat Team, on the left together with Rangers and a tank battalion. The Corps task was to land in the Gulf of Gela, from Cape Scaramia to Gela town, and capture the airfields at Ponte

Olivo, Comiso and Biscari, subsequently to make contact with Eighth Army in the area of Ragusa. Parachutists of 505 Regimental Combat Team were to be dropped on the night of D minus I/D-day about four miles inland and six miles east of Gela to capture the high ground and road junctions covering I Division's beaches. On the left of the Army front 3 Infantry Division, with a Combat Command of 2 Armoured Division, was to land in the area of Licata and capture the port and airfield. To support either of these assaulting forces a floating reserve sailed with the Army, consisting of the remainder of 2 Armoured Division and one Regimental Combat Team of I Infantry Division. In reserve in North Africa was the remainder of 82 Airborne Division, less those elements which had already been dropped before the landings, and 9 Infantry Division. The frontage of attack of the two Armies covered about a hundred miles, from Cape Murro di Porco to Licata.

The problem of assembling these forces for a simultaneous assault was perhaps the most complicated that ever faced a planning staff, for they were mounted from all over the southern and eastern shores of the Mediterranean and in part from the United Kingdom and United States. Of the British forces 5 and 50 Divisions and 231 Infantry Brigade came from Suez in ships; 51 Division came from Tunisia in craft and part of it staged at Malta *en route;* I Canadian Division sailed from the United Kingdom in two ship convoys. 78 Division, earmarked for reserve, was waiting in the Sousse – Sfax area to be ferried across in craft. Seventh Army used the ports west of Tunis, I Division came from the Algiers area, partly in ships and partly in craft; 3 Division from Bizerta and 2 Armoured and 9 Divisions from Oran, again partly in ships and partly in craft; 45 Division came from the United States, staging in the Oran area. Both the airborne divisions, I British and 82 United States, were based on Kairouan in Tunisia. From the command point of view also there was extreme dispersion. My Headquarters was originally near Algiers and later at La Marsa, near Carthage, with a small Tactical Headquarters on Malta. Seventh Army Headquarters was near Oran for the planning stage, subsequently moving to Bizerta, Eighth Army Headquarters was originally in Cairo and moved to Malta for the assault; Admiral Cunningham established his Headquarters also in Malta, and Mediterranean Air Command Headquarters and the Headquarters of the Tactical and Strategic Air Forces were all grouped around Carthage, adjacent to my main Headquarters.

Training was carried out at a number of different stations; it was not as thorough as I should have liked, but the pressing considerations of time and shortage of craft imposed serious limitations. The British forces mounted from Middle East carried out "dryshod"[12] training in the desert and had some very incomplete landing rehearsals in the Gulf of Aqaba. The Canadian Division had been well trained in the United Kingdom but its attempted exercise on the Ayrshire coast had to be cancelled as soon as it had begun owing to bad weather. 51 Division, which had no previous training or experience in combined operations, was put through a short course at Djidjelli, much hampered by shortage of craft. The American 3 Division trained at Bizerta and La Goulette and I Infantry and 2 Armoured Divisions at the old established training area of Arzew, near Algiers. 45 Division had been trained in Chesapeake Bay before embarking, and had a short rehearsal at Arzew after their arrival in North African waters.

The tasks of the Naval forces (British and United States) fell under four main heads: the cover of the whole operation against interference by enemy naval forces, the close support of the convoys to their destination and the delivery of the troops to the beaches, close support of the landings by gunfire, and the maintenance by sea of the forces landed, including the protection of shipping off the beaches. The Naval Covering Force, consisting of four battleships, two aircraft carriers, four cruisers and some eighteen destroyers, was concentrated in the Ionian Sea by 9th July. In this position it was well placed to meet any threat from the Italian Taranto fleet, or from the Spezia fleet if it should attempt to reinforce through the Straits of Messina. An additional force of two battleships, two cruisers and six destroyers, based at Algiers, provided cover for convoys on the North African coast and constituted a reserve for the reinforcement or relief of the covering force if required. A light covering force of cruisers and destroyers was despatched on 9th July to protect the northern flank of Eighth Army. The main bases of this covering force were Mers-el-Kebir, Alexandria and Malta, with fuelling and ammunitioning facilities at Tobruk and at Benghazi.

For the air forces of Mediterranean Air Command the battle for Sicily could be said to have begun with the last minute of the battle for Tunisia, or even, to some extent, still earlier, and D-day represented merely a peak of intensity. They were faced first by an administrative problem. After the enemy surrender in Tunisia many air force units required rest and refitting and an extensive programme of airfield construction in northern Tunisia was put in hand. Although, therefore, preparatory bombing of enemy installations began at once it was not intended to apply more than steady pressure until about one week before the assault. During the preparatory phase targets were mainly strategic but a steady programme of interference with the enemy ground and air build-up in Sicily was carried out. A particularly heavy scale of attack was directed against the Messina rail ferry. By 1st June only one of the original five ferry boats was still in operation and the harbour facilities at both ends were very heavily damaged. The traffic was continued by lighters and small craft. From about D minus 7 the air forces went over to a concentrated and powerful attack on the enemy air force; enemy airfields in the island were attacked both by bomber aircraft and, where within range, by fighter sweeps. Radar installations, which would give warning of the approaching invasion fleets, were also successfully attacked. We were thus able to ensure air superiority over the landing beaches and very shortly, when the captured airfields in the south-east came into use, over the whole island. The total aircraft, including transports but excluding gliders, employed in the operation came to over four thousand, divided into one hundred and ten British and one hundred and thirty-two American squadrons.

Enemy Strength and Dispositions.

It is now time to consider "the other side of the hill" and review briefly the strength which the enemy could bring to meet our attack. Since January the Axis had been reinforcing Sicily, but not on the scale which we had allowed for; it had produced the two German divisions we had expected but only one extra Italian division instead of three. My Intelligence Staff was able to follow with some success the enemy preparations for invasion. The Italian Order of Battle was fairly easily established but the German only became clear towards the end of June, a fact which reflects the tardiness with which the Germans reinforced the island. It will be realised that the task of establishing the enemy Order of Battle in Sicily was surrounded with many difficulties; normal means were not available as we were not in contact with the enemy and so good was the police and counter-espionage system in Sicily that we were unable to obtain any information direct from the island. It is gratifying to record that, in spite of these difficulties, one captured Italian general considered our Order of Battle to be superior to the official document in his possession.[13] I will not, however, detail the steps by which the enemy picture was built up, but give the situation as it was on the day of the invasion.

Command in Sicily was exercised by the Sixth Army (Italian), with headquarters near Enna. The Army Commander was General Guzzoni, a sixty-six year old officer who had recently been recalled from the retired list on which he was placed in 1940; he was assisted by a German liaison officer, General von Senger und Etterlin, later a Corps commander in Italy. The west of the island was commanded by XII Corps, headquarters Corleone, with 28 (Aosta) Division covering the Marsala – Trapani area with headquarters near Salemi and 26 (Assietta) Division covering the southwest with headquarters north of Santa Margherita.

The eastern and central portion of the island was the responsibility of XVI Corps, headquarters Piazza Armerina; its two field divisions were 4 (Livorno) at Caltanissetta, a nodal point of road communications in the centre of the island, and 54 (Napoli) north of Palazzolo, inland from Syracuse. The coastal defences were assigned to five "Coastal Divisions" and an autonomous coastal regiment; these forces played, in the event, little part in the defence of the island and need not be further considered. It will be seen that the Italians showed a tendency to concentrate greater strength in the western part of the island, the nearest to Tunisia, and had only one division in the south-eastern corner.

The original German forces in the island consisted mainly of drafts in transit to Tunisia. When resistance collapsed in Africa they were organised into a provisional division known first as "Division Sicily" but later as 15 Panzer Division,[14] in memory of one of the formations destroyed in Africa. Its commander was General Baade who had commanded a regiment of the original 15 Panzer Division in Africa and was later famous in Italy as the commander of 90 Panzer Grenadier Division. It was divided into three battle groups of all arms and these were dispersed to provide extra stiffening for the Italians at points considered vital: one battle group was in the extreme west between Marsala and Mazzara, a second in the centre of the island with divisional headquarters, and the third in the Catania area. There was a detachment from the central battle group covering the airfields at Biscari and Comiso. This central group, and divisional headquarters, moved west immediately before D-day in accordance with the enemy appreciation that that part of the island was our most likely target. The second German division was the Hermann Goering Panzer Division. Part of this formation had fought in Africa and been destroyed there, but the remainder, after re-forming in Italy near Naples, began to arrive in the island late in June. It was divided into two battle groups: one was in the Catania area, where it took under command the regimental group from 15 Panzer Division which was already there, and the second was established in the area of Caltagirone, from where it was able to operate against Gela or the Comiso airfields. This battle group had relieved the group from 15 Panzer Division which was moving to the west as already stated.

Besides their forces in Sicily the Germans were moving troops into other parts of the Italian homeland. By the beginning of July there were about five German divisions in southern Italy, one in Sardinia and a regimental group in Corsica. These were therefore available for the reinforcement of Sicily, though the event was to show that the Germans were prepared to reinforce the island from as far away as France.

To sum up, the enemy forces opposing me in Sicily amounted in round figures to about three hundred and fifteen thousand Italians and fifty thousand Germans, the latter total rising to ninety thousand when the reinforcing divisions which arrived after the attack began are included.[15]

Capture of Pantelleria.

Before the attack began General Eisenhower decided to assault and capture the island of Pantelleria and subsequently the minor islands of the Pelagian group. The original plan for Sicily had proposed that Pantelleria should be merely silenced by heavy bombardment, for any losses in amphibious equipment which might be incurred in an attempt to capture the island would directly reduce the resources available for the main operation; it was obviously more economical, however, to capture the airfield on the island for our own use rather than merely deny it to the enemy. A further advantage lay in denying to the enemy the use of the RDF[16] stations there. The operation, which was preceded by a very heavy Air and Naval bombardment, was carried out under direct command of General Eisenhower, using I (British) Infantry Division. It was entirely successful at negligible loss, and the use of the airfield was very valuable for the Sicilian campaign.

Invasion and Conquest of Sicily.

The period of planning for the invasion of Sicily was unusually prolonged and it was possible to devote a more intensive study to the subject than is generally the case. I have omitted, in the account given above, a good many of the stages in that planning but it is essential to give sufficient detail to make quite clear the nature of the problem with which we were faced and the solution which was eventually adopted. This has also made it possible to present the narrative of operations in a much briefer form since on the whole in this case the conventional phrase is justified and operations proceeded according to plan. I should like to take the opportunity now, before passing on to the narrative of events, of giving their due credit to the men who made success possible.

General Dwight D. Eisenhower, Commander-in-Chief, Allied Expeditionary

Force, was the man on whom fell the ultimate responsibility of taking the great decisions. He commanded directly all sea, land and air forces in the theatre. He and his staff could not have been more helpful to me throughout; I knew that when he had given his confidence he would support me through everything and I had already had the happiest experience in Tunisia of what that support could be. His great merits as a commander have been too well illustrated in all the campaigns in Europe to need further tribute from me but I would like to single out one aspect in which I think he excelled: the gift for managing a coalition of different allies in arms. In almost all the wars in which Great Britain has been involved we have fought as a member of a coalition and a British commander has, therefore, what I may call a deep historic sense of the difficulties of combining the efforts of an allied force; he can remember the controversies of Marlborough with the Dutch Field Deputies and Wellington going down on his knees to humour the fractiousness of a Spanish General. Throughout all the operations which I commanded in the Mediterranean the British and American forces fought not merely as two armies with the same general objective and the same war aims but as a single homogeneous army and, without for a moment derogating from the spirit of loyal co-operation of all commanders and men, there is no doubt that the inspiration which gave life and vigour to that co-operation derived originally from General Eisenhower.

The Commanders-in-Chief of the naval and air forces in the theatre came, in the chain of command, directly under General Eisenhower and occupied therefore a position co-ordinate with my own. It is for this reason that I have dealt only summarily in this despatch with their operations but I must at this point try to make clear the debt which land operations owed to the sister services. On Admiral Cunningham fell the weight of what was in some ways the most arduous, detailed and vital part of the operation, the actual conveyance of the troops to their objectives. I do not mean merely to point out the obvious: that to invade an island it is necessary to cross the sea; but to evoke to the imagination some picture of the gigantic nature of the task of convoying for such distances, assembling and directing to obscure and unlit beaches in an enemy territory an Armada of over two thousand ships and craft. I must mention only in passing the assistance of naval gunfire on the beaches and the silent strength of the covering forces waiting, and hoping, for the appearance in defence of its native soil of that fleet which once claimed to dominate the Mediterranean. It is a theme which can be adequately described only by a naval specialist, and one of which the Royal Navy and the United States Navy are justly proud. Air Chief Marshal Tedder, Commander-in-Chief of the allied air forces in the Mediterranean, was an old colleague from the Middle East. His mastery of air strategy was demonstrated in Africa, Sicily and Italy and his mastery of the art of war as a whole was shown by his subsequent appointment as Deputy Supreme Commander, of all three arms, to General Eisenhower for operations in France and Germany. I have referred elsewhere to the work of the allied air forces. To sum it up it is only necessary to say they gave us command of the air and to demonstrate it to point to the protection our troops enjoyed in the first critical days when the fighters swarmed over the great, vulnerable convoys and the fighter-bombers hunted up and down the roads of Sicily seeking and destroying enemy reinforcements moving up to the beaches. The Commander of the Tactical Air Forces, Air Marshal Coningham, was another old colleague from the Middle East. His headquarters moved always with mine and our contact was so close that the word co-operation is too weak; we were two parts of the same machine and worked as one.

Of the Armies under my command I had already had successful experience. General Patton, commanding Seventh Army, had already served under me in Tunisia and I had complete confidence in him. He had there taken command of a body of troops, the excellent material of which had been prevented hitherto from showing its full capabilities by a certain lack of experience and by difficulties of terrain and climate, and had transformed it by his inspiration into a fast-moving and hard-hitting force crowned with victory. Seventh Army was certainly fast-moving and hard-hitting and it undoubtedly owed these qualities to the leadership of its commander. General Montgomery was also a commander in whom I had every trust and confidence. He and his Eighth Army had served under my command since August, 1942. Fresh from a campaign where they had advanced eighteen hundred miles in six months to share in the capture of a quarter of a million prisoners, they showed in Sicily that they could apply the lessons learnt then to a very different type of terrain and style of fighting. I was glad to welcome, in addition to the veteran formations of the Desert, the splendid I Canadian Division, trained to a hair in the United Kingdom and eager and confident for battle. I also welcomed 78 Division, the most experienced of First Army's. As will appear, Eighth Army had to face the heaviest opposition from the Germans and had some of the hardest fighting of the campaign in their struggle for the plain of Catania. The stubbornness of the German defence was more than equalled by their stubbornness, and their skill and endurance in the heat of a Sicilian summer brought them the success they thoroughly deserved.

I must add here my thanks to my own staff. Most of the senior British officers had come with me from Middle East when I set up the headquarters of Eighteenth Army Group in Tunisia; of the Americans some had also served on that staff, some came from Allied Force Headquarters and elsewhere. They made a fine team, headed by my Chief of Staff, General Richardson and his American Deputy, General Lemnitzer.[17]

In the circumstances, therefore, it was natural for me to feel that everything that could possibly be done to make the operation a success had been done. We had a team of commanders and men who since the previous autumn had known nothing but success. I had no illusions that the task would be easy but I had confidence that we were bringing to this task the best that Great Britain and the United States could provide.

On the afternoon of 9th July the various convoys from both ends of the Mediterranean began to arrive in their assembly areas east and south of Malta and from there, when assembled, to move north to their landing areas. That afternoon the wind began to rise and the sea became suddenly choppy with the characteristic short, steep swell of the Central Mediterranean. It was a bad omen for the assault at dawn, but I was assured that these sudden storms were liable to drop as suddenly as they arose, and it would certainly be too dangerous to attempt a postponement at this stage. We had quite clearly, contrary to all reasonable expectations, achieved strategic surprise and evidence appeared to show that the Germans were, as we had hoped, thinning out in the assault area to reinforce western Sicily. After dusk that night I went down to Cape Delimara, the south-eastern point of Malta, to watch the gliders fly past for the landing in support of Eighth Army. As the tandem-wise pairs of tow and glider came flying low, now in twos and threes, now in larger groups, with the roar of their engines partly carried away by the gale and their veiled navigation lights showing fitfully in the half light of the moon, I took note that the first invasion of European soil was under way. On my right the quiet expanse of Marsa Scirocco waited for the Italian fleet which, two months hence, was to anchor there in humble surrender.

Shortly after midnight the wind began to fall off and the swell to subside. These conditions had favoured us in one respect, for at many places along the coast the hostile garrisons, which had been on the alert for weeks, were lulled into a sense of security by the bad weather and, believing that no one would attempt a landing under such conditions, relaxed their vigil.[18] Resistance was slight on the beaches on both Army fronts and by first light it could be said that all landings had been successful at the cost of very small casualties. The airborne attack had been less fortunate. The wind was still blowing at some forty miles per hour when the parachutists were dropped and the gliders slipped, and many of the pilots of the transport and tow aircraft, who had had no previous experience in actual operations, ran into difficulties with their navigation or were disconcerted by enemy anti-aircraft fire. The result was that the American airborne troops were scattered in small parties over an area of some fifty miles from Licata to Noto; in Eighth Army's area nearly fifty of the hundred and thirty-four gliders of I Airlanding Brigade which took off from Tunisia came down in the sea, about seventy-five came safely to land somewhere in south-eastern Sicily and only twelve landed in the correct dropping zone. The force which actually reached the bridge south of Syracuse, the Brigade's main objective, only numbered eight officers and sixty-five men, but they held the bridge until 1530 hours on D-day, when nineteen survivors were relieved at the last minute by 5 Division troops. However, in spite of this miscarriage, the effect on the nerves of the none too steady Italian troops of the descent of these airborne forces all over south-eastern Sicily was of the utmost value to the assault. Small isolated units of parachutists seized vital points, attacked roads and created widespread panic which undoubtedly disorganised all plans for defence.

Owing to the swell raised by the gale of the previous day some of the landings, especially on the more exposed Seventh Army beaches, suffered a slight delay; but the weakness of the defence soon allowed us to make up any time which had been lost. On the right 13 Corps made good its initial bridgehead, seized the high ground overlooking the coast road and, advancing over the bridge captured by I Airborne Division, entered Syracuse at 2100 hours on the evening of D-day. This was a particularly fine feat of arms. It involved a landing on a defended coast followed immediately by a march to a flank without waiting to consolidate the beachhead and, owing to the partial failure of the airborne operation, it had to be carried out in less strength and without the tactical advantages which had been planned. 30 Corps had captured all its beaches by 0545 hours, Pachino landing ground by 1000 hours and the town of Pachino by I330 hours. During the first day Eighth Army made no contact with any of the Italian mobile divisions or with any German troops; the men of the coastal divisions who were met made little difficulty in surrendering after slight resistance. Seventh Army had met equally poor opposition and easily seized all its D-day objectives Licata, Gela, Scoglitti and Marina di Ragusa were all in our hands and in the afternoon the floating reserve was ordered to disembark in the Gela area. This was the centre of the Army's front which now consisted of three separate bridgeheads: 3 Division at Licata, I Infantry and 2 Armoured at Gela and 45 Division on the right at the south-eastern end of the Gulf of Gela. The Gela bridgehead, now strengthened by the addition of the reserve, was the smallest, and enemy tanks had already been seen approaching from the north-east, a presage of what was to come on the morrow.

Next day, the IIth, Eighth Army continued to press on up the east coast in the direction of Catania. 30 Corps on the left extended its bridgehead to Pozzallo and Ispica, but the main weight of interest lay with I3 Corps which pushed on a marching column to Priolo, halfway to Augusta. The heat was intense and few vehicles were as yet ashore; contact was first made that day with the Italian 54 Division, outside Syracuse. On the American front, in the meantime, a more serious battle was developing. The battle group of the Hermann Goering Division which was disposed to cover the centre of the island and the Ponte Olivo airfields made a strong and deliberate counter-attack on I Infantry Division at Gela. From 0800 hours to I630 hours these attacks continued, supported by a battalion of tanks, and at one stage penetrated to the beach, but they were repulsed in hard fighting in which the direct fire of naval escort ships played a considerable part. By the end of the day landing strips were made available for our aircraft at Gela and Licata; in Eighth Army's sector we had Pachino, and the bridgehead was assuming very solid proportions.

The German Command put in the eastern group of Hermann Goering Division to defend Augusta but the impetus of our assault was such that, after being held up at Priolo all day of the I2th, 5 Division was able to capture the town next morning before dawn. Seventh Army had counter-attacked the Germans opposing them and by the I3th were firmly in possession of the three vital airfield areas of Comiso, Biscari and Ponte Olivo. Both Armies were pushing ahead impetuously and it seemed as though nothing could stop them. Ahead of the troops, the Tactical Air Force bombed intensively the lines of communication in the centre of the island to hold up the movements of enemy forces across Sicily. On my right General Montgomery was developing two thrusts, one with I3 Corps due north on to Catania, which he hoped to capture on the I6th, and one on the left with the Canadians whom he was hoping to send in a wide outflanking movement through Caltagirone and Enna to come in behind the enemy north of Mount Etna. This meant that Seventh Army would be free to pivot on its left and strengthen its grasp on the central portion of the island, preparatory to carrying out the task for which I had designated it. 30 Corps would be advancing straight across the front of Seventh Army's right wing where 45 Division, although fresh from the United States with no previous battle experience, had been making striking progress.

I issued orders for the new plan on I3th July. The new boundary between the two

Armies gave to Eighth Army the road Vizzini – Caltagirone – Piazza Armerina – Enna; it then ran due north to the north coast west of San Stefano, which was 30 Corps' ultimate objective. Eighth Army's attack on the right began on the night of the 13th, when I Parachute Brigade was dropped to capture the Primosole bridge over the River Simeto at the southern edge of the Catania plain. 5 Division, followed by 50 Division, were to attack northwards to make contact with the parachutists, establish a bridgehead over the river and advance on Catania. The parachutist operation was successful, though only about half reached the right area, and about two hundred men with five anti-tank guns seized the bridge, removed the demolition charges and prepared to defend the position until relieved. All day on the I4th they withstood enemy counter-attacks and only withdrew after dark to a ridge to the southward from which they could still cover the bridge. Early on the I5th contact was made with the main body which had been delayed by strong German counter-attacks, in one of which Augusta had been temporarily lost. The vital bridge was intact and on the I5th we succeeded in getting some troops across, though it was not until the I7th that we could consolidate our shallow bridgehead north of the river. This stubborn and partly successful defence was due to the arrival of German reinforcements. A regiment of parachutists from 7 Air Division[19] was taken from Tarascon, in Southern France, and brought by air via Naples to the area south of Catania. It was these excellent troops who were mainly responsible for the defence of the line of the Simeto.

On the right, therefore, we had been only partially successful; the capture of the bridgehead over the Simeto was a considerable advantage, but we had been halted south of Catania. In the centre, the sector of 30 Corps, we had made steady progress, but the nature of the country and the exiguous road-net meant that that progress had been slow. Vizzini was captured on the I4th, after strong resistance, by 5I Division assisted by 45 (United States). The Canadians then went into the lead capturing Grammichele and Caltagirone on the I5th and Piazza Armerina on the I6th.[20] Their next objective was Enna, the centre of the island and meeting point of a network of main roads against which the bomber effort of the air forces had been focussed during the first five days of the invasion. Seventh Army was now reorganising in order to meet the needs of its changed directive. On I5th July General Patton created a Provisional Corps Headquarters to command the left flank of the Army, consisting of 3 Infantry Division, with under command 4 Tabor of Goums,[21] old friends from Tunisian days, and 82 Airborne Division. II Corps continued to command the right flank with I and 45 Divisions, while 2 Armoured Division was under Army command. II Corps had made good progress northwards and 45 Division on its right had co-operated with 30 Corps in the capture of Vizzini and Caltagirone; on the I6th, however, the Division reached the new inter-Army boundary and started to transfer to the left wing of the Corps, behind I Division. 3 Division in the Provisional Corps made ground westwards along the coast and inland beyond Canicatti, which it had captured on the I2th. The Germans were now withdrawing across the front of Seventh Army from west to east. They had already decided that the most they could hope to hold was the north-eastern portion of the island and on the I6th I5 Panzer Division was reconnoitring the northern slopes of Etna. XIV Panzer Corps was arriving to take command in the island and its intentions clearly were to rely no further on the Italians but to secure a defensible position with its own German troops which would cover Messina, to ensure an eventual evacuation, and deny us as long as possible the airfields in the Catania plain.

On 16th July I issued a second directive to both Armies. In it I laid down three axes of advance for Eighth Army: northwards through Catania; from Leonforte to Adrano to sever communications this side of Etna; and via Nicosia – Troina – Randazzo to sweep round the northern slopes of Etna. I was already concerned with the problem of the Messina peninsula.

It is a long, mountainous, isosceles triangle with the great mass of Etna almost filling its base. The southern slopes of the mountain dominate the plain below and give perfect observation of any attack we could mount on the Gerbini airfields or the port of Catania. Our attack to drive the Germans from the island must therefore be canalized either side of Etna, in difficult country with few and bad roads. I hoped that Eighth Army would be able to mount a rapid attack on this formidable position before the Germans could assume a good position of defence. Seventh Army was ordered to protect the rear of this attack by seizing the central rectangle of roads around Enna and cutting the east-west road at Petralia. If it were found possible without involving heavy casualties General Patton was to capture Agrigento and Porto Empedocle, which would be useful for maintenance.

In accordance with this directive General Montgomery attacked northwards from his Simeto bridgehead on the night 17th/18th July. Two brigades of 50 Division made the attack but met very heavy resistance and gained little ground. The Air Force, at this period, was concentrating almost entirely on action to break the enemy's resistance at Catania. To this end, a continuous bombardment was maintained against all rail, road and air communications by which supplies might reach that area. The enemy had now concentrated the whole of the Hermann Goering Division in this area and added to it six battalions of I Parachute Division and two "Fortress" battalions rushed across from Calabria. The ground on this front was open but intersected with water courses which made difficult the employment of our armour. On the 19th General Montgomery informed me that he had decided not to persist with his thrust on the right, but to increase the pressure on his left. His first plan was to attack towards Misterbianco with 5 Division on the left of 13 Corps but this attack also met the same heavy resistance and could only draw level with 50 Division's bridgehead. 30 Corps now began to apply pressure. On the 20th 51 Division crossed the Dittaino River at Sferro and advanced on the Gerbini airfields but was driven back to the bridgehead by a counter-attack on the 21st. On 30 Corps' left the Canadian division, with 231 Brigade on its right, was still making the wide sweep as originally planned but it was now clear that Eighth Army would not have the strength to encircle Etna on both sides against the stout resistance of the Germans. The Canadians were therefore ordered to advance to Leonforte and then turn east to Adrano, the centre of the three original thrusts, abandoning the proposed encirclement through Randazzo. The Germans were continuing to reinforce, for we identified part of 29 Panzer

Grenadier Division opposing 30 Corps on the 20th. On that day General Montgomery ordered forward his reserve division, the 78th, from North Africa.

Seventh Army continued to make good progress following my directive of the 16th. The Provisional Corps took Porto Empedocle the same day and Agrigento the next, and II Corps captured Caltanissetta on the 18th. 15 Panzer Division had by now succeeded in making a rather scrambling retreat across Seventh Army's front, and were coming into line with the Hermann Goering Division to oppose 30 Corps' advance. There were therefore no German troops west or north-west of Seventh Army and there was no reason to anticipate effective resistance from the Italians on this front. Now that Eighth Army were stopped south of Catania I should need Seventh Army as the left arm of my enveloping movement round Etna. I therefore issued another directive to Seventh Army on 18th July. In this I ordered General Patton to push north after the capture of Petralia, which was provided for in my previous directive to him, and cut the north coast road. As soon as he had secured a line across the island from Campofelice on the north coast to Agrigento on the south he was to advance and mop up the whole western part of the island.

The rapid and wide-sweeping manoeuvres envisaged in this directive were very welcome to General Patton and he immediately set on foot the measures necessary to carry them out with that dash and drive which were characteristic of his conduct of operations. II Corps was given the task of securing the base in the centre of the island and cutting the north coast road, and the Provisional Corps, to which on 20th July he assigned 2 Armoured Division, was given that of the reduction of western Sicily. On the 20th the former entered Enna with the Canadians and the latter captured Sciacca, which had once been deemed an objective worthy of a separate amphibious landing. Progress was so good that I decided to push rapidly ahead with Seventh Army. On the 20th I directed General Patton to turn eastwards on reaching the north coast and develop a threat along the coast road and the road Petralia – Nicosia – Cesaro. This meant an alteration in the inter-Army boundary which entrusted the Americans with the operation north of Etna. In order to sustain this threat General Patton was ordered to capture at the earliest possible opportunity the port of Palermo and bring it into use as his main base of supply. American maintenance would then be switched from the south coast beaches and the ports of Licata and Empedocle to an axis running along the north coast from west to east.

The new directive was put into force with great rapidity and energy. The Provisional Corps entered Palermo on the evening of the 22nd and 45 Division of II Corps cut the north coast road east of Termini Imerese on the next day. These rapid advances had involved little serious fighting but considerable feats of endurance, for a large proportion of the troops had to march long distances in the sweltering damp heat of a Sicilian summer, far more trying than anything we had experienced in Libya or Tunisia. Seventh Army during this period took thirty-six thousand prisoners, nineteen thousand of them between the 16th and the 22nd.

The last week of July was characterised by a comparative lull on the Eighth Army front and the transference of the American effort to the axis of the north coast road and the road running parallel to it to the south. General Montgomery wished to rest his troops and await the arrival of 78 Division before resuming the offensive. I fixed on Ist August as the date at which both Armies should be ready to recommence active operations and I expected that after that date the process of clearing the island would be fairly rapid. The Germans had now four divisions in Sicily, Hermann Goering, I5 Panzer, 29 Panzer Grenadier and I Parachute, but they were not all complete and the first two had already suffered heavy casualties. General Hube, a man in whom Hitler was reported to have great confidence, had arrived to command them from the XIV Panzer Corps Headquarters. I moved my own headquarters over to Sicily and opened in a dusty but well-concealed site in an almond grove near Cassibile on 28th July.

Activity on Eighth Army front during this period was confined to the left flank where the Canadians and 23I Brigade continued to make ground. Nissoria fell on the 24th and Agira on the 28th. 78 Division had now arrived and it was General Montgomery's intention to use it in an attack down the axis Catenanuova – Adrano. The capture of Adrano would mean that the great mass of Etna was interposed between the two halves of the German force and the enemy's lateral communications would be pushed back to the far side of the mountain. On the night of the 29th 78 Division, with 3 Canadian Brigade under command, attacked and captured Catenanuova. There was further fighting before the bridgehead over the Dittaino was firm and on the night of Ist August the division proceeded to the attack on Centuripe. This hill city on an isolated pinnacle of rock was the main outpost of the Adrano position and was defended with fanatical vigour by troops of the Hermann Goering Division reinforced by 3 Parachute Regiment, perhaps the best German troops in Sicily. Fighting continued in the steep, cobbled streets of the town all the next day and it was not cleared until the morning of the 3rd. The storming of Centuripe was a particularly fine feat and its effects were widespread, for from that time the front once more became fluid. In face of the threat to Adrano the enemy position covering Catania became untenable.

Seventh Army in the meantime was pushing eastwards along the north coast. This was in accordance with my directive of 23rd July which called for the maximum pressure in this area. General Patton calculated that he could operate one division on each of the two roads and in order to keep up the pressure proposed to relieve the leading formations regularly. He therefore sent for 9 Division, his reserve in North Africa, which was to sail direct to Palermo.[22] 45 Division began the advance along the coast road and I Division on the southern road; on 25th July the former captured Cefalu and the latter Gangi. On the28th I Division took Nicosia and by 2nd August had advanced to near Troina. On the north coast 45 Division captured San Stefano on 3Ist July, where it was relieved on 2nd August by 3 Division. 9 Division was now in position behind the Ist on the southern road and the 45th behind the 3rd on the coast road and Seventh Army was in a position to keep up pressure continuously until they reached Messina.[23] Meanwhile, far to the rear, the whole of western Sicily had been cleared.

Operations were continuous and continuously successful from 3rd August onwards until the final reduction of the island. On that day Centuripe fell, I3 Corps began to advance on Catania and Seventh Army began the bloody attack on Troina. 5 Division, supported by the 50th on its right, began to attack on the night 3rd/4th August and by the 5th Catania, Misterbianco, and Paterno were in our hands. Adrano still resisted but it fell to 78 Division on the night of the 6th, together with Biancavilla in 5I Division's sector. All this time some of the fiercest and costliest fighting of the campaign was raging in and around Troina. I5 Panzer Division offered a desperate resistance lasting four days, though by the end of that period their position was becoming rather precarious, and 29 Panzer Grenadier Division offered an almost equally stubborn resistance on the coastal sector at Santa Agata and San Fratello. Troina was finally cleared on 6th August. General Patton now mounted a small amphibious operation on the north coast behind the enemy lines which was brilliantly successful and led to the capture on the 8th of Santa Agata which had been holding out against us for six days. On the southern road 9 Division passed through the Ist and captured Cesaro on the 8th. The next vital point north of Etna was Randazzo, the capture of which would leave the enemy with only one more lateral road across the peninsula. Both 9 and 78 Divisions were now converging on this point, though the latter had had some hard fighting for Bronte, which it captured on 8th August. Randazzo eventually fell on the I3th and 78 Division passed into reserve. On the coast road a further German line of resistance at Capo d'Orlando was turned by another seaborne hook behind it on the night I0th/IIth August. These two small amphibious operations were prepared at very short notice and were most ably executed. They were of the utmost assistance in accelerating the advance on the coastal road which was delayed by extensive demolitions. This road was in part built *en corniche* and the work of the American engineers in restoring it was worthy of the highest praise.

East of Etna the country offered many obstacles to a rapid advance. It is a thickly inhabited narrow strip, confined between the mountains and the coast, and the cultivation, especially the walls of the vineyards and olive groves, makes it excellent defensive terrain. 5 and 50 Divisions could make only slow progress, although the enemy had by now decided to evacuate and was seeking only to impose the maximum delay. Thanks to the difficulties of the terrain which I have already mentioned, he was able to extricate a high proportion of his troops, though not, of course, their heavy equipment. The Messina area was very heavily defended; anti-aircraft fire, for instance, was described by our pilots as worse than over the Ruhr. General Montgomery was anxious to bring a Corps into reserve to prepare for the invasion of Italy and on I3th August he pulled out 5 Division and I3 Corps Headquarters to join the Canadian Division in preparation for the new assault. 50 and 5I Divisions continued the pursuit. An attempted landing in rear of the enemy on the night of I5th August, in the style of those carried out on the north coast, was very nearly successful but the enemy were retreating too fast for any to be cut off.

On the night of I6th August the leading troops of 3 United States Division entered Messina. They were joined next morning by Commandos from 30 Corps. Just before dawn on the I7th, according to the German account, General Hube, the German commander, sailed from a beach north of Messina in the last boat to leave the island. Sicily had been conquered in thirty-eight days.

APPENDIX.

HQ FIFTEENTH ARMY GROUP

ADMINISTRATIVE REPORT ON THE SICILIAN CAMPAIGN.

10th July – 17th August, 1943.

THE PLANNING PHASE.

Planning for the Sicilian campaign began at Bouzarea, near Algiers, in February, 1943. Brigadier E.P. Nares and Brigadier-General Archelaus L. Hamblen, United States Army, were appointed for Administrative planning with British and American planning staffs representing Q (Maintenance), Q (Movements and Transportation), A Branch and the G-4 and G-I Branches.[24] To the above was added a strong R.A.F. team of planners which worked throughout in the joint scheme.

Considerations of concentration of force had originally suggested an attack by both Armies on the south-eastern corner of the island but this had been abandoned in the first plan on the administrative grounds that there was no port on the southern shores of sufficient capacity to maintain the forces in that area which could be captured. They would, therefore, have to be maintained indefinitely over the beaches. The lessons of TORCH Operation[25] had indicated that it was necessary to capture a suitable port within forty-eight hours. Consequently it was decided to proceed with the plan for the U.S. Seventh Army to assault in the area of Palermo and capture that port and for the British Eighth Army to capture Syracuse together with the airfields of Comiso and Ponte Olivo.

In May the Allied Commander-in-Chief directed that the administrative aspects of the original plan should be reviewed. After full examination, the administrative risks involved in assaulting in the south-east corner of the island were accepted and a plan of campaign using this area for the assault was evolved.

On 23rd May the staff of Eighteenth Army Group was dissolved, the Tunisian campaign having been concluded. Major-General C.H. Miller, MGA Eighteenth Army Group, was appointed MGA Force I4I (later known as Fifteenth Army Group) and the Administrative Staff was concentrated at Algiers to complete the planning of the Sicilian campaign. The War Establishment of Fifteenth Army Group initially approved included the Administrative Staffs of all Services and departments, but was not implemented in full, only those officers immediately required for planning being appointed. It was later decided that these Services and departments would not be required until the allied forces had been established on the mainland of Italy and that for the Sicilian campaign HQ Fifteenth Army Group would only fulfil the function of operational command and co-ordination as HQ Eighteenth Army Group had done during the Tunisian campaign.

In view of the unknown risks involved in maintaining the United States Seventh Army over beaches for an indefinite period, it was decided to set up a detachment of a United States Base Section in Syracuse on D plus I0 together with the British Base Area designated for that port and to include American ships in the D plus I4 convoy for discharge at I,000 tons per day at the expense of Eighth Army for the maintenance of Seventh Army. The object of this decision was to relieve the maintenance of Seventh Army over the beaches at the earliest date possible. It was further decided that HQ Tripoli Base Area (redesignated FORTBASE on arrival in Sicily) should move to Syracuse as early as possible after the capture of that port to co-ordinate shipping demands and maintenance between Eighth Army, Seventh Army and the Air Forces in accordance with the policy laid down by Fifteenth Army Group. In the event this co-ordination was not required since all the maintenance requirements of Seventh Army were successfully and adequately provided over the beaches and through Licata and Empedocle.

On 22nd June, the Naval and Army Task Forces together with the supporting Air Forces, both British and United States, taking part in the operation presented their outline plans before the Allied Commander-in-Chief and the three Service Commanders-in-Chief at Algiers.

On 24th June HQ Fifteenth Army Group moved from Algiers to the British Consulate at La Marsa, and on 4th July General Alexander moved his Tactical Headquarters to the Governor's Palace at Malta leaving Main Headquarters at La Marsa.

THE MOUNTING.

The operation was successfully mounted from North African and Middle East ports according to plan.[26] The mounting of this operation within two months of the conclusion of the Tunisian campaign was a very remarkable achievement on the part of all administrative staffs and formations responsible under AFHQ and GHQ Middle East, including the Naval and Sea Transport authorities concerned. It also involved very heavy commitments in the supply and maintenance of the large air forces operating in support from airfields in North Africa, Middle East, Malta, Pantelleria and Lampedusa.

THE OPERATION.

The assault on Sicily by Seventh and Eighth Armies, supported by the Royal Navy, United States Navy and the North-west African Air Forces, took place according to plan on I0th July I943, in spite of an exceptionally high wind. There was little or no opposition on the beaches Syracuse was in our hands by D plus I and was opened to receive the first convoy on D plus 3 by 86 Base Area (Brigadier H.C.N. Trollope) under command of Eighth Army. Licata was captured by 3 United States Division according to plan.

Beach maintenance was carried out by both Task Forces satisfactorily and the rate of discharge over the beaches was much higher than had been anticipated. From I0th July the weather was favourable and the sea calm; air and sea superiority was established and although there were some losses of craft and shipping due to enemy action, these did not seriously affect maintenance. No serious administrative shortages were encountered, and the DUKWS proved a marked success for transport from ship and landing craft to beach depot area.

By D plus I4 FORTBASE had taken over the general administration of the beaches and of the ports of Syracuse and Augusta from Eighth Army in accordance with the plan.

Seventh Army.

On the Seventh Army front in the western half of the island, the German forces retired eastwards towards the Messina peninsula, and there was no serious resistance from the Italian forces. The Commander-in-Chief directed that Palermo should be captured and the port opened up as the main base of supply for Seventh Army. This gave Seventh Army the port they needed and switched their main axis of supply for the final attack on the Messina peninsula from beaches and two small ports in the south to Palermo and eastwards along the north coast.

The main administrative problems confronting the staff of Seventh Army in the course of this operation ashore were:-

(*a*) To maintain the divisions in the initial advance to Palermo and the western end of the island from beach maintenance areas and from the small ports of Licata and Empedocle in the south.

(*b*) To open up Palermo port and to switch the convoys from the southern ports and beaches to the axis of supply along the north coast for the final drive against Messina.

(*c*) To get supplies of all natures to the troops over mountainous and narrow roads in poor condition with limited mechanical transport in the face of considerable demolitions that had been carried out on roads and railways by the enemy. In the final advance on Messina it was found necessary to supply the forward American divisions by sea from landing craft since the coast road from Palermo had been cut by demolitions.

(*d*) To maintain the Air Forces operating from Comiso and Ponte Olivo.

In spite of these problems and difficulties the troops never went short, and particular credit is due to the United States Engineer units who carried out repairs to roads and railways with great energy and speed.

Eighth Army.

On the Eighth Army front in the eastern half of the island strong German resistance was encountered on the general line south of Catania and to the west then running northwards round Mount Etna.

Maintenance over the beaches of the Pachino Peninsula and south of Syracuse was successfully achieved. Although some ships were lost owing to enemy air action no serious interference with maintenance resulted. The ports of Syracuse and Augusta were opened according to plan.

It was the administrative policy of Eighth Army to:-

(*a*) Form a main base of supply for Eighth Army at Syracuse.

(*b*) Utilise Augusta in the initial stages for the maintenance of I3 Corps on the eastern flank.

(*c*) Maintain 30 Corps from beach maintenance areas, but to close these down as soon as possible and shift the supply axis of this Corps on to the Syracuse main depot area.

The railways and such locomotives and rolling stock as were available were used to the maximum possible extent and Corps railheads were opened up as far forward as circumstances permitted. Roads were narrow and twisty but, with good Q (Movements) traffic control, presented no insuperable difficulties in the movement of mechanical transport, and all demands for ammunition and other supplies were adequately met.

After the capture of Catania, this port was used for the maintenance of Air Forces located on the Gerbini airfields and subsequently for the mounting of operations against the Toe of Italy. The port of Augusta was closed for maintenance and handed over to the Royal Navy, stocks in beach maintenance areas being cleared into Syracuse depots according to plan.

The outstanding administrative feature of this operation was the speed with which ports were opened to shipping immediately after capture and the efficient manner in which stores were off-loaded, transported into depots and moved by rail and road to the forward troops.

This was due to:-

(*a*) The fact that FORTBASE and most of the Base Areas and Sub-Areas concerned had had considerable previous experience in this type of work during the campaigns in the Western Desert.

(*b*) The high standard of co-operation which had been developed with the Royal Navy, the Air Forces and the Anti-Aircraft in opening up ports to shipping and in protecting them against enemy air attack.

(*c*) The efficient work of the Q (Movements and Transportation) Staffs and Transportation units concerned with all port working.

Maintenance of the Air Forces.

The main airfields in Sicily were located at Gerbini near Catania in eastern Sicily, and at Comiso and Ponte Olivo on the southern coast. The latter were rapidly captured by Seventh Army and the necessary supplies moved to them from the beach maintenance areas. Seventh Army Engineers arranged to erect bulk petrol storage at Gela and to lay pipelines from there to the Comiso and Ponte Olivo airfields, an operation which was successfully carried out and saved much transport. At Syracuse and Augusta, and later at Catania, bulk storage was found intact. After the capture of Catania, its port was used to maintain the Air Forces that occupied the Gerbini airfields.

Throughout the operation Air Force supplies were successfully maintained, although at times in the early stages the margin of safety was a small one. Considerable difficulties were encountered owing to the fact that American Air Force supplies were shipped from the United States at the same time as ground force supplies, the former were required for delivery at eastern ports in the neighbourhood of which the Air Forces were mainly located, and the latter at Palermo which was the main port of supply for Seventh Army.

Air Transport.

Transport aircraft were available in large numbers for the first time in the Mediterranean campaigns. Full use was made of them for the rapid conveyance of air force supplies, mails and urgent stores (particularly Ordnance stores), and for the evacuation of casualties to hospitals on the mainland. A very large proportion of the total sick and wounded, both British and American, were successfully evacuated by air, and there is no doubt that a certain limited number of aircraft under exclusive medical control are required to enable serious casualties to be evacuated promptly.

Medical.

Medical arrangements worked very well except that the organisation for calling forward hospital ships for evacuation from the ports of eastern Sicily was initially unsatisfactory and had subsequently to be improved. In view of the dangers of malaria in Sicily at this time of the year, preventive measures were taken by all troops before and during the operation. The incidence of malaria during the campaign was therefore not unduly high.

CONCLUSION OF OPERATIONS.

When the capture of Messina brought operations to a close on 17th August the Administrative boundary between Seventh and Eighth Armies was made to coincide with the Civil Administrative boundaries. The whole of Seventh Army, except for certain Artillery and Engineer units required in support of Eighth Army for the next operation against the Toe of Italy, was withdrawn to the western half of the island where it could be most easily and economically maintained. The United States Island Base Section assumed Administrative control of the port of Palermo and all American stocks were moved to this area except those required for local maintenance. The ports of Licata and Empedocle were closed.

Civil Administration under AMGOT[27] (headed by Major-General Lord Rennell) had been set up in all districts immediately behind the armies as they advanced.

All necessary Administrative arrangements were at once put in hand for mounting subsequent operations against the mainland of Italy. These were the responsibility of Seventh Army in the west and FORTBASE in the east.

The Administrative Organisation[28]

It was the Administrative plan of Eighth Army to move HQ Tripoli Base Area, which had been established under its command soon after the capture of Tripoli to carry out general and local administration of that area as the Advanced Base for the Tunisian campaign, into Sicily where it was to undertake similar duties at Syracuse and in eastern Sicily as soon as possible. The great advantage of this plan was that it retained the existing administrative organisation of Eighth Army and made use of a most experienced and efficient team under the GOC Base Area, which knew the Army's requirements and had its complete confidence as well as that of GHQ Middle East. On the other hand it meant that there could be no place in Sicily for the full establishment of the Administrative Staff, Services and departments of Fifteenth Army Group, and it was clearly unsuitable for the general administration of the mainland of Italy with a single axis of supply from North Africa and the West under AFHQ. It was, however, decided to adopt the existing organisation for the Sicilian campaign and not to make any change until the allied forces had been established on the Italian mainland except for placing FORTBASE under command of Fifteenth Army Group instead of Eighth Army when it arrived in Sicily.

The administrative organisation therefore for the Sicilian campaign can be summarised as follows:-

(*a*) Fifteenth Army Group was responsible for administrative policy and co-ordination of general administration of all ground and air forces in

Sicily, in accordance with the Army Group Commander's plan of operation.

(*b*) Seventh Army was responsible for general and local administration in western Sicily including the port of Palermo. This port was not taken over by the United States Island Base Section under CG NATOUSA[29] until operations had been concluded.

(*c*) FORTBASE assumed responsibility for general administration of all ports and beaches in eastern Sicily under command Fifteenth Army Group, whilst local administration in eastern Sicily was carried out by Eighth Army through the various Base Areas and Sub-Areas.

This organisation proved entirely satisfactory under the particular circumstances involving the capture of an island by two armies maintained initially on two separate supply axes with a view to a further advance across the sea to the mainland of Italy. It would, however, have been more satisfactory if Palermo had been taken over immediately after capture by the United States Island Base Section. The Army Administrative Staff would then have been free to devote its attention entirely to the maintenance of formations in battle.

Footnotes

1   Succeeded in May by (the late) Major-General A.A. Richardson. The Headquarters was "integrated", i.e., Anglo-American, but organised on the British Staff System, just as Allied Force Headquarters, also integrated, was organised on the American system.

2   Now Field-Marshal the Viscount Montgomery of Alamein, K.G., G.C.B., D.S.O.

3   The late Lieutenant-General George S. Patton Junior.

4   Now Admiral of the Fleet the Viscount Cunningham of Hyndhope, K.T., G.C.B., O.M., D.S.O.

5   Now Marshal of the Royal Air Force Lord Tedder, G.C.B.

6   Actually planning had been based on the appreciation that the mobile part of the garrison of the island would be more than doubled and I myself thought that the Joint Planning Staff had taken a rather unduly pessimistic view.

7   Now Lieutenant-General Sir Oliver Leese, Bt, K.C.B., C.B.E., D.S.O.

8   Seventh Army actually managed to raise this figure in practice to a thousand tons per day.

9   Major-General C.H. Miller, C.B., C.B.E., D.S.O.

10   13 and 30 Corps Headquarters, 5, 46, 50, 51, 78 and 1 Canadian Infantry Divisions, 231 Infantry Brigade and 1 Airborne Division.

11   II Corps Headquarters, 1, 3, 9 and 45 Infantry Divisions, 2 Armoured Division and 82 Airborne Division.

12   "Dryshod" was a technical term meaning exercises carried out on land simulating landings from craft.

13   *One serious error was made. By an extraordinary series of coincidences a body of evidence was built up which made it appear that an extra Italian division (103 Piacenza) was in the area south of Catania. This was in fact false, but the mistake was discovered before it could have any untoward effect.*

14   *It was not a real Panzer Division and had only one tank battalion; after the Sicilian campaign it was renamed Panzer Grenadier Division, which name it retained.*

15   *Enemy air force strength amounted to about eight hundred German and seven hundred Italian combat aircraft counting all those based in Sicily, Sardinia, Italy and South France. The Italian battle fleet included six battleships and two 8-inch cruisers.*

16   *RDF = Radio Direction Finding (now known as Radar).*

17   *Major-General Lyman L. Lemnitzer.*

18   *It was also of assistance in helping the craft to cross the off-lying sand bars which formed "false beaches" on some of the American beaches.*

19   *This was the original German airborne division which had been responsible for the invasion of Crete. It was at that moment engaged in splitting into I and 2 Parachute Divisions; 3 Regiment, which is the one in question here, was assigned, either already or later, to I Parachute Division.*

20   *War Office footnote. According to official records, Caltagirone was captured at 0400 hours, 16th July, 1943, and Piazza Armerina at 0600 hours, 17th July, 1943.*

21   *Goums are composed of French Moroccan native troops particularly skilled in mountain warfare. A Tabor is the approximate equivalent of a battalion.*

22   *One Regimental Combat Team was already in the island having arrived to reinforce II Corps on 15th July at Licata.*

23   *This was done by employing one regiment at a time on each axis for a short period of about forty-eight hours each, relieving continuously with the other two regiments of this division and then with the next division. This meant continuous fresh troops in action and must have imposed an intolerable strain on the German defence.*

24   *War Office footnote. G-4 and G-I Branches are the American equivalents of the British Q and A Branches.*

25   *Operation TORCH was the Anglo-American assault on French North Africa, 8th November, 1942.*

26   *War Office footnote. In addition I Canadian Division, ancillary units and 3,000 R.A.F. personnel were embarked in the United Kingdom and transported to Sicily. 45 U.S. Division (less I Regimental Combat Team) and ancillary units were mounted from the United States of America.*

27   *AMGOT = Allied Military Government of Occupied Territories.*

28   *War Office footnote. The following paragraphs deal with Administration from the Army aspect only. Mediterranean Allied Tactical Air Forces had its own Administrative organisation.*

29   *CG NATOUSA = Commanding General, North African Theatre of Operations, United States Army.*

2

ADMIRAL OF THE FLEET SIR ANDREW CUNNINGHAM'S DESPATCH ON THE INVASION OF SICILY

THE INVASION OF SICILY

The following Despatch was submitted to the Supreme Commander, Allied Expeditionary Force on the 1st January, 1944, by Admiral of the Fleet Sir ANDREW B.CUNNINGHAM, G.C.B., D.S.O.

> *Office of the Commander-in-Chief,*
> *Mediterranean.*
> *1st January, 1944.*

I have the honour to forward the accompanying reports on the Invasion of Sicily. Many of these reports have been forwarded previously to the appropriate authorities in order that there should be no delay in the digestion and application of the "lessons learnt." The reports of the naval Task Force Commanders, and of the Vice-Admiral Commanding, Force "H"[1], are very full and carefully compiled, giving a complete narrative of the operation in all its stages, and summarising a wealth of experience in the sound conclusions they have reached and suggestions they have offered.[2]

2. It is not my intention to add a further narrative to those already written nor to do more than comment on salient points of importance. Except in so far as stated in the succeeding paragraphs, I concur fully in the suggestions and recommendations of the Force Commanders.

Planning.

3. The following outstanding lesson emerged from the planning stage of this operation.

4. It is essential, if much time is not to be wasted and much confusion caused, that the responsible Commanders-in-Chief, together with the Task Force Commanders who will be responsible for the tactical conduct of the battle, should meet at the outset for the discussion and evolution of a sound basic plan which should not thereafter be changed except for reasons of exceptional urgency, such as a complete change in the enemy's dispositions or a major strategic upheaval.

5. In the case of "Husky"[3] this was not done, since both General Alexander and General Montgomery were absorbed in the Tunisian battle. In consequence, although the operation was authorised on 23rd January and combined planning headquarters set up on 12th February, the final firm plan was not approved until the 12th May. Thus, although five months were available for perfecting plans for the operation, all detailed planning had in fact to be compressed into two months, resulting in some confusion and considerable unnecessary duplication in the issue of orders.

6. It cannot be too clearly recognised that a combined operation is but the opening, under particular circumstances, of a primarily army battle. It is the function of the navy and of the air to help the army to establish a base or bases on the hostile coast from which the military tactical battle to gain the object must be developed. It is upon the army tactical plan for the fulfilment of its object that the combined plan must depend. The navy and the air commanders must join with the army commander to ensure that the base or bases selected for seizure are capable of achievement without prohibitive loss in the irrespective elements, and that, when seized, they will fulfil the requirements of the force; but it is of no use to plan on the seizure of bases unrelated to the realities of the military situation when ashore.

7. It was upon this point that the initial planning of "Husky" broke down. It maybe that the earlier plans would have succeeded equally well; but the fact remains that these plans in the end proved unacceptable to the army leaders called upon to fight the tactical battle for the object, and that, had it been possible for those leaders fully to study the tactical aspect at the outset, the undesirable last minute changes would have been saved.

8. A further point is that in the initial planning great weight was lent to the value of airborne troops for the softening of beach defences. The conditions of light required for the employment of paratroops were inimical to the secure and undetected approach of naval forces. As the result of much discussion and in view of the importance attached to the airborne attack, the date selected for the assault was one which was not favourable from the naval point of view. In fact the airborne troops were never used in the manner projected, but that they were not to be so used did not emerge until it was too late to change the date. In consequence, the navies, for no advantage, had to accept a disadvantageous light for approach, and a subsequent period of moonlit nights off the beaches which could have been avoided.

9. The Naval Commander Western Task Force comments at length and stringently on this subject in his report.[4] While I do not in all respects agree with his estimate of

the effectiveness of naval gunfire, I concur generally in his remarks, and, in particular, in questioning the wisdom of attaching a high degree of importance in the plan to the employment of airborne troops. A seaborne assault is unalterably committed to a date for some days in advance of D day. In tidal waters it is even more inflexibly bound by time and tide. It may well be that, on the selected date, airborne troops are weatherbound and cannot operate. It does, therefore, appear most necessary that airborne troops should be considered as a useful auxiliary rather than as a governing factor which may react to the disadvantage of other services involved.

10. Apart from the use of airborne troops, many other factors affect the selection of D day and H hour[5]: but a dominating factor must always be the high casualty rate inflicted by aimed machine-gun fire. Unless it can be guaranteed to the army that the enemy beach defences can be neutralised by naval gunfire or air attack or both – or by smoke – it is felt that darkness will always be chosen for the first waves to reach the beach. "Husky" gave but poor opportunity for judging the soundness of our choice since surprise was unexpectedly attained; but it is felt that, had the enemy been resolute and alert, it would have required more than the gun support actually available if the soldiers were to be landed in daylight without heavy casualties. Bomber forces were not available since they were occupied in neutralising the enemy air forces.

Preparation, Training and Mounting.

11. The training and mounting of "Husky" proceeded under difficulties, particularly in the case of Force "B"[6] of the Eastern Task Force, and to a lesser extent of the Western Task Force. Both these forces had to establish their base facilities in captured ports which had been considerably demolished, namely Sfax and Sousse for Force "B", and Bizerta and Tunis for the Western Task Force. Great credit is due to all concerned that these difficulties were ably surmounted in the time available. Force "B", in addition to other difficulties, was faced at short notice with the task of capturing Pantellaria but the task was taken in its stride and successfully accomplished without prejudice to "Husky", of which operation indeed it was an essential preliminary.

12. The reception and absorption in the station of the great number of landing ships and craft, and the establishment of their bases, presented a heavy problem to both navies. The probable performance of these craft, manned as they were by new and inexperienced officers and men but recently enrolled in their respective services, gave cause for some anxiety, and in the early stages of training they caused some slight wavering of confidence among the troops they were to land. The manner in which they buckled to and met and overcame their inexperience can best be measured by what they achieved, and deserves the highest praise.

13. Another cause of anxiety at this stage was the large demand for movement of troops, airmen and vehicles to their staging points or bases for the attack. This involved heavy and continuous running by the landing craft at times when they should have been training, and fear was felt, not only that their training would be inadequate, but that their engines would not stand the strain. These fears were happily disproved, and in fact the sea training provided by these voyages must have stood them in good

stead. That the craft themselves withstood the extra wear and tear is a tribute to those who designed and built them.

14. Additional difficulties in the way of training and mounting arose from late arrival of craft and material. This was particularly so in the case of Force "A"[7] of the Eastern Task Force which received its L.S.T.s[8] extremely late and had little or no opportunity of trying and practising with pontoons. This portion of the force was also separated by 900 miles from the L.C.T.s[9] which were to form a part of its assault. A high standard of staff work was required to knit these scattered components into an operational whole.

15. The Western Task Force was more fortunate in that opportunities for training and mounting were undisturbed, and all ships were concentrated. Although this force also suffered to some extent from late arrivals and rushed planning, as compared with the Eastern Task Force the Western Task Force was much better placed since the U.S. warships came into the Mediterranean for the specific purpose of the operation, and only very slight calls were made upon them for extraneous duties on the station. In the case of the Eastern Task Force, all ships, belonging as they did to the normal forces of the station, were heavily and continuously employed right up to the date of sailing for the operation, and in but few cases took part in any rehearsal or training. That their duties were performed so adequately when the time came reflects highly alike on the adaptability of their ships' companies and on the standard of maintenance achieved in spite of many months of arduous service at sea.

Collection of Beach Intelligence.

16. Much credit is due to the officers and men of the beach reconnaissance parties for their arduous and hazardous effort to obtain details of the beach gradients and sand bars. Credit is also due to the submarines of the 8th and 10th Flotillas which worked on beach reconnaissance in company with these parties.

Their casualties in this operation were unfortunately heavy; apart from natural dislike of such losses, the possibility of capture always gives rise to anxiety on grounds of security.

Location of Headquarters.

17. Much discussion was devoted to the best location for the combined headquarters from which the three Commanders-in-Chief should conduct the operation. Various alternatives were explored in an effort to find a common site satisfactory to all, but in the end communications problems, and, to a lesser extent, lack of suitable accommodation, caused an undesirable dispersion in that though the navy and army headquarters moved to Malta from Algiers, the Air Officer Commanding-in-Chief found himself unable to move from his existing headquarters at Marsa, where he was in close touch with his main forces.[10]

I am sure Malta was a wise choice from both naval and army viewpoints, and apart from an unexpected assault of sandflies which devastated my staff, the arrangements were in all respects excellent.

18. The separation of the Commanders did not in the event have serious reaction, but was manifestly undesirable and might have proved extremely awkward had things begun to go awry. In particular the navy and the air are closely interdependent in a sea assault, and with the exception of the coastal air component, the air plans of the operation had all along appeared to the other services to be somewhat nebulous, and their day-to-day exposition was necessary to make the picture clear.

The Approach and Assault.

19. The co-ordination and timing necessary to ensure the punctual concentration of this vast force in the assault areas, presented a problem of some complexity. The problem was to some degree complicated by the great distances over which the forces were initially dispersed[11], by the need for deceptive routeing to avoid disclosure of intention, by the bottleneck presented by the Tunisian war channel, and, finally, by the requirement for topping up the fuel of escort vessels before their arrival in the assault area.

Very detailed orders were issued regarding the routes and timing of the approach, backed up by track charts and the inevitable "Mickey Mouse" diagrams which are in my view essential to the clear understanding of a problem of this nature. Even so, everything depended, as always, on the seamanship and good sense of individual commanding officers and on the smooth working of the berthing and fuelling organisations of the several ports concerned.

My confidence in their abilities was not misplaced. The operation ran like a well-oiled clock.

20. The only incidents which occurred to mar the precision of this remarkable concentration were the loss by submarine attack of four ships in convoy, the CITY OF VENICE and ST. ESSYLT in K.M.S. 18B on the 4th July, the DEVIS in K.M.S. 18B on 5th July, and the SHAHJEHAN in M.W.S. 36 on the 6th July. The passage of the convoys was covered most effectively by the operations of the North-West African Coastal Air Force, of No. 201 (Naval Co-operation) Group, of squadrons operating under Air Headquarters Air Defence, Eastern Mediteranean, and, on D - 1 day, of the North-West African Tactical Air Force Squadrons based on Malta. Their problem was one of a complexity equal to our own. It was solved with conspicuous success, since no bomb was dropped on any convoy – the majority were not sighted by enemy aircraft – and all reports showed that the fighter cover was excellent.

21. An aspect of the approach which caused me concern was the slow speed of the L.C.T. convoys, and the necessity for their arrival at the assault beaches well before first light to provide the supporting arms the army needed. Throughout the planning stages, the estimates of speed of advance allowable for L.C.T. convoys had continually to be lowered as experience was gained. In the end it became clear that not more than 5½ knots could be counted upon in safety, even in calm weather. I was not sanguine of our ability to maintain surprise at any time after 1200 on D -1, since it appeared beyond doubt that the enemy must by then become aware of our concentration south of Malta: but it appeared to be beyond the wildest expectation

that he should be unaware of the L.C.T. convoys which must be within 20 miles of his coast at sunset.

It is, I suggest, a matter of urgency that some means be devised of landing supporting arms at an early stage from craft whose speed is at least in the region of that of the average infantry assault ship, if tactical surprise is to be aimed at.

22. Little anxiety had been felt on the score of weather, which is so rarely bad in the Mediterranean at this time of year. Nevertheless, plans had been made whereby a postponement of 24 hours could, if necessary, be ordered as late as 1200 on D - 1. Beyond this time it was felt impracticable to disturb the march of events, and it was also expected that in the event the weather would have sufficiently disclosed its intentions by this time.

Such was not the case however – at 1200 D – 1 the wind was blowing force 4 from the northwest but there was no evidence of imminent increase and no question of postponement arose. By 1700 the wind was force 6 to 7[12] and a nasty sea had risen. It was manifestly too late for postponement but considerable anxiety was felt, particularly for the small craft convoys making up against the sea. The wind mercifully started to ease from 2330 onwards, by H hour it was slight, and by morning had ceased, leaving only a tiresome swell and surf on the western beaches.

Attainment of Surprise.

23. This little blow had various effects but the most noteworthy was its contribution to our unexpected success in gaining complete surprise. The very efficient cover plan and the deceptive routeing of the convoys both played their parts. In addition the vigilance of the enemy was undoubtedly relaxed owing to the unfavourable phase of the moon to which we had been so unwillingly subjected. Finally came this wind which indeed came dangerously close at one time to making some, if not all, of the landings impracticable. These last two, to us, apparently unfavourable factors had actually the effect of making the weary Italians, who had been alert for many nights, turn thankfully in their beds saying "tonight at any rate they can't come!"

But they came.

The Landings.

24. In consequence of the wind not all assault waves reached the beach at H hour, but none was seriously late. Some of the L.C.T. convoys were very late, the most being that for BARK EAST[13] which was six hours late, having furthest to go against the wind. One L.C.T. was swamped and capsized. The performance of the small craft of both nations in this period was most creditable. They made valiant efforts to keep their rendezvous and in large measure were successful.

25. The assaults were landed in all sectors in the right place, nearly at the right time and with negligible opposition. In some areas some interference was encountered after daylight from coast defence and shore batteries, but in most cases they were readily silenced by ships' gunfire and the landings proceeded steadily with no appreciable interference other than the swell.

The Western Task Force, on their exposed western beaches, bore the brunt of opposition both by gunfire and surf, the latter particularly at CENT[14] beaches which were most nearly a lee shore. Losses of craft by broaching in this area were considerable. That the surf was in no wise allowed to interfere with the smooth progress of the landing reflects highly on the determination, resource and sound training of the Western Task Force.

26. After the landings the troops moved steadily inland on both fronts, apparently encountering but little opposition except inland of Gela in the DIME[15] area of the Western Task Force, where the floating reserve (Kool Force) was ordered to be landed in support. A determined counter attack by the Hermann Goering Panzer Division started to develop in this area from 0900 on D day and had some success, reaching almost to the beaches on the evening of D + 1. Naval gunfire played a prominent and praiseworthy part in stopping and turning this attack, being notably effective against tanks. By 2230 on D + 1 the situation had been restored and no further serious threat to the security of our bridge-heads developed. Syracuse was entered by our troops at 2100 D day and the port swept and open by 0830 D + 1.

Air Action during the Assault.

27. The degree of air opposition encountered in the assault and later could by no means be described as serious; but caused some casualties among shipping and had some nuisance value.

In this respect the Western Task Force was less fortunate than the Eastern Task Force and was somewhat bothered, particularly by fighter bomber aircraft coming low over the hills from inland in such a manner as to evade detection by radar.

28. The provision of S.E.[16] fighter cover in the assault areas prior to the capture of adequate Sicilian airfields, presented a difficult problem to the Air Command, with only the limited airfield facilities of Malta, Gozo and Pantellaria lying within reasonable fighter range. The number of fighter sorties necessary to maintain even squadron strength in both assault areas was prodigious.

The Air Command had to strike a balance in the allotment of their resources between the value of defensive patrols and offensive action at the enemy airfields – both having the same object – the security of the assault from enemy air interference.

It was pointed out in my operation order that much of the air's effort would be unseen by the naval forces, and the strength of fighters to be expected was outlined.

29. By results I consider that the air appreciation was proved sound. To one who had fought through the Mediterranean campaign from the beginning it appeared almost magical that great fleets of ships could remain anchored on the enemy's coast, within 40 miles of his main aerodromes, with only such slight losses from air attack as were incurred.

The navies (and consequently the armies) owed a great debt to the air forces for the effectiveness of the protection afforded them throughout the operation. Nevertheless, there was palpably room for improvement in the close air cover of the assault areas, and, in particular, in the effectiveness of the liaison between the Naval Force Commanders and the fighter forces upon which they had to rely. This improvement was in fact effected in the next major amphibious operation which was undertaken in this theatre.

Routeing of Troop-carrying Aircraft.

30. The routeing of aircraft carrying airborne troops to the attack was, from the beginning, recognised as presenting an awkward problem. Allowance was made in the naval approach plan, in conference with Air Plans, for a gap between assault convoys north of Malta through which the troop-carrying aircraft could approach and return without flying over convoys. These routes were promulgated in my operation orders.

In fact these attacks were delivered without interference between naval and air forces involved; but it was not until D - 3 that the airborne troops' plans became firm and that troop-carrier command were able finally to confirm the suitability of routes passing through the corridor laid down so long before.

These late decisions were in large measure due to the late crystallisation of the military tactical plan already referred to in paragraphs 5 to 7 above.

31. Later, airborne troop missions were flown on the night 10th/11th July to the Gela area and on the night 13th/14th July to the Catania area.

In the first instance, an ingress corridor over a deserted portion of coast between the two task forces was allotted and promulgated by signal. The aircraft were to fly inland by this corridor and withdraw passing to the north and west of Licata, well clear of the Western Task Force. In fact, owing to heavy ground A.A. fire and possibly due to bad navigation, large numbers of aircraft forsook the route and flew over the Western Task Force assault areas concurrently with an enemy air attack. Considerable losses resulted.

In the second instance, decision to carry out the operation was taken too late to enable routeing to be certainly promulgated to all ships. The airborne troops' representative at H.Q. was apprised of this danger at the time. This late decision in combination with the unexpectedly late sailing of a convoy from Augusta led to a number of aircraft being shot down by merchant vessel gunfire. In this instance too, enemy aircraft were present to complicate the issue.

32. These incidents led to an enquiry being held by Allied Force Headquarters with a view to eliminating such incidents in future. I concur in the recommendations of committee which are forwarded separately.

Though not easy, the routeing of troop-carrier aircraft prior to the main assault, while ships are moving in pre-arranged tracks and in perfect timing, presents a clear cut problem readily susceptible to solution by careful planning as was shown on the night of D - 1/D day in "Husky".

The major problem arises in the routeing of aircraft to make drops to fulfil military tactical requirements arising after the main assaults, when the situation has become fluid, convoys are being cleared as they unload, and signal communications are inevitably congested. It was under these conditions that the incidents quoted above occurred.

Naval Forces other than Assault Forces.

33. The work of the main covering force, the hinge pin of the operation, was dull and unspectacular as must ever be the case against a passive enemy. Force "H" was faced with the prospect of steady patrolling in waters within easy reach of the enemy's air bases, in conditions of moonlight and weather peculiarly suited to air attack and with a growing U-boat threat.

It was not until July 17th (D + 7) that the reduced congestion of Malta and my appreciation of enemy intentions combined to allow this force to be withdrawn into harbour at Malta. In the interval the INDOMITABLE had, not unexpectedly, been torpedoed and severely damaged. Force "H" achieved its object.

34. The effect of the diversionary operations, "Fracture"[17] by Force "Z" and "Arsenal"[18] by Force "Q" and coastal forces, cannot be accurately assessed. It is presumed that they contributed to the confusion of the enemy. Both were satisfactorily carried out in precisely the manner ordered.

35. The operations of Force "Q" patrolling nightly northward of the landings, were as necessary as they were unspectacular, and lacked incident. The torpedoing of CLEOPATRA by a U-boat, and the sinking of a U-boat by ILEX and ECHO were merely incidents of passage unconnected with the operational function of this force.

36. The operations of coastal forces, and, at a later stage, of the American P.T. boats[19] in the Straits of Messina were most gallant and determined. They nightly faced an unpleasant volume of gunfire and inflicted losses on the enemy.

37. The anti U-boat operations, both air and surface, which were instituted as soon as a U-boat concentration on the east coast of Sicily became apparent, did not succeed in making any kills. But the U-boat activity achieved little, and that this was the case was probably in no small measure due to the active measures which were taken to discourage their presence.

The U-boat kills which were made were fortuitous, notably the capture of BRONZO by the 13th Minesweeping Flotilla off Syracuse, and LAFOREY's rapid revenge for the torpedoing of NEWFOUNDLAND off Catania.

March of Events subsequent to the Assaults.

38. An outstanding feature of the operation was the rapidity of progress of the left wing U.S. 7th Army once they were firmly ashore. The whole of these operations both before and after the capture of Palermo was a model of amphibious tactics by the Western Task Force.

In particular, after the capture of Palermo on the 22nd July (D + 12) U.S. generalship showed that it had nothing to learn of the value of sea power and Task Force 86 under Rear-Admiral Davidson, U.S.N. that it had nothing to learn of the rapid planning and execution of outflanking operations.

The three "end runs" executed in the north coast of Sicily saved days of costly fighting.

39. Progress on the east coast was less spectacular and more costly. Augusta was entered by the army on the evening of 12th July (D + 2), after a rather exasperating

day in which our destroyers alternately entered the harbour triumphantly and were evicted by enemy shellfire to which they could not reply owing to inability to distinguish our own troops; but the situation did not really become cleared up and the port rendered safe for democracy until the morning of the 13th when the Port Party was finally installed and a valuable protected anchorage made available for our use.

Two small commando operations from two L.S.I. (H)[20] contributed to the capture of this port. From this time onward, however, no use was made by the 8th Army of amphibious opportunities. The small L.S.I.s were kept standing by for the purpose at the call of Rear-Admiral McGrigor (Flag Officer Sicily) and landing craft were available on call: but the only occasion on which they were used was on 16th August, 1943, after the capture of Catania, when a commando landing was made, but fell short of the flank of the retreating enemy.

40. There were doubtless sound military reasons for making no use of this, what to me appeared, priceless asset of sea power and flexibility of manoeuvre: but it is worth consideration for future occasions whether much time and costly fighting could not be saved by even minor flank attacks which must necessarily be unsettling to the enemy. It must be always for the General to decide. The Navy can only provide the means and advice on the practicability from the naval angle of the projected operation. It may be that had I pressed my views more strongly more could have been done.

41. Much use was made of naval gunfire to support the seaward flank of the 8th Army. Reports showed that such support was satisfactory and effective. Only on one occasion was heavy ship gunfire employed, when WARSPITE carried out a brief bombardment of Catania on the evening of the 17th July.

The End of the Operation.

42. The operation concluded with the entry of Messina on the 17th August, the U.S. 7th Army, thanks to their amphibious tactics and some prodigious road engineering feats, beating the British 8th Army by a short head for the prize.

Conclusion.

43. These remarks contain criticism where, in my view, criticism is due. Where possible the criticism is constructive and designed to avoid a repetition of such mistakes as were made. It is a cause for congratulation of all concerned that the criticisms are so few and the triumph so great.

44. I count myself indeed fortunate that, in the planning and execution of this, the greatest seaborne operation so far known in history, I met with a co-operation so complete and cordial as was accorded me by my colleagues General Alexander and Air Chief Marshal Tedder, and their subordinates.

45. Of the Navies, I can only say that I never wish to command better, and I count it a great honour that, through the person of Vice-Admiral Hewitt, I was privileged to command so large and efficient a force of the United States Navy. Both the Western Task Force, under Admiral Hewitt, and the Eastern Task Force, under Admiral

Ramsay, performed their unaccustomed tasks in a manner befitting the highest tradition of any fighting service.

(Signed) A.B. CUNNINGHAM,
Admiral of the Fleet.
General Dwight D. Eisenhower,
Supreme Commander,
Allied Expeditionary Force.
Admiralty,
*S.W.*1.
1st October, 1943.

I have the honour to forward herewith the report of proceedings of the Eastern Naval Task Force during the initial phase of operations for the capture of the Island of Sicily, known as Operation "Husky". These operations were wholly successful, but considering the large force involved and the time allowed for preparation, any other result could only have been most unexpected and disappointing.

2. By reason of the weakness of the Italian opposition, the success of the assaults in "Husky" cannot be considered as a reliable guide to what may be attempted or achieved elsewhere. Nevertheless, valuable experience was gained which will be of inestimable assistance in future operations, notably in regard to maintenance through the beaches, handling and serviceability of landing ships and craft, opening of captured ports and in the use of naval armaments in support of the army in subsequent operations along the coast.

3. Casualties to shipping and amongst landing craft were considerably less than had been anticipated and allowed for. This was gratifying and is considered to be due to:-

(*a*) the very high degree of air superiority achieved;

(*b*) the efficiency of the A/S[21] organisation;

(*c*) the unexpected attainment of a considerable degree of tactical surprise. That tactical surprise was effected is considered to have resulted from a combination of circumstances, such for example as the adoption of a waxing moon period for the assaults, the lack of enemy air reconnaissance on D - 1 day and a prolonged period of "alert" preceding D day, all of which, together with the unexpected high wind which got up p.m. on D - 1, lulled the enemy coast defences into a false sense of security.

4. The performance of landing ships and craft was uniformly good and, in the majority of cases, creditable seamanship was displayed by those in charge of them, having regard to their necessarily restricted training and lack of previous experience. The advantage enjoyed by the personnel of the flotillas which were sent to the Middle East in advance of the operation was very marked and much credit is due to Rear-Admiral T.H. Troubridge, D.S.O. (Rear-Admiral (G)) for the excellent training which he gave them.

5. *Period of Preparation and Planning.* – The conditions that would result from the large distances between the various headquarters had been foreseen, and, as expected, planning by telegram inevitably led to misunderstandings and a large number of amendments to the operation orders in the last few days. Due to the unavoidable delay in getting the operation orders to the various Task Group Commanders, considerable complications arose by the inclusion in some of their orders of matter which was properly the concern of higher authorities. This again increased the number of amendments necessary, and presented great difficulties to the smaller craft who received a mass of orders and amendments a few days before the operation.

6. *The Plan.* – There are two outstanding points about the plan which call for remark. The first has to do with the operational and the other with the administrative aspect. In my opinion the primary consideration is the operational aspect. The army must first examine the implications of the land campaign necessary to achieve the object in view. After this the administrative authorities must assess the administrative implications. In the early stages of planning for "Husky" too little importance and attention was paid to the operational aspect whilst too much was paid to the administrative, with the result that the outline plan given to the Commanders of the Eastern Task Force was operationally unacceptable. This situation was further complicated by the pre-occupation of the Army and Air Commanders with current operations and the wide dispersal of all planning authorities which resulted in a prolonged period of negotiation and delay.

In the end military necessity dictated the acceptance of administrative risks and the choice of a sound operational plan. It is to be hoped that plans for future operations will be based on operational requirements and not to suit the administrative appreciations, which incidentally always appear ultra-conservative in probabilities.

By the time the final orders were issued I felt entirely satisfied that the best plan available to us had been adopted, and my hopes that the weight of our attacks on a narrow front would overwhelm the enemy were, in the event, justified.

7. *Mounting of the Operation in the Middle East.* – From the moment of my arrival in Cairo on 2nd March, 1943, every possible assistance was afforded myself and my staff in the mounting and preparation for "Husky" by the Commander-in-Chief, Levant, Admiral Sir Henry Harwood, K.C.B., O.B.E., and his successors, Admirals Sir Ralph Leatham, K.C.B., and Sir John H.D. Cunningham, K.C.B., M.V.O., and the other naval authorities and departments in the Middle East. All the resources of the Levant Station, personnel, material and training, were made available and too great credit cannot be given to that Command for its share in the successful operations which followed.

Training in the Middle East was satisfactory. The rehearsals were carried out in the Gulf of Aqaba from 10th to 17th June but were necessarily limited in scope, as only four M.T. ships and four L.C.T. were able to be present, no L.C.I.(L)[22] were available, and a limit had to be placed on the number of beachings that could be made by operational assault craft.

8. *Move to Malta.* – With my staff I took passage to Malta in H.M.S. ORION,

arriving late on 2nd July. It had always been foreseen that there would be a large amount for my staff to do on arrival at Malta in the few days available previous to the operation, *e.g.,* the allocation of landing craft by numbers to flotillas and task groups, and the briefing of the large number of landing craft and smaller warships based there. The forethought given to these matters by Vice-Admiral Malta enabled the work to be undertaken expeditiously and with his full understanding. I cannot speak too highly of the assistance given by Vice-Admiral A.J. Power, C.B., C.V.O., and his staff throughout the period that I was in Malta. His organisation enabled the heavy and intricate programme of loading, sailing and refuelling, etc., to proceed without a hitch, and all my requirements were readily and efficiently met.

9. *Narrative of the Operation.* – A composite narrative for the Task Force is attached. More detailed narratives for each sector are included in the Task Group Commanders' reports.

The Eastern Naval Task Force came under my operational control at 1200 on D - 1, 9th July, and I was afloat on that and the following day with my flag flying in H.M.S. ANTWERP. Weather conditions were fair during the forenoon, and although the wind had risen slightly by noon, at which time I was in company with the four main ship convoys, south of Malta, I was not seriously concerned. The L.C.T. convoys from Tripoli and Tunisia had previously been spoken off Malta earlier in the day, and they and the ship convoys were all in their appointed positions. During the afternoon and evening the wind increased steadily from the north-west to a strength of at least 6 and by 1800 a nasty sea was running.

The effect of these conditions on the landing craft and at the beaches caused me some anxiety but postponement did not seriously enter into my mind. My reasoning was based on long acquaintance with Mediterranean weather conditions which led me to expect that the wind would go down suddenly before morning, together with the knowledge that all but one of my landings were to be made on a weather shore where conditions would not be too bad. It may be stated here that the wind and sea did start to drop soon after midnight and daylight saw the beginning of a perfect day with a clear blue sky and steadily decreasing swell. Except at BARK WEST,[23] where Force "V"[24] had to compete with a slight sea and swell, conditions at the beaches were perfect. It must be remembered, however, that the L.S.I, reached their release positions at 0030, before the wind and sea had abated to any extent, and the conditions in which the L.C.A.[25] were lowered with the first flight and when L.C.I.(L) came alongside to embark their troops were very unpleasant. The more credit is due to them for the fact that the initial landings were made as near to H hour as was the case.

I did not myself see any landing craft during the night, but all reports show that their performance together with that of the H.D.M.L.,[26] etc., was very satisfactory taking into account the prevailing weather.

10. The L.C.T convoy for BARK EAST, having been held up by the weather and having eventually made BARK SOUTH,[27] arrived close on six hours late, that for ACID[28] two hours late, and that for BARK SOUTH about two hours late, but the L.C.T. for BARK WEST, which had been given a shorter route than originally intended, passing east of Gozo, arrived only thirty minutes late. This latter convoy

had the worst of the blow, and their prompt arrival reflected high credit on Lieutenant-Commander K.A. Sellar, R.N., who led them.

11. In general the marking submarines were in their correct positions and navigational aids were working and were picked up by the convoys on approaching their release positions. The ships at the release positions were not apparently detected by the shore defences, and the only difficulties experienced in lowering and forming up landing craft were those imposed by the weather. It is clear that the allowance of two and a half hours from the arrival at the release position to H hour was in no way excessive as the majority of the assaults were a few minutes late.

12. The defences were taken generally by surprise when the assaulting formations landed and there was little organised resistance on the beaches. It is understood that a proportion of the coast defences were not, in fact, manned on that night; those that were manned were, in the majority of cases, not stoutly fought.

13. At first light there was a certain amount of shelling from shore batteries, but these were effectively dealt with by supporting monitors, destroyers and gun boats. The effectiveness of the supporting fire from our naval forces was a feature of the operation, and many tributes have been paid it, both by the army and by enemy prisoners.

14. Due to the late arrival of the L.C.T. convoys the only L.C.T. to beach before daylight were those at BARK SOUTH. Although these did so successfully, and on a shore that was generally rocky, insufficient experience was gained in the operation as a whole to show how far the beaching of L.C.T. in large numbers in darkness is a practical proposition. The problem of landing the supporting arms immediately behind the assault infantry cannot yet be considered to be solved, and it is recommended that comprehensive trials should be undertaken as early as possible to examine this matter. If difficulties are experienced, it is believed that a dark assault should be timed to be about one hour before first light, unless the army are prepared to rely on naval supporting fire for a longer period until first light.

15. It was unfortunate that the L.C.R.[29] were not able to soften the beach defences, but their subsequent performance suggests that they are well fitted for this role. L.C.G. (L)[30] engaged direct targets effectively at short range, and the moral effect of both the L.C.R. and the L.C.G. (L) firing from close inshore is reported to have been considerable.

16. The slow convoys arrived in accordance with the plan and in every case ships had moved to an inshore anchorage by 0800/10th July. No mines were found inshore.

17. Unloading of the M.T. ships was commenced without delay, and proceeded satisfactorily, despite bad exits and soft sand in the ACID sector and false beaches and soft sand at BARK WEST. It had always been known that BARK WEST beach was unlikely to be suitable as a maintenance beach, but it is clear that it was nevertheless correct to assault on it close on the flank of BARK SOUTH. It was generally considered by Task Group Commanders that the strength of the Docks Operating personnel in the M.T. ships was insufficient, and this was borne out in "Husky". It is probably correct to say that the bottleneck in maintenance through the beaches was the insufficiency of the Docks Operating Companies to work the ships

continuously. Casualties to landing craft due to enemy action were very small, but as in "Torch",[31] a few L.C.T. and L.C.M.[32] were put out of action due to bad seamanship displayed by their half trained crews.

18. Both the L.S.T. (2)[33] and the L.C.I. (L) proved invaluable in their respective roles, and it is considered that the speed with which both vehicles and personnel were landed was one of the principal factors of the operation from the naval point of view. Although at times the rate at which stores were unloaded appeared to be disappointing, the totals unloaded for the beaches were, in fact, greater than the planned figures. On 21st July 4,400 tons of stores were discharged at BARK SOUTH. This was of course an exceptionally good beach, and by that time the organisation there had been perfected and three beach groups were assisting, but the previous estimates for beach maintenance would seem to need revision. It appears that neither BARK SOUTH nor BARK EAST were worked to capacity during "Husky". The salient feature of this period was the success of the L.S.T. (2), L.C.I. (L) and the D.U.K.W.[34] of which the latter were making their first appearance in European waters: they fulfilled our highest expectations.

19. In general, it is considered that the beach organisations worked satisfactorily, although Naval Commander Force "V" reported that his S.N.O.L.[35] organisations were slow in settling down. The shortage of transport ashore to clear the beach dumps was commented on by Task Group Commanders, and was aggravated by the very quick forward advance of the army. This is not likely, however, to obtain in future operations undertaken against a more determined enemy.

20. The immunity from air attack was as surprising as it was satisfactory and considerably greater than I had been led to expect. Our ships were not attacked until 1015/10th July, when a raid was made on the ships at ACID. On subsequent days there were intermittent air attacks, principally on the east coast, and an increasing number at night. It was fortunate that more damage was not done by these attacks; only three M.T. ships and one hospital ship were sunk by them. The hospital ship TALAMBA was deliberately attacked and sunk and the ABA and DORSETSHIRE were also attacked whilst lying over five miles to seaward fully illuminated. It is regretted that the orders regarding the conduct of hospital ships were not sufficiently clear; it had always been my intention that if hospital ships had to remain off the beaches at night they should remain darkened and in the fleet anchorage, and that normally full illumination would only be switched on when five miles clear of the beaches and on passage to or from the assault area. It is clear that the illumination of hospital ships stopped offshore provides the enemy with a temptation to attack that is too great to resist and, in consequence, after the TALAMBA incident hospital ships were kept in the anchorages all night without lights. This procedure is recommended for future occasions.

21. Syracuse was occupied at 2100/10th July, the port party entered during the forenoon of 11th July and the D + 3 personnel convoy arrived there according to plan on 13th July: unloading all twelve ships and sailing them again at 1800 the same day was a notable achievement. Attempts were made to enter Augusta which was reported as having been evacuated at 0500 on 12th July but on her way to do so ESKIMO

with Naval Commander Force "A" on board was damaged in an air attack. Later in the day other ships of Force "A" again entered Augusta, and I myself went in in the evening in BROCKLESBY with Naval Commander Force "A". At this time the enemy on the outskirts of the town commenced to shell our ships intermittently with field guns and we had to clear out. I strongly support the recommendation of Naval Commander Force "A" that the foremost elements of the army should have some means of notifying their positions to supporting warships, as on this occasion we saw a large amount of M.T. which we thought belonged to the Eighth Army but which in fact belonged to the enemy. In consequence we missed an excellent and easy target.

22. In accordance with my instructions Naval Commander Force "V" took over the BARK sectors on 13th July in order that Naval Commander Force "B" could proceed to Syracuse to take over the duties of Flag Officer Sicily. On visiting that port on 15th July I found a certain amount of confusion existing in the naval organisation which was absorbing the attention of Rear-Admiral McGrigor, to the detriment of the performance of his functions as Flag Officer Sicily. As I was anxious that he should proceed to and carry out these functions in Augusta without further delay, and as I deemed it advisable that a naval officer of standing should be temporarily present in Syracuse to supervise the Naval Officer-in-Charge and put matters right, I directed Naval Commander Force "A" to proceed there forthwith and Flag Officer Sicily to carry on to Augusta.

23. A larger number of L.S.T. and major landing craft was found to be serviceable on D - 1 than had been anticipated, and as a result it was possible to commence loading the first flight of the ferry service before ships and craft which had been engaged in the assaults had returned. The Eighth Army plan was to clear the high priority vehicles and stores from Malta before working craft in any numbers from Sousse and Tripoli, and in the first seven days 56 L.S.T., 36 L.C.T. and 33 L.C.I. (L) cleared loaded from Malta. Some initial difficulty was experienced over the control of the Ferry Service, as the Military Movements organisation set up in Malta did not appear adequate to meet the demands made upon it, but after a shaky start things went much better, and the planned programme was finally completed earlier than anticipated.

24. It was decided, both to reduce signalling and to avoid delays to sailings, that the short passage between Malta and Sicily should be made by L.S.T. and major landing craft engaged in the ferry service without making any sailing signals. The organisation of a convoy was often only completed immediately before it sailed, and I am satisfied that this apparently casual method was fully justified in order to continue the build-up of the army as fast as possible. As far as I know there was only one mishap; WALLACE engaged an L.C.I. (L) on the night of 12th/13th July, but happily only one rating was wounded. It would not have been possible to continue to sail these landing craft convoys in this manner, unescorted or only lightly escorted as they were, had the weather not remained calm after D day, and had there not been an increasing period of moonlight. Although the first quarter of the moon at first sight appeared unfavourable for landing operations from the naval aspect, in the event it

proved greatly to our advantage against a weak enemy and with our possession of great air superiority.

25. Major landing craft seemed to keep running very well during the first few days of the operation, but my flag was struck at about the time when I imagine that defects were beginning to accumulate. It must always remain a difficult decision in future operations as to when to withdraw a proportion of landing craft for essential maintenance as the need for this must be balanced against the vital requirement of following up the initial blow as expeditiously as possible.

26. It is greatly regretted that a number of our troop-carrying aircraft were shot down by our ships off the east coast on 13th July. The question of the rules for the engagement of aircraft off the beaches was always a vexed one during planning, and the orders were twice altered by agreement with the R.A.F. As finally framed, ships were free to open fire at night at aircraft whose approach indicated hostile intent, and it was stated that if friendly aircraft had to fly over our convoys they would do so above 6,000 feet. All troop-carrying aircraft were routed in lanes to avoid our convoys on the night of D - 1/D, but for the second airborne attack on D + 3, they flew low over the Gulf of Noto. It is understood that Mediterranean Air Command had obtained the agreement of Commander-in-Chief, Mediterranean to this some hours earlier, and warning signals were at once sent by the latter to all ships and forces concerned. It is not certain that they did in fact reach all the merchantmen, and by unfortunate chance a small number of enemy aircraft was in the vicinity at the time our aircraft were approaching. As might be expected, firing which started spasmodically soon became general, and it is hard to blame ships for engaging low-flying aircraft which appeared to be menacing them during an air raid. It is considered that in only very exceptional circumstances should ships be deprived of their right to open fire at low-flying aircraft approaching them. The solution must be always to route transport aircraft clear of our shipping.

27. I cannot close this letter without paying tribute to the magnificent work throughout all stages of "Husky" of my Task Group Commanders, Rear-Admirals R.R. McGrigor, C.B., Sir Philip L. Vian, K.B.E., D.S.O., and T.H. Troubridge, D.S.O. – as well as that of Captain Lord Ashbourne. I could not have been more efficiently and loyally supported by them nor by my staff under Commodore C.E. Douglas-Pennant, D.S.C.

28. Although the enemy did not make a determined attempt to prevent our assaults, conditions were not always easy, and it is considered that in general a very high standard of seamanship and devotion to duty was shown by officers and men of the Eastern Naval Task Force.

(Signed) B.H. RAMSAY,
Vice-Admiral,
Naval Commander,
Eastern Task Force.
Commander-in-Chief, Mediterranean.

NARRATIVE OF THE OPERATION

D - L DAY.

Friday, 9th July, 1943.

Naval Commander Eastern Task Force assumed operational control of all his ships and craft at noon. Leaving Malta in his Headquarters ship, H.M.S. ANTWERP, at 0630, he proceeded to the southward to sight first the L.C.T. groups approaching from Sousse and Tripoli, carrying the supporting arms for the assault, and later the fast and slow assault convoys from the Middle East and United Kingdom, all of which were in their assigned positions and proceeding according to plan. The forces and landing craft starting from, or staging through, Malta sailed as arranged throughout the day to join their respective group or convoy. H.M.S. ANTWERP returned to Calafrana in the evening to land the Chief of Combined Operations, and sailed again after dark for the scene of the landings south of Syracuse.

Weather. – The weather which in the early morning was good deteriorated throughout the day until in the evening the wind was force 6 from the north-westward. A short steep sea resulted which, while it did not interfere with the timing of the ship convoys, had the effect of slowing down the craft convoys and driving them off their course to the eastward. The state of the weather caused a certain amount of anxiety regarding the suitability of conditions off the beaches for carrying out the assault, but the question of suggesting a postponement did not come to be seriously considered.

Enemy reports. – No reports of enemy aircraft were received during the day.

D DAY.

Saturday, 10th July.

Weather. – After midnight the wind commenced to decrease in strength and the dawn ushered in a perfect blue Mediterranean day.

The Assaults.

The detailed accounts of the various assaults are given in the reports of the respective Task Group Commanders, etc., and only a general outline will be found in this narrative.

A. BARK WEST.

The fast assault convoy (K.M.F. 18) under Naval Commander Force "V" anchored about half-an-hour late, in a position subsequently found to be two miles to the eastward of the planned release position.

(i) SUGAR Sector

Considerable swell was still running in this sector, but the first assault flight were quickly and successfully lowered, and moved off not more than ten minutes behind schedule. The second flight were at once lowered and were got away only fifteen minutes late (*i.e,* 0155).The two flights beached on their correct beaches five and eighteen minutes late respectively. A runnel with nine feet of water inside a bank off the beaches, of which warning had been received while on passage from U.K., was encountered but all craft were carried over it by the surf.

The loading of serials[36] was put under way immediately the other craft had departed, but was slow on account of the swell.

Shortly after 0330 success signals were observed and about 0415 a signal was received that the shore was ready to take serials.

The Royal Marine Commandos also successfully landed and reported about 0330. The batteries which formed their objective proved to be dummies, and they suffered only a few casualties.

These landings were made without surprise being lost and there was little opposition at the beaches; in fact it was not until the first flight was leaving the shore that machine-gunfire was opened.

The first L.C.A. reported back to their parent ship about 0430. Naval casualties amounted to two wounded.

(ii) ROGER Sector

Having regard to the runnel mentioned above an alternative plan was devised and ordered whereby the troops would embark in L.C.T. instead of L.C.A. at the release position and then be launched in D.U.K.W. on reaching the runnel.

The L.C.T. duly arrived and loaded from S.S. MARNIX VAN SAINT ALDEGONDE, but none reached H.M.S. GLENGYLE and on instructions from the Naval Commander Force "A" she loaded her L.C.A. as originally planned. This necessitated the reorganisation of her troops and it was not until nearly 0230 that her craft were ready for lowering and it was 0315 before the first flight got away owing to the second flight from S.S. DERBYSHIRE persisting in an attempt to form up at the same time. The beach was found without difficulty with the aid of the Folbot[37] from the marking submarine.

The first flight from H.M.S. GLENGYLE beached about 0500; the second flight from S.S. DERBYSHIRE at 0520; and the remainder from S.S. MARNIX at 0545.

The first flight from H.M.S. GLENGYLE was met by a little machine-gun opposition, which was effectively dealt with by L.C.S.[38] from S.S. MARNIX. There were no casualties to craft personnel.

ROGER GREEN I and II beaches were used for the assault as in the light of conflicting information they appeared to be the best. In the event all the ROGER beaches were found to be shallow with constantly changing sandbanks, except ROGER RED which, though very small and rocky, was shown by a survey to be the most suitable for all types of landing craft. There was also an appreciable and abnormal tidal effect and many L.C.M. were stranded and could not be re-floated for some time. H.M.S. BOXER, THRUSTER and BRUISER were unable to beach within a reasonable distance from the shore and had to be unloaded by L.C.T.

Slow assault convoy arrives. – The slow assault convoy K.M.S. 18 arrived on time at the release position and brought up in the appointed anchorage.

Inner anchorage occupied – Shortly before daylight, Naval Commander Force "V" in H.M.S. HILARY led into the intermediate anchorage after the approach channel had been swept. A searching sweep indicated that the inner anchorage was free of mines and at 0900 shipping was entered into the bay.

By midday both S.N.O.L. (R) and S.N.O.L. (S) had moved ashore. A reasonable rate of unloading was continuously maintained and at 1630 the L.S.I. (L) and L.S.P.[39] had completed disembarkation and sailed for Malta.

B. BARK SOUTH.

In spite of the weather which made station keeping by L.C.I. (L) very difficult, the assault convoy for BARK SOUTH was only fifteen minutes late when it anchored. L.C.A. were got promptly away from the L.S.I. (M), but the swell made it difficult for L.CI. (L), both in coming alongside and in embarking their troops.

However, at 0115 the signal for the assault party to proceed was given, and the craft moved off with the exception of some L.C.I. (L) which had not completed loading; these followed later direct to the beaches.

The landings on RED beaches were made to time though two to three hundred yards to the westward of the correct position in the case of RED III. The GREEN beaches were found correctly but owing to the weather more time than anticipated was required for the passage and the landings were forty minutes late.

Opposition was everywhere slight, surprise being complete or almost so. At the GREEN landings some casualties were suffered in L.C.I. from machine-gun fire and in the RED sector an L.C.A. received several direct hits from a mortar.

The L.C.T. convoy were late but proceeded direct to the waiting position arriving there at 0330. The majority had beached by first light.

All RED and GREEN beaches were found to be smaller than expected, and there was some congestion, particularly when the Reserve Brigade went in at first light. Notwithstanding this all L.C.I. and L.C.T. had beached and discharged by about 0745.

Between 0800 and 0900 reconnaissance of AMBER beach by land and water proved, as anticipated by the military, that this beach was only lightly defended. The only opposition was one burst of machine-gun fire, immediately silenced by a broadside from EGGESFORD.

By midday AMBER beach was in use, with L.C.I. beaching there in formation. A rocky promontory at the eastern end was found suitable for L.S.T. and needing only a little work to make it into an excellent hard. Elsewhere a false beach with three feet of water inshore caused some inconvenience and necessitated the use of D.U.K.W. and a pontoon.

The three L.S.I. (M) were sailed for Sousse at 1400 followed at 2100 by the first convoy of empty L.S.T. for Malta. Empty L.C.I. (L) had been proceeding to Malta in groups as, and when, ready since 0900. H.M.S. ROYAL ULSTERMAN was retained by S.N.O.L .(Q) as his headquarters.

C. BARK EAST.

When approaching Sicily it was found that the southerly set was stronger than had been anticipated but allowance was made for this and the convoy stopped in the correct position at 0030/10th July. All landing craft were lowered on arrival.

All flights touched down at the correct time, and the sea inshore being calm, all landings were made without difficulty. Surprise was lost fifty yards from the shore and light machine-gun fire and sniping were encountered by most on the beach. L.C.S. and L.C.F.[40] replied with effect and only slight military, but no naval, casualties were suffered. Only at RED beach was any serious opposition met and this was disposed of by troops landed on SCRAMBLE RED. Throughout the assault only one landing craft was lost – an L.C.P. [41] burnt out after being hit in the petrol tank by a shell splinter.

Although the beaches had been cleared, no progress could be made in the landing of supporting arms until nearly 0700 when the first L.C.T. arrived via BARK SOUTH, having been delayed and diverted by the weather.

At 0520 the coastal battery north of Pachino began a barrage on a line about 200 yards off the beaches without doing serious damage and in less than an hour-and-a-half was virtually neutralised by the Dutch gunboats SOEMBA and FLORES.

At 0615 the slow assault convoy arrived at the release position and a searching sweep by M.M.S. (L.L.)[42] and fleet sweepers having revealed no mines, at 0640 all ships were ordered to the anchorage. It was reached by the leading ships about 0740. The ferry service then started and all personnel were ashore by noon with army baggage and light stores soon after.

By 1400 S.N.O.L. (N) had transferred to H.M.S. ALYNBANK, and K.M.S. KEREN and the personnel ships sailed for Malta.

D. ACID SOUTH and ACID NORTH.

The marking submarine was in the correct position and no difficulty was experienced in picking up her transmissions and the screened signal lamp. Swell caused some difficulty in embarking troops in L.C.I. (L), and wind and sea made some formations late in getting underway.

The assault waves touched down up to thirty minutes late, but with one exception the correct beaches were all found.

Although the wind had considerably decreased the big ships were quickly set down to leeward: *i.e.,* the south-eastward: and the follow-up flights had considerably more than the planned distance to cover.

There was little organised resistance to the landings and after a short period of heavy machine-gun fire the defenders withdrew. A few casualties were caused by mines on one beach before it was cleared. Success signals were received from all beaches by 0500 and ships were then ordered to close the shore without waiting for the anchorage to be swept for mines.

From first light onwards there was considerable shelling from batteries inshore, but these were silenced by supporting destroyers and gunboats by 0800.

The arrival of L.C.T. with supporting arms was rather disorganised, and none beached before daylight. Two of the beaches at ACID NORTH intended for use by L.C.T. were found to be composed of large boulders instead of the shingle indicated by the air photographs, a fact which did not make easier the task of beaching the craft and discharging them. The slow assault convoy arrived an hour-and-a-half late, but all had taken up their anchor berths by 0700.

The first large personnel ship completed discharging by 0900 and all, with one exception, had disembarked personnel and baggage and hoisted their craft by 1415. With four exceptions they were on passage to Malta at 1500.

The rate of discharge of L.C.T. was slow, but the unloading of the slow convoy proceeded satisfactorily in spite of being unable to discharge L.S.T. and L.C.T. at most of the beaches without pontoon bridging and difficulties with wheeled vehicles due to heavy shingle and soft sand.

Gun Support.

The following details of gun support are available:-

A. BARK WEST.

Since the assaults met little opposition, fire from the destroyers in support was confined to a few rounds only and L.C.S. were able to furnish all the support needed on the beaches.

Between 0415 and 0542, when the battery was silenced, H.M.S. BLANKNEY at a range of 6,000 yards fired 80 rounds at P.4 battery in ROGER sector. At 0740 another 37 rounds were fired at the same battery, fire ceasing when our troops were seen in the vicinity.

H.M.S. ROBERTS carried out three shoots in the course of the day:

(i) at 0510. Impromptu from anchor at a range of 15,000 yards against the Casa Guiliano battery of five 149 mm. guns which had fired about a dozen rounds haphazard at landing craft without scoring a hit. After ten rounds from H.M.S. ROBERTS the battery was silenced.

(ii) 0540, another four rounds from 15,000 yards for the second time silenced the same battery which had again opened ineffective fire at craft on and close to the beach.

(iii) 1556, at the request of the army, fourteen rounds were fired at the southern outskirts of Spaccaforno and the area was observed to be well covered by the fall of shot.

H.M.S. BRISSENDEN also carried out several shoots:

(i) at 0645, at a range of 3,800 yards, six smoke shell to thicken the screen laid by L.C.S. on SUGAR RED beach. Result was good.

(ii) 1550 to 1600 at anchor, range 11,000 yards, with H.M.S. ROBERTS, at southern outskirts of Spaccaforno, 90 rounds in salvos seen to be spread with effect over the area.

(iii) 1825, on call from Forward Observation Officer 84 rounds fired at infantry at Casa Basile. Result very effective.

H.M.S. PUCKERIDGE.

(i) 0515, fire opened impromptu at flashes from four guns of 149 mm. of the Casa Chiusa battery which were firing irregularly and without success at landing craft. From anchor, range 9,200-8,800 yards, eight rounds. Result – battery ceased fire and was captured by troops soon after.

(ii) 0532, at gun flashes from Casa Guiliano battery when it opened fire again after H.M.S. ROBERTS' first shoot. Range 8,000 yards, eight rounds. Result – shot seen to fall in target area, and battery ceased fire.

(iii) 0600, the last mentioned battery again opened fire and H.M.S. PUCKERIDGE was ordered in to eliminate it. At ranges 6,000-4,200 yards, twenty rounds were fired under way and the battery which had constituted almost the only opposition to the landing was finally silenced.

Three of the four L.C.G. (L) in Force "V" engaged direct targets during the assault, and fired ten rounds H.E. full charge each. An ammunition dump was blown up by L.C.G. (L) 9 with her seventh round at 500 yards range.

B. BARK SOUTH.

(i) Between 0308 and 0420, three L.C.T. (R)[43] carried out pre-arranged shoots on flank targets at the beaches.

(ii) After daylight H.M.S. WHADDON and EGGESFORD gave close support and three L.C.G. also fired a few rounds. H.M.S. LAFOREY also joined in the silencing of machine-guns at Portopalo Bay.

(iii) Later in the day ships of the Bombarding Squadron (H.M.S. NEWFOUNDLAND, ORION, LAFOREY, LOYAL, LOOKOUT) direct shoots at areas five miles inland including Rosolini and Spaccaforno.

C. BARK EAST.

L.C.S. and L.C.F. replied with effect to the machine-gun fire and sniping encountered by the assault craft on beaching.

H.N.M.S. SOEMBA and FLORES engaged a battery 2,000 yards north of Pachino at 0533, which with five guns of 100 mm. had been firing at the rate of one round per gun per minute a defensive barrage on a line about 200 yards off the beaches. The two ships underway and keeping station on dan buoys, at ranges of 7,000 and 7,800 yards respectively, fired in periods until 0645 when the battery was virtually neutralised.

D. ACID SOUTH and NORTH.

Bombardments were carried out as follows:-

(i) By H.M.S. MAURITIUS.

(*a*) at 0600, fire was opened on a coast defence battery which had been worrying How and JIG beaches. After thirty-six rounds had been fired no further shelling occurred from this direction although great difficulty was experienced in locating the target.

(*b*) at 0840, in response to a call, a defended area was bombarded for five minutes, the shells appearing, from visual observation, to hit the required area.

(ii) By H.M.S. ESKIMO.

(*a*) at 0545 at a range of 10,000 yards, five salvos were fired at a battery concealed among trees north-east of Avola which had been dropping shells on How sector. The battery ceased fire.

(*b*) at 0610, at another battery shelling How beaches. The battery quickly ceased fire but opened up again soon after. The bombardment was resumed at 0715 and after the sixth salvo there was an explosion and fire at the position of the battery from which nothing further was heard.

(iii) By H.M.S. TETCOTT.

(*a*) at 0510, opened fire at a battery which had been shelling JIG beaches, and drew its fire which was very inaccurate.

(*b*) at 0559, changed target to another battery giving trouble at the beaches, but as H.M.S. MAURITIUS opened fire at about the same time, reverted to first target so as not to confuse her, the first battery having again come into action. The battery ceased fire as a result.

(*c*) at 0641, opened fire at a third battery of three guns, which ceased fire.

(iv) By H.M.S. TARTAR.

(*a*) at 0410, fire was opened at two searchlights in the vicinity of Avola, which were extinguished.

(v) By H.M.S. EREBUS.

(*a*) at 1415, fire was opened on an infantry defended post with six pill boxes. Target reported destroyed after twelve rounds at 12,600 yards had all been spotted and corrected upon the target, including two direct hits and seven within one hundred yards of the centre of the target.

(*b*) at 1945 at a range of 18,700 yards, six rounds fired at another infantry defended post. Five direct hits and target reported by Forward Observation Officer as destroyed.

Enemy Air Activity.

Prior to the landings enemy air activity against the expedition was non-existent and it was only slight throughout D day. Some details were as follows:-

A. BARK WEST.

Shortly after 2200, an attack was made on the anchorage in the course of which a stick of bombs fell close between H.M.S. HAMBLEDON and H.M.S. WALLACE. Flares dropped by the aircraft were effective but the anchorage was heavily protected by smoke and no damage was sustained.

B. BARK SOUTH.

There were indications of air activity, but no bombs were dropped. One low-flying aircraft was shot down after dark.

C. BARK EAST.

(i) At 0550 two Me.109 made a cannon-fire attack on RED beach; one stoker of an L.C.S. was wounded.

(ii) From 2010 to midnight there were intermittent attacks on the ships and H.M.S. ALYNBANK was near missed by a dive attack, two ratings being killed.

D. ACID NORTH and SOUTH.

While waiting to cover the later flights two L.C.S. (M) were machine-gunned by an aircraft and some minor casualties were suffered; the aircraft was seriously damaged. Then between 0630 and 0700 fighter bombers appeared overhead but no bombs were dropped. Next, at 1015 about ten Ju.88 and some F.W.190 dropped bombs in the vicinity of shipping. During the afternoon two L.C.T. were damaged by near misses and in further intermittent attacks, including an attack by forty aircraft at 1630, near misses on S.S. BERGENSFIORD and L.S.T. 407 were the only incidents of note.

Night attacks began soon after 2100 and a considerable number of bombs scored no direct hits until 2200, when the hospital ship TALAMBA, lying illuminated five miles to seaward of GEORGE sector, was sunk in a deliberate attack. Another hospital ship, ABA, was attacked at the same time, but escaped damage.

D + 1 DAY.

Sunday, 11th July.

Weather. – Weather and sea conditions continued to improve at all sectors, though some wind and surf persisted at BARK WEST and ACID.

Situation at beaches.

A. BARK WEST.

The beaches assaulted were unsatisfactory for maintenance owing to flat gradients, the sandbars already mentioned, and poor exits. SUGAR RED beach I was opened and proved satisfactory for L.C.M. and vehicles and guns were unloaded here throughout the day, while L.S.T. and L.C.T. discharged on to ROGER RED.

Unloading as a whole was slow, some of the delays being attributable to the inexperience of the men handling the Vehicle Landing Ramp, its liability to "snake" and the length of time required for adjustment when an L.S.T. came up to it.

H.M.S. BOXER, THRUSTER and BRUISER having completed, sailed with three M.T. ships for Malta, leaving twelve ships of the slow assault convoy to complete discharging.

B. BARK SOUTH.

Unloading of L.S.T. continued satisfactorily throughout the day and by nightfall nearly all of the first flight was unloaded and twenty had sailed for Malta with H.M.S. ROYAL ULSTERMAN, S.N.O.L. (Q) having landed and established himself and party ashore at AMBER beach. The General Officer Commanding 30 Corps had also disembarked during the afternoon and set up his headquarters ashore. At 1900 H.M.S. LARGS sailed for BARK EAST and the A/S patrol off BARK SOUTH was discontinued, the destroyers thus released reinforcing the patrol at BARK EAST.

C. BARK EAST.

Unloading at this sector was delayed as a result of the time required for discharging L.C.T. with 51 Division stores which had been transferred from BARK SOUTH owing to the poor beaches in the latter area. In addition, L.S.T. 9, also from BARK SOUTH, grounded on Isola Grande.

D. ACID SOUTH and NORTH.

The only outstanding incident was the successful launching of D.U.K.W. from L.S.T. over the ramp while the L.S.T. were underway. It was found that this method of discharge presented no difficulty in fine weather. Good progress was made with unloading M.T. and stores, the flow to the beaches increasing steadily and much of the arrears due to delays in discharging L.C.T. the previous day was made up.

Large L.S.I. sail from Malta. – Convoy M.K.F. 18 consisting of eleven large L.S.I. sailed from Malta westbound and soon after midday twelve similar ships left eastbound in M.E.F. 36.

Malta shuttle service begins. – The first empty landing ships and craft arrived back at Malta from Sicily and the shuttle service commenced. The first empty M.T. ships were also sailed from the beaches.

Gun Support.

Supporting fire was provided by ships at various points as required from time to time. In particular:

(i) between 0030 and 0250, at the request of 1st Canadian Division, H.M.S. ROBERTS fired from anchor four rounds in each of three prearranged shoots from 12,400 yards at high ground in the Pozzallo area. H.M.S. BLANKNEY and BLENCATHRA had earlier in the night carried out harassing fire on the same area. The object of these shoots, which was achieved, was to force the enemy to retire before the Division advanced at 0300.

(ii) between 1130 and 1205, simultaneously with a shoot by H.M.S. DELHI on Spaccaforno and by H.M.S. BRISSENDEN on Pozzallo, H.M.S. ROBERTS on request from 1st Canadian Division carried out a prearranged shoot on an area N.E. and S.W. of Rosolini in which the enemy were concentrating. At a range of 18,000 yards, 30 rounds were fired from anchor, the area being swept three times. All enemy troops who came under this fire were demoralised and surrendered promptly.

(iii) H.M.S. BRISSENDEN, under way, fired 40 rounds at a gun emplacement and 120 rounds at a building and area in the vicinity of Pozzallo. At the conclusion of the shoot a white flag was hoisted on the gun emplacement.

(iv) H.M.S. ORION carried out a bombardment of Medica at the rear of BARK WEST.

(v) H.M.S. UGANDA engaged a hostile battery at the southern end of Augusta Bay.

(vi) H.M.S. UGANDA and MAURITIUS bombarded the enemy's line of retreat in the vicinity of Augusta.

Enemy Air Activity.

There was rather more activity by enemy aircraft and it was more widespread than on D day. Some particulars follow:-

A. BARK WEST.

Sporadic attacks during the night D day/D + 1 day caused no damage to ships but were responsible for a few casualties.

B. BARK SOUTH.

No loss or damage was suffered, though there were several "Red" warnings.

C. ACID SOUTH and NORTH.

Several sharp raids took place and at 1235, S.S. BAARN at anchor off JIG sector was near missed by a Ju.88 and cased petrol in No. 1 hold set on fire. The fire became uncontrollable and in view of the risk of a serious ammunition explosion she was later sunk. Another M.T. ship JOSEPH C. CANNON off How received a direct hit at about 1900, but although the ship's bottom was penetrated no fire resulted as the hold was nearly empty and she was eventually able to proceed to Malta. Raids after dark were ineffective.

Syracuse occupied. – The army entered Syracuse at 2100 on 10th July, and at 0600/11th July, fleet sweepers and B.Y.M.S.,[44] escorted by H.M.S. NUBIAN and H.M.S. TARTAR, proceeded to sweep the approach channel into the port. No mines were swept; there was no opposition, and at 0830 H.M.S. WHITEHAVEN passed through the gate. Naval Commander Force "A" entered in H.M.S. CROMARTY shortly after, and the majority of the port party landed at the same time. The boom and gate were intact, though in poor condition in spite of the existence of spare gear on the spot. The town was almost deserted. There was no damage to port installations apart from that caused by our own aircraft on the night of the beach assaults. About 2130, Naval Commander Force "A" advised that all personnel ships of the convoys due on D + 3 day should proceed to Syracuse to discharge.

Pozzallo occupied. – Following the bombardment by H.M.S. BRISSENDEN mentioned above, the white flag was hoisted and H.M.S. BRISSENDEN closed the town of Pozzallo.

The Bombardment Liaison Officer and an armed party landed and accepted the surrender at 1315, returning on board with 98 prisoners. The port was found to be useless for unloading either vessels or craft.

A.A. cruisers transferred. – To strengthen the defence of the ACID anchorages which had so far borne the greater part of the enemy's air attacks, H.M.S. DELHI, hitherto at BARK WEST, was transferred to the orders of Naval Commander Force "A" from noon.

H.M.S. COLOMBO from Force "V" was transferred to the Western Task Force to reinforce the protection of Gela anchorage where enemy aircraft were also troublesome.

D + 2 DAY.

Monday, 12th July.

Weather. – Weather continued fine, and on the whole less inconvenience was experienced from swell at the anchorages and beaches, though it still retarded the rate of discharge at the western end of the area.

Situation at beaches.

A. BARK WEST.

"G" Naval Commando moved from SUGAR sector to BARK SOUTH and "N" Commando took over SUGAR sector in addition to ROGER.

M.T. continued to come in on SUGAR RED I beach and a number of L.C.T. beached at SUGAR RED II. The exits from these beaches were only moderate, and the roads behind bad, while approximately one vehicle in three was "drowned" getting ashore. Accordingly it was decided that S.N.O.L. (S) should transfer to BARK SOUTH (QUEEN sector) and receive the follow-up convoy, while S.N.O.L. (R) remained to complete the discharge of the assault convoy over ROGER sector. Stores began to come in at about midday, and an urgent call for petrol in the evening was met by unloading from L.C.T. throughout the night.

B. BARK SOUTH and EAST.

At 0600 the first follow-up convoy of L.S.T. arrived at BARK SOUTH and commenced to beach and unload during the forenoon. All the original L.S.T. and L.C.T. completed unloading by the afternoon. The rocky ledge at the eastern end of AMBER beach had been levelled and improved by this time to an extent which enabled five L.S.T. to be discharged at a time.

Two M.T. ships from BARK WEST arrived at BARK SOUTH and commenced to discharge by means of D.U.K.W.

Naval Commander Force "B" decided that as soon as the M.T. ships of the assault convoy were cleared BARK EAST beaches should be kept open mainly for 51 Division stores in L.C.T. which were becoming congested at BARK SOUTH and that S.S. DIOMED, the only follow-up ship destined for BARK EAST, should be diverted to BARK SOUTH.

Late in the evening the two Category "A" ships of the assault convoy completed unloading (the third had been sunk en route).

C. (i) ACID SOUTH.

Discharge was completed of the four Class "A" M.T. ships of the assault convoy and the stevedores thus released were transferred to the Class "B" ships.

(ii) ACID NORTH

At 1900 an additional beach, called BLUE, was opened at the northern end of the sector and proved satisfactory for both L.C.T. and L.C.M. though inadequate approaches and shortage of labour precluded its use for landing stores.

Gun Support.

Supporting fire was provided by ships as and when required and opportunity offered.
H.M.S. MAURITIUS had a busy day and carried out shoots as follows:-

(*a*) from 0830 to 0900, in response to an urgent call for support, Mellili was effectively engaged.

(*b*) at 0930, a coast battery was engaged and gave no further trouble.

(*c*) at 1115, in response to an immediate call, a battery north of Priolo which was holding up the army's advance was effectively engaged. After a short bombardment the Forward Observation Officer reported the target destroyed.

(*d*) at 1205, fire, reported effective from direct observation, was again opened on Mellili.

(*e*) at 1251, a strong point near Augusta was bombarded at the request of the army.

(*f*) at 1340, Mellili was again bombarded, direct observation indicating that the fire was effective.

(*g*) at 1403, the target was another defended post and the Forward Observation Officer reported the shoot as particularly satisfactory.

(*h*) at 1500, an accurate and successful shoot on a defended area near Augusta.

(*i*) from 1532 to 1541, direct fire in the Augusta area.

(*j*) from 1834 to 1843, a successful shoot at a coast defence battery.

(*k*) at 2006, an effective shoot on Augusta defences in support of a commando landing from H.M.S. ULSTER MONARCH.

H.M.S. TETCOTT, in support of the commando landing from H.M.S. ULSTER MONARCH,

(*a*) at 1930, engaged and silenced a light high velocity gun on the ridge overlooking Augusta.

(*b*) at about the same time, effectively bombarded at a range of three cables with 4-inch pom-pom and Oerlikon a cement works near the shore from which machine-gun fire was observed.

H.M.S. EREBUS was also well occupied during the day carrying out the following shoots:-

(*a*) from 0542 to 0602, coast defence batteries, range 1,800 yards, rounds 27. Target area covered.

(*b*) from 0628 to 0634, anti-aircraft battery, range 2,650 yards, rounds 10.Target area covered.

(*c*) from 0653 to 0658, coast defence battery, range 3,000 yards, rounds 6. Target area covered, probable ammunition dump blown up.

(*d*) from 0744 to 0747, coast defence battery, range 14,800 yards, rounds 6. Target area covered, and barracks observed hit.

(*e*) from 0749 to 0756, coast defence battery, range 3,000 yards, rounds 8. Target area covered and explosion observed.

(*f*) from 1018 to 1029, coast defence batteries, range 11,000 yards, rounds 13.Target area covered and explosion observed.

(*g*) from 1031 to 1033, same coast defence batteries, range 10,000 yards, rounds 7. Target area covered and on closing to two miles, guns in first target observed apparently intact but building immediately behind damaged. Guns of second target badly damaged.

(*h*) from 1050 to 1058, H.A. battery, range 12,600 yards, rounds 10. Indirect shoot, no spotting.

(*i*) from 1132 to 1142, town of Mellili, range 18,300 yards, rounds 12, of which 8 observed to fall in target area.

(*j*) from 1338 to 1400, town of Mellili, range 18,000 yards, rounds 32. Whole area of town covered.

H.M.S. ORION and UGANDA also carried out bombardments in the vicinity of Mellili and Augusta in the course of the day.

Enemy Air Activity.

Once again the northern end of the area experienced the heaviest attacks during a day when activity was on much the same scab as the previous day. Details:-

A. BARK WEST.

There was slight activity at dawn, and one aircraft was shot down by a night fighter controlled by the radar set in L.C.T. 305.

B. BARK SOUTH.

A raid warning in the early hours left BARK SOUTH untouched. On this occasion M.L.s[45] put up a very effective smoke screen. After nightfall, further warnings, with aircraft passing overhead, still produced no bombs.

C. BARK EAST.

The hospital ship DORSETSHIRE had arrived the previous afternoon and before nightfall had been sent to sea by S.N.O.L. (N) so as to be well clear of the assault area and illuminated during the night. Nevertheless, at 0500/12th July, she was attacked and sustained some structural damage and casualties from near misses. Though the attacks on the anchorage were of some weight no other damage was caused.

Following the experience of TALAMBA and DORSETSHIRE the latter and AMRA were for the night of 12th/13th July darkened and anchored close to the convoy so as to have the benefit of the anti-aircraft and smoke protection of the anchorage.

D. ACID SOUTH and NORTH.

At 0500, H.M.S. ESKIMO, when about three miles to the southward of Cape Murro di Porco on her way with Naval Commander Force "A" to investigate the situation at Augusta, was attacked by several aircraft and hit in Nos. 5 and 6 oil fuel tanks. The ship stopped and was ordered to Malta in tow of H.M.S. TARTAR; they arrived at 1700 without further incident.

At dawn an attack developed off JIG sector and a near miss at the fore end of S.S. OCEAN PEACE caused a fire in the cased petrol in No. 1 hold. The fire could not be controlled and the ship had to be sunk to prevent further disaster. The usual raids after dark on anchorage and beaches were again ineffective, causing only a few casualties ashore. A good smoke screen was put up before the raids began.

Augusta entered. – Late the previous night there had been a report that Augusta was being evacuated by the enemy and in execution of orders from Naval Commander Eastern Task Force, sweepers proceeded to sweep the channel at first light. They were not molested by coast defence batteries, which were under occasional fire from H.M.S. EREBUS to keep them quiet, but a field gun opened fire on the B.Y.M.S. (L.L.) when on their last leg out.

At 1045, H.M.S. EXMOOR, flying the flag of Naval Commander Force "A" – he had transferred from H.M.S. ESKIMO after she had been bombed – proceeded into the harbour. The gate was open and the boom vessel abandoned, and there was no sign of life until a field gun, or possibly a tank, concealed behind trees, began shelling the ship at short range. The fire was accurate, and as no target could be distinguished EXMOOR was ordered out. No counter shoot could be conducted owing to the proximity of our own troops.

N.C.E.T.F. enters Augusta. – H.M.S. EXMOOR with the Greek Hunt class destroyer KANARIS in company re-entered the port at 1600 followed later by H.M.S. BROCKLESBY flying the flag of Naval Commander Eastern Task Force. Again the ships had to withdraw because of fire from high velocity guns of 3 to 4-inch calibre to which no adequate reply could be made owing to uncertainty in regard to the exact whereabouts of our own troops. Much transport was seen in motion ashore, but could not be engaged as it was not known whether they were friend or foe – they were in fact enemy.

Late in the evening one of the brigades of 5 Division penetrated into the town, and the naval port party arrived from Malta. The army's hold was, however, precarious, and later the S.B. Squadron, S.A.S. Regiment[46] was successfully landed by H.M.S. ULSTER MONARCH as a reinforcement. In consequence of this uncertainty and a statement by the Brigadier that he might have to retire from the town, the Naval Officer-in-Charge temporarily withdrew his party except for some key ratings.

H.M.S. ROBERTS to Acid North. – H.M.S.ROBERTS from Force "V" was ordered to move to ACID NORTH ready to be called forward either to join Force "K" or to supplement the anti-aircraft defences of captured ports as and when required. In the meantime she was placed under the orders of Naval Commander Force "A".

U-boats. – Although it was estimated that some eighteen Italian U-boats were at sea in the area of operations of the Eastern and Western Task Forces there had so far been no contact with any. This day, however, several were encountered.

H.M.S. OAKLEY claimed a "probably sunk" in the vicinity of Sousse, and the Greek Hunt class destroyer PINDOS was unsuccessfully attacked two miles east of Cape Passero at 0445. The latter U-boat was counter-attacked, and one pattern of depth charges dropped, but though A/S vessels hunted until noon no further contact was obtained.

BRONZO captured. – While the 14th Minesweeping Flotilla were engaged in screening the cruisers bombarding Augusta, H.M.S. SEAHAM sighted a periscope shortly before 1300 and closed at full speed with the intention of ramming. The U-boat surfaced and fire was opened on it with all possible weapons and hits were observed on the conning tower with the 3-inch. The U-boat replied, but surrendered after a sharp engagement, which had lasted about half-an-hour. The U-boat was the Italian BRONZO, and she was towed by H.M.S. SEAHAM to Syracuse. Twenty prisoners were taken out of a crew of forty, the remainder including the Commanding Officer having been killed by gunfire or drowned when abandoning ship.

H.M.S. BLANKNEY and BRISSENDEN in collision. – While on A/S patrol off BARK WEST, H.M.S. BLANKNEY and H.M.S. BRISSENDEN came into collision. Both sustained damage and were detached to Malta for repairs, BRISSENDEN proceeding there p.m. 12th July and BLANKNEY p.m. 13th July.

D + 3 DAY.

Tuesday, 13th July.

Weather. – The weather remained fine, and the calm sea permitted the passage to Sicily from Malta of lighters and harbour craft for use in the captured ports.

N.C.F.V. takes over from N.C.F.B. – *In pursuance of orders given by Naval Commander Eastern Task Force when in Sicily the previous day, Naval Commander Force "V" at 0400 took over the BARK areas from Naval Commander Force "B" who proceeded to Syracuse to assume duty as Flag Officer Sicily.*

Situation at beaches.

A. BARK SOUTH.

S.N.O.L. (Q) left for Sousse during the forenoon and S.N.O.L. (S) from BARK WEST took over the sector.

The follow-up convoys, K.M.F. and K.M.S. 19, consisting of three personnel, fourteen M.T. ships and two petrol carriers arrived at BARK SOUTH at 0700. Unloading of M.T. by L.C.T. and of stores by a fleet of about fifty D.U.K.W. began at once. By 1630 the personnel ships, using L.C.I. (L) and L.C.M., had discharged and by 1930 sailed for Malta, in addition to four M.T. ships of the slow assault convoy for Tripoli. This left eight ships of the slow assault convoy and the newcomers remaining at the beaches.

B. BARK EAST and WEST.

Naval Commander Force "V" decided in the forenoon to continue his predecessor's policy of using BARK EAST only for L.C.T. when the assault convoy M.T. ships had been cleared. This entailed all ships, as opposed to craft, leaving BARK EAST p.m. and resulted in the S.N.O.L. ship H.M.S. ALYNBANK being withdrawn. The latter was in any case particularly needed to increase the anti-aircraft protection at BARK SOUTH.

In the afternoon, however, there was a partial reversal of this plan when, with a view to avoiding the increased concentration at BARK SOUTH which would result from the decision to close BARK WEST, the Naval Commander Force " V" ordered three nearly empty M.T. ships from BARK WEST to BARK EAST the following day. The one ship of the follow-up convoy for BARK EAST which had been diverted, was also sent back there.

The decision to close BARK WEST was reached because BARK SOUTH was in every way superior. L.S.T. and L.C.T. could beach at the eastern end without using a ramp, and L.C.M. could land stores almost dry shod at the western end which was backed by a good maintenance area.

In consequence of these changes S.N.O.L. (S) transferred to BARK SOUTH while S.N.O.L. (R) remained at BARK WEST and S.N.O.L. (N) moved ashore and set up his headquarters in a house on Isola Piccolo.

The two Category "A" ships of the slow assault convoy at BARK EAST sailed a.m. under escort to join the ACID portion of a convoy for Tripoli, and the three Category "B" ships cleared by the evening.

C. ACID SOUTH and NORTH.

The follow-up convoys M.W.F. and M.W.S. 37 arrived. The fast section entered Syracuse at 0945 and at once began to discharge. Such good progress was made that by 1800 all twelve ships were empty and away from the port. The slow section of thirty ships anchored off the beaches at 0900. Thirteen ships of the slow assault convoy having previously been cleared from the anchorage sailed immediately with the escort of M.W.S. 37. Of the new arrivals ten were ordered to enter Syracuse at first light the following day.

Gun Support.

Gun support units continued their activities as required.

The following are some particulars:-

H.M.S. MAURITIUS.
(*a*) from 0900 to 0930, an apparently effective shoot, using direct observation, at Carlentini.
(*b*) a few minutes later, at a battery at Campolato which had opened fire on the ship. One hit observed and battery ceased firing.
(*c*) at 1032 and from 1144 to 1240, spasmodic engagement of gun opposition ashore. Results probably not satisfactory, observation by Forward Observation Officer difficult and possibly an incorrect map reference received.
(*d*) at 1720, against a defended post near Catania. Result reported satisfactory by Forward Observation Officer.
(*e*) from 1753 to 1800, target Lentini.

H.M.S. TETCOTT.
(*a*) at about 2300, opened fire on a defended area south of Catania in support of commando landing from H.M.S. PRINS ALBERT at Murazzo Point. Enemy guns not completely silenced. Target engaged again after midnight with the result that the enemy guns ceased fire.

H.M.S. EREBUS.
(*a*) at 0938. Shore batteries near Carlentini, range 2,500 yards, rounds 10.
(*b*) at 1105. Catania Airfield, range 30,000 yards, rounds 10. Indirect fire.
(*c*) at 2140. Catania Airfield, rounds 20.
Results unobserved but a fire seen when bombardment complete.

Enemy Air Activity.

The only air attacks this day were in the ACID area. There were continuous though ineffective raids during the night 12th/13th July, as well as the usual dawn attack. The most serious incident occurred a little before noon when two fighter bombers scored hits on S.S. THOMAS PICKERING in the after hold. The ship, which had only arrived earlier in the morning, became a total loss.

Shortly before midnight intermittent attacks with bombs and torpedoes on the empty personnel ships from Syracuse caused some confusion but no damage or casualties.

Augusta. – The naval port party returned during the forenoon. The town was found deserted with considerable damage at the northern end but none at the southern end. There was no power and a shortage of water.

The conditions in the harbour varied in one part and another. Only the northern entrance was open, but there was a four hundred foot quay with twenty-two feet of water alongside and ample berthing for all types of landing ship. The Carlo del Molo harbour and jetties were, however, found to be completely obstructed. The floating dock was undamaged and, in addition to one large oil carrier and three small petrol carriers, lighters were available though without means of towage.

Commando landing. – After dark H.M.S. PRINS ALBERT successfully landed No. 3 Commando with little loss near Murazzo Point, north of Augusta. H.M.S. TETCOTT, escorting, effectively engaged a battery which opposed the landing and also sank one of three E-boats[47] which attacked.

Local Defence Forces. – In view of the progress made and in anticipation of the capture of Catania, Naval Commander Eastern Task Force re-allocated local defence forces as follows:-

1.   Syracuse.
      13th Trawler Group (A/S),
      153rd B.Y.M.S. Flotilla,
      6 H.D.M.L. from Force "A".

2.   Augusta.
      8th Trawler Group (A/S, M/S[48]),
      105th M.M.S. Flotilla,

4   H.D.M.L. from Force "B".

3.   Catania.
      4th Trawler Group (A/S, M/S),
      4 H.D.M.L. from Force "A",
      2 H.D.M.L. from Force "B".

4.   Group "P".
      Hunt class destroyers, CROMARTY, POOLE, BOSTON, SEAHAM
      and 22nd M.L. Flotilla to be based on Augusta when Catania
      occupied.

5.   20th M.G.B. Flotilla and 32nd M.T.B. Flotilla to be based on
      Augusta as ordered by Commander-in-Chief.

Inshore Squadron for army support. – In accord with instructions from the Commander-in-Chief, Naval Commander Eastern Task Force also placed under the orders of Flag Officer Sicily for service in the inshore squadron in support of the army the following: H.M.S. EREBUS, ROBERTS, D.S. FLORES, SOEMBA,

H.M.S. CROMARTY, POOLE, ROMNEY, SEAHAM, the 22nd M.L. Flotilla and temporarily two Hunts to be detailed by Naval Commander Force "A". It was stated that three L.C.R., three L.C.G. and four L.C.F. would also be available from Malta if required. The latter were requested forthwith by Flag Officer Sicily.

S.N.O.L. prepare to leave. – *At the end of the day proposals were submitted by S.N.O.L. (N) and (Q), with which Naval Commander Force "V" concurred, that they should withdraw from the Island on the 15th July with their staffs, leaving the Beach Commando and Deputy S.N.O.L. at BARK EAST and a nucleus beach party at BARK SOUTH. Naval Commander Eastern Task Force also concurred with this.*

U-boats. – *Further successes were recorded against U-boats at no great distance from the operational area of the Eastern Task Force.*

M.T.B. operating under the orders of the Commander-in-Chief encountered two U-boats southbound in position 38° 10'N.15°27'E. and sank one with a torpedo. The U-boat was not identified.

H.M.S. ECHO and H.M.S. ILEX, two of Force "H" destroyer screen, sank the Italian NEREIDE in position 37° 36'N. 16° 17'E., taking twenty-five prisoners. This boat was only twenty-four hours out from its base.

D + 4 DAY.

Wednesday, 14th July.

Weather. – Weather was unchanged at very fine.
    Situation at beaches.

A. BARK WEST.

All unloading was stopped over these beaches. The M.T. ships were divided between BARK SOUTH and EAST with their superior facilities and there was an improvement in the rate of unloading. All ships were clear of BARK WEST by 2030 and H.M.S. HILARY, headquarters ship Force "V", anchored at BARK SOUTH.

Six more ships of the slow assault convoy were sailed at midday.

B. BARK SOUTH.

S.N.O.L. (S) set up his headquarters in a house above Punta Portopalo with Deputy S.N.O.L. and a V/S[49] station in the centre of the stores beach.

L.S.T. were employed in addition to L.C.T. in transferring vehicles from the M.T. ships, as more transport was urgently needed at the front.

C. BARK EAST.

The three Category "B" ships of the assault convoy sailed at 1400 to BARK SOUTH to join convoy. This left only one M.T. ship in the anchorage.

D. ACID SOUTH and NORTH.

The remaining ships of the slow assault convoy were sailed for Tripoli at 0630.

JIG sector closed down and all M.T. ships and landing craft proceeded to Syracuse. GEORGE and HOW sectors were progressing well though the stevedores were very tired owing to the frequent night air raids. To alleviate this they had been sent to sleep ashore.

N.C.F.A. turns over to F.O.S.Y. – Naval Commander Force "A" turned over all operations from Syracuse northwards to Flag Officer Sicily who was by now at Syracuse in H.M.S. LARGS. In the evening, having finished at ACID, he proposed turning over to S.N.O.L. (H) with a view to proceeding to Malta the following day in H.M.S. BULOLO.

KM. 19Y ordered forward. – By noon the situation was such that the Commander-in-Chief ordered forward convoys K.M.F. and K.M.S. 19Y, *i.e.,* those parts of the follow-up convoys from the United Kingdom which had been held at Algiers until required.

H.M.S. CARLISLE to Augusta. – About midday Naval Commander Eastern Task Force ordered H.M.S. CARLISLE to be sent to Augusta as soon as Flag Officer Sicily thought fit, to provide long range air warning. Flag Officer Sicily had, in fact, released her the previous day as he had expected Syracuse to be empty that night except for H.M.S. LARGS and L.S.T. He was of the opinion, however, that she should return to Syracuse on 14th when M.T. ships were due, as the A.A. defences were still below minimum and somewhat extempore.

Gun support. – Ships continued to give supporting fire to the army as required but, apart from a bombardment of Lentini by H.M.S. MAURITIUS lasting from 0702 to 0730, there were no shoots of particular note.

Enemy Air Activity.

The night 13th/14th July was almost free of air raids and the customary dawn attack at ACID was less intense than on previous days. While on patrol at BARK SOUTH after dark H.M.S. MENDIP and H.M.S. WALLACE were bombed. The full moon and many flares dropped by the enemy made evasion difficult for the destroyers, which apparently were taken as substitute targets, since the merchantmen in the anchorage were quite invisible in the smoke screen put up. Several sticks of bombs fell within one to two cables of the destroyers but no damage or casualties were caused. There was much activity and many flares were dropped at about 2100 but no incidents occurred.

At BARK EAST in the evening smoke cover was also used most effectively, the ships being well backed up from the shore. After the smoke had become effective three M.T. ships and two hospital carriers made the anchorage safely. One circling torpedo was reported, but failed to find a target and neither at BARK EAST or at ACID were any ships damaged by bombs.

At Syracuse there were no daylight raids, and three night raids by single aircraft were ineffective.

Great confidence was inspired among the ships by the successes of night fighters, and A/S screening vessels also took toll of low-flying aircraft.

Own aircraft engaged by ships. – As a result of our own aircraft being engaged by our ships, in particular low-flying transport aircraft on the night 13th/14th July, the Commander-in-Chief issued orders that fire was to be withheld unless aircraft were clearly identified as hostile, and that the strictest fire discipline was essential.

A/S measures. – Implementing the Commander-in-Chief, Mediterranean's policy of employing every possible A/S vessel in active offensive measures against the known concentration of U-boats in the operational area, Group "W" of four Hunts was detached from Force "B" to devote all its time to systematic hunting.

D + 5 DAY.

Thursday, 15th July.

Weather. – There was no change in the weather which remained fine and calm.
Situation at beaches.

A. BARK SOUTH.

L.C.M. arrived from BARK WEST where there was nothing more for them to do, and the number of D.U.K.W. available was increased to about 160. By this time a number of L.C.M. were suffering from defects (though many continued to run satisfactorily on one engine), as the beach repair party were still at BARK WEST salvaging damaged craft.

By the end of a good day little M.T. remained to be discharged and two ships were sailed.

B. BARK EAST.

After a considerable quantity of stores had been discharged from the ships which had come round from BARK WEST they were sailed at 1800 to join a Tripoli convoy from ACID. Two further M.T. ships arrived during the evening from BARK SOUTH having discharged their vehicles there.

C. ACID SOUTH and NORTH.

Seven ships of the D + 3 day convoy completed discharge and sailed in convoy at about 1600.

H.M.S. BULOLO with Naval Commander Force "A" left at 1800 and S.N.O.L. (H) took charge of the area.

Ports. – The situation at Syracuse was not satisfactory, and it was decided by Naval Commander Eastern Task Force that Naval Commander Force "A" should take over there to permit Flag Officer Sicily to proceed to Augusta where he was urgently required. Accordingly the staff of Force "A" were placed at the disposal of N.O.I.C. Syracuse to help straighten matters out.

At Augusta the harbour and approach channel were both swept for mines during the day with negative result. A start was made with the establishment of coastal forces and landing craft bases.

N.C.E.T.F. visits ports. – Naval Commander Eastern Task Force visited Syracuse and Augusta in H.M.S. LAFOREY during the day.

Gun support. – The normal supporting fire was carried out when, and where, required by the army. The only incident of note was damage inflicted by H.M.S. ROBERTS upon herself while engaged in a bombardment. This included one 4-inch mounting put out of action and an Oerlikon wrecked.

Air activity. – Air activity was restricted to night raids in the north which resulted in nothing worse than some near misses. Heavy barrage from shore defences and extensive use of smoke probably prevented any attempt at precision bombing.

D.S. SOEMBA and FLORES to Augusta. – By order of Flag Officer Sicily the Dutch gun-boats SOEMBA and FLORES sailed from BASK EAST for Augusta.

D + 6 DAY.

Friday, 16th July.

Weather. – Fine weather still prevailed over the whole area of operations.
  Beaches.

A. BARK SOUTH.

Discharge of stores continued satisfactorily all day. The pontoon with three mobile cranes on it was used for discharging stores from L.C.T. and Scammels to off-load crates from beached L.C.M. Part of the beach repair parties having come round from BARK WEST, a repair park for craft was established on one section of the beach.

B. BARK EAST.

Good progress was made with the unloading of the three M.T. ships in the anchorage and L.C.T. with stores for 51 Division continued to arrive from BARK SOUTH for unloading. Four ships of the 14th Minesweeping Flotilla carried out a searching sweep in the approch to the anchorage.

C. ACID SOUTH and NORTH.

The last Class "A" ship of the D + 3 day convoy sailed to join a convoy from Syracuse.

F.O.S.Y. to Augusta – Flag Officer Sicily in H.M.S. LARGS transferred from Syracuse to Augusta.

K.M.S. 19B and C forward. – It was decided that K.M.S. convoys 19B and C, which had been held at Malta, should be sailed for Sicily the following morning. This was to relieve congestion at Malta and permit economic use to be made of escorts.

Gun support. – Supporting fire was given to the army as required, but there was again no shoot worthy of particular note.

Enemy air activity. – Only at the northern end of the area of operations was there any particular incident. Raids on a reduced scale were experienced during the night 15th/16th July at Syracuse and near misses resulted in some damage to H.M.S. BOSTON and a few minor casualties in that ship and H.M.S. POOLE. Aircraft mining was also reported south of Syracuse by H.M.S. ROOKWOOD.

D + 7 DAY.

Saturday, 17th July.

Weather. – There was no change in the weather which remained consistently favourable.

Beaches.

A. BARK SOUTH.

Unloading continued satisfactorily and four M.T. ships and two cased petrol carriers were cleared and sailed, leaving eight ships in the anchorage.

B. BARK EAST.

It was decided by Naval Commander Force "V" that after the completion of discharge of the three ships then present, BARK EAST beaches were to be closed. S.N.O.L. (N) was relieved in the evening by Commander R.W.D. Thompson, R.N. and Captain (D), 21st Flotilla assumed responsibility for the safety of the ships in the anchorage.

When S.N.O.L. (N) left, all landing craft in the sector with the exception of two L.C.M. and one L.C.T. were still in good running order.

Augusta. – The presence of two E-boats in the searched channel during the night 16th/17th July caused minelaying to be suspected. Convoy movements were held up until 0930 when the port was re-opened after a 100 per cent. sweep of the channel over a width of two cables on either side of the centre line had been completed without disclosing a mine of any type.

The E-boats were also reported by a patrol trawler to have fired torpedoes and H.M.S. MAURITIUS at anchor in the harbour observed two flashes resembling torpedo explosions outside. No damage was done.

Syracuse. – H.M.S. BULOLO sailed from Syracuse for Malta at 2000 with Naval Commander Force "A" on board, the situation being, by then, satisfactory with a new N.O.I.C., Captain A.N. Grey, R.N. temporarily in charge. It had previously been agreed between Naval Commander Force "A" and Flag Officer Sicily that a prolongation of the stay of H.M.S. BULOLO would eventually lead to confusion owing to divided control, and that the shore organisation would settle down more quickly when there was no doubt as to who was in charge.

Gun Support.

The Inshore Squadron once more gave its support to the army in their operations along the coast, but no call was made upon the bombardment cruisers.

In the evening between 1842 and 1902, H.M.S. WARSPITE bombarded Catania, firing 57 rounds of 15-inch at ranges opening at 15,000 yards and finishing at 11,200 yards. At the same time the accompanying destroyers engaged shore batteries of about 4-inch calibre to the northward of Guardia. The batteries engaged the destroyers intermittently and with little accuracy.

Enemy Air Activity.

Enemy aircraft were little in evidence and there was only one incident of moment. In the early hours of the morning, H.M.S. QUEEN EMMA with Royal Marine Commandos on board was near missed at Augusta, and a number of casualties were suffered among both the ship's company and the Commandos. In all about 18 were killed and about 70 wounded. In addition to superficial damage the ship sustained many holes in her sides and superstructure as well as fractures in fire main and piping systems.

H.M.S. WARSPTTE saw enemy fighters once, and some unidentified aircraft on another occasion, but no attack developed.

U-boats. – H.M.S. WARSPITE recorded that there were two doubtful reports of the presence of U-boats in her vicinity, but no contact was obtained, and no attack apparently made.

D + 8 DAY.

Sunday, 18th July.

Weather. – Favourable weather conditions still prevailed.

Beaches and Ports.

Unloading was steadily becoming a matter of routine, and at 0700 S.N.O.L. (N) with his staff sailed for Malta in H.M.S. BRECON.

At BARK SOUTH as a result of some re-organisation and re-allocation of craft the daily total was again increased.

At Syracuse, operations were hindered by a serious petrol fire at the Molo San Antonio, the fuelling point connected with the bulk installation inland, and all efforts failed to extinguish the fire which continually broke out afresh. As a result, two alongside berths in the harbour were rendered untenable and the bulk storage immobilised.

At ACID NORTH, a period of twelve hours this day, Royal Engineers constructed at BLUE beach a causeway sixty feet wide with a depth of 3 feet 6 inches at the seaward end.

Three ships of the KM. 19 Y convoy arrived.

In the course of the normal patrols off the ports there were no incidents.

Gun support. – *Support was given to the right flank of the army by L.C.G., gunboats and destroyers, and during the forenoon H.M.S. MAURITIUS and NEWFOUNDLAND bombarded Catania.*

Enemy air activity. – *This was on a small scale and the night 17th/18th July saw only one raid on Augusta. Two small fires were started ashore but no damage was suffered by port or ships.*

U-boats. – *A combined sweep east of Augusta was carried out during the night 17th/18th July by destroyers and A.S.V. aircraft.[50] Two U-boats were located by aircraft in positions 37° 26' N., 16° 22' E. and 37° 09' N., 15° 42' E. respectively. The first was attacked with depth charges, and the aircraft claimed to have inflicted severe damage. The enemy was last seen on a course 047° still on the surface, but the supporting destroyers failed to find it. The second U-boat also escaped.*

D + 9 DAY.

Monday, 19th July.

Weather. – Continued fine weather was experienced at all sectors.

Beaches and ports. – *At BARK SOUTH further re-arrangement resulted in the daily total of personnel, stores and vehicles which landed being still further increased.*

N.C.E.T.F. hauls down his flag. – *Naval Commander Eastern Task Force proceeded from Malta to Sicily for a final inspection during the day. At noon his appointment lapsed, his task being regarded as completed, and his flag was struck. The duties hitherto performed by him were assumed between them by the Commander-in-Chief, Mediterranean, Vice-Admiral Malta and Flag Officer Sicily.*

ERRATUM.

Supplement to The London Gazette of Friday, 8th October, 1948.

Naval Operations in the Aegean between the 7th September, 1943, and 28th November, 1943.

In paragraph 21, after "BEAUFORT" *delete* "(Lieutenant-Commander Sir Standish O'G. Roche, Bt., D.S.O.)" and *substitute* "(Lieutenant J. R. L. Moore, R.N.)".

Footnotes

1   *Force "H" – a British naval force under the command of Vice-Admiral A.U. Willis, C.B., D.S.O., which was employed as a covering force for this operation.*

2   *Only the report and narrative of operations of the Naval Commander, Eastern Task Force are reproduced here.*

3   *"Husky" was the code name for this operation.*

4   *The Western Task Force was an American Task Force under the command of Vice-Admiral H.K. Hewitt, U.S.N. The publication of the report of the Naval Commander Western Task Force is a matter for the United States Navy Department, and this report is therefore not included here.*

5   *H hour – the time at which it is planned that the first wave of landing craft should "touch down" on the beach for the assault.*

6   *Force "B" – a British Task Force under the command of Rear-Admiral R.R. McGrigor, C.B.*

7   *Force "A" – a British Task Force under the command of Rear-Admiral T.H. Troubridge, D.S.O.*

8   *L.S.T. – Landing Ship, Tank.*

9   *L.C.T. – Landing Craft, Tank.*

10 *Besides the accommodation and communications difficulties mentioned, time did not permit of the Air Officer Commanding-in-Chief changing the elaborate arrangements for controlling the air operations from Marsa.*

11 *Some of the British assault force was sailed from Egypt and the First Canadian Division from the Clyde. Part of the American assault force was mounted in the U.S.A., making only a short call at Algiers and Oran on passage to the assault beaches.*

12   Definitions in the Beaufort scale of windforce-
      Force 4 – moderate breeze (11-15 m.p.h. at sea level);
      Force 6 – strong breeze (21-26 m.p.h. at sea level);
      Force 7 – high wind (27-33 m.p.h. at sea level).
13   BARK EAST – one of the British assault beaches (see Plan).
14   CENT and DIME – American assault beaches, west of the Eastern Task Force assault
      area. DIME beaches were in the vicinity of Gela; CENT beaches were southeast of
      Gela, at places between DIME and Cape Scalambri.
15   (See foot note 14).
16   S.E. – single engined.
17   Operation "Fracture" – a bombardment of Favignana (an island off the western point
      of Sicily) and convoy feints towards the west of Sicily.
18   Operation "Arsenal" – a bombardment of Catania (east coast of Sicily).
19   P.T. boats – the counterpart of British Motor Torpedo Boats.
20   L.S.I. (H) – a type of Landing Ship, Infantry.
21   A/S – anti-submarine.
22   L.C.I. (L) – Landing Craft, Infantry (Large).
23   BARK WEST – one of the British assault beaches (see Plan).
24   Force "V" – a British Task Force under the command of Rear-Admiral Sir Philip L.
      Vian, K.B.E.
25   L.C.A. – Landing Craft, Assault.
26   H.D.M.L. – Harbour Defence Motor Launch.
27   BARK SOUTH – One of the British assault beaches (see Plan).
28   ACID – a sector in BARK EAST (see Plan).
29   L.C.R. – Landing Craft, Rocket.
30   L.C.G. (L) – Landing Craft, Gun (Large).
31   "Torch" – the code name for the landings in North Africa.
32   L.C.M. – Landing Craft, Mechanised.
33   L.S.T. (2) – a type of Landing Ship, Tank.
34   D.U.K.W. – an amphibious vehicle.
35   S.N.O.L. – Senior Naval Officer Landing.
36   Serials – convoys of ships or groups of landing craft when employed on regular ferry
      service between ports or from ship to shore, were organised as a "series" and each
      passage or trip was given a "serial" number.
37   Folbot – a collapsible rubber boat.
38   L.C.S. – Landing Craft, Support.
39   L.S.P. – Landing Ship, Personnel.
40   L.C.F. – Landing Craft, Flak.
41   L.C.P. – Landing Craft, Personnel.
42   M.M.S. (L.L.) – motor minesweepers.
43   L.C.T. (R) – Landing Craft, Tank (Rocket).
44   B.Y.M.S. – British Yacht Minesweeper.
45   M.L.s Motor Launches.
46   S.B. Squadron, S.A.S. Regiment – Special Boat Squadron, Special Air Service Regiment.
47   E-boats – motor torpedo boats.
48   M/S – minesweeping.
49   V/S – visual signalling.
50   A.S.V. aircraft – aircraft fitted with radar equipment.

3

ADMIRAL OF THE FLEET SIR ANDREW B. CUNNINGHAM'S DESPATCH ON THE LANDINGS IN THE GULF OF SALERNO

9 SEPTEMBER 1943

TUESDAY, 2 MAY, 1950

OPERATIONS IN CONNECTION WITH THE LANDINGS IN THE GULF OF SALERNO ON 9TH SEPTEMBER, 1943.

Admiralty foreword:-

The Naval forces taking part in Operation "Avalanche" were under the general control of the Commander-in-Chief, Mediterranean.

The Naval Task Force for the operation was under the immediate command of Vice-Admiral H.K. Hewitt, U.S.N., who was known as the Commander Western Naval Task Force. This Force was charged with the escort to and the landing of the Fifth Army at Salerno and with the subsequent support of this Army until it was firmly established on shore.

The Western Naval Task Force included the Northern Attack Force (Force "N") composed of British and American Ships and Craft and under the command of Commodore G.N. Oliver, R.N., and the Southern Attack Force (Force "S") composed of U.S. Ships and Craft and under the command of Rear-Admiral John L. Hall, Jr., U.S.N.

The Naval Covering Force (Force "H") was under the command of Vice-Admiral Sir Algernon Willis, while the Naval Air Support Force (Force "V") was under the command of Rear-Admiral Sir Philip Vian.

The report of the Commander Western Naval Task Force on this operation will be published by the U.S. Navy Department in due course.

The following Despatch was submitted to the Lords Commissioners of the Admiralty on the 8th March, 1945, *by Admiral of the Fleet Sir ANDREW B. CUNNINGHAM, K.T., G.C.B., D.S.O.*

Office of the Commander-in Chief,
Mediterranean Station,
Allied Force Headquarters.
*8*th March, *1945.*

I have the honour to forward the report of the Naval Commander Western Task Force on the Operations in connection with the landings in the Gulf of Salerno on 9th September, 1943[1].

2. Owing to the unavoidable delay in forwarding the report of the Naval Commander Western Task Force due to more urgent demands on the time and facilities of his staff, it is not my intention to do more than comment on the salient features of this operation, the more so since many of the lessons learnt have been incorporated in other operations which have been carried out subsequently in this and other theatres. Except insofar as is stated in the succeeding paragraphs, I fully concur with the suggestions and recommendations of the Force Commander, whose report is very full and covers every aspect of the operation.

Planning.

3. My detailed remarks on the planning of Operation "Avalanche" are contained in Appendix I.

4. Having decided that the mainland of Italy was to be invaded on the West coast, it was clear that the seizure and development of the port of Naples was of paramount importance, since no other port in Western Italy could maintain the Military forces which it was intended to deploy.

5. The choice for the actual point of attack lay between the Gulf of Gaeta and the Gulf of Salerno. The former had the advantage of having an open plain as its immediate hinterland and it was clear that a successful landing in this area might lead to the early capture of Naples. On the other hand, its beaches were, at the best, indifferent and were beyond the reach of adequate single seater fighter cover based on Sicily. The first of these disadvantages might have been overcome, the second was insurmountable. Therefore, despite the fact that on 27th July information was

received that H.M.S. UNICORN, acting in the capacity of a light Fleet Carrier, and four Escort Carriers could be made available from outside my Command, it was decided that the landings must take place in the Gulf of Salerno. Here the beaches were superior to those of the Gulf of Gaeta but the area immediately inland could be covered by artillery fire from the adjacent hills. Further, the roads to Naples led through narrow defiles, which could be easily defended. These disadvantages had, however, to be accepted.

6. Once again, as in Operation "Husky"[2] the choice of D-Day was largely governed by the period of moon required for the employment of paratroops. The date finally selected for this operation was thus not entirely favourable from the Naval point of view, and the assault forces had to accept a disadvantageous light for the approach. In the event, airborne troops were not employed for the assault.

Preparation, Training and Mounting.

7. Due to the short time available between the final conquest of Sicily and mounting of Operation "Avalanche", there was little time available for rehearsal. In fact, as is stressed by the Naval Commander Western Task Force, it was necessary to overhaul the landing craft at first priority. Every possible repair facility in North Africa was pressed into service and the fact that more craft than had at first seemed likely were overhauled in time to take part in the operation enabled a faster build-up to be achieved than had been expected, and reflects great credit on the repair staffs concerned.

8. In this connection, however, I cannot concur entirely with the remarks of the Naval Commander Western Task Force in Part IV, Section I, paragraph 18 of his report, in which he states that "Naval Planning for Operation 'Avalanche' was affected by the late receipt of orders from higher authority and changes in the composition of the Naval Task Forces brought about by unforeseen releases of Landing Craft from Operations 'Husky' and 'Bay town'[3]." The increases in the numbers of Landing Craft assigned were largely due to the great efforts of the maintenance personnel. Further changes in the numbers and types of Landing Craft available were caused by the omission of the Naval Commander Western Task Force to provide six L.S.T.s, as required by my Operation Orders, to lift Air Force stores from Milazzo in Northern Sicily to the assault area. To take the place of these L.S.T.s a number of L.C.T.s were diverted from the Messina/Reggio ferry service at considerable expense to the Eighth Army build-up. This is referred to more fully in paragraph 21 of this report.

9. During the loading stages an unfortunate incident took place at Tripoli, due to the loading without proper authority of some smoke containers into an L.C.T. already containing ammunition. Spontaneous combustion of the smoke led to the explosion of the ammunition which put out of action four L.C.T.S which could ill be spared. This incident serves to stress the necessity for careful supervision of the loading of assault convoys.

Italian Armistice.

10. The fact that an Armistice had been signed between the Allies and the Italians was broadcast by the B.B.C. on the evening of D-1. It had been fully realised that this announcement might well engender an unjustified sense of security in the minds of those taking part in the assault. Accordingly, the Commander-in-Chief, Mediterranean and the Task Force Commanders sent signals warning all ships taking part in the operation that strong opposition from German forces must still be expected. There can, nevertheless, be no doubt that many took no heed of these warnings and viewed the proceedings with a sense of complacency which was not substantiated in the event.

Intelligence.

11. In general, the intelligence proved reliable and it is satisfactory to note that both beach intelligence and intelligence on fixed Coastal Defence installations were found to be accurate; the only additional defences encountered over and above those estimated being of the mobile type. That the security of the operation was not all to be desired was due to a variety of reasons, the chief of which were:-

(*a*) The logical selection of the beaches (from the enemy's point of view) for the reasons given in paragraph 5.

(*b*) The Armistice.

It is interesting to note, however, that although the assaulting forces were sighted by air reconnaissance on the 7th September, it was not until 0230 on 9th September that Alarm Number 3 ("Landing imminent or in progress") was instituted by the Germans.

Assault.

12. The assaults, with a few minor exceptions, went according to plan. The forces arrived at the correct lowering points at the times laid down in the orders. The distances of these lowering points for the deep draught L.S.I. (L)s – 9 and 10 miles from the shore – was forced upon the Task Force Commanders by an expected minefield along the 100 fathom line. This expectation was fulfilled.

13. One Brigade of 56 Infantry Division was landed to the South of its allotted beach and became mixed with the other Brigade which had spread North of its sector, thereby causing considerable confusion for some hours.

The Scout Boat marking UNCLE GREEN beach was too far to the South, thus causing a gap in the 46th Division landing, which left an enemy strongpoint unneutralised. This strongpoint subsequently caused considerable trouble to the Division.

14. The landing of the Rangers[4] at Maiori was without opposition, but the Commando landing on Vietri was opposed by the gunfire of the shore batteries. Both these landings, however, were able to make considerable progress and to secure the left flank with the X Corps landing.

15. The organisation for clearing Landing Craft and Boats of Military stores on arrival at the beaches left much to be desired. In a large number of cases boats' crews had to clear their boats themselves, with consequent delay in returning for further loads. Further, in the stress of events in the early stages after the assault, arrangements for the transfer of stores from the beaches to disposal areas further inland were inadequate. Consequently there was much congestion on the foreshore: but, by D+2 and onwards, 3,000 tons per day were being discharged over the British beaches.

Naval Forces other than Assault Forces.

16. The existence of the main cover force, Force "H", was rendered unnecessary by the Italian Armistice, and two Divisions of the Battle Squadron were employed to cover the passage to Malta of such units of the Italian Fleet as succeeded in making good their escape (Operation "Gibbon"). In addition, four Cruisers were diverted to Bizerta on D-2 to load elements of the First British Airborne Division for discharge at Taranto (Operation "Slapstick"), a course of action rendered possible by the Italian Armistice.

17. The chief object of Force "H", therefore, became to provide fighter cover over the Escort Carrier force (Force "V").

Air Activities.

18. Fighter cover over the beaches was provided by Naval fighters from Force "V", and by land based fighter aircraft of the 12th Air Support Command. Fighter cover over Force "V" was provided by the Fleet Carriers of Force "H".

19. The high accident rate suffered by the Escort Carriers, which was at the time attributed almost entirely to the lack of natural wind, must, in the light of more recent experience in Operation "Dragoon"[5], be considered largely due to insufficient deck landing practice immediately prior to the operation. Wind speeds experienced during Operation "Dragoon" were very similar to those prevailing throughout Operation "Avalanche", but in spite of the fact that during the former operation the Carrier forces operated for six days and the fatigue of the pilots thereby increased considerably in the later stages, the number of deck accidents was relatively smaller.

20. The plan assumed that Monte Corvino airfield would be captured on D-Day and put into operation for shore based fighters on D+l. The Escort Carriers were, therefore, only intended to operate for two days. There was, however, considerable delay in capturing Monte Corvino airfield and even after capture it was under constant artillery fire from the neighbouring hills. It was, therefore, necessary to construct an air strip near Paestum nearer to the coast, and for Force "V" to operate at sea for 3½ days after which it was withdrawn to Palermo. Before doing so 26 aircraft were flown ashore to operate at Paestum.

21. Had the Military progress proceeded according to plan considerable embarrassment would have been caused by the late arrival of Air Force material for the preparation of Monte Corvino airfield. This was caused by the non-arrival at Milazzo of six L.S.T.s destined to ferry these stores to the assault area.

Enemy Air Activity.

22. Enemy air activity was not on a heavy scale and on the average only ten red alerts per day were experienced. Indeed, so light was the scale of attack that the fighters of Force "V" had few combat opportunities. This operation was notable, however, as being the first occasion on which several new types of missiles were used by the German Air Force. These new bombs caused considerable losses and damage.

Events Subsequent to the Assault.

23. On the whole, the Fifth Army was unable to establish itself ashore as quickly as had been planned. This was due in part to the fact that it had been anticipated that the coast defences would be manned by Italians, whereas in fact the Germans had taken over these defences a few days prior to the assault.

24. The port of Salerno was opened early on D+2 but by 1900 the following day the port was again under enemy gunfire and at 1500 on D+4 it was necessary to withdraw the port party for the time being.

25. Thus, despite the initial successes which attended the landings, by D+4 the Military situation had become unfavourable. The German Command had rallied quickly from the disorganisation caused by the liquidation of their erstwhile brothers-in-arms and had concentrated sufficient armoured forces with supporting infantry to drive a wedge into the Fifth Army defences and at one point had almost penetrated to the beaches,

26. By the following day, the situation had further deteriorated, all unloading ceased, and the Naval Commander Western Task Force requested me to provide heavier Naval support fire. Accordingly, H.M.S. VALIANT and H.M.S. WARSPITE were ordered to proceed to the "Avalanche" area, so as to arrive as soon as possible after first light on D+6. In addition, three cruisers from Force "V", EURYALUS, SCYLLA and CHARYBDIS, were ordered to proceed at their utmost speed to Tripoli to embark further Military reinforcements. Throughout D+7 Naval gunfire of all calibres shelled enemy formations and strongpoints and by 1400 on D+8 the situation was restored. It was while returning from these gun support duties that H.M.S. WARSPITE received two direct hits and one near miss from radio-controlled glider bombs. H.M.S. WARSPITE subsequently reached Malta in tow without further damage.

27. There can be little doubt that the psychological effect upon our troops of seeing these heavy ships bombarding close inshore played a large part in relieving a situation which at one time showed every indication of becoming extremely grave.

The End of the Operation.

28. The Military situation, stabilised on D+6, 15th September, gradually improved; indications of a general German withdrawal were seen on D+7. On 19th September, Eboli and, on 20th, Campagna and several other towns in the vicinity were captured. Five days later the port of Salerno was reopened, followed quickly by the capture of Castellammare on 28th and of Torre Annunziata the next day. Naples was entered on

1st October and with its capture, Operation "Avalanche" drew to a close. The port of Naples had been carefully and methodically wrecked by the withdrawing enemy, but even so, two days later five Liberty ship berths, six coaster berths and eight holding berths were cleared. By the 6th October discharge over the Salerno beaches was almost completed, the port of Naples was functioning slowly, and on that day Operation "Avalanche" was officially deemed to have been completed.

Lessons Learnt.

29. Owing to the considerable period which has elapsed since Operation "Avalanche" was carried out and the fact that the experience gained therein has been embodied in other operations, it is redundant to remark at length upon the lessons learnt. Owing to the short period which had elapsed between Operations "Husky" and "Avalanche", but few of the difficulties brought to light in the first operation were remedied in time for the second. My remarks on Operation "Husky" still hold good, but to some extent these mistakes have now been rectified and it is not intended to elaborate upon them further.

Conclusions.

30. Operation "Avalanche" was the most ambitious amphibious operation so far launched. That it succeeded after many vicissitudes reflects great credit on Vice-Admiral Hewitt, U.S.N., his subordinate Commanders, and all those who served under them. That there were extremely anxious moments cannot be denied. The enemy employed new types of weapons and defended his positions with a ferocity which we have now come to regard as normal, but at the time it provided a severe test to our Military Commanders. I am proud to say that throughout the operation, the Navies never faltered and carried out their tasks in accordance with the highest traditions of their Services. Whilst full acknowledgment must be made of the devastating though necessarily intermittent bombing by the Allied Air Forces, it was Naval gunfire, incessant in effect, that held the ring when there was danger of the enemy breaking through to the beaches and when the overall position looked so gloomy. More cannot be said.

(Signed) ANDREW CUNNINGHAM,
Admiral of the Fleet,
Late Commander-in-Chief,
Mediterranean.

APPENDIX I

PLANNING

On completion of the Sicilian Campaign there were many and changing factors involved in the decision as to the location of the main assault on the Italian coast. Not until August 19th was it decided that the planning and mounting of Operation "Avalanche" should be given first priority. Plans involving landings in the Gulf of Gioija[6] (Operation "Buttress"), in the Gulf of Taranto and on the Italian coast North of Brindisi (Operations "Musket" and "Goblet"), were all examined and progressed to a certain extent. Operation "Buttress" was in fact fully planned and detailed orders were issued to the ships concerned. This uncertainty led to an immense amount of work for my planning staff and for the British Naval Commanders involved, all of whom had two or more problems to examine.

2. It was the intention that the "Buttress" Force would become the Northern Assault Force for "Avalanche" and that an American force would provide the "Avalanche" Southern Assault Force. By this means it was hoped that it would be practicable to switch from Operation "Buttress" to Operation "Avalanche" without upsetting the detailed planning to any marked extent. For a variety of reasons this combination proved not to be so simple as had been imagined, the chief difficulty being that "Buttress" involved the use of only one port, namely Vibo Valencia, whereas in "Avalanche" the plan had to allow for the eventual capture and development of Salerno, Castellammare, Torre Annunziata and Naples.

3. As a result of the several plans under consideration, planning for Operation "Avalanche" was conducted almost simultaneously on the levels of the Commander-in-Chief, Mediterranean, the Western Task Force Commander, who had no other operation to plan, and the subordinate Task Force Commanders, one of whom, Commodore G.N. Oliver, R.N. (the Northern Assault Force Commander), was planning in detail for both "Buttress" and "Avalanche" concurrently.

4. Naval planning memoranda were issued as for previous operations in this theatre to disseminate the building of the plan to the subordinate Commanders. It is no exaggeration to say that without this system these subordinate Commanders could never have produced their own orders in time for the operation, as planning was taking place on all levels simultaneously, as stated in the preceding paragraph.

5. Further difficulty was experienced through the frequent changes of plan introduced by the Fifth Army, many of which took place at a very late date. The Commander Western Naval Task Force comments strongly on this point in his report.

6. The sailing and routeing of the assault convoys called for careful timing and accurate navigation, as many of the convoy tracks had perforce to cross each other,

due to the fact that the troops embarked in convoys sailing from Oran were required for the Southern Sector of the assault beaches. A special channel was swept through the minefields between Sicily and Tunisia to allow the assault forces to pass West of Sicily.

7. The decision by Commanding General Fifth Army to advance H-Hour by 30 minutes was not taken until 24th August and was one which involved a considerable number of alterations to the convoy sailing and routeing programmes, all of which had to be signalled, as by that time the Operation Orders were in course of distribution.

Footnotes
1   See Admiralty foreword.
2   Operation "Husky" – the landing in Sicily.
3   Operation "Baytown" – the assault across the Straits of Messina, 3rd September, 1943.
4   Rangers – the American counterpart of British Commandos.
5   Operation "Dragoon" – the landing on the South coast of France in August, 1944.
6   Gulf of Gioija – on the North-West coast of Calabria.

4

FIELD-MARSHAL LORD ALEXANDER'S DESPATCH ON THE CAMPAIGN IN ITALY

3 SEPTEMBER 1943 TO 12 DECEMBER 1944

The War Office, June, 1950.

THE ALLIED ARMIES IN ITALY FROM 3RD SEPTEMBER, 1943, TO 12TH DECEMBER, 1944.

PREFACE BY THE WAR OFFICE.

This Despatch was written by Field-Marshal Lord Alexander in his capacity as former Commander-in-Chief of the Allied Armies in Italy. It therefore concentrates primarily upon the development of the land campaign and the conduct of the land battles. The wider aspects of the Italian Campaign are dealt with in reports by the Supreme Allied Commander (Field-Marshal Lord Wilson) which have already been published. It was during this period that the very close integration of the Naval, Military and Air Forces of the Allied Nations, which had been built up during the North African Campaigns, was firmly consolidated, so that the Italian Campaign was essentially a combined operation. The very intimate relationship between the three Services was undoubtedly one of the governing factors in securing victory.

The following Despatch was submitted to the Secretary of State for War on 19th April,1947, by HIS EXCELLENCY FIELD-MARSHAL THE VISCOUNT ALEXANDER OF TUNIS, K.G., G.C.B., G.C.M.G., C.S.I., D.S.O., M.C., former General Officer Commanding-in-Chief, Fifteenth Army Group.

I have the honour to submit my Despatch on the Allied Armies in Italy during the period from 3rd September, I943, to I2th December, I944.

The Despatch is divided into the following four parts:

Part I - Preliminary Planning and the Assault.

Part II - The Winter Campaign.

Part III - The Capture of Rome and the Advance to the Arno.

Part IV - The Gothic Line Battles.

The War Office, June, 1950.

PART I.
PRELIMINARY PLANNING AND
THE ASSAULT.

Strategic Basis of the Campaign.

The invasion of Italy followed closely in time on the conquest of Sicily and may be therefore treated, both historically and strategically, as a sequel to it; but when regarded from the point of view of the Grand Strategy of the war there is a great cleavage between the two operations. The conquest of Sicily marks the closing stage of that period of strategy which began with the invasion of North Africa in November, I942, or which might, on a longer view, be considered as beginning when the first British armoured cars crossed the frontier wire into Cyrenaica on IIth June, I940, the morrow of Mussolini's declaration of war. The invasion of Italy was part of the next period in European strategy which was destined to culminate in the invasion of the West and the destruction of the German armies. When the last German fled across the Straits of Messina the first aim of Allied strategy had been achieved: to clear the enemy from Africa and to open the Mediterranean to the shipping of the United Nations without fear of interruption; in the next phase the Mediterranean theatre would no longer receive the first priority of resources and its operations would become preparatory and subsidiary to the great invasion based on the United Kingdom. It was now called on to break up the victorious team of armies trained in its hard school and to surrender to the West the picked divisions which were to form the spearhead of the assault on the beaches of Normandy.

   The nature of the break between the Sicilian and Italian operations is clear from the contrast between the directives for them issued by the Combined Chiefs of Staff. The Casablanca conference treated the invasion of Sicily as a continuation of the clearance of North Africa and looked no further ahead; its orders were clear-cut and definite. The "Trident" conference which met in Washington, in May 1943 took a wider view. On 26th May, the Combined Chiefs of Staff informed the Supreme Allied Commander[1] in the Mediterranean of their decision that the major attack on Europe would be made from the United Kingdom, probably in the early summer of 1944. He was therefore instructed to plan such operations in exploitation of the conquest of Sicily as would be best calculated to eliminate Italy from the war and to contain the maximum number of German divisions; which of the operations should be adopted and thereafter mounted would be decided by the Combined Chiefs of Staff. Here were no geographical objectives pointed out but two *desiderata,* one political and the other, the containing of the maximum number of German divisions, from its very nature indefinable. It is essential that this directive be constantly borne in mind, for it continued to rule all strategy in Italy up to the final surrender of the German armies in the field, and the campaign can only be rightly understood if this is firmly grasped. The campaign in Italy was a great holding attack. The two parts of the directive aim at the same purpose: the diversion of German strength to a theatre as far removed as possible from the vital point, the Channel coast. To eliminate Italy would mean the loss to the Axis of fifty-nine divisions amounting to some two million men[2]; they were admittedly not good troops but they were useful as garrisons in occupied territory. To replace these, and at the same time to provide the troops which would have to be sent to hold the line in Italy, would represent a formidable commitment for Germany at a time when she was faced once more with war on two fronts. The comparison with the contribution of the Peninsular War to the downfall of Napoleon is hackneyed but fully justified.

In order to carry out the tasks assigned by this directive the Supreme Allied Commander was allotted all the ground forces available in the Mediterranean theatre except for four American and three British divisions, which were to be held available for return to the United Kingdom by Ist November,[3] and two British divisions held in readiness to fulfil our commitments to Turkey. These forces were estimated at the equivalent of nineteen British and British-equipped divisions, four American and four French, but of these many were under strength in men and material and others were not fully trained. Other divisions, again, had to be retained for internal security duties in the Middle East and for garrisons of the principal ports of North Africa, while the threat of a German attack through Spain, though already remote by now compared with 1942, could not be entirely disregarded. Our air strength, though slightly reduced, particularly in heavy bombers, would remain adequate for the support of operations[4]. On the sea we were now not likely to meet the Italian fleet and fully confident of our ability to defeat it if met. More serious was the intention to withdraw almost all the landing craft from the theatre for use in the west; this programme did not take effect until later but it represented a severe curtailment of our amphibious mobility.

A further contrast between the campaigns in Sicily and in Italy is provided by the nature of the planning which proceeded them. For Sicily we had had a period of almost six months to study in detail a problem which was not, in its essentials, a complicated one. For the operations in exploitation of success in Sicily we were in the first place not given any definite geographical objectives and the problem of deciding between the available alternatives was complicated by a number of unknown factors which would only be resolved by the outcome of the preceding campaign. It was realised from the first that the decision between the various courses of action which would then be open to us would have to be deferred to a later date and might have to be taken rapidly. Our aim in planning was therefore extreme flexibility and I think it is fair to say that few operations of war of this magnitude have been so distinguished by the speed with which they were mounted and the shortness of the time between the decision to undertake the invasion and its launching. This speed was made possible by the flexibility of strategy permitted by the nature of amphibious operations and the geographical configuration of the theatre, and it was encouraged by the challenge of a constantly changing military and political situation. A certain amount of preliminary planning began as soon as the plan for Sicily was firmly established. This was done in the first place at Allied Force Headquarters, since my own staff were fully engaged on the Sicilian operation. I shall therefore pass over this preliminary period as briefly as possible, but in order to understand the background to the operations carried out under my command it is necessary to give some account of the way in which the problem of an invasion of the Italian mainland was first approached and the basic reasons for the strategy which was eventually adopted.

General Considerations Governing Operations against Italy.

To carry out the terms of the directive from the Combined Chiefs of Staff one course of action had obviously pre-eminent advantages. Italian troops could be found and fought at any point of the deeply indented northern coastline of the Mediterranean from Thrace to the Pyrenees, or in the many off-lying islands, but to eliminate Italy from the war an attack on the mother country offered clearly the best solution. We were already committed to the conquest of Sicily, for reasons, as I have explained, of African and Mediterranean strategy, but it was the opinion of the Intelligence Staff at Allied Force Headquarters that not even the complete loss of the island would bring Italy to sue for terms. Nor was it likely, in the prevailing state of mind in Italy, that the loss of Sardinia in addition would produce that effect. To eliminate Italy from the war we should have to land on the mainland of the peninsula. We should have to do so in any case as soon as the Italians capitulated, whether or not we had made it our main theatre of effort, for we should want to occupy the country as quickly as possible and begin to put its resources to use against the Germans. That being the case, our weakness in available formations rendered it advisable not to split our efforts but to concentrate on one geographical objective.

It was my opinion, therefore, that an invasion of the peninsula was by far the best means of carrying out the first part of the directive and I decided, after considerable study, that it would also offer the best chances of achieving the second object of our strategy, to contain as many German forces as possible. First of all the elimination of Italy, for which an invasion of the peninsula was essential, would of itself, as I have already pointed out, throw a heavy additional strain on Germany. In the summer of 1943 Italy was still performing important garrison duties for the Axis in the Mediterranean theatre; she had seven divisions in Southern France, extending as far west as Marseilles, and no less than thirty-two in the Balkans, together with many non-divisional anti-aircraft and coast defence units in both theatres. If the Germans could no longer count on these forces they would have to replace them at once with German troops: they could not leave south-eastern France ungarrisoned with the Allies loose in the Mediterranean in overwhelming superiority on the sea and in the air; resistance movements in the Balkans would also get completely out of hand unless they took over the areas vacated by the Italians. It was, in fact, not unreasonable to hope that in the Balkans at least, where they far outnumbered the Germans, the Italians might attempt to resist; the resistance was not likely to be prolonged but it would help in diverting German troops. However, apart from these automatic results of Italian capitulation, we should be in a position, by invading the peninsula, to force the Germans to a more damaging diversion of effort than the mere increase in occupational commitments, which could be entrusted to lower category formations, including foreigners and satellites. They would have to put into the field a strong force of good quality troops or see Italy lost by default and the Anglo-American armies appearing on the southern frontier of the Reich. That southern frontier is strong enough by nature, but to abandon Italy, especially the industrial area north of the Apennines, would add a serious loss of war potential to a disastrous loss of prestige. Perhaps even more serious for the Germans would be to allow us to make use of the airfields of Italy from which our strategic Air Forces could develop attacks against hitherto immune targets in Southern and South-eastern Germany, in Hungary and against the vital Ploesti oilfields. For all these reasons I felt sure that the Germans would not stint troops for the defence of Italy and that nowhere else should we be able to draw in and contain so many.

There was, of course, the objection that a campaign in Italy would canalise the whole effort of Great Britain and the United States for 1943 into a comparatively narrow peninsula. The objection, though based on ignorance of our resources and misappreciation of the general strategy of the war, appears superficially sound but omits any consideration of what alternatives were open; as Mr. Churchill said on a later occasion: "We have to fight the Germans somewhere, we can't merely sit and watch the Russians." It would serve no useful purpose to keep the forces available in the Mediterranean in idleness, and plans had already been prepared to make the largest contribution in men and amphibious means which could be transferred in the time available to the Western assault. To say that Italy was a secondary theatre is not a valid objection; it is the nature and function of a holding force to attack secondary objectives while the main force is preparing to attack the main objective. It would be a valid objection, if it could be proved, that the Allies employed unduly large forces in attacking a secondary objective: in fact, as I shall show, our forces in Italy never at any time enjoyed any but the slenderest margin of superiority over the Germans, and usually not even that, and, above all, the invasion of the West was never deprived of any resources in men or materials by the needs of the operations in Italy. The Italian campaign fulfilled its function in the strategic scheme of the war against Germany, and I am convinced that no other possible strategy would have fulfilled that function so well.[5]

It was clear, therefore, that an invasion of the mainland of Italy was the most advantageous course to pursue in the exploitation of success in Sicily. It was also clear, gazing at the relief map of Southern Italy, that it would be an operation of great difficulty. We must get up that long leg as quickly as possible and preferably start as far north as possible, but the limits were laid down by the availability of air cover. I had had experiences in Burma of fighting against an enemy with control of the air which I was not anxious to repeat, and the loss of "Prince of Wales" and "Repulse" off Malaya was a reminder of what could happen, in those circumstances, even to great warships, let alone convoys of merchant ships and landing craft. The experiences of the United States Navy in operations against comparatively isolated Japanese-held islands in the Pacific under cover of aircraft from large groups of carriers were not applicable to the situation facing me in the Mediterranean, and in any case I was assured by Admiral Cunningham[6] that there was no chance of getting such a force of carriers. My air cover would have to come from land-based fighters and, taking the Spitfire with 90 gallon long-range tanks as the standard, this gave me a circle of operations of a hundred and eighty miles. Assuming that we could construct sufficient airfields in the north-eastern corner of Sicily, in the area of Milazzo and Messina, where there was at the moment only one small landing strip, this would mean that the area within which an assault landing was possible would be bounded by an arc of a circle drawn across the peninsula from west to east through the island of Capri, just north of Salerno, north of Potenza in Lucania and cutting the shore of the Gulf of Taranto some fifteen miles short of Taranto itself. The prospects within this area were not inviting. The provinces of Calabria and Lucania are the poorest and most undeveloped in Italy and yield to none in the complexity and difficulty of their mountain structure. In the whole area so circumscribed, there were no major strategic targets the possession of which would be worth the effort of a full-scale assault and whose loss would induce the Italians to sue for terms. There were two great prizes just outside the range of fighter cover; the naval base of Taranto to the east and the port and city of Naples to the north; but a direct assault on either of these heavily defended places would be sufficiently hazardous even with the fullest scale of air support and quite impossible without it.

Calabria was obviously the first objective to be considered. It was the nearest to Sicily, for one thing, and the Navy was bound to be anxious to have the Straits opened as soon as possible by clearing the opposite shore. Our forces would be operating from a firm base and, if the attack were made directly across the Straits of Messina on to the ports of Reggio and San Giovanni, the always hazardous venture of an amphibious operation would be reduced almost to the proportions of a river crossing, with full support from the artillery deployed on the Sicilian shore. If this were considered too modest an operation it could be supported by landings further up the Toe of Italy which could be given the fullest air support and which would quickly allow a junction with the force which had crossed the Straits. Calabria therefore offered a safe but not spectacular investment for the profits of Sicily. The main disadvantage was that the nature of the ground would permit the enemy to block any northward advance with the employment of minimum forces. The country is mountainous and the road-net undeveloped; and there are three isthmuses: Gioia - Locri, Francavilla - Squillace, and Scalea - Castrovillari - Villapiana, the narrowest of which is eighteen miles from sea to sea and the widest only thirty-seven. The *massifs* of Aspromonte and the Sila, both rising to six thousand feet in height, would assist the defence and the summer season would be drawing to its close before Sicily could be secured and the first landings in Calabria mounted. There was a danger of the strategic effort of 1943 finding itself stuck for the winter in a *cul-de-sac* among inhospitable mountains in the most barren and least important part of the Italian peninsula.

It was clear to me, therefore, when the first stage of planning was reached in May, that it was desirable to carry the war to the mainland at the earliest possible moment. It was also clear that a decision would have to be taken whether the landing was to be made in an area where success would be comparatively easy but unproductive or in an area at the extreme end of our range where the risk would be greater but vital objectives within closer reach. These decisions need not and could not be taken yet; much would depend on the progress of operations in Sicily, which were planned to open in July. Only then could vital questions be answered: what would be the value of Italian troops fighting in defence of their native soil, what would be the German reaction to the increased threat to Italy, what was the value of our own amphibious technique and what resources would remain to the Allies, in manpower and landing craft, after a successful invasion of Sicily.

In the meantime there was another possible operation to be considered, against Sardinia and Corsica. This had already been studied as an alternative to Sicily and, though rejected in this role, still offered certain advantages. To put it on the lowest terms: if, after the conquest of Sicily, the enemy were found to be so strongly posted on the mainland that invasion would be impracticable, an operation to capture Sardinia and Corsica would at least mean that we retained the initiative and, since there was little risk of failure, would score another encouraging success. Our shipping in the Mediterranean would also benefit from the elimination of German air bases in the islands. From a superficial glance at the map it might seem that the islands could act as stepping stones for an attack on the South of France, as an alternative to an advance up the Italian peninsula. In fact, however, they offered poor bases for such a strategy and the attrition of our dwindling stock of landing craft would mean that the eventual assault could only be on a small scale. Moreover we were not anxious to attract any more German forces into France but rather away from it, into Italy and the Balkans. Admittedly it would be useful, when the invasion of Northern France began, to be in a position to make, or at least threaten, a diversionary attack on the French Mediterranean coast. We calculated, however, rightly as the event showed, that a successful invasion of Italy would not only draw German forces away from France but also give us Sardinia and Corsica with little trouble. If we locked up our whole force in the islands without invading Italy (and we could certainly not do both) it would mean a long period of inactivity until the early summer of 1944 when a threat from Corsica could begin to play its part in the grand strategy of the invasion of Western Europe. This would be to give the Germans a welcome breathing space and forgo the chance of inflicting casualties on them. To sum up: an operation against Sardinia and Corsica, though clearly feasible, would be inconsistent with the directive laid down for Mediterranean strategy. If the loss of Sicily had not caused the elimination of Italy from the war it was unlikely that the loss of Sardinia in addition would do so, and the number of German divisions contained would be small.

First Stages of Planning.

Detailed planning may be said to have begun with a memorandum produced by Allied Force Headquarters on 3rd June, 1943. It was recognised that, in view of the considerations brought out above, there were two operations which were likely: against Calabria and, as an alternative, Sardinia. For Calabria it might be possible to rely on Eighth Army, assaulting across the Straits of Messina, but that would depend on what shape it was in after the Sicilian campaign. It would be better to have fresh forces available for exploitation, if at all possible, and our two spare Corps Headquarters, of 5 and I0 Corps, could plan the operation, since Eighth Army was not in a position to do so. It was therefore proposed to study two operations, both to be mounted from North Africa: against Reggio by I0 Corps (Operation BUTTRESS) and against Cotrone[7] by 5 Corps (Operation GOBLET). These two headquarters came under my command on 5th June, together with one armoured and four infantry divisions.[8] The Cotrone landing was intended to hasten the capture of the airfields in that area, the only useful ones in Calabria, and would take place about a month after the original landing. Target dates were Ist September and Ist October respectively. The operation against Sardinia (Operation BRIMSTONE), only to be undertaken if success on the mainland appeared unlikely, was entrusted to the United States Fifth Army under General Mark W. Clark. He was ordered on I0th June to prepare a plan for this operation, employing VI United States Corps of two infantry divisions and the British 5 Corps, composed as for the Cotrone landing. General Giraud[9] on I5th June was asked, and agreed, to nominate a commander and staff to prepare a plan for the capture of Corsica (Operation FIREBRAND). I kept in touch with all this planning activity for operations which, if mounted, I should be required to command, but could do little more since this was now the critical period just before the Sicily invasion.

A clearer conception of the detailed implications of future operations is set out in a memorandum from the Executive Planning Section of Allied Force Headquarters dated 30th June. This represents the stage to which Allied strategic thought and planning had been brought before the actual experience of the invasion of Sicily allowed modification in a more optimistic direction. The possibility of such a future modification is fully realised in the opening paragraph: experience alone would show the value of the Italian forces, the extent to which Germany was prepared to reinforce Italy and what Allied resources, particularly in landing craft, would still be available and when. In the circumstances appreciation of Allied capabilities could scarcely be over sanguine. Exploitation into Calabria was estimated as likely to be slow, since the first assaulting force was not expected to be within striking distance of Cotrone, only eighty air miles from the original landing point, by the end of the first month and a subsidiary landing was therefore planned to seize that port thirty days after the original landing. Even if these two operations should be successful the terrain and the weather were likely to offer severe difficulties to our advance, while the number of landing craft available would be so diminished as a result of them that further amphibious operations on a scale large enough to seize a major port such as Naples or Taranto would be impracticable. The maximum number of divisions we could maintain in Calabria was reckoned as six. There were, therefore, now two reasons for invading Sardinia: one, if it was decided that resistance on the mainland would be so strong as to make any landing impracticable, and the second if it was appreciated that, though a landing could be made, the result would be to lock up six divisions in the Toe of Italy without prospect of being able to exploit rapidly either towards Naples or Taranto. I was, however, most reluctant to be forced back into so unproductive a course.

More optimistic possibilities were, of course, considered, based on the possibility of an Italian "collapse", a term never specifically defined. It was the view of the Joint Intelligence Committee that, although Italian morale, both civilian and military, was then low and would sink still further as a result of the loss of Sicily, no complete collapse was likely until the Allied forces had landed on the mainland and had made a considerable advance northwards.[10] However, it was necessary to be prepared for such an eventuality. If Italian resistance ceased, our aim was to move rapidly overland on Naples with the minimum force necessary to seize the airfields and port, to build up our forces to a strength of six divisions and forty-three squadrons of the Tactical Air Force and then to exploit to seize Rome. Subsequent operations could be either into North Italy or across the Adriatic. The timing envisaged on the "most optimistic" development, which gave us Naples by lst October, hit on the right day with an accuracy rare in the forecasts of the best inspired oracles. On the timing considered more likely, that date would see us just assaulting Cotrone and, in the worst case, we should be just appearing off the coast of Sardinia.

Effect on Planning of the Progress of Operations in Sicily.

The result of the first few days fighting in Sicily brought a breath of actuality into the process of planning, hitherto tentative and rather academic, and with it a full gale of optimism. Two of the questions which had dominated previous planning were answered: what was the value of the Italian forces on their own soil and what would remain of our own resources after the reduction of Sicily. Both answers were more favourable than we could have hoped. The Italian coastal divisions, whose value had never been rated very high, disintegrated almost without firing a shot and the field divisions, where they were met, were also driven like chaff before the wind. Mass surrenders were frequent. Moreover, the civilian population seemed well disposed and, when once we were firmly established, were prepared to welcome the Allies as liberators. On the other hand our casualties in men and equipment, and particularly in the all-important categories of landing craft and assault equipment generally, were much lighter than had been expected. We were, however, fully prepared to exploit this success and my staff worked out a plan to improvise an operation against Calabria. Assuming that Eighth Army continued to make such good progress up the east coast as it had in the first few days it would, within five days of the capture of Messina, pass a brigade from l3 Corps across the Straits, assisted by commandos and parachutists. 78 Division would then follow up into Reggio and 46 Division from North Africa would make an assault landing in the Gulf of Gioia. I agreed to this tentative plan and obtained the concurrence of Admiral Cunningham - in fact we even considered assaulting Calabria before the fall of Messina, using Catania as a port of departure - but the premises on which it was based failed to materialise. German reinforcements blocked the way to Catania and 78 Division, following the original plan, had to be thrown into the heavy fighting for Centuripe. However, the feeling of justified optimism and the positive gains represented by the lightness of the Allied casualty list still remained. It was possible to contemplate bolder strokes which promised more valuable results than the capture of the incidental objective of Sardinia or locking up the Allied forces for a winter in Calabria in circumstances reminiscent of the Allied situation at Salonica in the 1914-1918 War.

It was with these considerations in mind that I attended a conference at Carthage on 17th July with General Eisenhower, Admiral Cunningham and Air Marshal Tedder.[11] We then decided that "the mainland of Italy is the best area for exploitation with a view to achieving our object of forcing Italy out of the war and containing the maximum German forces." In order to retain complete freedom of action to avail ourselves of any possibilities which might offer themselves we agreed to prepare for the following eight courses of action:

(*a*) A quick exploitation across the Straits by Eighth Army, assisted by one or more divisions from North Africa.

(*b*) A full scale assault landing by 10 Corps to capture Reggio.

(*c*) A quick exploitation from the "Toe" (Reggio) to the "Ball" (Cotrone).

(*d*) A full scale assault landing by 5 Corps to capture Cotrone.

(*e*) Repeated outflanking operations up the coast of Calabria by small amphibious forces.

(*f*) A large-scale amphibious operation against Taranto by Fifth Army, to be known as Operation MUSKET, dependent on sufficient landing craft being available.

(*g*) "Introducing a reinforcing force into Naples after the port has been captured as a result of our land advance."

In this schedule of future courses (*b*) was intended as an alternative to (*a*) and (*d*) as an alternative to (*c*), if the overland drive had become held up before it reached the Cotrone area. Course (*e*) reflected the healthier situation of our landing craft resources; it was expected that we should be able to unblock ourselves if halted by strong resistance and overcome the difficulties of the Calabrian terrain by swift "seaborne hooks" in brigade strength. So far, however, there was little change from previous conceptions of the progress of future operations except that the speed of the advance was appreciated as likely to be greater; but the last two courses for which preparations were now to be made were more ambitious.

An assault on Taranto had been considered earlier but rejected on what then seemed sufficient grounds. At the date proposed, 1st November, the weather was likely to be unsuitable for beach maintenance, we should have lost too many landing craft in the three previous assaults (i.e., Sicily, Reggio and Cotrone) and air cover would be impossible since Taranto would be out of range of the majority of our fighters operating from the airfields in north-eastern Sicily. These reasons were no longer cogent. No degree of success could change the November weather in this stormy part of Italy but it would ensure our being able to mount the assault earlier, and a provisional date of Ist October could now be contemplated with some confidence. More landing craft were now available as a result of our light losses in the landings in Sicily and we had considerable hopes that it might be unnecessary to carry out one or other of the assaults at Reggio and Cotrone, perhaps even both, with a consequent further saving in resources. As for air cover we now had hopes of a rapid advance to seize the airfields at Cotrone and in any case, if the Italian defences in Apulia were as feebly manned as in Sicily (and the German forces in the area were weak), a lesser scale of air support might be acceptable. The advantages of the operation were considerable. It would give us the possession of ports through which a large force could be built up and it would place us in a geographically protected area on the same side of the Apennines as Foggia, the capture of whose numerous airfields for the use of the Strategic Air Force was one of our first objectives in Italy. On 22nd July, therefore, Fifth Army was directed to prepare plans for an operation "to seize and secure the Heel of Italy east of the line Taranto - Bari inclusive," with target date Ist October, to be carried out under my command. Planning for the assault on Sardinia had already been cancelled on the 20th and responsibility for this operation, together with that against Corsica, was handed over to the French. With this decision the western islands passed out of the strategic picture; in the event the Germans withdrew from both, with a precipitancy which they probably later regretted.

The last of the possible courses for which preparations were to be made provided for the introduction of a force into the port of Naples after it had been captured by an overland advance; this was given the codename GANGWAY. It had been contemplated already, but only as a possibility which would be open in the event of an Italian collapse. What we hoped, was that, with the Italian forces disintegrating and the Germans withdrawing to safer positions further north, a small mobile force, necessarily restricted to the minimum by difficulties of maintenance, might be able to push rapidly across the tangled mountains of Calabria, Lucania and Southern Campania to seize the port for the entry of Fifth Army. In the first optimistic days of the invasion of Sicily Fifth Army had been directed (on I5th July) to prepare plans for an unopposed landing in Naples. This directive was still in force, but priority had now been shifted to the operation against Taranto. Nevertheless, the great prize of the capture of Naples still glittered; it would give us control of an area capable of maintaining any Allied force which could be placed in Italy in 1943, it would establish our armies well on the road to Rome and it would oblige the Germans to withdraw not only from Calabria but probably from Apulia as well. But if the required conditions were unfulfilled there were weighty arguments against an assault landing in so well defended an area; in particular the lack of air cover and the time which must elapse before our troops advancing from Calabria could make contact. We were likely to capture Cotrone, from which we could cover operations against Taranto, sooner than Scalea, the first place from which we could cover Naples; exploitation overland from Cotrone to Taranto would be much easier than from Scalea to Naples; for the present the priority of the Taranto operations must stand.

Fall of Mussolini.

On 25th July Radio Roma announced the fall of Mussolini, the suppression of the Fascist party and the accession to power of Marshal Badoglio. Although we had often considered the possibility of this, the actual announcement came as a surprise, for the secret of the *coup d'état* had been well kept, as was natural with so few persons involved in the plot. It was not a case of a popular rising nor even of a wave of popular discontent, for the Italian people in general was still sunk in its usual apathy; though, of course, claims to that effect were subsequently put out, mainly by Italian exiles in Switzerland. If there had in fact been any such occurrences we should have been less surprised, and so would the Germans, who were struck with consternation. We had a certain advantage over them, as we were aware of the discontent of some senior officers in the Italian services, and there had already been some cautious approaches by Italian commanders in the Balkans which showed a willingness to abandon a lost cause and a now unpopular alliance.

This dramatic news introduced a new factor into our delicately poised calculations, and one which clearly brought nearer the long hoped for collapse of Italy. That Badoglio had declared "The war continues" deceived nobody and proposals for a capitulation were confidently awaited. But the Allied side need not wait until Badoglio felt secure enough to move; the optimism of the early days of the Sicilian invasion, which had become dashed with more sober reflections as the deadlock before Catania continued, was reborn. At a conference at Carthage next day, 26th July, attended by General Eisenhower, Admiral Cunningham, Air Marshal Tedder and myself, we decided that greater risks might now legitimately be taken. Accordingly on 27th July General Clark, commanding the Fifth Army, was directed to prepare plans for seizing the port of Naples "with a view to preparing a firm base for further offensive operations." The target date was to be 7th September and an outline plan was to be submitted by 7th August. The September date was the earliest we could possibly hope for. All our available troops were engaged in Sicily, where the two reserve divisions, American 9th and British 78th, had just been committed in order to speed up the completion of the campaign. We hoped to finish in Sicily by mid-August, after which the troops there engaged would be available, with the important exception of those earmarked for return to the United Kingdom. More decisive, for if a real opportunity had offered no doubt we could have scraped together some troops to take advantage of it, was the fact that we had no craft to move them as we were still dependent on craft for the maintenance of our forces in Sicily. It was calculated that the first week of September would be the earliest time by which sufficient would be available and serviceable. The moon would be at its most suitable between 7th and 10th September.

Plans for Assault Landing in the Naples Area.

Operation AVALANCHE, as the Naples assault was called, was to be carried out by VI United States Corps, organised as for the invasion of Sardinia, and 10 British Corps.[12] Theoretically each Corps consisted of one armoured, two infantry and one airborne division, but this was liable to revision in view of the difficulties of providing shipping and airlift; we knew, for instance, that we should only have air lift for at most one airborne division and would probably, as turned out, not be able to lift much more than three divisions in craft for the assault wave. There were difficulties about the British contingent. Since the plans for Calabria were still in force, and we could not yet say whether that was to be the main attack or only subsidiary, it was necessary for 10 Corps to be prepared, at short notice, to attack either Naples or Reggio, and only time could show which. The solution reached was to devise loading tables common to both plans and to ensure that 10 Corps' allotment of landing craft was not varied to meet the exigencies of one or the other.

The directive of 27th July specified the Gulf of Salerno as the site for the initial landings for the assault on Naples. This choice was much argued, both at the time and subsequently, and I think it as well to consider at some length the reasons for the decision, of whose correctness I am convinced. To sail straight into the Bay of Naples was impracticable. The sea approaches were strongly defended by minefields and net barrages and the whole area was heavily covered by permanent fortifications, including over forty coast defence guns; moreover, it was almost certain that, whatever else the Germans might do, they would hold Naples in strength to deny us so great a prize for as long as possible and to cover the withdrawal of their forces from the south. The choice therefore fell between landing north or south of Naples. The former course had many advantages and was originally favoured by General Clark. The plain of Campania, between the Volturno and Naples, is one of the few plains along the west coast of Italy not dominated by nearby mountains, a fact which would permit the rapid deployment of large forces and the full use of our armour, and a quick success there would cut the communications of all the German formations in the south, perhaps forcing them to evacuate Naples before they had had time to carry out extensive demolitions. The Germans also appear to have expected us to attack in this area rather than further south; they moved two divisions there immediately after the evacuation of Sicily whereas it was only shortly before our landing at Salerno that a division was brought across to there from Apulia. But there were two serious objections to the northern assault area; the beaches were unsuitable for landings, and in parts obstructed by off-lying sandbars, and it would be well beyond effective fighter cover. The first might possibly have been accepted but the second was decisive. The plans for the landing involved sufficient risks already, as the event was to show; without fighter cover it might well have been a disaster.[13]

The Salerno beaches are undoubtedly the best for an assault on the whole west coast of Italy. There is a continuous strip of beach twenty miles long running from Salerno southwards; sea approaches are good and offshore gradients vary between one in forty and one in eighty, allowing landing craft to come close inshore.[14] The coastal defences in the area were not impressive and were almost exclusively fieldworks. From the air point of view a fine prize was within our grasp in the Montecorvino airfield, capable of taking four fighter squadrons, which lay less than three miles from the shore. Conditions for an assault, therefore, are ideal but the trouble begins inland from the beaches. The coastal plain is compressed by a line of mountains, rising abruptly at distances varying between two and ten miles from the coast, which would afford the enemy excellent observation and fire positions commanding the plain and a strong defensive position to which to withdraw if our bridgehead were expanded. Still more serious is the fact that, even if the landings should be completely successful, a formidable obstacle still bars the way to Naples: the rocky spur of the Monti Picentini which runs down into the Sorrento peninsula. Towering sheer above Salerno, this wall of bare mountain is pierced only by two passes, running through narrow gorges offering admirable defensive positions. For all these disadvantages, however, there was one decisive factor in the choice of Salerno: it was the furthest north and the nearest to Naples that we could strike without losing fighter cover.

For the present the proposed landing at Salerno took second priority to the gaining of a lodgement in Calabria, for General Montgomery[15] considered he would need I0 Corps as well as I3 Corps for the latter operation. I was already of the opinion, however, that we could exploit into Calabria on a much cheaper scale, using only the troops from Sicily, for I felt certain that there would be no serious German resistance and that the Italians would do no better than in Sicily. This proposal was accepted at a further conference of Commanders-in-Chief on Ist August; we agreed that a lodgement in Calabria was necessary but hoped to be able to achieve it without using I0 Corps at all. In any case our strategy was flexible enough to allow us to switch I0 Corps to either objective and this was laid down in a directive issued after another Carthage conference on 9th August. The relevant paragraph directed: "every effort will be made to seize a bridgehead in Calabria with the resources available after the allocation of the necessary landing craft to I0 Corps." I informed General Montgomery on 23rd August that he would almost certainly have to undertake the operation with his existing resources and without the assistance of an additional assault landing by I0 Corps. On I3th August I3 Corps Headquarters, with under command I Canadian Division and 5 Division, had already been withdrawn from operations in Sicily in order to prepare for the assault across the Straits.

Final Decisions on Invasion Plans.

At a Commanders-in-Chief conference at Carthage on I6th August the final decisions were taken on which the invasion of Italy was based. The campaign in Sicily was practically over and the Germans were being more successful than we had hoped in evacuating men and light equipment over the Straits. Evacuation was actually completed by dawn next day, I7th August. It was known that new German troops were pouring into Italy, mainly re-formed divisions from the old Sixth Army destroyed at Stalingrad. By the end of the month there were to be as many as eighteen German divisions in Italy, including five armoured divisions. We should not be able to get an equivalent number of divisions into the country until December. Nevertheless, the decision was taken to proceed at the earliest possible moment to a full-scale invasion on the lines of the boldest plan which had been considered. First I3 Corps were to land in Calabria; the date, to be as early as possible and probably between Ist and 4th September, was left to my subsequent decision. Secondly, the

Salerno assault was to be launched with a target date of 9th September. This date could be postponed not more than forty-eight hours if necessary. Fifth Army came under my command on 17th August, just over three weeks before it was to assault the Salerno beaches.

Fifth Army's outline plan for the operation, which it had been ordered to prepare on 27th July, was presented on 15th August. Only slight modifications were necessary and the final Operation Order was issued on 26th August. The most important change was in the use of airborne troops. We only had sufficient aircraft for one division and 82 (United States) Airborne was nominated; in the event this too was removed from the order of battle in circumstances which will be described later and there was no airborne operation as part of the assault. The troops to be employed in the initial assault only amounted to three divisions with a floating reserve of one Regimental Combat Team. On the left the British 10 Corps, Lieutenant-General McCreery,[16] with under command 46 and 56 Divisions, was to assault between Salerno and the Sele River, seize Salerno and the Montecorvino airfield and establish a firm beach-head, including the mountain passes north-west of Salerno. When firmly established it was to advance and capture the port of Naples and the airfields at Capodichino and Pomigliano. On D-day it was to be assisted by three American Ranger battalions and two British Commandos, attacking on its left flank, and on D plus 4 it was to be reinforced by 7 Armoured Division. On the right the United States VI Corps, General Dawley,[17] was to assault, with 36 Division and one tank battalion, the beaches south of the River Sele, establish a firm beach-head and secure the Army right flank. The Army floating reserve consisted of one Regimental Combat Team of 45 Division under the divisional commander. As a follow-up, when shipping became available after the assault phase was over, the remainder of 45 Division was nominated, and subsequently 34 Division. In the original plan a Regimental Combat Team of 82 Airborne Division was to be dropped north of Naples in the valley of the River Volturno to seize the bridges at Triflisco, Capua and Cancello and prevent the arrival of enemy reinforcements from the north. This drop was subsequently cancelled, to the great detriment of the operations.

It will be seen that the forces available for the invasion of a hostile coast at the extreme limit of air cover and well out of touch with any supporting force were not large, though I need not say that they were the largest we could manage. Only three infantry divisions were to make the assault, with an armoured division to start disembarking on D plus 4, and subsequent reinforcement would be slow. The provision of landing craft was now our acutest problem. Many of those needed could not be withdrawn from Sicily before 19th August, after which they had to be hastily refitted at Bizerta, undergo such repairs as might be necessary, and sail to their loading ports; the many uncertain factors in the programme made it impossible to be sure how many would eventually be available. We were prepared to strip 13 Corps of its craft as soon as it had got itself established across the Straits, in fact we took some Landing Ships, Tank, away on D-day of that operation. Convoy problems were difficult for the Navy. VI Corps was to sail direct from Oran in a single convoy, but 10 Corps had to be loaded into many different types of ships and craft and sail from

Tripoli and Bizerta in a series of convoys of various speeds and composition. All convoys were to pass west of Sicily and then proceed, on D minus I, on a northerly course, turning eastwards towards Salerno only after last light. A great part of the route would be along narrow lanes specially swept through the enemy minefields where, if opposed, alterations of course would be impossible and the force would have to fight its way through. Force "H", comprising four battleships, two aircraft carriers and I2th Cruiser Squadron, was to cover the assault convoy from attack by the Italian battle fleet in Spezia and Genoa while two battleships at Malta watched Taranto and were available to replace casualties. A support carrier group of one light fleet and four escort aircraft carriers was to provide additional fighter cover for the landing and was itself covered by aircraft from the fleet aircraft carriers of Force "H".[18]

The task of the Air Forces was twofold; first and most important to neutralise the enemy air effort and secondly to disorganise his power of movement. The opening stage in the air plan was designed to force him to evacuate his air bases in Southern and Central Italy and to disrupt the Italian communication system by attacks on key-points. From D minus 7 until the bridgehead had been firmly established a concentrated effort would be made against the Naples - Salerno area to render useless the airfields there and, as far as possible, to isolate the battlefield from enemy reinforcement. When this was deemed to be accomplished, and dependent upon the measure of success attained, close bomber support would become available for general operations. Fighter cover was to be provided by a continuous patrol from bases in Sicily,[19] supplemented by the Seafires of the Carrier Support Group, until airfields or emergency air strips ashore were available. It was hoped that Montecorvino airfield could be captured on D-day and that seventy-five aircraft could be flown into it by D plus I.

The orders for the Calabrian landing (Operation BAYTOWN) were also issued on I6th August. It was a simple plan which was carried out without any but minor variations. The troops to be employed were only two infantry divisions, I Canadian and 5 British, reinforced by an armoured and an infantry brigade and various Commando units. The artillery support for the actual crossing, however, was almost as heavy as Eighth Army had ever had, including an Army Group Royal Artillery, 30 Corps artillery and four battalions of American mediums from Seventh Army assisted by naval supporting fire.[20] In the air, the attack was to be supported by the Desert Air Force, with elements both of XII U.S. Air Support Command and of Tactical Bomber Force temporarily under its command.

Italians Open Negotiations for Surrender.

The military situation on I6th August was thus clearly defined. The final decisions as to the manner of the invasion of the Italian mainland in Calabria and at Salerno had been taken and the planning of the operation was in an advanced stage. On the next day we received the news that the political situation had once more undergone a sudden change. On I5th August a General Castellano, of the Italian Commando Supremo,[21] presented himself at the British Embassy in Madrid; he was travelling under an assumed name as a civil servant and had no written credentials but he claimed to be an accredited representative of Marshal Badoglio and bearer of a message on the latter's behalf. The Marshal stated that when the Allies invaded Italy the Italian Government was prepared to order the immediate cessation of hostilities against the Allies and to join them forthwith, with all available forces, in the fight against Germany. This was the news we had been awaiting since 25th July, when Mussolini fell. The delay had been caused, not by any reluctance to accept the formula of "unconditional surrender," but because Badoglio was anxious to establish himself firmly in power and also because this was the first good opportunity which had presented itself to get in touch with the Allies unknown to the Germans. The cover employed was that Castellano was going to Lisbon as one of the party sent to meet the Italian ambassador returning from Chile. However, the date was well chosen since Mr. Churchill and Mr. Roosevelt were at that moment conferring in Quebec, accompanied by the Combined Chiefs of Staff. They were able, therefore, immediately they were notified from Madrid of this new development, to direct General Eisenhower, in a signal received on 17th August, to send two representatives to Lisbon where a further meeting with Castellano had been arranged at the British Embassy. The two emissaries, Generals Smith and Strong, Chief of Staff and Assistant Chief of Staff, G-2,[22] of Allied Force Headquarters, left on 18th August and returned to Algiers on the 20th.

The nature of the Italian capitulation and the reasons which led to it were not generally understood by the public at the time and have been widely misrepresented since. This is not the place for a discussion of the political aspects of the situation but I feel that in order to explain its effect on our military appreciation of the problems of the invasion of Italy and give the proper strategical background to our subsequent operations I should deal as briefly as possible with the motives behind the Italian offer. Italy in 1943 was in a very different position from Germany in 1945. Germany capitulated when the country had been almost completely occupied by the victorious Allies and when the prospect of resistance, even for a few days more, had been almost totally excluded by the complete disintegration of the armed forces and the disappearance of central control. This was not the case with Italy; she still had large armies in the field (her forces in the peninsula alone were numerically superior to anything the Allies could bring against them) and, although their morale was shaken and their quality inferior, there were sufficient German forces in the country to stiffen them. Resistance was certainly still possible. The events of the next twenty-one months showed that the German forces alone were sufficient to impose a most serious delay on the Allied occupation of Italy and the experience of the Republican Fascist Government showed that an Italian Government could have continued to function and exercise authority over the greater part of Italy for a long time to come.

Nor was it true that capitulation was dictated by internal unrest and popular demand. There were, indeed, continuous reports during this period of disturbances in the industrial towns of Northern Italy, reports spread for the most part by exiled Italian politicians who had also claimed the credit of provoking the fall of Mussolini by similar disturbances; but these reports, like the earlier ones, were known to be greatly exaggerated. A reference once more to subsequent events will show the unimportance of this factor: no unrest among the civilian population played any significant role in diminishing the German capacity to resist in Italy;[23] it cannot therefore have been the main factor in disposing the Royal Government to capitulate nor, if they had decided to fight on at the side of their German allies, would popular unrest have been any more of an embarrassment to them than it was to their Republican successors. The plain fact is that the Italian Government did not decide to capitulate because it saw itself incapable of offering further resistance, nor because of any change of heart or intellectual conviction of the justice of the Allied and Democratic cause; it decided, as Italian statesmen had decided in the past, that the time had come to "spring to the aid of the victors".

It was largely a General Staff decision. On a cool calculation, inspired by that "sacro egoism" recommended by Salandra in 1914, the chief military authorities had decided that the fortunes of war had turned at last against the Axis. A similar calculation, false as it turned out, had brought them into the war in June 1940. The moment then had been carefully chosen; now also they hoped that, by changing sides at this juncture, they would have just enough fighting to do to justify a claim, when the actual end of the war came, to a place among the victorious allies. It would involve sacrificing for the present their troops in the Balkans and South France but they hoped that their armies in Italy itself would remain reasonably intact. The calculation was acute in one sense, in that they clearly saw that resistance at the side of the Germans could still have been prolonged for some time; but there was one serious miscalculation which they undoubtedly regretted bitterly later on and but for which they would probably have postponed their offer of capitulation. Lacking a proper appreciation of the difficulties of amphibious warfare, and grossly misinformed by their Intelligence services of the strength and capabilities of the Allied forces in the Mediterranean theatre, the Commando Supremo assumed that we were able to put on shore, at any point of the Italian coastline we chose, a force of such a size that, with the assistance of the Italian troops in the country, the Germans would either be destroyed or driven from Italy in rout. The least they hoped was that the Germans would be forced to evacuate all Italy south of the Apennines, the later "Gothic" line. In that case the authority of the Royal Government would continue over the greater part of the country, the capital would be secured, the Italian Armed Forces, though reduced in size, would remain in being with the position of the Commando Supremo unimpaired, and Italy would be able to take her place among the United Nations.

I have dwelt at some length on the military conceptions underlying the Italian offer because, unless they are thoroughly grasped, the progress of negotiations and subsequent operations will be misunderstood.[24] They were clearly brought out at the meeting in Lisbon between Castellano and General Eisenhower's emissaries. The latter began by presenting the Allied Armistice terms; these had already been prepared on the news of the fall of Mussolini in anticipation of an approach by the Italians and the approval of the Allied Governments obtained on 1st August. They were short and straightforward, dealing only with military matters; the full terms were not yet presented but the Italian Government, in accepting the short terms, was to undertake to sign the more comprehensive instrument at a later date. Castellano's reaction was as might have been expected from the circumstances of the Italian decision; almost disregarding the question of surrender terms, which he said, indeed, he was not authorised to discuss, he declared that his purpose was to concert the means by which Italy would transfer her allegiance from the German to the Allied side.[25] What he was interested in was our plans for the invasion of Italy, to see what help we could give to the Italian forces in resisting the Germans. He was told that there was no question of our revealing our intentions; not only was this an obvious measure of security in so dubious a situation but also, and more important, if the Commando Supremo had been apprised of the fact that the utmost we could do was to land three divisions no further north than Salerno they would undoubtedly have decided to postpone capitulation to a more propitious date. Castellano was therefore merely informed that, if the Italian Government accepted our terms, cessation of hostilities would take effect from a date and hour to be notified later; this would be five or six hours before the main Allied landings, which would be in considerable strength. At that time the Supreme Allied Commander would broadcast an announcement of the armistice; the Italian Government must simultaneously make a similar announcement and order its forces and people to collaborate with the Allies and resist the Germans, its fleet and shipping to sail to Allied ports and its aircraft to fly to Allied bases, and ensure that all Allied prisoners in danger of falling into German hands should be released. Italian formations in the Balkans should be ordered to march down to the coast preparatory to evacuation.

With this Castellano had to be content; there was a considerable element of bluff in our attitude but it seemed likely that the bluff would be successful. It was clear throughout that his interest was centred, not on the distastefulness of surrender, but on apprehensions of what the Germans might do. One threat with which the latter had made great play was to employ gas against the Italian cities. For our part we did not allow ourselves to be carried away by the prospect of invading Italy with Italian assistance. I was sceptical as to the amount of assistance we should actually receive and determined not to attempt any rash operation, such as trying to land our three divisions out of range of air cover, in reliance on such assistance. This judgment, based on past experience, was justified in the sequel; I had expected a little more resistance to the Germans than was actually offered, but not much more. Any help, however, was welcome, for the German forces in Italy were growing at an alarming speed. At any rate the Italian Government was clearly in earnest, as it proved by the subsequent despatch to Lisbon of General Zanussi and General Carton de Wiart.[26]

Our next direct contact with General Castellano was on 31st August at Cassibile in Sicily. I had moved my headquarters there on the 28th. The scene of a historic disaster in 413 B.C., which marked the downfall of the Athenian empire, it was now destined to be the scene of the signature of an armistice which sealed the dissolution of the Italian empire and the disappearance of Italy from the ranks of the Great Powers. General Smith, representing General Eisenhower, Admiral Cunningham, Air Marshal Tedder and I were present, and General Clark also attended. It was clear that the Italian Government was prepared to accept any terms we offered but that it was obsessed by the fear that the Germans would be able, when the armistice was announced, to seize control of the whole country in spite of any resistance their troops might offer. German troops continued to pour in; from Naples southwards there were the four divisions which had been evacuated from Sicily, reinforced by two armoured divisions which had not yet been engaged, but there were between ten and twelve divisions in the rest of Italy, including two well placed for a stroke against Rome. Castellano now said that his government could not accept our terms unless we revealed our intentions, so that they could judge whether we were coming in sufficient force. He pleaded with us at least to assure him that the landing would be made north of Rome and in strength not less than fifteen divisions: he even seemed to think that we could land a force of that size in the area of Leghorn.[27] To show our hand was obviously impossible; the bluff must be played out to the end for we too were deeply concerned by the German reinforcement of Italy; but unless we could do something to counter this fear of the Germans all might yet be lost. An offer was therefore made that we would fly an airborne division into the Rome area, to land on airfields already seized by the Italians, which would co-operate with the five Italian divisions around the capital[28] in holding it against the Germans until our invading force could effect a juncture. The risk was obvious; not only might we lose the division flown in (82 United States Airborne Division was nominated) but it would also mean that it would not be available for its very important rôle in the Salerno assault, the forces for which were already quite weak enough. We decided, however, that the risk must be taken and on Ist September General Eisenhower informed me of a message received from the President and the Prime Minister: "We highly approve your decision to go on with AVALANCHE and to land an airborne division near Rome on the conditions indicated".

An unexpected difficulty now arose because Castellano claimed he had no authority to sign the armistice and must first consult his Government. He was told plainly that our terms, including the new offer, must be accepted or rejected by the night of Ist-2nd September and that, whatever their decision, we should proceed with our plan for carrying the war to the Italian mainland. I have wondered since whether we should have been able to make good those bold words if the Italian decision had been negative, but at the time I had no doubt they would accept. On the other hand the military situation had been changing to our disadvantage every day since the plan for Salerno had first been proposed, in view of the constant arrival of fresh German forces.[29] However, the bluff was not called; within our specified time on Ist September the King and Badoglio agreed to our terms and at a quarter past five on 3rd September General Smith, on behalf and in the presence of General Eisenhower, and General Castellano, on behalf of Marshal Badoglio, signed the Military Terms of Surrender. The scene of the signature was a tent in an almond grove near Cassibile; thirteen hours before, to the thunder of six hundred guns in the Straits of Messina, the Eighth Army had begun the first invasion of the continent of Europe.

German Dispositions in Italy.

Before proceeding to an account of our operations in Italy I must complete the picture of the problems which faced us by detailing the enemy forces opposing us and the strategy which they had decided to adopt. On the latter point we were fairly well informed and had acquired an additional source of information in General Castellano who told us all the Germans had so far revealed to their allies. In order to give a true picture I must step back a little in time and fill in the background of the general German strategic position in 1943.

At the beginning of the year the German High Command saw themselves faced with the certainty of a serious defeat in South Russia and the high probability of complete disaster in Africa. The loss of Stalingrad would tear a great gap in the southern end of the Eastern Front; the loss of Tunisia would open all southern Europe to the attack of the Anglo-American forces in North Africa. For the moment the danger in the east was the greater. Tunisia was still holding out and was expected to continue to do so; indeed both Kesselring and Jodl have since stated that they had expected to be able to retain the bridgehead in Tunisia indefinitely; all the available reserves therefore, less those already allotted and *en route* for Africa, must be sent to Russia. These reserves came, as always previously in times of stress on the Eastern Front, from France, which was still being used as the place where battered divisions were re-formed and new divisions activated. No less than nineteen divisions were despatched in January and February from France to Russia; they were successful, aided by the coming of spring, in stabilizing the front. But as the thaw on the steppes brought the long opposing battle lines to a standstill, 7 Armoured Division entered Tunis through the Bardo Gate and a German Commander-in-Chief wandered disconsolately down from the low hills of Cape Bon to surrender to an officer of 4 Indian Division. To the twenty divisions lost at Stalingrad there were now to be added over one hundred and thirty thousand men[30] swallowed up in Tunisia, as a final item in the balance of losses already sustained in two years of fruitless campaigning in Africa.

The first German reaction was to reinforce the Balkans. By the end of May their forces there had risen from seven to thirteen divisions and by the end of August to nineteen; in particular a strong corps of four divisions, including a crack armoured division from France, was formed in the Peloponese. It was necessary, however, to give some attention to Italy. It might be felt that the Alps were sufficient protection to the Reich without a glacis to the south of them but there were disadvantages involved in the abandonment of Italy which rendered such a course intolerable except *in extremis*. The loss of an ally, involving the disappearance of the Rome - Berlin Axis from the political scene, the loss of useful auxiliary troops who were, numerically, playing the greater part in the garrisoning of the Balkans, the direct threat to the Balkans themselves from attack either across the Adriatic or across the relatively lower Julian Alps, the loss of airfields from which strategic attacks against Germany herself could be greatly augmented and directed against hitherto immune areas, and the loss of Italian industrial production, were dangers to be avoided at almost all costs. There were also two psychological factors which weighed strongly with Hitler, on whom the decision rested; the well-known reluctance, exhibited both previously and subsequently, to yield any ground without a fight, and, to some extent at least, loyalty to his old ally Mussolini. It was decided, therefore, that German troops should assist in the defence of Italy and that the Allies should be held as far south as possible.

By this time good progress had been made with the re-formation, in France, of the twenty divisions destroyed at Stalingrad, and other exhausted divisions from the Eastern Front were resting there. If the precedent of 1942 had been followed these re-formed divisions should have been employed once more in Russia; instead, any idea of a serious offensive in the east was renounced and they were to be made available for the defence of the southern front. There were no organisational difficulties in their employment in Italy for there were already in existence there the installations which had served for the transit of divisions bound for the war in Africa and Kesselring, the Commander-in-Chief, South (Oberbefehlshaber Süd),was already on the spot. The first necessity was to provide for the security of the islands; two divisions went to Sicily and one to Sardinia and an S.S. brigade to Corsica. More were to follow, when available, for the defence of the peninsula but at the Feltre conference on 19th July Hitler informed Mussolini that he could not spare more than twenty divisions and could not guarantee more than to hold northern Italy north of a line roughly from Pisa to Rimini. The first week of the Sicilian campaign had already shown the uselessness of the Italian Army.

The fall of Mussolini came as a great shock to the Germans, who had had no warning of its imminence. Orders were hurriedly issued to all German troops in Italy to avoid any behaviour which might appear provocative and many observers report how apprehensive and nervous all ranks appeared. For the moment there was no open cause for alarm since Badoglio had declared "The war continues" but it was perfectly clear that the Italians had lost confidence in an Axis victory. It was necessary, therefore, to provide for the safety, not only of the southern frontier of the Reich, but also of the German troops in Italy who might at any moment find themselves at the mercy of a hostile population and attacked in force by their erstwhile brothers in arms. The programme of reinforcement had already been laid down; it was necessary to speed it up and throughout July and August, while the German troops in Sicily were holding a line around Mount Etna and while they withdrew across the Straits of Messina into Calabria, new German forces continued to pour into Italy over the Brenner, out of France and over the north-eastern passes. The main concentration was in northern Italy, where Field-Marshal Rommel was appointed to command; he was also to be responsible for Slovenia and Northern Croatia, from which Italian troops were to be withdrawn.

The last occasion on which the Germans and Italians consulted together on their plans for the defence of Italy, as far as can be ascertained, was at Casalecchio near Bologna, on 15th August, a conference attended by Roatta, the Italian Chief of Staff, and three other Italian Generals on the one hand and by Rommel, Jodl and Rintelen on the other[31]. After some ugly bickering between Roatta and Jodl over the question of German troops being used for the "protection" of the Brenner route the two plans for the defence of the country were produced. The Italians wished for twelve German divisions of which nine were to be in Southern and Central Italy, one in Corsica, and only two in Northern Italy and Liguria; this figure excluded the four divisions from Sicily. This plan might reasonably appear to be based on the Italian desire to have the defence of the whole pensinsula provided for; but after the capitulation it was used by Hitler as the basis of a charge that Badoglio had schemed to draw the German forces far down into Italy, as far as possible from their bases, and dispersed in small groups which could be easily dealt with by the Italian troops in the same areas. The German plan for the disposition of their sixteen divisions (i.e. including the four from Sicily) put eight in Northern Italy under Rommel, two near Rome and six in Southern Italy; the latter two forces were to be under Kesselring. This plan was the one adopted in the event. Proposals for the employment of Kesselring's forces, as reported to us by General Castellano, were still fluid and would be based on the Germans' own strength when the invasion came and their appreciation of the Allies' strength. In principle they intended to defend the line of the Apennines from Massa Carrara to Pesaro, the later "Gothic" line, though if the Allies were to attack this in great strength they would withdraw to the Po. If, however, the Allies showed little strength the Germans would attempt to hold a line from Grosseto, through Monte Amiata to Perugia and thence to Ancona.[32] Finally, if the circumstances and relative strengths were particularly favourable, an attempt would be made to stand south of Rome on the line Gaeta, Isernia, Vasto. This was a line which the Italians had already surveyed, and defences were already being prepared at certain points.[33]

There is no need to detail the various stages of the German reinforcement of Italy and I will pass on to the situation as it presented itself on 3rd September.[34] For the immediate purpose dispositions in South Italy are the most important, and they were the best known at the time. Four divisions had been evacuated from Sicily; of these 29 Panzer Grenadier Division remained in Calabria, I5 Panzer Grenadier and Hermann Goering Divisions moved to the Naples area to refit and I Parachute Division, less certain elements, moved to Altamura in Apulia. In addition to these there were two newly formed armoured divisions south of Naples: 26 Panzer Division[35] in Calabria, based on the isthmus of Catanzaro and I6 Panzer Division covering the Gulf of Salerno. In the general area of Rome there were 2 Parachute Division on the coast near Ostia and 3 Panzer Grenadier Division around Viterbo. These were Kesselring's eight divisions already mentioned; they were organised, under Headquarters Tenth Army (Colonel-General von Vietinghoff), into two corps: XIV Panzer Corps north and LXXVI Panzer Corps south. Directly under Kesselring was XI Flieger Corps (Air Corps); this had been moved from Avignon when the two parachute divisions, Ist and 2nd, came to Italy. It was responsible for the training and administration of all parachute units (and directly commanded 2 Parachute Division) and for the defence of the Rome area and the west coast between a point north of the Gulf of Gaeta and Kesselring's northern boundary.

In North Italy was Army Group 'B', Field-Marshal Rommel, with headquarters on Lake Garda, commanding all forces in Italy and Italian-occupied Slovenia north of a line from Grosseto to Rimini. By the beginning of September it totalled an equivalent of ten divisions (including one and a half divisions in Sardinia and Corsica which were technically under the local Italian commanders) of which two were armoured divisions. Reinforcement had been proceeding throughout August and at the same time an extensive development of lines of communication and administrative facilities had been rapidly pushed ahead, in particular the creation of a very large staging and maintenance area around Verona. There were four Corps Headquarters under the Army Group, the most important being LXXXVII Corps which, with four divisions, was responsible for the protection of Liguria and Tuscany.

The effect of these dispositions was, first of all, to ensure German control of Northern Italy. For the rest forces were disposed to meet an Allied invasion at the points considered most threatened: Calabria, Gaeta - Naples - Salerno, the Rome area and Genoa - Spezia. All these points were considered as possible Allied objectives with the degree of probability increasing towards the north. Any landing we made, except in Calabria, would be strongly opposed. The chief lesson the Germans claimed to have learned from Sicily was that it was vital to destroy the assaulting forces actually on the beaches and not to hold back defending forces for a deliberate counter-attack. But an intention to resist a landing in the hope of a spectacular victory is quite consistent with a decision on general principles not to hold Southern and Central Italy if an invasion were successful. It was a decision rather at variance with ordinary German, and in particular Hitlerian psychology and appears to have been based on two misappreciations the usual over-estimate of Allied strength and too gloomy a judgment of the dangers which Italian treachery would involve. Although the Germans had no higher an opinion of their Axis partners than had the Allies they realised that Italian defection would at least leave many doors open for the invader and, in the worst case, Italian arms turned against them might lead to more serious disaster; they also expected, as we did to a certain extent, that the allegedly turbulent population of Northern Italy would present them with a grave security problem which would engage the attention of all the troops allotted to that area. There was also the danger of a complete breakdown of all facilities, such as transport and power, with an additional strain on German resources in consequence which might be more than they could stand unless control was limited to the Northern Italian area. This was a factor on which we also placed some hopes; it seemed reasonable to expect that the workers in these industries would, even if they took no other action, at least achieve a high degree of "absenteeism". It was natural, therefore, in the midst of such dangers and uncertainties, that the German High Command should decide to restrict its ambitions to what seemed within its powers and not wish to risk disaster by attempting too much.

I must touch, in closing, on a question which was hotly debated both at the time and subsequently; whether the Germans expected us to land in the Naples area and, more particularly, at Salerno. It is essential to be clear what is meant by the question.[36] Certainly the Germans expected us to land somewhere in Italy and almost certainly on the west coast. It is standard form for all armies to prepare appreciations to meet all possible cases and there was undoubtedly somewhere in Kesselring's headquarters an appreciation based on the assumption that we should launch an assault on Naples and one of the sub-headings undoubtedly considered a landing in the Gulf of Salerno. What we have to consider in order to arrive at a just conclusion is not all the possibilities that passed through the mind of the Commander-in-Chief but what actual physical steps he took; his dispositions will give the answer. As I have already pointed out, he had made dispositions to meet attacks in the Naples area, the Rome - Civitavecchia area and the Genoa - Spezia area. Turning to the first mentioned, the reasons, which I need not detail again, that urged Naples as an objective so strongly on us must have been obvious to the Germans as well. In the circumstances I consider it surprising that they should have allotted only three divisions, two of which had scarcely recovered from their severe losses in Sicily, to cover the whole stretch of a hundred and fifty miles of coast from Gaeta to Agropoli. That they knew of our intention to land actually in the Gulf of Salerno I do not believe, nor do I believe that they even considered it the most likely hypothesis. They had disposed two divisions to cover Naples and the beaches to the north, either side of the Volturno, and had only brought over the third, I6 Panzer Division, from Apulia to Salerno at the end of August. Actions speak louder even than wisdom after the event. I have already described the excellence of the Salerno beaches. Four battalions of infantry and a battalion of tanks, even adding in the divisional reconnaissance and engineer battalions, are a very slender force to defend over thirty miles of coast; although there were Italian troops also in the line Sicily had clearly demonstrated their uselessness and the Germans should have suspected, though the evidence is clear that they did not know, that Marshal Badoglio was about to follow the example of General Yorck in I8I2.

Eighth Army Landings in Calabria.

While the negotiations for the armistice were in progress planning for I3 Corps' assault had proceeded rapidly under great pressure and overcoming continual crises. It was difficult to work strictly within the craft limitations imposed by the necessity of giving priority to the Salerno operation and there were times when there were considerable differences of opinion between the military and naval staffs. Every effort was made to mount the attack as early as possible; for some time it looked as though the night of 4th/5th September would be the earliest, but we managed eventually to put it forward to 0430 hours on the 3rd. The attack was a complete success. Opposition was light and we met no Germans; by the morning of D-day Reggio had been captured and in the evening of the same day Bagnara was in our hands. The reinforcement and supply of our forces were exceeding expectations. Demolitions were the main factor delaying our advance and there was reason to hope that if these enemy tactics were continued, and providing Eighth Army pressed resolutely forward, it would not be as far out of supporting distance of Fifth Army's Salerno landings as had been feared. It must be emphasized, however, that the roads were few and inferior, the Army was on a light scale of transport and the further it advanced the more difficult would be its maintenance. I will deal with this point later, when I come to discuss the administrative crisis which developed late in September.

Attention and interest could now be switched to the major operation impending on the 9th. In order to exercise proper control, I found it necessary to move back to Bizerta where I opened a small Tactical Headquarters on 7th September. This was dictated mainly by the necessities of the Commander-in-Chief, Mediterranean, who wished to control naval operations from his command ship there, H.M.S. LARGS. It was also convenient for the air forces who were already established at La Marsa, where was also General Eisenhower's Command Post. It was vital to have the closest contact with the Naval and Air Forces during the difficult initial stages of an amphibious operation, but I planned to return to my Main Headquarters in Sicily as soon as possible.

Further Operations to Exploit Italian Surrender.

With our limited resources it was inevitable that we should have to pass over many opportunities for exploiting the situation brought about by the Italian surrender which in other circumstances would have looked most attractive. Certainly with Badoglio's signature in our pocket we looked out on a very different map of the Mediterranean from that to which we had long been accustomed and to the superficial observer we might seem to be faced with an embarrassing number of choices. Areas of vital strategic importance garrisoned by Italian troops would now go to the first claimant. The Dodecanese, for example, which ever since 1940 had so often been described as a ripe plum ready to fall into our hands, was now in fact ready to fall but the hands which would gather it would be German. Crete was not in the ripe fruit category as it was mainly garrisoned by Germans already but there would certainly be an interregnum in the Western Balkans which would offer tempting opportunities of easy gains at small initial expense. I was particularly reluctant to see Corfu go by default. But none of these subsidiary operations would bear close examination; however inexpensive they might appear in the early stages the subsequent cost was bound to be high and, above all, by dispersing strength to secondary objectives we should offend against the great principle of concentration. With an assault force of only three divisions a commander must choose carefully his course and, when chosen, persevere in his choice without dissipating his resources. "War," said Wolfe, "is an election of difficulties." I have given the reasons why we had decided on the mainland of Italy as our next objective and we had no troops to spare for any other objective, however attractive. Every available man who could be lifted in every available craft was already earmarked for the Salerno operation and there was no-one who did not from time to time fear that even this might prove too little. AVALANCHE had already been weakened by the withdrawal of 82 Airborne Division for the Rome operation; it would be impossible to weaken it any further.

There were, however, two other areas where action on the small scale possible for us could have useful and lasting results. Sardinia and Corsica had already been prepared for, as I have explained, and General Giraud's task was likely to be made much easier by the Italian surrender as there were four Italian divisions to one German in Sardinia and three to a German brigade in Corsica; encouraging odds since in these islands, if nowhere else in Italy, the Italians would be in direct touch with Allied sea-power. But over and above the forces the French could scrape together for the liberation of Corsica (and these could not have been used elsewhere) there was one Allied formation available, I British Airborne Division. It was available because there were only sufficient transport aircraft in the theatre to lift one division, and 82 American Airborne Division had been the one selected to support Fifth Army. There were, of course, no craft available for it either and it could not, therefore, make an assault landing; but if the Italians could ensure for it an unopposed landing at a suitable port it could be transported there in warships. We did have some warships available, for the cruisers and attached destroyers of the I2th Cruiser Squadron would now not be needed to help cover the Salerno assault convoys from surface attack by the Italian fleet.

I decided, therefore, to use I Airborne Division to seize Taranto. We had always considered it essential to capture and bring into use as early as possible the south-eastern ports in order to provide for Eighth Army's maintenance, which would eventually have to be shifted to the Adriatic coast to follow the Army's proposed axis of advance. It was not in any way a diversion of effort, for it would be pointless to put any more troops into Calabria, rather it was an acceleration of Eighth Army's build-up. The chances of success were high, since the Germans were known to have no more than the equivalent of a regiment of parachutists in the whole area south-east of Altamura. General Hopkinson,[37] commanding I Airborne Division, was therefore summoned to my headquarters on 4th September and instructed to prepare to land part of his division at Taranto on the 9th with the tasks of securing the port, airfields and other installations and making contact with the Italians in the area of Brindisi. As soon as this was achieved, and when sufficient landing craft became available, it was proposed to bring in 78 Division from Sicily, followed by 8 Indian Division from Middle East. The codename for the operation - SLAPSTICK - an undignified term to denote the seizure of the main naval port of Southern Italy, at least illustrates happily the *ex tempore* nature of the planning. At the same time the Cotrone operation (GOBLET) was cancelled and 5 Corps Headquarters became available. I therefore ordered General Allfrey,[38] General Officer Commanding to prepare to move to the Heel of Italy with his Corps Headquarters to take over command of such troops as were already there (I Airborne and such of 78 Division as had landed) and 8 Indian Division when it arrived. His task was defined as to secure a base in the Heel of Italy covering the ports of Taranto and Brindisi, and if possible Bari, with a view to a subsequent advance on my orders. 5 Corps was to come under operational command of my headquarters from 5th September, but I planned to put it at a later date under command of Eighth Army, when the latter should have advanced sufficiently to make contact with it. The result of this decision was that our build upon the mainland of Italy, no longer restricted to the beaches of Salerno and the minor ports of Calabria, would be considerably accelerated and Fifth and Eighth Armies would each have an independent axis of supply, on the west and east coast respectively.

Situation on 8th September.

The plans for AVALANCHE were completed and the various convoys sailed on 3rd, 4th, 5th, 6th and 7th September, but arrangements for the acceptance of the Italian surrender and the descent of 82 Airborne Division on Rome remained to be made, and at feverish speed. For the former the main task was to prepare instructions for Italian shipping and aircraft, to be broadcast at the appropriate moment, giving recognition signals, routes, and ports and airfields to which they were to proceed. The latter was altogether a riskier operation and it was decided that we must have first-hand knowledge of the actual situation before a final decision on its launching could be taken. It was decided, therefore, to send Brigadier-General Taylor,[39] of the United States Airborne Forces, to Rome to report from there the chances of success; he was instructed, if he decided against the operation, to include a specific innocent-sounding code-word in his signal. He sailed in a British motor torpedo boat from Palermo on 7th September and transferred, off Ustica, to a light Italian naval craft. At the same time details were agreed with the Italians to ensure that there should be no possibility of misunderstanding over the announcement of the armistice. We were already in direct wireless communication with Marshal Badoglio by means of a set given to Castellano in Lisbon, but in case this should break down it was arranged that the BBC should broadcast at stated times two short talks on German activities in the Argentine as a sign that that was the day. At 1830 hours on that day (i.e., 8th September) General Eisenhower was to broadcast the announcement of the Italian surrender and simultaneously Badoglio was to broadcast a similar announcement. Immediate steps would then be taken to ensure that the news was spread as widely as possible all over Italy by radio and leaflet.

On 8th September the dispositions of the Allied invasion forces were as follows. The assault convoys for Salerno were at sea north of Sicily steering a northerly course preparatory to turning east after last light, I Airborne Division was concentrated at Bizerta on its warships, ready to sail for Taranto when Badoglio's announcement should have confirmed that the Italians were ready to surrender. The troops of 82, Airborne Division were at Licata in Sicily, ready to emplane for the drop on Rome. In Calabria I Canadian Division on the right had entered Locri, Cittanova and Polistena without contact with the enemy; 5 Division on the left had reached Rosarno and the line of the River Mesima; 23I Infantry Brigade, supported by Commandos, made a landing at Pizzo, the same morning, which was intended to get in behind the enemy's rear but which actually made contact with his last elements retreating more rapidly than had been expected. Meanwhile a new crisis was brewing at Bizerta where at 1100 hours a conference of Commanders-in-Chief, presided over by General Eisenhower, was in progress.

Italian Surrender Announced.

At the end of the conference two messages from Rome were brought in. One was from General Taylor advising against the airborne operation; the pre-arranged codeword was present and the decision had to be accepted. 82 Airborne Division were stood down only a short while before they were actually due to emplane; not merely were they not used in Rome, where their presence perhaps would have made little difference to the development of the situation, but it was also too late for them to be switched back to their original role in support of the Salerno landings. This was a serious blow. The other message was from Marshal Badoglio. He stated that because of the presence of strong German forces in the neighbourhood he was unable to guarantee the security of the three airfields on which the airborne division was to land and therefore the landing could not be attempted; consequently it was impossible for him to announce the armistice until the seaborne invasion had proved successful. The statements in the first part of the signal were not strictly accurate, or at least exaggerated, for the Germans made no move until after the announcement of the armistice and General Taylor based his decision to cancel the airborne operation on the obvious disorganisation and vacillation in Italian military circles rather than on the danger from the Germans. As to delaying the announcement of the armistice, it was quite impossible for us to accept Badoglio's change of attitude, or rather reversion to his original attitude, since he had all along been anxious to see our hand exposed before taking the final step. The troops were at sea facing an operation whose risks were already considerable; it would be intolerable to add to those risks. If we allowed the Italians to break the agreement with us there was a danger that, when they saw the smallness of our force, they might repudiate it altogether. It was not true that they had had insufficient time to make the necessary military dispositions, and in the frame of mind which then reigned it is doubtful if any further allowance of time would have produced a better result.

Marshal Badoglio was therefore reminded in vigorous terms of the obligations he had assumed and the dishonour which would follow their repudiation. Although the airborne operation, on his own showing, would have to be cancelled, we were eager to undertake it again as soon as possible; in the meantime his five divisions should suffice to provide temporary protection for the capital. Whatever Badoglio did, finally, the Allies would announce the existence of the armistice at the hour originally planned. No reply came to this signal and when at the appointed time, 1830 hours, Badoglio did not broadcast as arranged it seemed that the worst had happened. But it was only a final instance of vacillation; at 1945 hours he at last was heard reading in a depressed and subdued voice his statement that Italy had surrendered unconditionally. That night he and the King fled from Rome by car to Pescara and thence in a warship to Brindisi. They left no orders behind for the defence of Rome, where all was in confusion, and scarcely any response was made by the Italian armed forces or civilian population to the rather vaguely worded order in Badoglio's broadcast that, whilst ceasing resistance to the Allies, they were to resist "any attack which might come from another quarter". It was only at the last minute that Badoglio had decided that he could not honourably order his people directly to take action against the Germans.

The result was a fatal apathy and disorganisation. Only the fleet carried out wholeheartedly the surrender terms. The air force endeavoured to do so, but with only partial success. On land no real resistance was offered to the Germans and we derived little positive benefit from the armistice as a result. The five divisions in the Rome area made only a brief and unco-ordinated resistance to 2 Parachute Division and the hastily summoned 3 Panzer Grenadier Division; all was quiet there by 10th September, so much so that the Panzer Grenadiers could be sent on almost immediately to the front in Campania. In North Italy the Germans were faced with a considerable logistical and organisational problem in the mere physical difficulties of taking over control of so extensive an area with so many large industrial cities; but these difficulties were not aggravated, or only insignificantly, by the resistance either of the armed forces or of the civilian population. The great city of Milan, for instance, with a strong garrison of regular troops and an allegedly turbulent and liberty-loving proletarian population, surrendered to a small force of S.S. troops. We had not expected much from the Italians; twenty-one years of Fascist corruption and inefficiency had quenched any spark of patriotic feeling in a not naturally warlike people.

The Battle of Salerno.

The news of the Italian armistice could not be kept from the troops who were even then heading up the Gulf of Salerno nor was it either honourable or advisable not to inform them that the Italians were now pledged to fight on our side. But in spite of the fact that they were warned that the assault would continue as planned and that they would certainly meet resistance on shore from the Germans there was a definite feeling of optimism among the assaulting troops. The Germans were also surprised by the news with opposite results; the shock was the greater as they had just heard that our invasion fleet was at sea. That afternoon at 1600 hours, two and a half hours before General Eisenhower's broadcast, 16 Panzer Division had been informed that thirty-six ships, escorted by destroyers, had been sighted twenty-five miles south of Capri; the division ordered "State of Alarm II."[40] When the news of the surrender came, however, there was still nine hours in which the Germans could act. They at once proceeded to take over the Italian coast defence positions and disarm the troops. By the time the first Allied troops landed the Germans were ready for them.

The fighting on the beaches of Salerno was among the fiercest of the whole Italian campaign, in spite of the fact that the advantage of strategic surprise enabled us to bring three divisions against one; but war is never a matter of mathematics and least of all are amphibious operations. Of the Allied formations only 46 Division had had much previous experience in action and that experience had been occasionally unlucky; 56 Division had had only a few days fighting on the Enfidaville line in Tunisia, with varied success; 36 Division was entirely inexperienced. The time available for training and planning had been very short; some units landed on the wrong beaches. This was the first time we had met real resistance, including the use of German tanks actually on the beach. The result of the tactics employed by 16 Panzer Division was that, at the cost of severe casualties to itself, it succeeded in imposing serious delay and some degree of disorganisation and thereby gained time for reinforcements to arrive. Once given this breathing space the German rate of reinforcement by land was bound to be greater than ours by sea. They determined to devote all their efforts to throwing us back into the sea and for a week they disregarded all other factors for this purpose, including the steadily growing threat from Eighth Army.

The first three days of the operation went relatively successfully though our progress was not as great as we had hoped. In the next three days the Germans launched a series of counter-attacks which produced a very serious crisis on the I4th. By the I5th the Germans had admitted defeat. It was a dramatic week. The first reports spoke of heavy fighting on the beaches but steady progress. The greatest gain in ground was made on the southern flank where VI Corps by the night of IIth September had captured a line from Altavilla to Albanella and back to the coast at Agropoli; at its furthest point this represented an advance of some ten miles inland. Resistance in this sector had been very heavy on the beaches but considerably lighter when the first beach-head had been consolidated. The enemy resisted much more strongly on I0 Corps' front, both on the beaches and further inland; Salerno was captured on the morning of the I0th and Montecorvino airfield, one of the Corps' most important objectives, on the evening of the IIth, but it could not be brought into operation as yet since it was still under artillery fire. Very heavy fighting raged on the I0th and IIth around Battipaglia, the most important road junction in the plain; by the night we had a battalion in the town, fiercely engaged by the enemy.

Fighting of this intensity showed how different the Sicilian campaign would have been had we been opposed on the beaches by German troops and seemed to augur ill for the time when enemy reinforcements should arrive. On the afternoon of I0th September, I signalled to General Montgomery to the effect that if the Germans had dealt successfully with the Italians in the Naples - Rome area I was anxious about their possible rate of concentration against Fifth Army. It was of the utmost importance that he should maintain pressure upon the Germans so that they could not move forces from his front and concentrate them against AVALANCHE.

The Germans were indeed reinforcing fast. From the north-west the Hermann Goering Division and part of I5 Panzer Grenadier Division were rushed down to oppose I0 Corps, followed by 3 Panzer Grenadier Division, its task of pacification in the Rome area completed. LXXVI Panzer Corps was ordered to accelerate its disengagement from Calabria and despatch to the Salerno battlefield 29 Panzer Grenadier Division, all but a battle group of 26 Panzer Division and the third regiment of I Parachute Division from Apulia. Eighth Army's advance was henceforward to be delayed almost entirely by geographical and logistical difficulties while Kesselring sought to snatch a quick success over Fifth Army. There was an obvious danger that the German build-up would be quicker than ours at a time when only our initial objectives had been reached and we had neither a port nor an airfield, and to meet the threat all means of increasing our fighting troops in the bridgehead, even at the expense of their administrative units, must be sought. It was fortunate, therefore, that there were at Oran eighteen Landing Ships, Tank, *en route* for India; permission was asked and granted on IIth September for these to be employed at Salerno; they were to be released again by I2th October at the latest.

Before this reinforcement programme could take effect large-scale German counter-attacks had begun and soon caused grave anxiety. The critical period was I2th to I4th September. On the I2th a strong attack drove VI Corps out of Altavilla and on the I3th the enemy advanced down both banks of the River Sele, threatening to cut our bridgehead in half. This latter attack made dangerous progress and on the night of the I3th/I4th VI Corps withdrew from Albanella to a shorter line on the La

Cosa creek to conform with the withdrawal on its left. Our lines had been pushed back at one point to within a thousand yards of the beach. Even more dangerous was the attack on the I0 Corps front. On the I2th the enemy succeeded in driving us out of Battipaglia, inflicting heavy losses on I67 Infantry Brigade which had to be relieved by 20I Guards Brigade. In a signal which I received early on the I3th from General Clark he described I0 Corps' situation as unfavourable and 56 Division as exhausted. The enemy pursued his advantage; regrouping his forces he attacked again in strength from Battipaglia and Eboli on the night of the I3th/I4th, clearly intending to break right through to the beaches. The I4th was the critical day and the attacks on all parts of our front were pressed with the greatest vigour. We suffered heavy casualties and lost ground in some places, but by the use of every remaining reserve and by employing administrative troops in the line the enemy was held. It was an impressive example of stubborn doggedness in defence, for the sea at our backs was very close and all troops were exhausted by six days of uninterrupted struggle.

We had taken such steps as we could to improvise extra assistance but there was not much we could do which would have immediate effect. Admiral Cunningham ordered "Warspite" and "Valiant" at full speed to the Gulf, in spite of the danger of German air attacks, which had been scoring some successes with the new radio-controlled bombs. Their accurate and deadly shooting against the troop concentrations at Battipaglia and Eboli, reinforcing the fire of the British and United States cruisers and destroyers already on the spot, undoubtedly contributed very considerably to the defeat of the counter-offensive in the most dangerous area. An equally valuable contribution was made by heavy bombing attacks by the Strategic Air Force. To bring sea and air power to bear was a relatively easy and rapid affair, but other reinforcement could not be so speedy. On the I2th I had ordered Eighth Army to press on with all possible speed, accepting the administrative risks involved, and sent General Richardson[41], my Chief of Staff, to General Montgomery to explain the full urgency of the situation. On the I3th I made arrangements to put 82 Airborne Division into the bridgehead as quickly as possible and bring 3 United States Division from Sicily on top priority. A Regimental Combat Team of 82 Division was dropped by parachute behind our own lines on the night of the I3th-I4th and went into action at once, another was dropped in the same way the next night and the third came in by landing craft on the I5th. We also dropped a battalion of parachutists in the Avellino area to disrupt enemy communications there; this was originally requested for the night of the I2th-I3th but could not be mounted before the night of the I4th-I5th. This was fairly quick work; the first elements of 3 Division, on the other hand, could not begin to arrive before the I8th.

I went to the bridgehead myself on I4th September and was able to see both the acute difficulties of the situation and the gallant efforts of the defence. By the evening of that day I felt that the crisis was past and the situation beginning to turn in our favour. 7 Armoured Division had begun to disembark in I0 Corps' area on that day and a Regimental Combat Team of 45 Division also landed and came into Army reserve.[42] These moves were part of the original programme and the emergency moves on which we had decided were also beginning to show their effect. Before I left on the I5th I signalled to General Eisenhower to the effect that although I was not actually happy about the situation I was happier than I had been twenty-four hours earlier. The troops were tired but on the whole in good heart. I informed him that I had issued certain instructions, details of which I would give on my return next day. I also said that I had asked for I,500 British Infantry replacements from Philippeville to come as early as possible. I asked him to inform Admiral Cunningham and Air Marshal Tedder that our air bombing and ships' gunfire had been great morale raisers to the troops.

The Germans in their counter-attacks had been working under definite limitations of time. They had, deliberately, as good as broken contact with Eighth Army in order to fling the troops coming up from Calabria against Fifth Army, but they could not ignore Eighth Army's advance beyond a certain date. By the I5th they decided that they had failed; on that day reconnaissance elements of 5 British Division were at Sapri, about fifty miles south of the VI Corps position, with patrols forward, and by the I6th the whole division was concentrated in the area Lagonegro - Sapri - Maratea with a brigade at each place. On the same day patrols of 5 Reconnaissance Regiment made contact with patrols from VI Corps five miles west of Vallo and the Canadians were in a position to threaten Potenza. The enemy had already begun to withdraw in front of VI Corps, and with that confession of his inability to destroy our bridgehead our hold on the mainland of Italy could be considered firm.

PART II.
THE WINTER CAMPAIGN

Planning.

On 2Ist September I issued instructions to both Army Commanders giving the broad basis of our plan for future operations. The situation at that date was briefly as follows. Fifth Army had just advanced VI Corps, on its right, northwards to follow up the German withdrawal which was taking the form of a great wheeling movement, pivoting on the Salerno peninsula; I0 Corps was regrouping and reorganising after the heavy fighting of the past week and was preparing to launch a direct attack on the Naples plain through the gorges north of Salerno. Eighth Army was halted in the Potenza area, having made contact with Fifth Army on its left and 5 Corps on its right; it was now necessary to pause after the rapid advance to the assistance of Fifth Army while the administrative "tail" of the fighting troops could be brought up and the new axis of supply established through the Heel ports. 5 Corps Headquarters had landed at Taranto on I8th September and on the 22nd a special force under command of Headquarters 78 Division, and including elements of that division and of 4 Armoured Brigade, was due to land at Bari for mobile operations against Foggia. I Airborne Division had reached a line from forward of Bari to near Matera, where they were in contact with I Canadian Division; all the area southeast of this line, including the ports of Bari, Brindisi and Taranto, was clear of the enemy. The Italian fleet and air force had surrendered in accordance with the terms of the armistice in so far as they were not prevented by the action of the Germans but the Italian army had been eliminated except for a few poorly equipped formations in the south and the troops in Sardinia and Corsica. Mussolini had been rescued from his prison on the Gran Sasso but this, though irritating, was not considered likely to add to our difficulties in Italy, an appreciation which proved wholly justified. The "Quadrant" conference at Quebec had broken up and I was informed of its main decisions regarding the Mediterranean on I8th September. No change was made in the allotment of forces to the theatre; this involved the withdrawal to the United Kingdom of eight good divisions, to be replaced in part by French divisions as the latters' equipment progressed, reduction of the bomber strength by about a hundred and seventy aircraft by December I943 and a considerable withdrawal of troop-carrying aircraft and assault shipping and craft.

My plan of campaign had to be based on these considerations. It had to be flexible and general in terms and as I put it to my Army Commanders it was rather a general directive on the method of conducting the coming operations and an indication of the bounds of our advance. Our object I defined as "the seizing of certain vital areas which contain groups of all-weather airfields, ports and centres of road communications. On these firm bases the Armies can be regrouped, reorganised and balanced, and from them strong offensive operations can be developed to destroy the

German forces in the field. Light mobile forces and patrols will be operating ahead of these bases against the enemy continuously. This advance screen harasses the hostile rearguards, obtains information of all natures, and aids us to keep the initiative".

I indicated four phases into which our advance could be divided. The first was the consolidation of our present position on the line Salerno - Bari; the second was to give us the port of Naples and the airfield centre of Foggia. The third aimed at securing Rome and the airfields round it and the important road and rail centre of Terni. For the next phase I indicated as eventual objectives the port of Leghorn and the communications centres of Florence and Arezzo; but this was well in the future, dependent on the enemy reaction, the strength of our own forces, how our ports and communications were functioning and so on. Throughout the advance I planned "to take full advantage of our control of the sea and skies to put ashore small but hard-hitting mobile forces behind the enemy so as to cut him off". In the event I was only able, for reasons which will appear later, to carry out two of these amphibious operations, at Termoli and Anzio.

Capture of Naples and Foggia.

The first phase of this plan was already practically completed when I wrote and, after the pause, we proceeded with the second phase. Fifth Army had a hard struggle for the passes leading down into the plain of Naples but by 28th September 10 Corps was through and the King's Dragoon Guards entered the great city at 0930 hours on 1st October. Eighth Army's principal objective, Foggia and its airfields, had fallen four days before on the 27th. On both fronts the pursuit went on, but it was slower now. On 6th October Fifth Army stood along the line of the Volturno River and realised that it would have to force a crossing against strong resistance; Eighth Army had also left behind the early days of rapid advance across the open country of Apulia and the line ran clear across Italy through the mountains from Termoli to Benevento and Capua and down to the Tyrrhenian at Castel Volturno. My plan had been based on the German intention to withdraw to the Pisa - Rimini line and that intention had now been revoked on the highest authority; but before proceeding to discuss the effect of this new situation I must pause to describe the problems of administration which now faced us.

Administrative Problems.[43]

The most serious and most urgent problem was the imminent danger of the complete breakdown of the maintenance of Eighth Army. This situation, though no doubt it should in theory never be allowed to occur, did not reflect any discredit on anyone but was the result of a deliberate decision to accept an administrative risk for the sake of urgent and vital operational advantage. It would obviously be absurd at such a time, to sit down and do nothing until our administrative resources and plans were perfect, nor was there any simple solution available, for we had rightly decided not to create a proper base in Sicily and were therefore still based on North Africa and

Middle East and, to a certain and increasing extent, directly on the United Kingdom and United States. It would have been equally absurd to confine our operations to Calabria until we could build up a cast-iron administrative backing. The early days of the landings had gone smoothly enough; the small ports of Reggio, San Venere and Cotrone were put into use for the maintenance of the forces in Calabria and although the initial maintenance of the hastily planned operations at Taranto was not entirely satisfactory this was natural enough in the circumstances[44]. The administrative staffs were a little surprised to get their first positive confirmation of the operation simultaneously with the news of the landing but were soon mollified by reflecting on the importance of the speedy capture of Taranto and Brindisi undamaged; indeed this was of vital importance in averting the threatened breakdown. It was when I began to be worried about the situation at Salerno that I ordered General Montgomery to push ahead at all risks and he complied in spite of the warnings of his staff that so rapid an advance would risk a complete administrative breakdown. Hardly was the danger to Fifth Army averted when the expected difficulties materialized and Eighth Army found itself with virtually no reserves at all.

Taranto and Brindisi, however, were now available so that if our administrative tail could be switched from the Toe to the Heel there would be the considerable advantage of a shorter line of communication and better roads and ports, and even railways, with which to operate. On the other hand to carry out this switch and at the same time continue to support the Army in its operations was an extraordinarily difficult task and placed a tremendous strain on the very limited resources available. It was a great achievement and it took the rest of the month of September before the situation could be said to be stabilized again, though even then it was far from satisfactory. On the 29th General Montgomery informed me that when he had reached a line from Termoli through Campobasso to Vinchiaturo he would have to pause for ten or fourteen days as he had absolutely no reserve stocks. Our administrative machinery had been overdriven and could not sustain any more shocks for the moment; as I told the Chief of the Imperial General Staff[45] in a signal on the 30th "Men can go hungry but a truck just won't".

Eighth Army were thus rather breathless after their splendid gallop through Calabria, Lucania and Apulia; Fifth Army had had sterner fighting but their maintenance position was much easier, for they could use the ports and beaches at Salerno and Torre Annunziata, which were close behind their front line, and would shortly be able to bring Naples into use. At first sight this looked a disheartening problem. The port had been most thoroughly blocked and all the port facilities - cranes, quays, lighters, etc. - destroyed. Ships of all sizes, including ten thousand ton cruisers, hospital ships and two large liners, had been sunk alongside nearly all the quays and in the fairway inside the moles. In all, some three hundred lighters, the total number available in the port, and all the tugs and small craft had been sunk at their berths. I need hardly mention that mines and booby traps were cunningly dispersed everywhere from the harbour gates to the water's edge. But we had had fair experience in opening demolished ports and by the second week in October the discharge capacity was already reaching five thousand tons per day. This was a splendid effort and entirely removed any apprehension as to Fifth Army's maintenance.

Our next problem, now we were firmly established in Italy, was the rate at which we could reinforce or, in the universally accepted expression of this war, our "build-up". We were definitely inferior in numbers to the Germans and their land communications would enable them to reinforce much faster than us. The solution of the problem depended on availability of formations and shipping to move them. The former consideration was not likely to influence the situation before 1944 since, although the number of formations in the Mediterranean was in fact limited, and although the majority of these were deficient, in one way or another and would therefore only become available for operations with a varying degree of delay, there were at present as many fit for battle as the means of transport could deal with. An estimate prepared for me on 6th September showed that by the end of the month we should have available in the Mediterranean one armoured and eleven infantry divisions and an airborne brigade; this figure did not include the divisions due to return to the United Kingdom but included one division earmarked for operations against the Dodecanese.[46] By 1st January this figure should have risen to twenty infantry divisions, five armoured divisions and possibly one airborne division. I must emphasise, however, that this was the total for the whole theatre and out of it must be deducted the four divisions required for the garrison of the Middle East and North Africa and the forces intended and promised for the support of Turkey if that country should enter the war.[47] Our position is therefore clearer if we contrast these forces not merely with the nineteen German divisions already in Italy but with the fifty-odd in the Mediterranean theatre from South France to the Balkans.

Our build-up in Italy could not be very fast. A paper prepared on 2nd October estimated that by mid-October we should have on the mainland ten infantry divisions, one and a third armoured divisions, two airborne divisions and the equivalent of five independent brigades. Three of the infantry divisions had had heavy casualties and were considered only seventy-five per cent. effective; one armoured division and one airborne division were due to be withdrawn to the United Kingdom and in the event the other airborne division went also, leaving only a brigade group behind. By February, 1944, we expected to have in Italy eighteen and a half divisions (of which two were armoured). In actual fact we managed to increase this figure to the equivalent of over twenty-one divisions (as against a German total of twenty-three) but of these, two infantry divisions and an armoured brigade were only in process of arriving and an infantry division was leaving. This increase was due to the allotment of extra shipping and the delaying of the move of the Strategic Air Force. The move of the latter represented a serious slowing down of our build-up and required a very nice adjustment of priorities.

It had originally been intended to move the Strategic Air Force to bases in the Rome area when captured but on 15th September this was changed and it was now to be moved to Italy as quickly as possible and based on the many airfields around Foggia. It was planned to move the whole of the Tactical Air Force, the whole of the Strategic Air Force, elements of the Coastal Air Force, the Photographic

Reconnaissance Wing and the Troop Carrier Command, together with most of the Service Command and the supporting services, to the Italian mainland by the end of December, 1943. This could only be done at the expense of the Army, both the build-up of the formations already engaged and the reinforcing formations. The Tactical and Coastal Air Forces, the Reconnaissance Wing and Troop Carrier Command were, of course, of vital importance to the success of the campaign in Italy; the move of the Strategic Air Force, on the other hand, was dictated by considerations of general European strategy outside Italy, that is the furtherance of POINTBLANK, the strategic bombing programme against German Europe which was in full swing from the United Kingdom. In itself, therefore, from the purely local point of view, the move represented a positive disadvantage to the progress of the Italian campaign, though the capture of Foggia and its employment in this manner had been one of the main objects of the invasion of Italy. The necessary lift for the Strategic Air Force came to rather more than the equivalent of two divisions and their maintenance requirements were nearly as great as those of Eighth Army on the east coast. We eventually decided to slow down the move and spread it out until March, with the proviso that six heavy bombardment groups (equivalent to about two hundred and fifty four-engined aircraft) should be in Italy and operative by the end of the year.

The vital question in all discussions of build-up was the availability of shipping. I have already pointed out that the Mediterranean now took second priority to western waters and that, besides surrendering eight veteran divisions, we were to lose most of our amphibious equipment. The effect of the reduction was to remove eighty per cent. of our Landing Ships, Tank and Landing Ships, Infantry and two-thirds of our assault craft of all natures. The loss of Landing Ships, Tank was most serious for we could move a vehicle across the Mediterranean in a week by craft that would take a month to do so by ship. The careful destruction by the Germans of Italian lighters had left us terribly short of small craft for harbour working. We wanted a minimum of fifty-eight Landing Craft, Tank but it looked as though we should, on this programme, be reduced to nine; by vigorous representations I got this increased to twenty-four but even this was still below the number required. I mention these details not with any intention of querying the decision to concentrate the maximum resources in the west, which was obviously the right one, but to show more clearly the difficulties of our position in Italy and, in particular, why we were unable to make greater use of our command of the sea.

Enemy Change of Plan.

Up to the beginning of October we had been planning on the assumption that the Germans were intending to withdraw by gradual stages to a line in the northern Apennines but in the first week of that month we became aware that a radical change had been made.[48] Hitler had decided that the withdrawal should stop and Kesselring was to hold a line as far south as possible in Italy. There had been time enough to recover from the gloomy apprehensions with which the Germans had regarded the situation on the Southern Front at the time of the Italian surrender. The country was perfectly quiet, except for the north-east where the Slovenes were giving trouble, so that the internal security commitment was much reduced, and a better knowledge of the Allied Order of Battle showed that the Germans enjoyed a considerable numerical advantage and were likely to continue to do so. The terrain of southern and central Italy is admirably suited for defensive warfare; the whole of the area between Rome and Naples, except for the Volturno plain at its southern end and the Pontine Marshes at its northern end, is mountainous and unfavourable to manoeuvre and offers on the east coast a continuous series of river lines. The weather in autumn and winter would hamper Allied offensive operations and curtail the value of our air superiority. To hold a line south of Rome was eminently practicable; from the German point of view, therefore, it was eminently desirable. The forces under command of Field-Marshal Kesselring had been engaged in a continuous retreat for almost a year, since November, 1942, a retreat which had brought them from just short of Alexandria to just north of Naples and it was time to put a stop to it. I have mentioned the other reasons which urged the retention of as much of Italy as possible; there was now an additional reason, to give a certain semblance of authority to the recently created Republican Fascist Government by retaining as much territory as possible for it to govern under German supervision.

The line which it was decided to hold, known as the "Winter Line"[49], had been reconnoitred by the Germans before the armistice. It was based on the east coast on the River Sangro and on the west on the Garigliano backed by the Aurunci Mountains on the coast and the strong Cassino position rising to the *massif* of Monte Cairo; the centre of the peninsula, the rugged mountains of the Abruzzi, where bears roamed in the fastnesses of the National Park, was considered too difficult to admit of manoeuvre by large forces. On this line the Italian peninsula is at its narrowest, only eighty-five miles from sea to sea. Delaying positions could be held in front of it in order to gain time for the weather to deteriorate still further and allow artificial defences to be constructed to add to the natural strength of the position. There was little hope of holding permanently the Volturno and Biferno, but a stronger defence of these positions could reduce the Allied impetus and give still greater depth to the Winter Line. This new decision involved a reorganisation of the command. Rommel's Army Group "B" in the north was dissolved and on 21st November Kesselring assumed command of the whole theatre. The armoured divisions in North Italy, which would be of little use in the mountains, were relieved for employment in Russia, to be replaced by infantry, including a Mountain Division from the Leningrad front, and the remainder of the forces were put at Kesselring's disposal.[50]

This German decision to stand south of Rome did not affect my general plan of campaign though it was, of course, destined to affect its timing. It was, as can be seen, a positive assistance to me in carrying out the Combined Chiefs of Staff directive, for if the Germans had adhered to their original intention it would have made it very difficult for me to carry out my mission of containing the maximum enemy forces. An orderly withdrawal up the peninsula would have required only a comparatively small force, aided by the difficulties of the terrain, and although a larger force would be eventually required to hold the selected line, even this would not be immediately required since our build-up in front of that line would be necessarily slow. This peculiar feature of the strategy of the Italian campaign remained unchanged to the end: we had the initiative in operations but the Germans had the initiative in deciding whether we should achieve our object since they were free, other considerations, psychological or political, being excluded, to refuse to allow themselves to be contained in Italy. Had they decided to withdraw altogether, for instance, they could have defended the line of the Alps, or one of the strong river lines in north-eastern Italy, with the minimum forces and, instead of us containing them, they would be containing us. All danger of such an alarming result was removed by Hitler's decision. From the moment of that decision the German Army undertook a commitment as damaging and debilitating as Napoleon's Peninsular campaign, the final result of which was that it saw itself next summer under the deplorable necessity of pouring troops into Italy to retrieve disaster there at the very moment when the Allied invading forces were storming the breaches of the crumbling Western Wall. One further result of the German decision to stand was to remove the necessity, and the possibility, of a Balkan campaign. I had considered at one time a possible plan of first capturing Naples and Foggia and then, from this firm base in South Italy, launching an operation across the Adriatic. The Germans placed much greater importance on the retention of the Balkans than on the defence of Italy as was shown by the way in which, while withdrawing hastily from Sardinia and Corsica, they turned and struck with all the strength they could collect at a minor British incursion into the Dodecanese. If they continued to withdraw in Italy it would be difficult, as I have just explained, to contain any large force there but we should be certain of a violent reaction if we landed on the eastern shores of the Adriatic. We should also get some military support from the Partisans, though by October the Germans had a pretty firm hold on the coastal areas at least. It would have been a good way, therefore, of carrying out our directive, though we should have required a large increase in our allotment of amphibious equipment and reinforcement in troops. However, now the Germans had decided to allow themselves to be contained in Italy, there was no need for us to go further afield; Campania and Latium were far enough from France. And if there was no need there was certainly no possibility; now that all the German divisions in Italy were to be made available for the southern front we were actually outnumbered and would remain so for some months; there was even the possibility that the enemy might, if we let him, assume the initiative in an attempt to snatch a hasty victory, which would have come as a very welcome present to the German people at the beginning of a hard winter. I devoted my attention, therefore, to the exclusion of adventures further afield, to the task of containing, and manhandling as far as possible, the German forces facing us in Italy.[51]

Battles of Termoli and the Volturno.

Now that the Foggia plain had been overrun the sector allotted to Eighth Army was a mountain and foothill region separated from the Adriatic Sea by a narrow coastal plain. The lower slopes of this area offer only moderate difficulties to an advancing army; but on the left the centre of the pensinsula is in all places steep and precipitous, completely unsuited to the manoeuvre of armour, for all movement is confined to the roads. The coastal plain with its gentle slopes presents greater opportunities but here trees and intensive cultivation also favour the defence by limiting the field of view and the effectiveness of weapons. Major rivers cross the whole region at approximately ten mile intervals, at right angles to our line of advance; in the mountains they are swift-running streams usually between high banks and in their lower reaches they spread out into broad sandy and gravel beds where the streams meander widely, normally shallow but liable to sudden flash floods. We could expect plenty of rain in the autumn, up to five inches a month[52], and snow above two thousand feet as early as December. This would assist the effectiveness of bridge demolitions and render movement off the roads most difficult. The only good continuous roads forward lay on either side of the Army sector, forty miles apart; these were the coast road through Termoli and Vasto (Route 16) and a mountain road through Vinchiaturo and Isernia (Route 17). A number of first or second class laterals connected these roads by tortuous routes over mountains and along river valleys, and between them lay other less direct routes forward which could be used by up to one division.

Eighth Army's maintenance situation was now better and likely to improve and General Montgomery decided to seize with light forces a line including Termoli, where there was a small port which might be of use, and Vinchiaturo, a communications centre on Route 17. After this it would be necessary to pause to establish our administrative facilities on a firmer basis before advancing to contact the main German winter line on the Sangro. The enemy on this front consisted of the LXXVI Panzer Corps with I Parachute and 29 Panzer Grenadier Divisions, holding a front from the Adriatic to Benevento. 26 Panzer Division, originally under command of XIV Panzer Corps in the Benevento area, came under command after the beginning of October, operating south of the Benevento - Isernia road with a detachment operating on the Foggia - Isernia road. General Montgomery's plan was to employ 13 Corps for his advance with 78 Division right and I Canadian Division left while 5 Corps took command of the remaining formations, I Airborne, 5 Infantry and 8 Indian Infantry Divisions, with the task of organising the administrative build-up, securing the Army lines of communication and protecting the left flank of 13 Corps. On 3rd October the Royal Navy landed 2 Special Service Brigade (Commandos) at Termoli ahead of the advance of 78 Division and captured the town and port intact, together with a number of prisoners. They made early contact with the leading brigade of 78 Division across the Biferno but the difficulties of the crossing rendered this contact precarious. A brigade of 78 Division was therefore landed in the bridgehead area on the night 3rd/4th October and a further brigade was taken in by sea on 5th October. The enemy reacted violently and rushed over 16 Panzer Division from Army reserve in the western sector. Fierce fighting continued for some days. The Biferno rose in flood and cut communication by road, but by the 7th the enemy had accepted defeat and drew off westward to his next line behind the River Trigno.[53]

While the fighting at Termoli was in progress I Canadian Division was advancing up Route 17 against skilfully conducted German rearguards who forced our troops to deploy against every defensible position without themselves imperilling their withdrawal. 5 Division came under command of I3 Corps on 9th October; it was put in on the right of the Canadians on IIth October and on the I3th entered Casacalenda on Route 87. On the I4th the Canadians captured Campobasso and on the I5th Vinchiaturo. The first part of the Army Commander's plan was thus completed and the necessary pause ensued.

On the west Fifth Army's maintenance position, from its nearer bases, was much easier and by the end of the first week in October both I0 and VI Corps had reached the River Volturno. They were now faced with a difficult military problem in the crossing of this broad and swiftly flowing river and the recent change in enemy intentions made it certain that the defence, though not pushed to the last extreme, would be stubborn and protracted. The weather was miserable. It was originally hoped that VI Corps would be able to force a crossing on the night 9th/I0th October and I0 Corps on the following night, but delays were imposed by heavy rain and bad going, combined with extensive demolitions and mining. The enemy forces opposing Fifth Army consisted of XIV Panzer Corps with, from east to west, 3 Panzer Grenadier, Hermann Goering Panzer and I5 Panzer Grenadier Divisions. In the lower reaches they had the advantage of a higher flood bank on the northern side of the river and superior observation from Monte Massico, just in rear. Sites for a crossing were restricted, by the difficulties of the going, to existing sites and the river continued to rise and fall in a baffling manner.

The attack eventually went in on the night of the I2th. I0 Corps made diversionary attacks with 56 Division at Capua and 7 Armoured Division at Grazzanise and a main attack by 46 Division at Cancello. The latter was successful but heavy fighting followed in difficult and open country while 56 Division at Capua, as had been feared, was unable to force a crossing. VI Corps, however, got across in the more mountainous area east of Capua and by the use of its bridges 56 Division also crossed on the I5th. By the 25th both Corps had firmly consolidated their bridgeheads and were ready to engage the next enemy delaying line, based on the ridge of mountains from Monte Massico on the sea coast, through Monte Santa Croce to the Matese Mountains on the boundary between Fifth and Eighth Armies. Only two passes pierced the line of hills, at the two defiles followed by Routes 6 and 7 and called after Mignano and Sessa respectively.

On 4th October I moved my headquarters to the small village of Santo Spirito, north-west of Bari. I intended to move eventually to the Naples area but there was no hope of accommodation there for the moment and if I wanted to move to Italy, as was clearly necessary, the relatively undamaged areas of Apulia offered the only suitable sites.

Plans for the Winter Operations.

Both at Termoli and on the Volturno the Germans had shown a new determination and stubbornness, and this, together with the slowness of our build-up, made the decision as to the correct strategy to be adopted in Italy still more difficult. My most recent directive from General Eisenhower, called for the capture of air bases in the Rome area; the general directive under which all forces in the Mediterranean, and mine in particular, were working was to tie down and divert from other fronts the maximum German strength; it was not easy to see how, with the forces available or in prospect, either of these objects could be attained or to what extent the pursuit of one might hinder the achievement of the other. One thing was certain; for either purpose it was essential to retain the initiative which we then had. It would mean a hard and costly fight, now that it was known that the Germans no longer intended to withdraw by stages to the north, but for the sake of the greater objects in view it was necessary to accept this cost and not give the enemy any rest.

I reviewed the situation in the light of these considerations on 21st October. In Southern Italy eleven Allied divisions were opposing nine German in a position eminently suitable for the defence, while in the north there were some fourteen more, a known total of twenty-three divisions.[54] Eleven against nine was no great numerical superiority and with their great resources in the north, where the internal security commitment was now quite unimportant, the Germans could easily convert it into a positive inferiority; at the least they could carry out constant reliefs of their formations in the battle area and oppose our attacks with constantly fresh troops. This was what they proceeded to do. There was no practical limit to the number of troops they could bring into Italy; it was calculated that their lines of communication were adequate to support up to sixty divisions should they wish to employ such a force there. Our build-up, on the other hand, was severely limited, as I have already explained; we expected to have thirteen divisions by the end of November, fourteen or fifteen by the end of December and sixteen to seventeen by the end of January. Since the Germans had decided to stand we were committed to "a long slogging match" with no possibility, in view of the shortage of landing craft, actual or about to exist, of amphibious operations against the enemy's flanks.

Admittedly the disparity of our relative strengths showed that we were doing our duty in containing the enemy. Indeed he seemed to be going out of his way to assist us in attaining that object; I pointed out in my appreciation "the German reinforcement of Italy seems greater than warranted by the internal situation or by purely defensive requirements".[55] There was a serious possibility, which I had to consider, that if he saw a chance of seizing an easy success in Italy he would take it, for its psychological value at such a time would be very great. Any relaxation of effort on our part would allow him to seize the initiative and use it either, as just suggested, for a strong counter-offensive - aiming for instance at the recapture of Naples, a glittering prospect - or to reduce his forces on the defensive front to a minimum and make available for elsewhere the divisions thus saved. This same result, the relieving of German forces from Italy for the Eastern or, subsequently, Western front, would also follow, and in greater measure, from a successful enemy counter-offensive, provided it were delivered before the spring of 1944. On the other hand, if we could keep the enemy "on his heels" until then, we should be certain of retaining in Italy the divisions already there; we might even (and this, though unexpected, actually occurred) draw still more into the theatre, while still keeping him sufficiently off-balance to be unable to seize the initiative from us; finally, if he were to launch a great counter-offensive next spring, we should welcome it, for the more successful it was the more troops it would draw off from the defence of France, and success there was well worth the price of a possible set-back in Italy.

I presented this appreciation at a conference at Carthage with the Commanders-in-Chief on 24th October. It was agreed by General Eisenhower and signalled to the Combined Chiefs of Staff. The conference agreed that it was essential to retain the initiative and approved my plan of campaign which I reported at the same time. Eighth Army's advance up the east coast was running into a *cul-de-sac* of rather unimportant country; but General Montgomery was of the opinion that if he could establish himself on the high ground north of Pescara, after crossing the Trigno, Sangro and Pescara rivers, he could then strike south-westwards down Route 5, the Via Valeria, to Avezzano and threaten Rome from the east. In conjunction with this south-westerly attack by Eighth Army, Fifth Army was to attack north, directed on Rome. Both attacks were to be assisted, if at all possible, by amphibious flank attacks, on the east in the strength of about a brigade group and on Fifth Army's front of at least an infantry division with some armour. Since landing craft were so short the latter attack would have to wait until those used in the former had been brought round to the west coast; even then they might not be sufficient for the scale of attack I proposed. The signal to the Combined Chiefs of Staff therefore concluded: "it is certain that more landing craft will be required for a limited time if we are to capture Rome in the near future and avoid a slow, painful and costly series of frontal attacks."

A further review of the situation produced more definite proposals. On 31st October, General Eisenhower again approached the Combined Chiefs of Staff with a full review of the need for landing craft and the resources necessary to meet those needs. The tasks for which the craft were required were threefold. The first was the build-up of auxiliary units to complete formations already in Italy. Secondly it was essential to be able to mount an assault behind the enemy lines in the strength of about a division, probably on the west coast. Thirdly it was necessary to meet the demands of the Strategic Air Force, which included not only the move of the operational formations themselves but also large numbers of airfield construction and servicing units. The Foggia airfields, though the principal base in South Italy for the Italian Air Force, were not all-weather and very large quantities of steel plank had to be transported. The requirements of the Strategic Air Force had also been largely increased by the decision, communicated on 23rd October, to set up the XV United States Air Force in Italy. With our present resources, that is adhering to the existing programme of returning craft to the United Kingdom, the first of these tasks would not be completed before 15th December and there would remain only sufficient lift for one brigade or regimental combat team, which would be quite inadequate. If, however, we could keep until 15th December all the British Landing Ships, Tank (between forty-eight and fifty-six) and twelve United States, it would be possible both to complete the build-up of present formations and to mount a divisional amphibious assault. Even then only about a third of the task of establishing the Strategic Air Force in Italy would have been carried out; but if the craft could be retained for a further three weeks, until 5th January, the whole programme could be completed.

Another Commanders-in-Chief conference was held at Carthage on 3rd November. I confirmed the plan presented at the previous conference with the proviso that Eighth Army would have to make a short pause after the capture of the Pescara line before exerting pressure south-westwards down Route 5. Fifth Army was to press on up Route 6, the Via Casilina, and attempt to break through the enemy opposition on that axis coincident with Eighth Army's drive on Rome; it was hoped that it would retain sufficient impetus to reach the Frosinone area. At this point we would, if we had the means, launch an amphibious assault south of the Tiber and subsequently other assaults north of the Tiber. In order to carry out these contemplated manoeuvres it would be necessary to move in for Fifth Army two French divisions plus the necessary services and non-divisional troops in order to maintain the impetus of the attack: the bulk of the troops in Fifth Army had been fighting continuously, and heavily, since 9th September. Moreover, their mobility and maintenance were severely hampered by the fact that about two thousand five hundred urgently needed vehicles were still held up at Bizerta awaiting landing craft to move them. In reply to a signal sent at the conclusion of the conference we were authorised by the Combined Chiefs of Staff to retain the sixty-eight landing craft until 15th December. With this, planning could go ahead with greater confidence.

Advance to the Winter Line.

After the advance to the Termoli - Vinchiaturo line Eighth Army continued active patrolling while they reorganised for the attack on the Winter Line. 5 Corps took over the right flank on 11th October with 78 and 8 Indian Divisions under command; the latter was a new formation, though of experienced units, but distinguished itself in this its first action. 78 Division managed to seize a bridgehead over the River Trigno, on the axis of Route 16, on the night of the 22nd-23rd, and by the next night all the enemy in the Corps sector were back behind the river. The main position here was on the San Salvo ridge, a dominant feature overlooking the west bank. The Trigno near the coast is a broad stream, liable to very sudden flooding and the ground on either bank is a very heavy clay soil in which it was almost impossible to construct a firm track. The first attack on San Salvo, on the night of the 27th, was frustrated largely owing to these difficulties, aggravated by a heavy fall of rain, and a full-scale attack was therefore necessary. This opened on the early morning of 3rd November, when 78 Division attacked San Salvo and 8 Indian Division, on their left, the village of Tufillo on a high spur above the river. There was heavy fighting for both villages but San Salvo was clear by the 4th and Tufillo by the 5th. The enemy, having now offered as much delay as possible on this line - and 16 Panzer Division, which was not fresh when it went into action, had had heavy losses - began to withdraw to his next, the "Bernhardt" line, which on Eighth Army's front ran from north of Isernia along the range of mountains forward of the Sangro. In the Sangro defences itself Kesselring had disposed 65 Infantry Division which he had brought down from the north. As a result of this withdrawal we were able to enter unopposed the important road junction of Isernia on 4th November.

On the Fifth Army front the first task, which fell to 10 Corps, was now to secure

Monte Massico, the high razor-back ridge north-east of Mondragone. Apart from being an important stage in our advance northwards, this position was also vital to complete the covering screen defending Naples if it should be necessary at any time to go on to the defensive; present enemy strength and his constant reinforcement had, as I have already mentioned, brought such considerations more into the foreground. Two new German divisions, 305 and 94 Infantry, had already been brought down into the line from North Italy. The operation, which led to the capture both of Monte Massico and Monte Santa Croce to the north, began on 28th October and was successfully completed by 4th November, at which date 46 and 7 Armoured Divisions reached the lower Garigliano between the bend opposite Monte Iuga and the sea. The enemy had intended to offer delay on this line, the southern extremity of the "Barbara" line, as shown by his reinforcing; but the dangers inherent in standing for long with a broad river immediately in rear, coupled no doubt with apprehensions of a seaborne outflanking move, decided him to pull back his right, when pressed, behind the Garigliano. In the meantime VI Corps had pushed forward up, and then across, the Volturno and driven the left wing of XIV Panzer Corps back to the "Bernhardt" line based on Monte Camino, Monte Maggiore and the hills on the north side of the Mignano defile from above Venafro (captured on 4th November) to above Isernia.

The idea of an amphibious landing continued to be entertained. On 23rd October General Clark signalled to me (I was then at the Commanders-in-Chief conference in Carthage) that he was contemplating a landing near Formia in the Gulf of Gaeta in the strength of a regimental combat team and two Ranger battalions, in connection with the attack of 10 and VI Corps. Naval opinion, however, condemned this as impracticable owing to the strength of the coast defences and minefields. The only apparent alternative, a landing between Gaeta and Sperlonga, was clearly impossible as yet, and until the forces advancing overland were within supporting distance.

Attack on the Winter Line.

On 8th November I received a new directive from General Eisenhower. It began by reaffirming the objectives given on 25th September, the capture of Rome and the maintenance, subsequently, of maximum pressure on the enemy. Rome, of course, had great political value but we did not regard it primarily as a prize to be won but rather as something which we knew the enemy intended to defend and for which we could make him fight his hardest. To draw him into battle and destroy his forces was our real object. The directive recognised that the enemy "intends to resist our occupation of Southern Italy to a greater degree than hitherto contemplated." Priority was therefore given, in the first phase, to the build-up of our land forces and of such, air forces as were specifically required to assist them in their task. However, six heavy bombardment groups of the Strategic Air Force must be in Italy and operating by the end of the year for use in the bombing programme against Germany. Finally I was directed, after the capture of Rome, to secure possession by occupying a general line to cover Civitavecchia and Terni, the former being taken into use as a port.

On the same day I also issued a directive intended in particular for the guidance of Fifth Army in the operations to secure their objectives. My directive must be read against the background of the severe exhaustion of Fifth Army. The winter rains had started at the end of September and were steadily increasing, making roads and by-passes extremely difficult and turning the open country into a sea of mud. The mountains in front were the most formidable we had yet encountered and the enemy, who had already reinforced his flanks with two fresh infantry divisions, was now bringing over part of 26 Panzer Division from Eighth Army's front. This meant that there were five enemy divisions opposing our five, and the Fifth Army troops were more tired than the enemy. The Germans were showing a stubborn spirit of resistance at all parts of the front and it was clear that a co-ordinated effort would be required to drive them from their positions. I therefore directed Fifth Army, on the completion of its present operations, to pause and regroup, allowing Eighth Army to strike first. The latter was to get astride Route 5 from Pescara to Popoli and Collarmele and be prepared to threaten the enemy lines of communication via Avezzano. Then Fifth Army would attack up the valley of the Liri and Sacco to reach Frosinone. This is the classical route for an army marching on Rome from the south and the only practicable one for a large force; the Via Appia, Route 7, becomes too involved with the Aurunci Mountains and the Pontine Marshes. Our troops, I think, got a little tired of hearing the Liri Valley described as "The gateway to Rome" during the long months when the gate was shut so firmly in their faces, but the description is true nevertheless. Finally, when the main body reached Frosinone, a seaborne landing would be made south of Rome, directed on the Alban Hills.[56] All available air support would go to Eighth Army in the first phase and to Fifth Army in the succeeding phase.

Between 5th and 15th November Fifth Army continued their attempts to break into the Winter Line in their sector. This enemy position, as I have already explained, was not so much a line as a belt of terrain about nine miles wide; its forward edge, in front of which our troops now stood, was the "Bernhardt" line, its rear, based on the high ground behind the Garigliano and Rapido, was the "Gustav" line, with the key fortress of Cassino. On the south the two lines coincided and the German defences utilised the plain forward of the Garigliano, the river, swift-flowing and deep, and the Aurunci Mountains to the west of it which command every part of the plain. To the north are the mountains commanding the Mignano Gap through which Route 6 passes, dominated by Monte Camino to the south and Monte Sammucro to the north; in the gap itself there are three isolated masses of high ground, Monte Lungo, Monte Porchia and Monte Trocchio, rising abruptly like rocks in a fairway. North of Monte Sammucro the mountains rise even higher to the central ridges of the Apennines, impossible country for large-scale operations.

The first objective was the Monte Camino *massif*, including the two subsidiary peaks of Monte La Difensa and Monte Maggiore, and the task of the assault was given to 56 British and 3 American Divisions under 10 and VI Corps respectively. From 5th to 12th November the attack was pressed against rock-hewn defences, steep slopes up which all supplies had to be man-handled, constant enemy counter-attacks and bad weather. Ground was gained by both divisions, but it was impossible to remain and impossible to push on in the weakened condition to which the divisions had been reduced.[57] On the 12th General Clark decided to withdraw, an operation which was successfully accomplished on the night of the 14th. Meanwhile VI Corps had been driving at the northern defences of the Mignano Gap. 3 Division had already been successful in capturing Monte Cesima, an outlying hill mass on the north side of the gap, and 45 and 34 Divisions battered their way into the mountains in front of them to extend the line northwards. But Monte Lungo, in the mouth of the gap, was a harder nut to crack. It is a great, bare, scrub-covered mountain ridge dominated from either flank by higher enemy-held ground and 3 Division was tired after fifty-six days of continuous operations. On 13th November General Clark represented to me that the time had come to pause and regroup; any further repetition of the attacks we had been making would exhaust divisions to a dangerous degree.

While Fifth Army was attempting to break into the Winter Line on the west coast, Eighth Army in the east was advancing to make contact with the left flank of the same line. This was based in their sector on the line of the River Sangro from the mouth for some fifteen miles upstream and then on the forward slopes of the great Maiella *massif* behind the Casoli - Pescocostanzo road. The strongest part of the line was the extreme north, where defences had been under construction since early October. The Sangro here runs in a channel varying from three hundred to four hundred feet wide and a foot deep but after heavy rain it rises rapidly, filling the entire river bed with a depth of five feet or more and a rate of flow measured on one occasion at seven knots. There are steep hills on the right bank, giving good observation; on the left bank there is a flat plain for about two thousand yards and then a steep escarpment, rising abruptly some hundred and fifty feet. It was on this escarpment that the main enemy defence works were established. "Our position," wrote the Commander of the German 65 Division in an Order of the Day, "is naturally very strong and it is rendered considerably stronger by our numerous and excellent defence works."

78 Division reached the right bank of the river from the mouth to as far south as Paglieta on 8th November and immediately began to organise patrols across it to dominate the plain on the left bank. 8 Indian Division, the left hand formation of 5 Corps, was longer in forming up to the line and the enemy did not withdraw completely across the river in their sector until 19th November. At that time the coastal sector was held by the recently arrived 65 Infantry Division, a relatively inexperienced formation, with 16 Panzer Division supporting it in reserve. To the south I Parachute Division held a front of some twenty-five miles in the mountains. Before the main Eighth Army attack began 16 Panzer Division was withdrawn to proceed to the Eastern front; after the attack went in 26 Panzer Division had to be hurriedly brought back from the Mignano sector, where it had been as hurriedly sent when Fifth Army's attack looked serious, and 90 Panzer Grenadier Division was brought down from northern Italy.

General Montgomery's plan for the attack envisaged a heavy, well-prepared assault on the coastal end of the line. 5 Corps was to command the main thrust with 78 and 8 Indian Divisions, and the recently arrived New Zealand Division, under Army Command, was co-operating on their left. 8 Indian Division had continued to advance on the left of the Corps' front until the Sangro was reached; it was then relieved by the New Zealanders and went into reserve behind 78 Division. The latter was to seize a bridgehead, the Indians were to break into the line, then 78 Division was to come into the lead again and exploit on to Pescara and simultaneously the New Zealanders were to strike across the river directed on Chieti, from where they were to swing south-west down Route 5 to develop the desired threat against the Avezzano area. D-day was laid down as 20th November in orders published on the 16th, but both the timing and execution of the plan were strongly affected by the weather. It was essential to make full use of our command of the air and our superiority in armour, and both depended on reasonably fine weather. On the 20th the weather broke completely and we could only establish a small bridgehead; on 23rd November the river was in flood and rendered all bridges useless; the same happened on 25th November when the attack had again been scheduled. The main attack eventually went in on the 27th with 8 Indian Division leading. Mozzagrogna, a key point in the defences, was captured on the 29th and by the next day a bold use of our armour against ground considered impassable by the Germans gave us the whole ridge above the Sangro from there to the sea. In the meantime the New Zealanders had got across the river and on 2nd December captured Castelfrentano. The Division's next objective was Orsogna, which was attacked unsuccessfully on 7th December and again on the 14th equally without success. The enemy had been reinforced and the weather was abominable. Further to the right 8 Indian and 78 Divisions advanced to the River Moro, capturing Lanciano and San Vito on 3rd December, I Canadian Infantry Division now relieved 78 Division, which had suffered ten thousand battle casualties in the last six months.

The battle of the Sangro had driven the enemy from strong prepared positions and inflicted on him heavy casualties. But thanks to the difficult nature of the ground and the violence of the winter weather, and the enemy's ability to relieve tired troops with fresh, Eighth Army had been unable to break through the enemy's dispositions or seize any vital ground. The difficult "ridge and furrow" country of the Molise offered few chances of a decisive success to an Army attacking, as Eighth Army had always done, across the grain of the country. The further north we pushed our advance the more numerous and close together were the river lines. The prospect was little better for the time when the Army should have turned westwards into the gap between the Gran Sasso and the Maiella where the Via Valeria runs through a series of terrifying defiles. It was one of our most serious handicaps in this winter campaign that our front was divided so rigidly into two by the spinal barrier of the Apennines. It meant an inevitable loss of flexibility, for the two armies were often fighting what were almost independent battles and, owing to differences in nationality and equipment it was not easy for me, as it was for Kesselring, to switch units and formations from one side of the barrier to the other.

During the period of Eighth Army's attack on the Adriatic sector Fifth Army had been resting and regrouping its troops in accordance with the orders of 16th November. The next operation was divided into three phases. The high ground dominating the Mignano Gap was to be captured in sections, first that to the south, and then that to the north; in Phase I, that is to say, Monte Camino, Monte La Difensa and Monte Maggiore were to be captured and in Phase II Monte Sammucro, combined with an attack westwards along the Colli - Atina road; Phase III, the main advance into the Liri valley, was only to be initiated on Army orders after the completion of the first two phases. Of the three British and six United States divisions in Fifth Army at the beginning of the period, two, 7 Armoured and 82 Airborne, (less one Regimental Combat Team) were being withdrawn to the United Kingdom. I United States Armoured Division began arriving at Naples and I Special Service Force, six battalions of specially trained mixed American and Canadian troops, also came under command.[58] 2 Moroccan Division was due to arrive in the first week of December. II Corps Headquarters arrived from Sicily in October and took over command of the centre of the line with 3 and 36 Divisions on I8th November; VI Corps now commanded on the extreme right with 34 and 45 Divisions. I Armoured Division remained in Army reserve; it was not expected that it would be used until the Liri valley was reached, when it would debouch through II Corps. The Germans had also been reinforcing; 29 Panzer Grenadier Division came in from reserve and 44 Infantry Division, an Austrian formation, from Slovenia. 5 Mountain Division arrived from Russia in December.

The first phase of the new attack, the capture of the mountains on the south side of the Mignano Gap, was planned as a very deliberate operation, as an example of how a large, semi-isolated mountain mass should be captured. The assault was to be made by two Corps, I0 south and II north, supported by very heavy artillery fire and the greatest weight possible of air attack. The enemy was to be made to believe that our intention was to attack further south, across the lower Garigliano, by various measures, including naval bombardment between Minturno and Gaeta and feint attacks by 23 Armoured Brigade in the plain between Monte Massico and the river. The operations began with a subsidiary attack on the southern end of the mountains on the night of Ist December and on the next night, while the heaviest concentration of artillery yet fired in the Italian campaign pounded the enemy positions on the heights, 56 Division started for the second time up the steep slopes of Monte Camino. Simultaneously I Special Service Force and 36 Division attacked the northern third of the mountain mass to gain Monte La Difensa and Monte Maggiore. Air support on that day was heavy and for the first time was not reduced by weather. Both Corps' attacks were successful. On 6th December I0 Corps captured the summit of Monte Camino, which they had almost secured on the 3rd but failed to hold against counter-attacks, and on the 9th Rocca d'Evandro was captured. This brought I0 Corps to the Garigliano all along its front. II Corps captured La Difensa on 3rd December and held it against strong counter-attacks, and on the 8th captured and mopped up Monte La Remetanea. 36 Division's attack on Monte Maggiore, the northern most and lowest peak, had succeeded by the night of the 3rd; counter-attacks were repulsed and by the 7th the position could be considered secured. Between then and the IIth I0 Corps took over the whole of the feature from II Corps.

Between 29th November and 9th December VI Corps on Fifth Army's right made diversionary attacks along the axes of the Colli - Atina and Filignano - Sant' Elia roads. Very little ground was gained in tangled and difficult country, with peaks rising to over twelve hundred metres. 2 Moroccan Division began to relieve 34 Division on the Corps' right on 8th December. Phase I of the Army Commander's plan was now, however, completed with the capture of the Camino *massif* and Phase II was ordered to start on 7th December. In this phase I0 Corps had a minor defensive rôle; the principal objective was the clearing of Monte Sammucro and this was assigned to II Corps. VI Corps was to continue to drive westwards along the roads to Atina and Sant' Elia but on a larger scale facilitated by the accession to its strength of the fresh and mountain trained Moroccan Division. It was hoped that by attacking on so wide a front the enemy would be sufficiently stretched to prevent him massing for the defence of Cassino.

The bitterest fighting took place for Monte Sammucro and the village of San Pietro in Fine below it. The attack began on 7th December; the first two high points on Sammucro were seized without exceptional difficulty but after that our troops were held until the I3th by severe German counter-attacks and heavy mortar and artillery fire. On the 8th the Italian Motorised Group failed in an attack on Monte Lungo, in the throat of the gap. The second battle for San Pietro opened on the I5th and succeeded, though at heavy cost in casualties, by the I7th; Monte Lungo was also occupied and, north of the village, we forced our way further along the knife-edge of Monte Sammucro. This was bitter mountain fighting, with great use of artillery and gains in territory small compared with the time consumed and the losses suffered. There was still another enemy position, almost equally as strong as San Pietro, just a short distance ahead, based on the western end of Monte Sammucro and the lower hills covering the village of San Vittore. But 36 Division was exhausted and on 29th December had to be relieved by the 34th before San Vittore was taken. The VI Corps attack on the right had also made little progress against difficulties of ground and stubborn enemy defence; by the end of the year it could only be said to have kept level with the advance of II Corps with gains of approximately three miles. The German Winter Line had been broken into but not broken; there were still some miles of mountain before the rear line of the position, the "Gustav" line, should be reached and the difficulties of that line were already the subject of serious study.

It was during this period that we received the only serious blow which the German Air Force was ever able to strike us during the campaign. On the night of 2nd December an air raid by about thirty aircraft on the port of Bari took the defences by surprise and caused very heavy damage. Seventeen ships of various sizes were sunk and thirty thousand tons of cargo lost, mainly by the explosion of two ammunition ships. The port was not permanently damaged but we lost five days' working.

At the turn of the year the Mediterranean theatre, which had already lost so many of its best troops, now lost two of its senior commanders for the benefit of the Western campaign. On I0th December, 1943, General Eisenhower was informed of his appointment as Supreme Commander, Allied Expeditionary Force; he actually handed over to General Wilson[59] on 8th January, 1944. General Wilson's appointment was announced on 27th December and on the same day was made the announcement of General Montgomery's transfer to command of Twenty-first Army Group. General

Montgomery was succeeded, on Ist January, I944, by General Leese,[60] who had commanded 30 Corps in the desert and in Sicily. In the new organisation in the Mediterranean, Allied Force Headquarters now had a wider authority, including those areas which had previously come under General Headquarters Middle East. To a large extent, therefore, its preoccupations were political and logistical; I was accordingly instructed that for the conduct of the campaign in Italy I was given a free hand. For this reason the title of my headquarters was changed from Fifteenth Army Group to Headquarters Allied Armies in Italy[61] and my administrative staff was reorganised and put on a proper level with the operations staff. At the same time I was relieved of the duties of Deputy Allied Commander-in-Chief, being succeeded in the appointment by Lieutenant-General J.L. Devers of the United States Army.

I had had the pleasure of serving under General Eisenhower as Supreme Allied Commander for about a year. I have already expressed, in my Despatch on the Conquest of Sicily, my appreciation of his gifts as a commander and I need not repeat it here; but I will say that, apart from our professional relationship, the footing on which we stood personally was of close friendship and understanding. General Wilson, of course, was a member of the old Middle East team, having commanded Ninth Army in Syria and subsequently the Persia and Iraq Command. He had succeeded me in command at General Headquarters, Middle East when I took over command of Eighteenth Army Group on I9th February, I943. His diplomatic gifts and his experience in negotiations with various nationalities made him the natural first choice for the command of Allied Force Headquarters in view of its new rôle; in particular his knowledge of the Balkans made it essential that he should continue to be in charge of that area which was now under Algiers. My military relations with him were slightly different in principle, as I have explained, from those with General Eisenhower but our personal relationship was excellent and I must record my gratitude here for the comprehension and support which he never failed to afford me.

The Cassino Position.

I have already described the Liri valley as the gateway to Rome and alluded to the strength of the defences of the gate. A description of the terrain now facing us will make clear the reasons why this one sector was the only place where we could hope to develop an advance in strength and why I was obliged to transfer there ever-increasing forces until by next May the bulk of my Armies was disposed in the Tyrrhenian sector. The Adriatic coastal plain in which Eighth Army had been operating leads nowhere except, eventually, to Ancona. The centre of the peninsula is filled by the Apennines which here reach their greatest height; they were now under deep snow and even in summer are quite impracticable for the movement of large forces. The west coast rises steeply into the trackless Aurunci and Lepini Mountains and the coastal road runs close to the seashore, except for a short stretch in the plain of Fondi, until it debouches into the Pontine Marshes which the Germans had flooded. The Aurunci and Lepini Mountains are separated from the main Apennine range, however, by the valley of the Liri and, further to the north-west, by the valley of its tributary, the Sacco. The gap thereby formed, through which runs Route 6, the Via

Casilina, varies in width from four to seven miles. When it reaches the eastern end of the Aurunci chain the Liri meets the Rapido (known also as the Gari for the stretch between Cassino and the confluence) flowing from due north at right angles to its course and the joint stream, now called the Garigliano, flows due south to reach the Tyrrhenian Sea east of Minturno. From the confluence with the Rapido to Ceprano, where the Sacco joins the Liri, the valley is about twenty miles in length with the river on the south side and the road on the north. Undulating and well-wooded towards the north-west the valley gradually loses these characteristics, and open cornfields in the vicinity of Aquino give way to flat pasture land nearer the Rapido. Numerous transverse gullies break up the surface, the most important being the Forme d'Aquino.

The mouth of the valley was closed by formidable defences. To enter it, it is first necessary to cross the Rapido river which, as its name shows, is very swift-flowing; the banks are generally low but marshy, in fact most of the land here is reclaimed land. The Rapido might be compared to the moat before a castle gate and on either hand are two great bastions. To the south Monte Majo, rising to just under three thousand feet, sends down spurs to the river running along its eastern side. The key of the position, however, lies on the north. Here Monte Cairo, over five thousand feet, rears its head as the southernmost peak of a great spur of the Apennines. From its summit a ridge thrusts out, terminating abruptly in Monte Cassino. This is a bare, rocky promontory, seventeen hundred feet high, whose sides drop sharply into the plain beneath. It had been selected for its natural strength and inaccessibility by Saint Benedict as the site of his first monastery and by the Italian General Staff as an example of an impregnable position. Before we could advance on Rome by this route, and there was no other way except by sea, we should have to storm this bastion defending the gate, for from it the Germans could command the whole floor of the valley.

Plans for an Amphibious Landing.

The desirability of employing our control of the sea in amphibious outflanking movements had been well in the forefront of all our planning ever since we first set foot in Italy. For lack of resources in men and craft only one operation had so far been attempted, Eighth Army's small-scale but successful landing at Termoli, but I had also been constantly examining the possibilities of a "seaborne hook" on the west coast where it seemed to promise still greater advantages. General Clark had endeavoured to fit in such an operation as a feature of almost all his attacks so far but, in spite of his great keenness, had been unable to find a suitable target for the resources available. Now that we were approaching the narrowest part of the peninsula the advantages of an amphibious strategy became even more obvious. With the shortening of their line and the strengthening of their defences, with only one really vulnerable point in their front, the Liri valley, the Germans could economise in troops while we, however well our build-up might progress, would have difficulty in bringing our full strength to bear. The advantages of an outflanking move were not, of course, limited to assisting the advance on Rome and extending the area on which the Germans would have to fight us; they included also the possibility of the destruction of part of the force opposing us. It was on these grounds that I had urged this strategy at the Carthage conferences on 25th October and 3rd November and it had been agreed that an amphibious landing should be made south of the Tiber when Fifth Army had advanced to within reasonable supporting distance. I had proposed to use for this I British Infantry Division, which had been originally intended for Eighth Army. The landing craft situation was quite uncertain. I pointed out on 8th November that, on the present programme, my Armies would still be ten thousand vehicles short by Ist January and that it would be impossible to mount an amphibious operation before 25th December. If the craft were then withdrawn it would be impossible to lift as much as a division with what would remain. However, we decided to go on planning on the assumption that sufficient might be available. The SEXTANT conference was due to open in Cairo on 22nd November and General Eisenhower agreed to press there for the retention of the landing craft which I thought necessary.

My operation instruction of 8th November had directed that in the third phase of the operations then envisaged an amphibious landing would be made south of Rome directed on the Alban Hills. The choice of this objective was made for obvious geographical reasons. Rising just south of Rome this large *massif* of volcanic origin dominates both routes from Rome to the enemy's line on the Garigliano, Routes 6 and 7, the Via Casilina and the Via Appia. The latter can be cut with ease by landing almost anywhere on the west coast, but the Alban Hills mark the first point where the inland route is not protected by the almost trackless Aurunci and Lepini Mountains. If we could seize them the enemy's communications would be cut and Rome almost within our grasp. It would, admittedly, be rather in the nature of a bluff, for a really strong-nerved commander might still hang onto his positions - although, of course, we intended to attack them frontally in force simultaneously with our landing - and try to raise a force from somewhere else to fight his communications free. Such a course would certainly mean reinforcements from outside Italy, which would be an assistance to the other fronts, and I felt myself that, provided we got firmly on to the Alban Hills and across Route 6, Kesselring would not dare to take the risk of retaining his positions at Cassino.

With the objective thus designated, detailed planning became a Fifth Army responsibility, in conjunction with Rear-Admiral Lowry,[62] United States Navy, who was appointed as naval commander for the force. The codename SHINGLE was given to the operation. On I2th November, Fifth Army set up a planning staff; they were instructed by my Headquarters to work on the assumption that the force would number about twenty-three thousand men and that the target date would be 20th December. The planning staff quickly decided on the area around Anzio as the site of the landing. This would give immediate access into relatively open terrain, though broken by water obstacles, over which good roads lead directly to the Alban Hills only twenty miles away. The beaches were definitely poor, with very shallow under-water gradients and off-lying sandbars, but they were the best to be had south of the Tiber; there were three possible landing sites, one east and one west of Anzio and one in the port itself. The beach to the west was particularly shallow and had, in fact, to be abandoned after the initial assault. The weather was likely to be bad for beach working and forecasts promised only an average of two good days out of seven. Conditions would be much improved, however, if the port of Anzio, which the Germans had been using for coastwise maintenance, could be captured undemolished. As to opposition to the landing, it was not expected that the enemy would have any large force in the area. Our estimate of the prepared defences likely to be met was made difficult by the fact that the first photographic coverage showed an enormous number of defences of all kinds in the immediate vicinity of Anzio. It was learned, however, that the area had been a much-used training ground for Italian troops before and during the war, and nearly all the defences were marked as unoccupied; in the event the masses of trenches and strongpoints which dotted the coast on the defence overprints issued to the troops played no rôle in resistance to the assault.

The first plan for SHINGLE was approved on 25th November. The operation was to be timed to coincide with the arrival of the main body of Fifth Army on the general line Capistrello - Ferentino - Priverno and was to be in the strength of one infantry division,[63] reinforced by some armour and anti-aircraft artillery. It was intended to make contact with the main body within seven days. We were to retain the necessary landing craft until 15th January but we now thought it unlikely that we should be within supporting distance until at least 10th January. By 18th December it was clear that even this date could not be met and General Clark signalled to me "reluctantly" recommending the cancellation of the operation on the grounds that the arbitrary date set for the surrender of landing craft made it impossible to mount the attack under the conditions necessary for success. I signalled this decision to General Eisenhower on the 21st but informed him that I was still studying the problem in the hope of being able to prepare a modification of the original plan for a later date.

I fully shared General Clark's reluctance to see ourselves forced back on a strategy of frontal assault in the present unfavourable conditions. There was now no hope that Fifth Army could arrive within supporting distance of a landing at Anzio within the proposed time; no advantage would be gained by a landing nearer to the present front under the abrupt southern slopes of the Aurunci; I therefore began to consider the possibility of making the SHINGLE force much stronger, strong enough to hold its ground by itself, for a longer time than we had previously considered. I put up this proposal, which virtually amounted to a new plan, at a Commanders-in-Chief conference in Tunis on 25th December. The Cairo conference had just broken up and it had there been decided that General Eisenhower should take over the command of the invasion of North-west Europe, to be succeeded in the Mediterranean by General Wilson. Both were present at the conference, as was also the Prime Minister who was passing through on his way back from Cairo to London. I proposed we should assault with two divisions reinforced by some armour. The conference decided that, by a readjustment of the programme for the repair and refitting of landing craft in England, it would be possible for sufficient to remain in the Mediterranean long enough to carry out the assault without diminishing the numbers available for the invasion of North-west Europe.[64] We also had a lucky windfall in the arrival of fifteen

Landing Ships, Tank on their way home from the Indian Ocean where a proposed operation for which they were earmarked had been cancelled. It was decided, therefore, that all preparations should be made for carrying out SHINGLE with two assault divisions on or about 20th January. The objective, as before, was to be the Alban Hills.

It was now necessary to press on rapidly with the planning of the new assault. The composition of the force caused some discussion as it would be difficult to compose a homogeneous Corps quickly enough. I decided, in agreement with General Clark, to use the VI United States Corps Headquarters, General Lucas commanding, which was then out of the line, with I British Division, plus some Commandos and armour, and 3 United States Division, also supported by American armour, parachutists and Rangers, I Division had just arrived in Italy and was not yet committed, 3 Division had already been engaged on planning SHINGLE and was the obvious choice. I should like to mention, in this connection, a typically understanding signal I received from General Eisenhower, almost the last he sent me before leaving the Mediterranean. "The disadvantages of employing a mixed Corps," he said, "are of course as obvious to you as to me. I have wondered whether or not you may have been influenced by either of the following factors: that you felt it undesirable, because of the risks involved, to hazard a Corps of two American divisions when you as a British officer have the deciding responsibility or that you may have thought it undesirable from a political viewpoint for a Corps of two British divisions to be given the opportunity for the direct capture of Rome. In my opinion neither of these factors should be allowed to outweigh the military advantages of launching your assault by any troops you believe best fitted and most available. In giving these views I merely wish to remove any political difficulties that may occur to you in order that you can launch the best military operation that can be laid on in the time available." I replied that the composition of the Corps was based solely on the best formations available in the time: "the political aspect is of no consequence but I do think the sharing of risks and hazards together is of importance."

Orders for the operation were issued on 2nd January. The objective was defined as to cut the enemy communications and threaten the rear of the German XIV Corps. In the last paragraph Fifth Army was ordered to make "as strong a thrust as possible towards Cassino and Frosinone shortly before the assault landing to draw in enemy reserves which might be employed against the landing forces and then to create a breach in his front through which every opportunity will be taken to link up rapidly with the seaborne operation." For this 10 Corps was being reinforced by 5 British Infantry Division. This was the second division I had taken from Eighth Army, for I Division had been originally intended for it, and I was shortly afterwards to take three more. The Adriatic sector was now of secondary importance to the western sector. The intention was to launch successive attacks by the three Corps on the main front: the French Expeditionary Corps on 12th January against the high ground north of Cassino, II Corps on the 15th to capture Monte Porchia and Monte Trocchio and reach the Rapido river and 10 Corps on the 17th to cross the lower Garigliano in the Minturno area and attack northwards up the Ausente river valley towards San Giorgio a Liri. Finally, II Corps, with its left and right thus protected, would on 20th January force the Rapido in the area of Sant' Angelo and exploit rapidly, supported by armour, westwards and north-westwards. Two days later VI Corps was to land at Anzio and threaten the rear of the enemy who, it was hoped, would by then be already hard pressed on his main front.

I was still a little anxious about the time limit for the return of landing craft because of the needs of maintenance and my Chief Administrative Officer, General Robertson,[65] gave me his opinion on 5th January that the plan was not sound administratively. I managed eventually a slight readjustment of the programme, as a result of a conference on 8th January, which gave us a reasonable guarantee that we should be able to supply the force landed. I also planned to land in the first follow-up convoy a mobile, hard-hitting force from I United States Armoured Division and 45 Infantry Division. Later the remainder of these divisions was to follow. This meant that in two months SHINGLE had grown from a first tentative figure of twenty-three thousand men to an expected eventual strength of one hundred and ten thousand. It was hoped that the Germans would not be able, with the resources available to them in Italy, both to block off this force and to hold the "Gustav" line.

Having made the outflanking force as strong as possible it was now essential to give the maximum strength to the frontal attack, which must have sufficient momentum to carry it well up the Liri valley. I therefore decided to withdraw the New Zealand Division from Eighth Army, to be concentrated in the Naples area by 26th January, D plus 4 for SHINGLE. This division, of good fighting quality, well motorised and with an armoured component, was the most suitable readily available for such exploitation. It gave me an Army Group reserve under my hand, for the first time, with which to influence the battle; as the events of the following May were to show, operations in the Liri valley and from Anzio must be treated as an Army Group battle. It was the third division taken from Eighth Army to increase our concentration at the vital point; I intended to put it at the disposal of Fifth Army when a suitable opportunity for its employment in an exploiting rôle could be foreseen.

Operations Preliminary to the Anzio Landing.

On the Adriatic sector General Montgomery still continued with his attempt to break through the enemy's defensive system and reach Pescara but with even less success as the weather worsened and the enemy's strength increased. The immediate objective was now Ortona, a small port surmounted by a medieval Old Town with a dilapidated castle and an outlying New Town of modern solidly built houses. It was hoped that we should be able to use the harbour for maintenance. On 6th December I Canadian Division and on 7th December 8 Indian Division crossed the Moro and drove on Ortona. Every advance was most bitterly contested by 90 Panzer Grenadier Division, which had now arrived complete; instead of the passive defence of 65 Division the Panzer Grenadiers spent lives recklessly in savage counter-attacks. But the acme of stubbornness was reached in the defence of Ortona itself by I Parachute Division which had been brought across from its hitherto inactive front on the Maiella. These parachutists were undoubtedly the best German troops in Italy - in the German army,

The invasion of Sicily, Operation *Husky*, underway on Saturday, 10 July 1943; this picture shows Axis prisoners of war marching along the beach to waiting ships being watched by Royal Marine Commandos. A Landing Craft Infantry (Large) and two Landing Craft Tanks, can be seen on the beach in the background. The large scale amphibious and airborne operation was followed by six weeks of land fighting. (ww2images)

The Allied invasion of Italy gets underway. This image shows British troops and vehicles from 128 Brigade, 46th Division being unloaded from LST 383 onto the beaches at Salerno, 9 September 1943. The main invasion force landed around Salerno on the western coast in Operation *Avalanche*, while two supporting operations took place in Calabria (Operation *Baytown*) and Taranto (Operation *Slapstick*).(ww2images)

Part of the Allied invasion force pictured heading towards the Italian coast as part of Operation *Shingle*, the Allied amphibious landings at Anzio which began on 22 January 1944. (Historic Military Press)

Tanks of an American armoured regiment are pictured disembarking from a Landing Ship, Tank – LST 77 – in Anzio Harbour as the US Fifth Army's VI Corps builds up its forces in Italy. In due course, LST 77, originally part of the US Navy, was decommissioned (on 24 December 1944) and commissioned in the Royal Navy. (US National Archives)

A vertical photographic-reconnaissance photograph taken over the docks at La Spezia, Italy, showing destroyed sheds, storehouses and workshops in an area of the naval dockyard north-east of Bassin I (lower centre), as a result of the raid by aircraft of Bomber Command on the night of 18/19 April 1943. (Historic Military Press)

Axis prisoners of war are pictured being guarded by British and American soldiers on 19 September 1943, as the push inland from the Salerno beachhead begins – the hills and mountains in the distance would be the scene of bitter fighting in the days and weeks to come. (Historic Military Press)

British troops go ashore at Salerno. (Historic Military Press)

A German *Fallschirmjäger*, or paratrooper, observing the lower ground from the heights of Monte Cassino, Italy, during February 1944 – an image which illustrates the scale of the challenge that Allied troops faced. (Bundesarchiv, Bild 146-1974-006-62/Czirnich/C C-BY-SA)

A photograph of a 240mm howitzer of 'B' Battery, 697th Field Artillery Battalion, US Fifth Army, taken just before it fires into German-held territory around Monte Cassino, Italy, on 30 January 1944.

German vehicles destroyed during an Allied air attack north of Cassino, Italy, in 1944. The halftrack artillery tractor carries the identification plate WH1028 348. (US National Archives)

Bombs lie on an Allied airfield in Italy ready to be loaded into RAF Consolidated B-24 Liberators during January 1944. (US National Archives)

The aftermath of one of the most successful German attacks on Allied shipping of the Second World War. During the raid on Bari Harbour on 2 December 1943, 105 Junkers Ju 88s of *Luftflotte 2*, achieving complete surprise, bombed shipping and personnel operating in support of the Allied campaign in Italy, sinking twenty-seven cargo and transport ships and a schooner in Bari harbour. (The James Luto Collection)

Another view of the devastation at Bari during the *Luftwaffe* attack on 2 December 1943. Not for nothing has the raid been called, with some justification, "The Second Pearl Harbor". One of the merchant vessels destroyed – the U.S. Liberty Ship *John Harvey* – had been carrying a quantity of mustard gas bombs which exploded with devastating consequences. (The James Luto Collection)

British gunners are pictured preparing to fire on enemy positions during the fighting in and around the Serchio Valley in late 1944. The Allied intention was to dislodge German troops from a number of well-defended, but important, positions. (Historic Military Press)

A Consolidated B-24 Liberator of No.205 Group flies over the target area during a daylight attack on the port of Monfalcone, Italy. Smoke from exploding bombs can be seen rising from the shipbuilding and repair yards and other installations in the harbour.

US troops in action during the Battle of Garfagnana, 26–28 December 1944. Known to the Germans as Operation *Unternehmen Wintergewitter* ("Winter Storm") and nicknamed the "Christmas Offensive", this was an Axis offensive on the western sector of the Gothic Line in the north Tuscan Apennines, near Massa and Lucca. (US National Archives)

some said - and Ortona gave magnificent opportunities for street fighting. For over a week, from 20th to 28th December, the Canadians were engaged in the most violent hand-to-hand struggle. Street fighting, especially in a town of masonry houses, calls for the greatest skill and courage as Stalingrad had shown and the Canadians came triumphantly out of a test as severe as any in the war. On the 28th the parachutists were finally driven from the town. All our attacks on Orsogna in the meanwhile had failed and the enemy remained in possession for another five months. For the rest of the period no advance was made east of the Apennines; the Germans took the opportunity of the pause in operations to complete the relief of 65 Division by the newly arrived 334 Division.

On the Fifth Army front advances by II Corps and the French Expeditionary Corps between 3rd and 15th January drove the Germans back through the depth of their winter positions on to the final "Gustav" line. It was a strongly contested advance; the Germans had reinforced their front here in December with 44 Infantry and 5 Mountain Divisions and 7I Infantry Division was on the way. San Vittore was captured on 6th January and Monte Porchia on the same day; Monte Trocchio, the last hill before the Rapido, was abandoned by the enemy on the I5th. Meanwhile the French Expeditionary Corps, of 2 Moroccan and 3 Algerian Divisions, had also made contact with the "Gustav" line further north where they had captured Monte Santa Croce across the upper Rapido, and Monte Pile, west of Viticuso. This represented an advance of about ten miles by the northern arm of my pincers aiming at Cassino and caused considerable alarm to the Germans; the newly arrived 5 Mountain Division made a poor showing in its first battle in Italy and had to be reinforced with detachments from the 3 Panzer Grenadier Division which had been intended for the Adriatic.

Opening of the Battle for Rome.

On 20th January I moved my headquarters over to the west of the Apennines and opened in the Royal Palace at Caserta. General Richardson had been succeeded as my Chief of Staff shortly before by General Harding[66] who, after commanding 7 Armoured Division in the desert, had had command of a Corps in England.

It will be useful at this point to pause and describe the order of battle of the opposing armies as they stood on 22nd January, the day of the Anzio landing.[67] On our side there were at that time eighteen divisions[68] and six brigades, equivalent to rather over twenty divisions; however 3 Carpathian Division and 5 Canadian Armoured Division were not yet available for employment. Eighth Army had two Corps in the line, 5 and I3, with four divisions and two brigades, and two divisions arriving in the Army area. Fifth Army had three Corps in line, French Expeditionary, II United States and I0 British, with six divisions in line and one in reserve; VI Corps, landing at Anzio, had two reinforced divisions, to be followed shortly by elements of two more. There was one division in Army Group reserve.

Total enemy strength was between twenty and twenty-one divisions. On the main front Tenth Army had thirteen divisions (facing ten to twelve on our side) under LXXVI Panzer Corps in the east and XIV Panzer Corps in the west. The remainder were in North Italy under Fourteenth Army; some of the eight there were still in process of forming. In view of the weak state of some of these the German High Command considered it necessary to reinforce Italy with the equivalent of three good divisions, and allow the retention of a fourth, in order to meet the threat presented by Anzio.

The operations to which the Anzio landing was to be the climax began with the attack of I0 Corps across the Garigliano on I7th January. This was delivered by three divisions, the 5th, 56th and 46th but the last played only a minor role in the opening phases; the object was to crush the enemy's extreme right behind the lower Garigliano, and then turn northwards and, breaking through the hills between Minturno and Castelforte up the valley of the Ausente river, to appear in the Liri valley at San Giorgio. The attack began well. The German 94 Infantry Division, a relatively inexperienced formation, had not been expecting an attack and was surprised by the weight of its delivery, for the arrival of 5 Division had been well concealed. The Germans reacted rapidly to what they imagined to be our main effort, finding confirmation of this appreciation when II Corps attacked across the Rapido on 20th January. 90 Panzer Grenadier Division was brought down from the Eighth Army front and 29 Panzer Grenadier Division from the Rome area; the latter move was rather gratifying and unexpected, for it was the division which had been expected to oppose the Anzio landing; in addition the Hermann Goering Division was also put in on the lower Garigliano in spite of orders which had been received to transfer it to France on 20th January to prepare for the invasion battles of the coming summer.

The I0 Corps attack looked the more dangerous to the enemy; by the I9th 5 Division had captured Minturno and the 56th was in the outskirts of Castelforte. General von Vietinghoff decided to rely on the strong defences of the Rapido to hold off the frontal attack of II Corps. In this he was justified although the attack by 36 Division was pressed with great gallantry. A small bridgehead was seized on the 2Ist but it was eliminated on the 22nd. Meanwhile the Germans were preparing a powerful force to counter-attack I0 Corps. On the morning of the 22nd all the three newly-arrived mobile divisions, 29, 90 and Hermann Goering, were thrown into the attack; every division of the Tenth Army was thus actively committed at the moment when VI Corps was landing at Anzio.

The assault force had sailed from Naples at 0500 hours on 2Ist January in perfect weather conditions and with the prospect that the weather would continue fine. The convoy was made up of two hundred and forty-three warships, transports, landing craft and various other vessels of the United States and Royal Navies, supplemented by Dutch, Greek, Polish and French ships. The assault force consisted of some fifty thousand American and British troops and over five thousand vehicles. The voyage was uneventful and the force was neither observed nor intercepted by the enemy. The first assault troops touched down on the beaches at 0200 hours on the 22nd; opposition was negligible and it was clear that complete surprise had been obtained. The enemy defences, except for a few coastal artillery positions, were unmanned and it was soon discovered that the only German unit in the area was a battalion of 29 Panzer Grenadier Division which had been so severely reduced in the recent fighting that it had been sent there the day before to rest and refit and to acquire some training in demolition by blowing up, at its leisure, the small harbour of Anzio.[69] Fortunately it had made no progress with the task before its training was interrupted. The failure of enemy reconnaissance is undoubtedly to be ascribed at least in part to a heavy air raid we had laid on for the purpose against the enemy's long-range air reconnaissance base at Perugia on 19th January. This was so successful that no reconnaissance was flown between 19th and 22nd January. A local diversion was made by the Navy who bombarded Civitavecchia and simulated landings there on the night of the 21st; the feint was taken seriously at first by the enemy who flew a reconnaissance over the area - the pilot asked where the landing was. Army Group "C" informed the German High Command at 0600 hours that a landing had taken place directed at Rome and requested the reinforcements which had been agreed for that case; but the first real news that the landing was taking place at Anzio was given by a Messerschmidt at 0820 hours, six hours after the assault troops landed.

Consolidation of the Bridgehead.

The first phase of the operation had thus gone better than we had reason to hope; we had gained both strategical and tactical surprise and had got our forces ashore with scarcely any fighting. The exploitation inland, however, was slower than I had planned and failed to reach our objective, the Alban Hills. This is in part to be ascribed to what is always a potent factor in all military operations, the delayed effect of preconceived ideas on a situation to which they no longer apply. At the time when the orders for the operation were issued Fifth Army's Intelligence Staff estimated that enemy resistance would be in the strength of one division (viz. 29 Panzer Grenadiers), four parachute battalions from Rome, a tank and an anti-tank battalion and other miscellaneous units, to a total of fourteen thousand three hundred men. VI Corps was therefore expecting to have to fight an assault landing and have some trouble in consolidating its beach-head. Although the enemy dispositions assumed in this appreciation had been radically altered, and VI Corps had, of course, been apprised of this fact before the landing, the effects of the original conception of the task undoubtedly remained. The fact that the whole nature of the operation had fairly recently been changed from a relatively small flanking assault designed to join up quickly with the advance of the main body of Fifth Army to one employing five times the force, intended to be self-supporting for an indefinite period, combined with the fact that the enemy withdrawals which had left the coast clear at Anzio had reduced the chances of rapid progress by the main body, undoubtedly contributed to the decision to secure first, and consolidate, a sound defensive perimeter before proceeding to the main objective, the capture of the Alban Hills. The increase in the size of the force no doubt persuaded the Corps Commander that it was now practicable to proceed, if not cautiously at least deliberately, rather than hazard a dash inland at the very beginning of the operations. There was a mechanical factor making in the same direction; the beaches were so bad that the landing of the guns, tanks and heavy equipment was delayed beyond our expectations and it was some time before the troops could be wedded to their supporting weapons.

At the time, therefore, I considered that our progress in the first days of the landing had been rather too slow. On the other hand, now that we have the inestimable advantage of wisdom after the event and know what steps the enemy was prepared to take, I find it interesting to speculate whether a deep and rapid thrust inland, ignoring what the Germans could bring against us, would have been successful or not. Certainly my experience of German reactions on such occasions has been that, though they are easy to deceive, they are not easily panicked. Every time we attacked Kesselring in Italy we took him completely by surprise, but he showed very great skill in extricating himself from the desperate situations into which his faulty Intelligence had led him. I feel now that he would not, in these circumstances, have altered his dispositions on the main front to any great extent until he had tried every means to eliminate the threat in his rear. The risk in such a course is obvious; on the other hand, VI Corps, with the resources available to it, would have found it very difficult both to be secure on the Alban Hills and at the same time retain the absolutely necessary communications with the sea at Anzio. There are too many hypotheses involved to make further speculation valuable; but such conclusions as can be drawn are at any rate satisfactory: that the actual course of events was probably the most advantageous in the end.

The area of the bridgehead, as decided on previously, was about seven miles deep by fifteen miles wide with a perimeter of twenty-six miles. On the left the flank rested on the Moletta river and was covered by a system of *wadis*. In the open central sector the line ran across fields to meet the western branch of the Mussolini canal south of Padiglione, and then along its course eastwards to Sessano and southwards to the sea. The canal between Sessano and the sea is a considerable obstacle, with steeply sloping sides like an anti-tank ditch, and a shallow stream in the middle sixteen feet wide. The right flank was therefore very strong and could be held with minimum forces. This original beach-head line was reached all along its extent by the evening of the 23rd after some small actions on the night of the 22nd on the Mussolini canal with elements of the Hermann Goering Division. The British beaches on the western flank had been found wholly unsuitable and abandoned after the landing of the first assault troops; but the port of Anzio had been opened, practically undamaged. Ninety per cent. of the personnel and equipment of the assault convoy had been landed by midnight on D-day and the return and follow-up convoy programme was running to schedule.

Enemy reactions to the landing were rapid. Kesselring's first decision was to build up as hastily as possible, and with every available means, some form of blocking force to contain the beach-head. There were already in the Cisterna area some elements of the Hermann Goering Division, notably part of the divisional tank regiment with some artillery; a regiment of 3 Panzer Grenadier Division, which was on its way to Eighth Army front, was halted and brought back to the Alban Hills where it was joined on the evening of the 23rd by a regimental group from I5 Panzer Grenadier Division, the successful defenders of the Rapido. The latter two forces were put under command of a regimental commander of 4 Parachute Division, Colonel Gehricke, and were rapidly joined by the remainder of this division which came down by battalions at a time from Perugia, where it was in process of forming. The rest of the Hermann Goering Division came up from the lower Garigliano, where the offensive it had joined in on the 22nd was called off by the end of the day. It was clear that the enemy intended both to hold the "Gustav" line, where he had now blunted our first attacks, and to seal off the bridgehead in his rear with a view to destroying it later if possible. This intention was soon reinforced by an order from the Fuehrer's Headquarters which was directed to be read out to all ranks: "The 'Gustav' line must be held at all costs for the sake of the political consequences which would follow a completely successful defence. The Fuehrer expects the bitterest struggle for every yard". This verbal intervention by Hitler was followed by more fruitful actions than was to be usual later; the Italian theatre was to be reinforced. Kesselring was informed that he would receive two semi-motorized infantry divisions, three independent reinforced regiments and two heavy tank battalions, together with an extra allotment of G.H.Q. medium and heavy artillery. Further, he was told he could retain in Italy for the present the Hermann Goering Division. With these reinforcements he was expected not merely to contain but to eliminate the Anzio bridgehead. Not only was this essential militarily in order to continue holding in Italy with the minimum forces but also psychologically and politically it would be a most valuable gain to defeat ignominiously the first seaborne landing made by the Allies in I944, a year which was fated to see other and still more dangerous landings.

By 30th January there were already elements of no less than eight divisions assembled south of Rome. Admittedly these forces were extremely mixed and hastily organised, but they were in the main experienced troops and accustomed by now to working independently of their parent formations. The first four divisions represented were, as already stated, 3 and I5 Panzer Grenadier, 4 Parachute and Hermann Goering. They were joined by 26 Panzer Division which was rushed across at top speed from the Adriatic sector, bringing with it three battalions of I Parachute Division. Meanwhile 65 Infantry Division, which was reorganising at Genoa after its losses on the Sangro, was hurried down to the west of the bridgehead to assist Gehricke, and advanced elements of 7I5 (Motorized) Infantry Division had already arrived. Command was exercised by Fourteenth Army, General von Mackensen, with two Corps Headquarters, I Parachute and LXXVI Panzer Corps. The tank strength available amounted to above one hundred and eighty and the artillery deployment was already formidable.

The first attempt to enlarge the bridgehead position was on 25th January when 3 Division advanced towards Cisterna. This attack was halted by the Hermann Goering Division after gains of up to two miles. The advance was resumed on the 27th but was again halted well short of its objective; 3 Division was still three miles from the town and it was evident that a more concentrated and better prepared attack would be necessary, I Division in the meanwhile was endeavouring to push up the main road from Anzio to Albano with Campoleone as its first objective. An attack on the so-called "Factory Buildings" (actually the first buildings of Mussolini's new town of Aprilia) was successful on the 25th, though it met strong resistance from 3 Panzer Grenadier Division; but we could only advance a mile and a half beyond the

"Factory" and it was clear that Campoleone, like Cisterna, could only be taken by a strong and consolidated attack. I had returned to the bridgehead on the 25th, after being there on D-day, and as a result of my observations ordered General Clark on the 27th to press the advance with the utmost energy, before the enemy reinforcements could arrive; they were then suffering considerable delay from our air attacks on communications. I told him I considered that, with the prospect of the balance of 45 Division arriving in the bridgehead shortly, risks must be taken and I suggested that all efforts should now be concentrated on full-scale co-ordinated attacks to capture Cisterna and Campoleone, followed by a rapid advance on Velletri.

General Clark, who had set up an Advanced Command Post at Anzio, replied that the main attack could not be launched, for various reasons, before 30th January. The results of the attack were disappointing. 3 Division failed to capture Cisterna and suffered heavy losses, particularly among the Ranger battalions which were under command. I Division reached the railway embankment at Campoleone, a difficult obstacle, but was unable to advance beyond it, leaving itself in a dangerous salient protruding into the enemy lines. On 31st January I again visited Anzio by destroyer, returning on 2nd February. It was clear to me that until we had captured Cisterna and Campoleone it would be impossible to undertake any important offensive operations. I therefore ordered a renewed attack on Cisterna in full strength with a properly prepared Corps plan and all possible concentration of artillery and air attacks. Next my plan was to gain ground on the left of I Division, clear up our centre and organise our communications so as to be able to mount a solid offensive to cut Route 6.

Before these instructions could be carried out the Germans on 3rd February launched a counter-attack on the salient which I Division had established, stretching north from Carroceto to Campoleone. The position, held by 3 Infantry Brigade, was untenable against a heavy attack and it was only by committing 168 Brigade of 56 Division, which had landed as a reinforcement on 3rd February, that it was possible to extricate our troops from the salient by the night of the 4th/5th to a line covering Carroceto and the "Factory". VI Corps then went over to the defensive in preparation for the enemy counter-attack in force, of whose imminence there was strong evidence. Two positions were to be prepared in rear of the present front lines; the last, corresponding with the initial bridgehead, was to be the final line, I and 3 Divisions, both reinforced, plus the newly arrived I Special Service Force and a regimental combat team of 45 Division, were in the line; the remainder of the 45th and I Armoured Division, less one Combat Command, were in reserve. As the dimensions of the enemy threat became more apparent I decided that more reinforcement was necessary and sent in the remainder of 56 British Division; this arrived between 13th and 18th February and relieved I Division on the 13th. On 25th February 18 Infantry Brigade, from the British I Armoured Division in North Africa, began to disembark at Anzio.

Renewed Attack on the "Gustav" Line.

Although the attempt by 10 Corps to envelop the southern flank of the "Gustav" line had been halted after an initial success by the enemy's counter-attacks, and the frontal attack by II Corps across the Rapido had failed, it was still vitally necessary to breakthrough as soon as possible in order to gain the maximum advantage from the Anzio landings. There was little chance of a further advance through the Aurunci Mountains for the enemy were strongly posted and prepared and we had had to weaken I0 Corps by withdrawing 56 Division for Anzio. I therefore decided to strengthen the northern arm of my pincers and ordered II Corps to shift its weight to its right flank and, in conjunction with the French Expeditionary Corps, to seize the high ground above Cassino and envelop the position from the north. If we could seize Cassino, the northern bastion, we should be able to advance up the valley without worrying about the southern flank.

It was difficult for Eighth Army to provide much distraction to tie down the enemy on their front. When General Leese took over he found that the heavy battles from the Sangro to Ortona had left the enemy, though no longer in his planned winter positions, still strongly posted on an easily defensible line and our own troops severely depleted in strength. There was no vital objective within our grasp on this front; the enemy could easily afford to give ground if really necessary and had already prepared strong defensive positions in rear. On 22nd January General Leese told me that he hoped to be able to mount a major operation, using 4 Indian, I Canadian and 78 Divisions, by mid-February. I replied that this would probably be too late and that what we needed was to prevent the enemy withdrawing troops from opposite Eighth Army, which he was doing at that very time. On further consideration, however, I saw clearly that that was impossible and I therefore decided, on 30th January, to follow the enemy's example and reinforce the vital points at the cost of weakening the Adriatic sector.

The first attack north of Cassino, between 24th and 3Ist January, had had limited success. 34 United States Division, in hard fighting, secured a bridgehead over the Rapido about two miles north of the town and, pressing up into the hills beyond the river, captured two outlying spurs and the village of Cairo. To their north the French, supported by an American Regimental Combat Team, captured Colle Belvedere and pushed further into the mountains towards Terelle. II Corps was now in a position to swing the direction of its attack from west to south. 36 Division, still weak from its losses in the Rapido crossing, was brought in to guard the western flank by holding Monte Castellone, captured by 34 Division on Ist February, and the 34th began attacking on the 2nd along the ridge from Colle Majola on to the rear of Monastery Hill. Hopes were high and General Clark signalled me on that day: "Present indications are that the Cassino heights will be captured very soon". He asked for a directive on the employment of the New Zealand Division.

I had already decided that the development of the situation at Anzio and the stubborn enemy resistance on the main front made necessary a reinforcement of General Freyberg's[70] forces if they were to be able to carry out the task assigned. I had therefore ordered General Leese on 30th January to despatch 4 Indian Division, which had newly arrived in the country, to come under command of General Freyberg in an *ad hoc* New Zealand Corps. 4 Indian Division had had the longest experience in actual operations of any Allied formation and had recently been doing some training in mountain operations.[71] I told General Leese: "I fully realise that this will put out of court any possibility of offensive operations by you". On 3rd February I put the New Zealand Corps under command of Fifth Army, from Army Group reserve. I still felt the need for a formation under my hand to influence the battle and therefore signalled Eighth Army on the 4th to be prepared to release 78 Division within seven to ten days. General Leese was naturally very perturbed at this proposal to take away a fifth division; not only would it render any offensive action quite impracticable and upset the system for reliefs of tired formations but he feared that it might even lead to a loss of security on his front. This, however, was a risk which I was prepared to take; the Adriatic sector was now unimportant to either side; both were gathering their maximum strength for the decisive battle under the snows of Monte Cairo and among the canals of the Pontine Marshes.

The attack by 34 United States Division continued to make progress but the enemy was now steadily reinforcing. Leaving 5 Mountain Division to oppose the French he decided to strengthen the mixed group of 44 and 7I Divisions which was defending Cassino itself and the Monastery with 90 Panzer Grenadiers, brought down from the Anzio front. Against these excellent troops II Corps was unable to make progress. It had got into the outskirts of the town and was within striking distance of the Monastery hill; indeed it was only a mile from Route 6 down below, but it was a mile packed with defences held by fanatical troops and broken up by mountain ridges and gullies. The first battle of Cassino was a German success; its retention now was a matter of German prestige.

I had refused to commit the New Zealand Corps, my *Corps de Chasse,* until it was certain that II Corps could not take the position. The New Zealanders had relieved the Americans south of Route 6 on 6th February to allow the latter to concentrate for the attack; but it was now clear that they would be obliged, not merely to debouch through a gateway flung open for them, but to capture the gate themselves. II Corps went over to the defensive on I2th February. My plan now was for 4 Indian Division to capture Monastery Hill while the New Zealanders would seize a bridgehead over the Rapido. The Corps would then exploit up the Liri valley, but this was not to start until weather conditions were favourable enough to allow the movement of armoured forces off the roads. At the same time I ordered Fifth Army to make plans for resuming the offensive with VI Corps.

Time was urgently pressing, for it was known that a great enemy counter-attack against the Anzio bridgehead was being prepared. In the event the two attacks went in on the same day, 16th February. A preliminary to the New Zealand Corps attack was the destruction of the Monastery of Monte Cassino by air bombardment and artillery fire. This famous building had hitherto been deliberately spared, to our great disadvantage, but it was an integral part of the German defensive system, mainly from the superb observation it afforded. It is doubtful, however, whether the ruins after the destruction were not more valuable to the enemy than the intact buildings; as we were to find in the town of Cassino below, heavy bombardment often produced better defensive positions than it destroyed. The attack which went in on the I6th made no progress. 4 Indian Division ruefully decided that the Cassino position was almost as strong as Keren, still their invariable standard of comparison. The only gain below the mountain was a small bridgehead over the Rapido opposite the railway station. 78 Division, which had been put under command of New Zealand Corps on the 8th, arrived in the area on the 17th, having been held up by deep snow on the way from Eighth Army front. On the 24th it took over from the New Zealanders south of the railway, the latter relieved 34 United States Division in the north end of Cassino and the remaining elements of II Corps, on Monte Castellone, were relieved by the French Expeditionary Corps on the 26th.

Fourteenth Army's Counter-attack at Anzio.

The preliminary moves in the enemy's planned counter-offensive against the bridgehead took the form of an attack to clear the "Factory" area to secure a firm base for the assault. This began on 7th February and the intention was to capture the whole area in a night attack. In actual fact the stubborn resistance of I Division and counter-attacks by 45 United States Division meant that five days of heavy fighting were necessary before the objective was secured on the 12th. VI Corps was now back on its "intermediate" line astride the Anzio - Albano road and it was clear that this road would be the axis of the enemy's main attack. To meet it VI Corps relieved I Division and handed over the sector to 56 and 45 United States Divisions. On 17th February General Truscott, Commander of 3 United States Division[72] was appointed Deputy Commander of the Corps. He directed, with great success, the defence against the great German counter-offensive and on the 23rd succeeded General Lucas as Corps Commander. It was a new rôle, for General Truscott had made his reputation, and continued to increase it, as a dashing commander of hard-hitting offensives; indeed the defence was a new rôle altogether for our armies in Italy. The troops showed, however, that they were fully equal to the demands made on them, encouraged by the massive support of our concentrated artillery fire, which was augmented by the big guns of the Allied Navies and the bombs and machine-gun fire of the Air Forces.

By the time the German attack began two more divisions had been brought in to reinforce Fourteenth Army: II4 Jaeger from Jugoslavia and 362 Infantry from North Italy, and the three independent regiments and two heavy tank battalions already mentioned had also arrived. This gave the Germans the equivalent of about ten divisions against an Allied strength of rather less than five. German morale was particularly high; a special order from Hitler was read out to all troops before the attack in which he demanded that this "abscess" must and would be eliminated in three days. They were told that they would get massive air support from the Luftwaffe, combined with numbers of heavy tanks, employed for the first time in Italy, and would have the privilege of operating for the first time on any front the new secret weapon, the "Goliath" remote-controlled explosive tank. The plan was to attack on a very narrow front of some four thousand yards straight down the Albano - Anzio road on to Anzio itself, only eight miles away. The loss of Anzio would mean that the bridgehead would be split in half and deprived of its port; this would have made further defence hopeless and even evacuation would have been almost impossible for the beaches were already known to be entirely inadequate. The assault was to be made by four divisions, reinforced by eleven battalions, led by the crack Lehr Regiment, the Infantry Demonstration Regiment from Döberitz, pride of the German Army. Four hundred and fifty-two guns supported the attack. Two mobile divisions, 26 Panzer and 29 Panzer Grenadier, reinforced by two battalions, one of Tiger and one of Panther tanks, were echeloned behind them to exploit the success of which no one doubted.

The attack began at 0630 hours on 16th February after half an hour's artillery preparation, with massed infantry covered with smoke and supported by tanks. By the end of the day a salient of some two thousand yards had been driven down the road in the sector of 45 Division. The airstrip at Nettuno had been rendered unserviceable by long-range artillery fire, which also destroyed four aircraft as they were about to take off; fighter cover, as a result, now had to be flown wholly from the Naples area. Before midnight the attack was resumed. Fighting on the 17th was even heavier; the enemy made fewer diversionary attacks and concentrated on his drive down the Anzio road. By now there was a wedge two and a half miles wide and over a mile deep in the centre of 45 Division's front. Against this wedge the whole of VI Corps' artillery was directed, supported by all the air resources available, some seven hundred bomber sorties. The enemy was now getting very near the "Final Beach-head Line" and General Truscott moved two brigades of I Division into that line in rear of 45 Division.

The 18th was the most critical day. After infiltration during the night into the shoulders of the salient the enemy moved forward under a lowering and overcast sky which prevented a repetition of the previous day's tremendous programme of air support. Once more waves of infantry attacked in the morning and in the afternoon Mackensen threw in his *Corps de Chasse,* not now to exploit a breakthrough in the Allied lines but to make one. For four hours the battle raged east of the road on the final beach-head line. The honours of the day go mainly to the United States 179 Infantry Regiment and I Battalion of the Loyals, and to the Corps artillery which did deadly execution in the attacking masses. The enemy was held, and that night it was clear that he was pulling back to reorganise. The time had come for the planned counter-attack. On the 19th an armoured force from I United States Armoured Division together with elements of 3 United States Infantry Division attacked the eastern flank of the German salient and gained some fifteen hundred yards causing disorganisation and panic. In the afternoon 2 Brigade of I Division cleared up some enemy penetrations and re-established the final line. A last, badly mismanaged enemy attack on I Loyals on the morning of the 20th, repulsed with heavy losses, was the end of the German offensive. It was clear that they would attack again, for Hitler was insistent, but their losses would render essential a pause to reorganise.[73]

Fresh Plans of Campaign.

The failure of the main offensive attempts by both sides, by the Allies in the second battle of Cassino and by the Germans at Anzio, left us with the same problem as before and the necessity of thinking out some new solution for it. I felt confident now that the bridgehead could be held, for, unless they could find fresh formations, a renewed German attack would have to be made in much reduced strength. I could concentrate, therefore, on Cassino and try to find some new method of taking this fortress which had twice defied our best efforts. I still had one division uncommitted, the 78th, but the weather was very bad and the Liri valley a sea of mud; it was no good putting my last fresh troops into a repetition of our former attacks unless I could produce some new tactics to give us a better chance of success. In this frame of mind I decided to try the effect of a really heavy air bombardment. General Cannon,[74] Commanding General of the Tactical Air Force, was anxious to make the experiment too; he hazarded the opinion that, given good weather and all the air resources in Italy, we could "whip, out Cassino like an old tooth." Of course both of us regarded the plan wholly as an experiment, without any certainty as to how it would work out, for we had never tried anything on that scale before; but I was very willing to try it on for I felt that if successful we should have found a way of capturing positions like this without the loss of life which more normal methods must involve.[75] Accordingly, on 20th February, after discussing the plan with General Clark and General Freyberg, I decided we would next attempt to capture the town of Cassino, after a heavy bombardment, with the New Zealand Division which would then push past the southern face of Monte Cassino along Route 6, make contact with the Indians north-west of the Monastery and thus encircle the enemy positions. This would give us a big bridgehead over the Rapido and an entry into the Liri valley.

At the same time I decided to carry out a thorough regrouping of forces and reorganisation of command, the main lines of which were reported by General Harding, my Chief of General Staff, to Allied Force Headquarters in an appreciation dated 22nd February. In this the object of operations in Italy is defined as "to force the enemy to commit the maximum number of divisions in Italy at the time OVERLORD is launched."[76] To attain that object the most effective way was not merely to push back the enemy's line but to destroy enemy formations in Italy to such an extent that they must be replaced from elsewhere to avoid a rout. But, as Nelson said, "Only numbers can annihilate"; my own calculations were that "to have a reasonable chance of effective penetration against organized defences in Italian terrain, it is necessary for the side that takes the offensive to have a local superiority of at least three to one in infantry". It is important to note that I said local, not overall superiority. At the time the Germans had between eighteen and nineteen divisions south of Rome and some five divisions, including three still forming, in the rest of Italy; as against this we had about twenty-one divisions. To remedy this it was proposed to initiate immediately a scheme of reinforcement to bring the Allied Armies by mid-April up to the total of twenty-eight and a half divisions, four of which, however, would be armoured divisions, of less value than infantry for fighting in Italy.

The details of the regrouping carried out can be better described in connection with the actual opening of the spring offensive. Briefly, the effect was to bring Eighth Army Headquarters over west of the Apennines to take command of all British troops, except for a Corps on the Adriatic and the two divisions at Anzio, and with these to capture Cassino and advance up the Liri valley. Fifth Army would attack on a parallel axis to the south through the Aurunci Mountains and from Anzio on to Valmontone to cut Route 6 in the enemy's rear. This was the plan with which we were successful in May, unaltered except for the minor point of timing that the VI Corps attack was held back until the main attack had made good progress. It was not certain that our big attack would be made from the same positions as those held in February but I was already prepared for that. This had certain advantages. A major offensive from these positions gave the best chance of achieving our object, for between the main front and the bridgehead we were certain to trap and maul so many German divisions that reinforcements would have to be sent at the expense of the resistance to OVERLORD. If, on the other hand, our spring offensive found the Germans holding a connected front south of Rome, or withdrawing up the peninsula to the "Gothic" line, they would be unlikely to need reinforcements so urgently and, indeed, in the latter case, might be able to release formations for the west. However, our regrouping would take a long time and I estimated mid-April as the earliest possible date which could be expected for the resumption of the offensive.

General Wilson, in replying to my proposals, showed anxiety about the possible effects of a pause in operations. He began by stating that as far as operations in Italy were concerned, these must be conditioned mainly by the air factor. His general plan for Italy was to use the air to deprive the enemy of the ability either to maintain his existing positions or to withdraw his divisions out of Italy in time for OVERLORD. There was indeed, considerable optimism at Allied Force Headquarters about the ability of the air forces so to damage the enemy's communications as to force him to accept the alternatives of starvation, and reduction of ammunition reserves below the danger level, or withdrawal. This was based largely on an over-estimate of the disorganisation caused by bombing attacks on marshalling yards; but even the more effective policy of creating blocks at defiles, especially by the destruction of bridges, which was subsequently adopted with the support, and, in part, on the advice of my staff, never in fact achieved this desirable result though, it did seriously reduce the enemy's margin of maintenance.[77] General Wilson estimated, in the signal referred to, that the Mediterranean Allied Air Forces' bombing plan would make itself felt by the end of April and the effect would be to compel the enemy to withdraw "at least to the Pisa - Rimini line". The land forces would be required to keep up a continuous pressure during this time, otherwise the enemy might withdraw and the spring offensive would be a blow in the air. I could not consider it likely, on the basis of past experience, that the enemy would withdraw, and I was convinced that our spring offensive would find him still offering a most determined resistance. It was for this reason that I considered a regrouping absolutely vital to bring our full strength to bear at the critical point, while a continued attack in our present circumstances would merely weaken us to no good purpose. First, however, I would try once more to eliminate Cassino and seize some kind of a bridgehead; this would mean that there would be no serious lull in the fighting. Commenting on the air plan I limited myself to hoping: "that the weather will improve in time to give our air forces a chance to carry out their part of your plan. At present it is atrocious and shows no sign of change".

I explained my plan, on the lines of the appreciation of 22nd February, to the Army Commanders at a conference at Caserta on the 28th. We decided to relieve 5 British Division in I0 Corps by 88 United States Division at once and the former should then move to Anzio to relieve 56 Division. 56 Division had been severely reduced in fighting value during its short period in the bridgehead; General Truscott on the 26th reported it as inadequate to hold its present front.[78] We decided further that, at a later date, 34 United States Division should also move to Anzio. Steps were also taken to prepare the major reorganisation of the front for the coming offensive.

Fourteenth Army's Second Offensive at Anzio.

While the weather held up our renewed attack at Cassino it was already clear that the enemy was preparing another offensive at Anzio. He no doubt calculated that he had time enough before our threat to the "Gustav" line became serious and experience had given him a justified confidence in the strength of his defences there. His renewed attack could not be made in the same force as the first; there were large gaps in his divisions and morale had suffered the inevitable depression that follows the failure of an offensive of which much had been hoped. Mackensen therefore planned an attack on a smaller scale, using LXXVI Corps only; it was designed to narrow down the bridgehead by driving a wedge into the eastern flank to cut off the troops defending the Mussolini canal. If this were successful a further process of attrition might reduce the bridgehead to dimensions too small for safety. Four divisions, including two panzer divisions, were to make the assault, with a mobile division in reserve: it was to be combined with diversionary attacks on both flanks. VI Corps was prepared for the attack on 29th February and it was a complete failure: artillery fire and the firm defence of 3 Division broke up most of the attacks, a small penetration was made but was soon ironed out and by the afternoon of Ist March the enemy had acknowledged defeat.[79] He never again resumed the offensive and I now could consider the Anzio bridgehead secure, especially after we had captured Fourteenth Army's order of 4th March directing the assumption of the defensive. In March three German mobile divisions, 26 Panzer, 29 Panzer Grenadier and Hermann Goering Panzer, were withdrawn from the line, followed by II4 Jaeger. On the Allied side 5 Division relieved the 56th between 5th and IIth March and on the 28th 34 Division relieved 3 United States Division, which had been sixty-seven days continuously in the line. 56 Division went to the Middle East but the 3rd remained at Anzio in Corps reserve.

I reported on the situation after the repulse of these attacks in a signal on 5th March, when I had returned from another visit to Anzio. It was now much improved and, I added, "a more healthy feeling of confidence prevails throughout". I took the opportunity of summing up the balance of the six weeks fighting with reference to the rather misleading accounts which had been given publicity:

"From various reports I have read from home it appears that public opinion imagines that after the initial landing no effort was made to advance further. This is most distressing to me and the troops. Reference should be made to the many casualties sustained by the British in taking Campoleone where they were finally held at the foot of the Colli Laziali, and also the losses suffered by the Americans in trying to take Cisterna, where all attacks failed. After this, superior German forces attacked us in strength and threw us on to the defensive and we had a bitter struggle to maintain the bridgehead intact after being driven back from Campoleone. A man may enter the backdoor of a house unperceived save by the kitchenmaid who raises the alarm. But unless the inhabitants hide upstairs there will be a fight in the passage for the possession of the house. We are now fighting in the passage".

All this time the New Zealand Corps, now strengthened by the addition of 78 Division, was waiting for suitable conditions for the next attack on Cassino, which was intended to be our last attack before the spring offensive. In order to give our experiment in the use of heavy air attack its best chance we had laid down two conditions: there should be three fine days before the attack to ensure that the ground was dry enough for the use of tanks, especially in the exploitation into the Liri valley, and there should be good visibility on the day of the attack for the benefit of the bombers. For a fortnight after the repulse of the second German offensive at Anzio General Freyberg waited at twenty-four hours notice until, on the 14th, these conditions appeared likely to be fulfilled and the attack was ordered for the next day. The total weight of high explosive showered on Cassino amounted to over eleven hundred tons of bombs and nearly two thousand rounds of artillery fire, but when the New Zealanders advanced into the town they found the enemy still resisting. This was an extraordinary feat and much to the credit of I Parachute Division.[80] After personally witnessing the bombardment it seemed to me inconceivable that any troops should be alive after eight hours of such terrific hammering, let alone should be able to man their defences. I doubt if any other division in the German Army could have done it. With the defenders showing such spirit the heaps of rubble raised by the bombardment were actually an assistance to them, not least in preventing the use of tanks. However, we succeeded in clearing the greater part of the town and capturing Castle Hill. That night, contrary to the forecast the weather broke; torrential rain turned the valley, with its mass of craters, into a bog and deprived the night attack of the advantage of the moon. The same spirited defence was made on the mountain as in the town beneath. "Hangman's Hill", a small knoll protruding from the glacis of Monte Cassino a short way below the Monastery, was captured by 4 Indian Division on the 16th; this marked the limit of our gains in the heights above the town. Fighting continued in the town and by the 18th most of it was in our hands; but on the 19th an enemy counter-attack re-took a point between "Hangman's Hill" and the Castle hill. Our garrison of the former, which had been reduced by casualties, was cut off and progress in the town was halted.

On 20th March I informed both Army Commanders:

"The slow progress made so far in attacking the town of Cassino with the consequent delay in launching the attack on the Monastery, combined with the necessity of preparing the maximum forces for a full-scale offensive in the second half of April, makes it essential to decide in the course of the next twenty-four or thirty-six hours whether (*a*) to continue with the Cassino operations in the hope of capturing the Monastery during the next three or four days or, (*b*) to call the operations off and to consolidate such gains of ground as are important for the renewal of the offensive later".

Renewed attacks on the 2Ist and 22nd again made no progress and on the 23rd the attack was called off. The decision was taken to consolidate Castle Hill and the eastern part of the town; as a result the isolated troops on "Hangman's Hill" were withdrawn on the night of the 24th, and 4 Indian Division was relieved by the 78th. On 26th March I3 Corps took command of the sector and the New Zealand Corps was dissolved.

The three attacks on Cassino had failed to achieve what we had hoped from them but they left us with solid advantages. We had the greater part of the town, which gave us a bridgehead over the Rapido to use when we could concentrate the proper force for a renewed offensive. We could look forward to the next phase with confidence. Not only had we the Cassino bridgehead but we also held a large salient into the enemy's southern flank, won by I0 Corps' attack in January, which was of the very greatest value to Fifth Army in May; above all we had established, far in the enemy's rear, a strong Corps of good troops well supplied, in a position to cut all the enemy's communications when they should break out, or to threaten directly the possession of Rome on which the Germans set such value.

It was natural, perhaps, that some disappointment should be felt at home in view of the length of the pause which we now proposed before renewing the offensive. I felt it necessary to explain, on 2nd April: "The date is influenced by our ability to regroup the necessary formations for battle, marshal our forces and prepare the stage for an all-out, sustained offensive which will best assist OVERLORD in drawing in and destroying the maximum number of German divisions which would otherwise be employed against the Western invasion". It could indeed be said, reviewing the results of the winter campaign, that the Allied Armies in Italy were already making the greatest possible contribution consistent with their strength to the plan of diverting German attention to what was now a secondary theatre. Twenty-three German divisions, including many of the best in the German Army, were held down in Italy; Anzio alone had meant the equivalent of four divisions being lost to other fronts. The size of the German garrison in the Balkans was also influenced by the potential threat from Italy and by aid to the Partisan movements which could be provided from Italian bases. All this was achieved without our once having that numerical superiority usually considered necessary for offensive operations, with a mixed force of many nationalities and with little opportunity of flexibility in their employment. And it was already likely that the enemy, now forced on to the defensive in so awkward a two-fronted position, would be unable to meet our next offensive without drawing once more on his dwindling central reserve to prevent a great disaster.

PART III.
THE CAPTURE OF ROME AND THE ADVANCE TO THE ARNO.

Regrouping for the Spring Offensive.

In planning the strategy to be used when the Allied Armies in Italy should be able to resume large-scale operations I had laid down at the start that "to have a reasonable chance of effective penetration against organised defences in Italian terrain, it is necessary for the side that takes the offensive to have a local superiority of at least three to one in infantry". It was to the attainment of this prior condition that I devoted my attention during the month of April. My general superiority in divisions in May would be of the nature of just under one-and-a-quarter to one; these were, however, the best odds I ever enjoyed in Italy. But to convert this slight overall superiority into a local superiority of three to one at the critical point would not be easy. Neither side enjoyed any particular advantage in ease of lateral communications and, if Kesselring correctly appreciated our intentions, he could concentrate his strength opposite the threatened point as fast as we could. And it must surely be easy for him to form a correct appreciation; we could not be going to attack up the Adriatic, which led nowhere; our main effort must come somewhere west of the Apennines and almost certainly on the axis of the Liri valley. So much was obvious from the configuration of the ground and would be confirmed by the move across to the west, which we could not hope to conceal, of Eighth Army Headquarters and the majority of the British troops under its command.[81]

The directive on which Kesselring was acting, dating from the previous October but still in force, was to hold the Allies as far south of Rome as possible. He had been successful, at great strain and risk, in achieving this object during the winter months, but this very success had made his task more difficult. For the very reason that he had kept the Allies out of Rome for seven months the retention of Rome had acquired a still greater value for prestige, a consideration which might overrule the requirements of sound strategy; indeed for the same reason, though acting here with slightly lesser force, the Cassino position had acquired a semi-sacred character which would dictate a special effort to hold it. However, there was no reason for Kesselring to suppose that the task laid on him would be beyond his powers. He had twenty-three divisions to our twenty-eight, two of them Panzer and four Panzer Grenadier divisions. He had been receiving very strong drafts all through the winter, amounting on the average to fifteen thousand men a month, and his formations were therefore well up to strength.[82] New equipment, particularly an increased divisional allotment of assault guns, had arrived and the April lull had been used to good advantage in training. Morale was high and the troops could be relied on to give a good account of themselves.

Of the twenty-three German divisions in the country eighteen were in the two armies actively engaged;[83] as the battle developed all but one were drawn in, together with five more from other theatres. One of the two Panzer divisions, the Hermann Goering Division, was earmarked for France and was already halfway there, as it was re-forming around Leghorn, but in the event it too was drawn into the battle in Italy. 162 Infantry Division, a formation of Soviet subjects, mainly Turko-mans, had been brought in from Slovenia to take over responsibility for the Tuscan coast. During the lull in April the mobile divisions in Tenth and Fourteenth Armies were pulled out of the line into reserve. The infantry divisions in the line also thinned out wherever possible; in the Adriatic sector Russian troops were employed in the line to relieve Germans and even west of the Apennines battalions were occupying sectors formerly held by regiments. The enemy, therefore, was theoretically in a good position to meet our offensive owing to the presence of strong mobile reserves. It was our prime object to see that these reserves should be directed to the wrong sectors.

One thing was clear to the enemy: the Allies would have to make an attack up the Liri valley whatever else they did, and here the German plan of defence rested on three fortified positions known as the "Gustav", "Adolf Hitler" and "Caesar" lines. The first of these was the present main line of resistance which represented the rear line of the old "winter position", dented and endangered in some parts by the Allied offensives from January to March, but in principle the same as planned. It had stood the test of many furious attacks, which had revealed as nothing else could have done its strength and its weaknesses, and during the April lull these lessons had been applied in the form of much work on the improvement of the defences. However even before this, in December 1943, work had been started on a second line in rear which was given the name of "Adolf Hitler" until its fall seemed imminent, when it was changed to the colourless "Dora"; we usually called it the "Piedimonte - Pontecorvo line". Its function was to bar the advance up the Liri valley to a force which had succeeded in forcing the Rapido, and for this its left rested on Monte Cairo, descending to the valley through Piedimonte, and its right on the Liri at Pontecorvo; south of the Liri there were few permanent defences on this line for the country was very difficult. In the plain the defences were by May very strong; they included extensive belts of wire, anti-tank ditches, minefields and steel pillboxes, many of the latter formed by "Panther" tank turrets sunk in the ground. Against a frontal assault, therefore, the line was most formidable but it had one serious weakness: the presence of a strong Allied Corps many miles behind it at Anzio. A break-out from there, cutting Route 6, would make the "Adolf Hitler" line useless. The Germans therefore began to construct, in March, a third line of defences known as the "Caesar" line. This was a position to which Tenth and Fourteenth Armies would withdraw when, and if, the Allies forced a junction with the Anzio bridgehead; it might be called the last-ditch defence of Rome though, if it could be held, it gave reasonable depth forward of the city. Its main purpose was to block the gap between the Alban Hills and the Prenestini mountains through which run both Route 6 and the Alatri - Palestrina - Tivoli road. To the west of this gap the line continued across the Alban Hills to the left flank of the bridgehead, and to the east of it, it ran via Avezzano and

Celano to positions on the Saline river west of Pescara. Only the right flank of the line, where it actually covered Rome, had had much work done on it but the positions here were naturally strong.

This was, in brief outline, the problem which faced me in planning the battle for Rome. The solution eventually adopted was first given expression in an appreciation of 22nd February and the plan there proposed was agreed on at an Army Commanders' conference at Caserta on 28th February. In essence it involved making Fifth Army responsible for the sea flank, including Anzio and the Aurunci Mountains south of the Liri, and bringing the weight of Eighth Army into an attack up the Liri valley. It would mean a great effort of regrouping and would take a considerable time. This would in any case be inevitable, for all troops in both Fifth and Eighth Armies were exhausted and time was necessary, not only for them to be rested, but also for the arrival of reinforcements.

Two main problems faced the administrative staff: the maximum number of divisions which could be maintained in Italy by the existing port facilities and the practicability of maintaining the bulk of these on an axis west of the Apennines. The agreed figure for the first was twenty-eight divisions, which coincided well enough with the maximum number we actually had available. The second problem was made easier by the fact that the original plan for a rigid division between the lines of communication of the two Armies had not been adhered to and there were already bases and depots both in Apulia and the Naples area which allowed us the requisite flexibility at the cost, well worthwhile as it turned out, of a certain duplication. The administrative plan for the spring offensive was that Fifth Army should be maintained on its existing west coast axis; Eighth Army should have two axes, one for the Army, less the Polish Corps, on the west and one for the Poles on the east, and 5 Corps, which was to be under direct command of my Headquarters, should have an independent axis of its own on the east coast.

Orders for the regrouping were issued by my Headquarters on 5th March; the change of Army boundaries took effect from 26th March. I need not describe the actual steps by which we carried out the various reliefs but in order to understand their effect it will be useful to anticipate by giving our dispositions on the main front as they were on IIth May, when the operation began.[84]

In the sector from the Tyrrhenian Sea to the confluence of the Liri and the Gari Fifth Army had two Corps in line: on the left II Corps with 85 and 88 Divisions, and on the right the French Expeditionary Corps with four divisions, I Motorised, 2 Moroccan, 3 Algerian and 4 Moroccan Mountain Divisions and three Groups of Tabors of Goums.[85] In Army reserve on this part of the front was 36 Infantry Division. Eighth Army's sector extended from Fifth Army's right boundary to a line running from the highest peak of the Maiella, through the summit of the Gran Sasso and so generally north-west. The striking force was on the left. From the Liri to Cassino town was I3 Corps with four divisions, 6 Armoured, 4, 78 and 8 Indian Infantry, and behind it, ready to pass through or come into line on its left as the situation should demand, was I Canadian Corps with I Infantry and 5 Armoured Divisions and 25 Tank Brigade; on its right, poised and concentrated for the attack on Cassino, was the Polish Corps with two infantry divisions, 3rd and 5th, and an armoured brigade.[86] I0 Corps held the right of the Army's front, the mountainous centre of the peninsula, with a miscellaneous group of forces based mainly on 2 New Zealand Division; it included a parachute brigade, two armoured car regiments and an Italian brigade group. In Army reserve was 6 South African Armoured Division which was not yet complete in the country; its motor brigade was under command of I0 Corps at the time the battle opened. On the Adriatic coast was 5 Corps, under direct command of my Headquarters; it consisted of 4 and I0 Indian Infantry Divisions and was intended to play a containing rôle only.

Plans for the Offensive.

A conference of the two Army Commanders was held at my Headquarters in Caserta on 2nd April and I explained my plan for the battle. Eighth Army's task I defined as "to break through the enemy's main front into the Liri valley and advance on Valmontone"; Fifth Army's "to secure the Ausonia defile and advance *via* Esperia to the south of the Liri valley" and "to break out of the Anzio bridgehead and advance on Valmontone." Timing was also discussed. The programme of reliefs, in particular the move of I0 Indian Division from the Middle East, was taking a little longer than was expected and we now estimated that it should be possible to complete all preparations by 3rd to 5th May. I had originally calculated that, in order to give the best support to the western invasion, our attack should precede it by fifteen to twenty-one days; I was unaware at the time of the date chosen for OVERLORD but I was given to understand that a date for our attack in early May would suit General Eisenhower. It would also suit well with the phases of the moon. For the sake of troop movements at night it is always most useful to have a good moon and it would be full on 8th May. I eventually decided on a tentative D-day of I0th May.

There as a good deal of discussion as to the relative timing of the assault on the enemy's main line and the break-out from Anzio. There was much to be said for making all attacks simultaneous but the main disadvantage of this was that it would mean splitting our air effort between the bridgehead and the main front. My original idea was to lead with the Anzio attack so as to threaten or, if possible, sever the enemy communications between Rome and Cassino and thereby make easier the task of the assault up the valley. I decided against it, however, because the enemy's mobile reserves around the bridgehead, for reasons which will appear later, were strong and there was a possibility that an attack there might get held up short of its objectives and, secondly, because the enemy seemed to expect us to make our major attack there and I wanted to surprise him; as long as he remained in that frame of mind he would tend to regard our attack on the main front as subsidiary only. It was decided, therefore, to lead with Eighth Army's assault on the valley and Fifth Army's into the Aurunci. The force at Anzio was to be ready to open an attack on or after D plus 4 at twenty-four hours notice. I modified the original proposal to put another infantry division into the bridgehead; instead the remainder of I United States Armoured Division would be moved in (as late as possible to avoid unnecessary losses from shelling in the rear assembly areas) and 36 United States Division would initially be held in Army reserve, ready either to support the main drive or to move to the bridgehead at short notice.

The prospects of an operation against Elba were also discussed at the conference. This operation (codename BRASSARD) had been for some time under consideration at Allied Force Headquarters. If it could be carried out without subtracting from the resources for the main attack the capture of the island would have important results in the disruption of the enemy's seaborne traffic and would also greatly assist our cover plan. General Wilson was prepared to use 9 Colonial Infantry Division (French) from Corsica. His Chief of Staff attended the conference and promised to examine the possibilities of the attack urgently. On 7th April, however, I was informed that, for various reasons, it would be impossible to launch the attack before May and 25th May was chosen as the target date. This considerably reduced the value of the operation as there was reason to hope that by that date enemy coastal traffic south of Elba would be diminished by reason of our overland advance and he would not be likely to pay much attention to a threat to his right flank when he knew that all our strength was committed on the southern front.

A final conference was held on Ist May, also in the War Room at Caserta, at which decisions were taken on the remaining outstanding points. D-day was fixed at IIth May and H-hour at 2300 hours; postponement would only be on account of bad weather and would be for periods of twenty-four hours, the decision to postpone being taken not later than I600 hours on D-day. The breakout from Anzio, which it had already been agreed should be prepared for D plus 4, would take place when a penetration of the enemy's second line of defence on the main front (i.e. the "Hitler" line) had been achieved. It was hoped that there would be sufficient air resources to meet all the demands of both Armies but, if not, priority would go in the first phase of the attack to Eighth Army and in the second, the breakout from Anzio, to VI Corps. Until the attack was about to open the air forces would continue with their existing plan of attacks on enemy lines of communication. The effects of this were most valuable but, since this was the first time we had tried anything of this nature, there was a certain tendency to overestimate them. I felt it necessary to emphasize that our intelligence staff credited the Germans with at least four weeks supplies at full operational rates and ventured the prophecy that we should have at least twenty-one days actual fighting, quite apart from days spent in movement, before the enemy could be defeated. It was actually twenty-four days from the opening of the offensive to the entry into Rome.

The definitive order for the attack, Operation Order No. I, was issued on 5th May.[87] This added little new information to the decisions already taken at the preceding conference. Reference was made for the first time to 9I United States Division which was now beginning to arrive in North Africa and was due to move to Italy during the latter part of May and the beginning of June, to join Fifth Army. It had arrived in North Africa at the end of April from the United States and was originally assigned to Allied Force Headquarters but one Regimental Combat Team was ordered to Italy, arriving at Anzio on Ist June; the remainder of the division joined Fifth Army after the fall of Rome. I British Armoured Division, which was expected to arrive in June, could not in fact be brought over from North Africa until July.

General Leese worked out his plan for Eighth Army at a series of conferences for Corps Commanders and did not issue any written operation orders. The Army's task was to break through the enemy's front in the Liri valley and advance on Rome. This involved breaking through, or turning, both the "Gustav" and "Hitler" lines, and the Army Commander divided the former task into two phases. In the first phase 2 Polish Corps would isolate the area Monastery Hill - Cassino from the north and north-west and dominate Route 6 until a junction should be effected with I3 Corps, subsequently capturing Monastery Hill. I3 Corps would secure a bridgehead over the Rapido between Cassino and the Liri, isolate Cassino from the west by cutting Route 6 and effecting a junction with 2 Polish Corps, and then clear the town and Monastery Hill and open up Route 6. In the second phase the Poles were to gain contact with the "Hitler" line north of Route 6 and develop operations against it with a view to a breakthrough. I0 Corps, covering a wide front, was to secure the right flank and demonstrate in force in the direction of Atina with the object of leading the enemy to believe that an attack was being made in that direction, a plan which had at one time been considered but rejected. I0 Corps was also to be prepared to relieve formations as the battle progressed, I Canadian Corps, in Army reserve, was to be held in readiness either to assist or to pass through I3 Corps, as the situation required. 6 South African Armoured Division was also in reserve; it was not yet quite complete and it was intended to use it for exploitation. The total strength in the attack was about six to seven infantry divisions and three armoured divisions.

The task of Fifth Army on the main front was described as to "capture the Ausonia defile and advance on an axis generally parallel to that of Eighth Army but south of the Liri and Sacco valleys." In his Field Order No. 6 of 20th April General Clark further defined this as "to advance with both Corps abreast, secure the Ausonia defile and advance south of the Liri River to cut the Pico - Itri road." Subsequent advances would be made on Army orders. The advance to the first objective was divided into four phases. In the first the intermediate objective was the Ausonia - Formia road; the French Expeditionary Corps, on the right, was to take Monte Majo and secure the defile at Ausonia while II Corps, on the left, was to seize the high ground west of Castel-forte and Santa Maria Infante, thus threatening the southern end of the Ausonia road. These attacks were to be simultaneous with each other and with the Eighth Army attack. In the second phase the French were to advance across the River Ausente and drive through the central part of the mountains to capture Monte Revole from where they could threaten the Pico - Itri road. II Corps were to cross the Formia - Ausonia road and capture Monte La Civita and Castellonorato. In the third phase the French were to cut the Itri - Pico road near Itri and direct their main strength on the capture of Monte d'Oro, overlooking Pontecorvo on their right. II Corps was to advance on the left to Monte Campese and Monte Scauri and on the right towards Itri. The fourth phase would put Fifth Army all along the Itri - Pico road, ready for a further advance. This division into phases was only to be regarded as an indication and it was expected that, after the "Gustav" line had been broken, the progress of operations would be fairly fluid. The total strength in the attack was six infantry divisions, plus twelve thousand "goumiers," with one infantry division in reserve.

Enemy Dispositions.

On the main front, held by Tenth Army, Kesselring adapted his dispositions to a fairly close copy of our own. On the Adriatic sector he organised a holding force which defended along stretch of front from the sea to Alfadena, in the centre of the mountains, with three infantry divisions; this was put under General Hauck of 305 Division and called the "Hauck Group"; in function it corresponded to 5 Corps on our side. From Alfadena to inclusive Cassino was LI Mountain Corps with three divisions, including I Parachute in Cassino. XIV Panzer Corps commanded the Liri valley sector, the Aurunci mountains and the west coast as far as Terracina. In the valley was a "Blocking Group" in regimental strength from 305 Division (Hauck) plus a regiment of I5 Panzer Grenadier Division; in the Aurunci mountains were two infantry divisions strengthened by three battalions from a third in LI Corps and the remainder of I5 Panzer Grenadier Division guarded the west coast. Fourteenth Army, at Anzio, had five divisions, one a Panzer Grenadier division, in line and a Panzer division in reserve.

These dispositions, especially when considered together with the location of the German mobile reserves, which I shall come to shortly, were gratifying evidence of the success both of our security measures and of our cover plan. As I have already explained, in order to achieve a secret concentration against the vital point in sufficient strength to give us the necessary superiority it was essential not merely to conceal our troop movements but also to induce the enemy to believe that the troops whose whereabouts were concealed from him were intended to be employed in a totally different direction. I therefore early decided that we would take steps to simulate the intention of launching another amphibious landing on the west coast, this time directed against Civitavecchia. The fact that, as was well known to us, the enemy constantly overestimated our total strength in the theatre and, from his own lack of experience of amphibious operations, was bad at assessing the probability of such a threat, would help us in our design; moreover I considered that the surprise which had been sprung on him at Anzio would make him more than ever willing to believe such a landing possible and more cautious in guarding against a repetition of his surprise. Such a cover plan had the further advantage that Kesselring would be bound to expect that, as in January, we should begin with a strong attack on the Garigliano so that the actual opening of the offensive would not cause him to revise his appreciation. Orders to put this plan into effect were issued on 18th April. The forces which were notionally to be employed in the amphibious operations were to be I Canadian Corps with its two divisions and 36 United States Division. They were directed to simulate wireless traffic and take other measures to create the impression that they were training in the Naples - Salerno area for the proposed operations.

Besides the positive measures of deception it was necessary to carry out negative measure of concealment and camouflage on a very large scale. This presented great difficulties, since almost the whole of the front of attack was overlooked by the enemy and he had particularly good observation in the Cassino and Liri valley sectors. This observation covered not only the forward areas and approaches but also many of the gun areas and ammunition dumps and even, in the case of the Poles, Corps Headquarters. In this particular sector it was necessary to erect a vertical screen over a mile long to conceal vehicles passing along the road to the Headquarters of 3 Carpathian Division, which was in full view from Monastery Hill. Many new tracks had to be constructed in I3 Corps' sector leading down to the chosen crossing sites over the river, and these had to be carefully concealed with brushwood. All moves forward were made by night and dummy tanks and vehicles were left in the areas vacated by armoured formations. The new artillery positions were so well camouflaged that hardly a shell fell on them before the battle opened, although some of the guns had carried out registration from their new positions. The French concentration was particularly well concealed. Into their Garigliano bridgehead, with a radius of only some four thousand yards, they packed twenty battalions, five batteries and two divisional headquarters; the enemy only credited them with one division forward on the whole Corps sector. An even greater feat was the concealment of the entire Canadian Corps. This was vital to the success of the whole scheme for if the enemy had discovered their true location our bluff would have been exposed.

The plan succeeded perfectly; that it had done so was clear to us at the time from Kesselring's dispositions and was confirmed by documents subsequently captured. All the available German mobile formations were disposed up the west coast. Between the "Gustav" line and the bridgehead was I5 Panzer Grenadier Division (less a regimental group); between the bridgehead and the Tiber was 90 Panzer Grenadier Division (less elements in Tenth Army reserve); north of the Tiber in the Civitavecchia area was 29 Panzer Grenadier Division. In the last area there was also 92 Infantry Division, which had not yet finished training but was fairly complete. The other two mobile divisions were on the Anzio front, one, 3 Panzer Grenadier, partly in the line and the other, 26 Panzer, in reserve; these two also were regarded as available for use against a seaborne landing.[88] A natural corollary of this misappreciation was that Kesselring badly underestimated the forces which we could bring against his main front. As late as I2th May, the day after our attack, he calculated that between Cassino and the west coast we had six divisions in line, against which his four should be quite adequate, considering the strength of his defences; in actual fact we had the equivalent of over thirteen. By this means we ensured that we had our three to one superiority at the vital point, that the German reserves were far away and that they were eventually committed, when Kesselring had at last realised the trap into which he had fallen, reluctantly, piecemeal and too late.[89]

Opening of the Offensive.

In the Order of the Day issued before the attack I stressed the connection between the blow about to be delivered to the enemy in Italy and the assault from the west for which the world was waiting. The Combined Chiefs of Staff had directed that, for the sake of security, the connection could not be directly asserted and, after careful consultation with Washington and London, the most I was allowed to say was "From the East and the West, from the North and the South, blows are about to fall which will result in the final destruction of the Nazis and bring freedom once again to Europe, and hasten peace for us all". But, however concealed, no-one could miss the significance of the event and no sentence was more gratifying to those who had long years of Mediterranean campaigning behind them than the words which followed: "To us in Italy has been given the honour to strike the first blow".

In the late afternoon of IIth May the guns at Cassino and in the Liri valley ceased fire. By an odd coincidence the German artillery also ceased fire and a strange, impressive silence fell on the front. This caused much conjecture; the reason, we subsequently discovered, was that the Germans were intending to carry out reliefs at Cassino that night and were anxious to avoid hostile reaction. After an hour or two of this suspicious silence we opened up again with moderate harassing fire. On Fifth Army front also the day wore on quietly, with desultory artillery fire. The weather was cloudy with a little rain but the night was fine, except for ground mist in the Liri valley, and the forecast for the next seven days was good. At 2300 hours the whole of the artillery of Fifth and Eighth Armies, some two thousand guns, opened with a violent counter-battery programme. The Fifth Army infantry attack followed immediately, I3 Corps three quarters of an hour later and the Polish Corps two hours later, at 0I00 hours on the I2th. It was soon clear that, having already achieved strategic surprise, we had now added tactical surprise. Besides the reliefs already mentioned which were going on at Cassino Tenth Army was carrying out a reorganisation of command in the Liri valley. The headquarters of 44 Division, from north of Cassino, was being brought down to take command of the five German battalions then opposing I3 Corps. As a result of the attack it never took over and went back to its old sector again; the confusion caused can be imagined and must have both assisted our attack and prevented the German higher command from forming a true picture of the situation.

The first definite success was the capture of Monte Faito by the French, four hours after the attack began. II Corps made some progress into the enemy's line of defences but met most violent opposition, as did the French after their first local gains. North of Cassino the Poles attacked with great dash across the broken rocks and scrub, seamed and pitted by four months of bitter battles and, at the cost of heavy casualties, seized "Phantom Ridge," north-west of the Monastery. It was an exposed position and, as soon as damaged communications were restored, German artillery and mortars made it untenable. The Corps Commander therefore ordered a withdrawal to the start line at I400 hours on the I2th. In I3 Corps sector 4 British and 8 Indian Divisions each assaulted the crossings of the Rapido with two brigades up. The stream was flowing fast, both sides were putting down smoke to add to the thick mist provided by nature and, though the enemy artillery had been very largely silenced, the infantry in their deep dugouts were much less affected. Once across the river the leading troops soon plunged into a thick and continuous network of bunkers, wire, minefields and concrete emplacements. 8 Indian Division managed to make good its footing on the west bank and two bridges were completed by next morning in the divisional sector; 4 Division was unable either to enlarge its narrow bridgehead or, for the whole of the next day, to replace its precarious ferries with bridges.[90] The Eighth Army position, therefore, by the evening of I2th May was not quite as favourable as I had hoped; the right hand Corps was back where it had started, the left hand Corps had gained only about half of the objectives which it was intended to capture in the first two hours. Fifth Army, too, had made no significant progress and were still heavily involved with the strong enemy defences facing them without having achieved a breakthrough. Nevertheless I felt justified in reporting that evening that both Army Commanders were reasonably satisfied with the opening stages of the battle. Provided we could bring our full strength to bear before the enemy could reinforce all would go well but, I added, "there is no doubt that the Germans intend to fight for every yard and that the next few days will see some extremely bitter and severe fighting." The forecast was fully justified.

The firm resistance offered to Fifth Army on the first day of the attack began to weaken on the I3th. The two German divisions facing our six had been ordered to resist to the last in their prepared positions; this meant that when their resistance was overcome there would be few survivors to oppose our further advance. The French enjoyed a particularly heavy numerical superiority - and exploited it with great *élan* - and the advantage of good training in mountain warfare. On this day they succeeded in capturing Monte Majo, the key to the whole "Gustav" line in their sector, and pushed I Motorised Division up the Garigliano, capturing Sant' Andrea, Sant' Ambrogio and Sant' Apollinare and thereby clearing the whole west bank of the river. II Corps made small advances in the coastal area, but were still meeting very stubborn resistance. It was clear, as I reported that night, that the Germans still intended "to fight it out where they stand." This was particularly noticeable on I3 Corps' front also. It had seemed likely to me that, once the "Gustav" line was breached by a successful crossing of the Rapido, the Germans would offer only delaying resistance in front of the "Hitler" line in order to preserve sufficient strength for a successful defence of that line. They could scarcely hope to eliminate our bridgehead by counter-attack for they had practically no mobile reserve for such a purpose. However they showed no signs of weakening but fought with the utmost vigour to resist any advance up the valley, pulling in every spare battalion, and even company, which they could detach from formations not heavily engaged, particularly from the central sector. Nevertheless we continued to make progress here also. By great efforts a bridge was completed in 4 Division sector on the morning of the I3th, the reserve brigade was immediately passed over and gains of up to two thousand yards made. By the evening both divisions in I3 Corps were only a little short of their second objectives, and the bridgehead was secure.

This completed the first phase of the operation. I3 Corps was now directed to employ its reserve infantry division, the 78th, to accomplish the second phase: to cut Route 6 and isolate Cassino in conjunction with the Poles who, having regrouped and reorganised, were warned to be ready to renew their attack on the morning of the I5th. The move forward of 78 Division was delayed by difficulties in the river crossing and congestion and bad going on the west bank. It was clear that I3 Corps would not be in a position to cut Route 6 by the morning of the I5th and the Polish attack was accordingly postponed. 4 British and 8 Indian Divisions continued to make good progress and with 78 Division moving in between them we should be able to develop a good degree of strength; but it was now certain that the latter would have to make a deliberate attack against stiffening resistance, rather than the rapid exploitation which had been hoped.

In the meantime Fifth Army was now finding the going rather easier. In the hard struggle which had marked the breaching of the "Gustav" line the two German divisions had suffered crippling losses; once forced out of their strong prepared positions their weakness was even more evident and their collapse was rapid. On the 14th the French captured Ausonia and cleared all the country to the north between it and the Liri, thus exposing the right flank of the Germans opposing 13 Corps as far west as San Giorgio a Liri. II Corps captured Santa Maria Infante, for which they had been fighting since the attack began, on the 14th; next day they were able to advance three miles beyond it and capture Spigno and Castellonorato. The whole of the German right flank had collapsed and its casualties had been such that it was never to form a coherent line again. The most significant point was the great hole which had been blasted in the centre of the line where 71 and 94 Divisions, or what remained of them, had left a gap as they fell back in different directions, one towards the Liri and the other towards the coast. Into this gap General Juin[91] launched his Goums, with the order to advance west across the trackless mountains north of the great ridge of Monte Petrella and cut the Itri - Pico road, far in the enemy's rear. Almost unopposed they pressed on through country regarded by the enemy as impassable; by the 16th they had captured Monte Revole and their mountain guns were shelling the road. On their right 3 Algerian Division was that day attacking Esperia.

Fall of Cassino.

In the Liri valley the Germans continued to resist unaffected by the disaster to their right.

13 Corps was now, however, almost through the "Gustav" defences and ready for the final assault, with the Poles, on the Cassino bastion. General Leese decided that the Canadian Corps would have to be employed on its left for the attack on the "Hitler" line and it began to cross the river on the evening of the 15th, relieving 8 Indian Division. Next day 78 Division opened their attack northwest-wards through the last remaining defences of the "Gustav" line and made such progress that the same evening Eighth Army ordered the Poles to launch their attack on the morning of the 17th. The Poles had been obliged to carry out extensive reorganisation to fill the gaps caused by the losses of the earlier attack but, though their strength was reduced, they had gained experience. Once more they attacked the strong enemy positions on the ridges west of the Monastery and by 1800 hours had secured both "Phantom Ridge" and the commanding height of Colle Sant' Angelo. By the same time 13 Corps had cut Route 6. There was a narrow gap between, over the bare mountain side, which the Germans succeeded in keeping open that night long enough to pass through a large proportion of the garrison. In the morning of the 18th the town

of Cassino was finally cleared and at 1030 hours the Poles raised the red and white standard with the white eagle over the ruins of the Monastery.

The fall of Cassino immediately brought a radical change in the shape of the battle in the Liri valley. The enemy now had no reason for attempting to stand forward of the "Hitler" line; indeed he had already spoiled his chances of a successful defence by his obstinacy in holding Cassino, mainly for propaganda purposes. Another incentive to withdrawal was the discovery of the original misappreciation; up to the 15th the German radio had still referred to our attack as "diversionary" but the identification of the Canadian Corps on the 16th showed Kesselring the trap into which he had fallen and the overwhelming strength of the assault which was about to be launched against the diminished garrison of the "Hitler" line. So weak, in fact, and so disorganised were they that Aquino, the northern bulwark of the line in the valley, was almost carried by a *coup de main,* on the evening of the 18th, by a small armoured force of the Derbyshire Yeomanry.

It was impossible to provide reinforcement from elsewhere. On the right 71 Division had suffered a blow from which it did not recover for nearly two months. To save the southern end of the line 90 Panzer Grenadier Division, which was intended for the valley, had to be diverted south of the river to block the Esperia defile. It came up in detail and was defeated in detail; this was to be the fate of all Kesselring's mobile divisions. 15 Panzer Grenadier Division, the next to be engaged, was split already; part was in the Liri valley; part, recalled from its coast-watching rôle, was now put in west of Formia to buttress 94 Division which was being hard pressed by II Corps, and part moved back to Sant' Oliva, at the mouth of the Esperia defile. Here they came under command of 26 Panzer Division. The latter had been originally intended as the armoured reserve for Fourteenth Army against a breakout from the bridgehead but it had been grudgingly committed, again in small detachments, on 18th May. Its initial losses were extremely heavy.

On the 18th, while the attempt was being made to rush the "Hitler" line at Aquino, the Canadian Corps on 13 Corps' left was advancing to contact with the line. South of the Liri the French had captured Esperia and Sant' Oliva and the two mountains overlooking Pontecorvo, Monte d'Oro and Monte della Commune. II Corps had captured Formia and was about to enter Itri and Gaeta, both occupied next day. The battle had become fluid, and I took steps to increase the pressure. It was almost near the time for the breakout from Anzio and I therefore ordered 36 United States Division to the bridgehead; its arrival was spaced out over four days and we hoped it would pass unnoticed. It was extremely difficult to decide on the exact date for the VI Corps attack. General Truscott, the Commanding General, had asked for three days' notice, rather than the twenty-four hours in the original orders, so as to give him two nights to get his assault troops into position; it would have to be done by night, for by day the enemy had too good observation. This faced me with rather a difficult problem in prophecy, for the breakout would have to be timed carefully to fit in with Eighth Army's advance and it would not be easy to forecast where they would be in three days' time. On the main front Eighth Army were ordered "to use the utmost energy to break through the 'Adolf Hitler' line in the Liri valley before the Germans have time to settle down in it". The Poles were directed to press on to Piedimonte to turn the line from the north and the French, after reaching Pico, were to turn northwards, if at all possible, and envelop the southern end. If they could strike into the rear of the enemy facing Eighth Army, directed on Ceprano, we should be able to surround a good proportion of their force.

The operation for the capture of Pico proved to be a major one. Fearing just such a manoeuvre as I had planned Kesselring had strongly reinforced the area with his best troops from reserve, 26 Panzer and 90 Panzer Grenadier Divisions (both less large detachments) and was bringing over to their assistance the greater part of the two divisions from the Adriatic sector.[92] As a result the French made little progress on the 19th but on the 20th captured Monte Leucio, a high and dominating mountain between Pico and Pontecorvo. They were driven off it by a German counter-attack on the 21st but recaptured it on the 22nd; on the latter date, after two days of violent and fluctuating fighting, they finally captured Pico. This delay meant that their thrust northwards would now have less chance of cutting off any important German forces, for Eighth Army was about to assault the "Hitler" line and expected, once that was broken, to make fairly rapid progress, especially on the left. II Corps, to the south, were pushing on, entering Fondi on the 20th and reaching Terracina on the 23rd. The French were therefore ordered to advance north-west as well as north, directed on Castro dei Volsci and Ceprano. The main assault would be a combination of two great drives; by Eighth Army through the "Hitler" line and up the Lin and Sacco valleys and by VI Corps from Anzio on to Valmontone. The French and II Corps were to clear up the mountainous triangle between the two drives.

Breach of the "Hitler" Line.

In spite of their losses since the attack began and the defeat of their right wing, Tenth Army were still determined to defend the "Hitler" line in the valley between Piedimonte and Pontecorvo. The defences were even stronger than in the "Gustav" line which had already given Eighth Army so much trouble; they varied between five hundred and a thousand yards in depth and the main system, of reinforced concrete emplacements, was linked by tunnels and communication trenches into a mutually supporting whole. The main weakness was the lack of troops to man the defences but Kesselring had all the same ordered the strongest resistance. Eighth Army between 20th and 22nd May was preparing for the assault. Following the failure of the surprise attack on Aquino on the evening of the 18th heavier, but still hasty, attacks had been mounted on the 19th by 78 Division on the right and I Canadian Division on the left; these ran into heavy fire which showed the defences to be as formidable as had been expected. An attack in full strength would be necessary. The main blow was to be delivered by the Canadian Corps north of Pontecorvo while 13 Corps would maintain pressure at Aquino and concentrate forward ready to advance abreast of the Canadians. The Poles, who had captured Villa Santa Lucia on the 19th, were to continue the attack against the strongly defended hill town of Piedimonte which they had started on the 20th. 8 Indian Division, after its relief by the Canadians, had been sent back east of the Rapido; General Leese now decided to bring it forward again to reinforce I3 Corps, together with 6 British Armoured Division. These moves led to considerable congestion, a foretaste of the serious traffic jams which were to be a feature of the Liri valley operations.

The Canadian attack began at 0600 hours on the 23rd and met very stiff resistance. Our casualties were heavy, particularly in I Division, and the equally severe enemy losses showed the effort which had been made to hold the line. By noon on the 24th, however, we had cleared the whole position, except for Aquino, and 5 Canadian Armoured Division was exploiting rapidly towards the River Melfa which crosses the valley at right angles to the course of our advance and offered the next delaying position for the enemy's rearguards. It was certain, however, that it could only be a delaying position; the Germans must now withdraw in as good order as possible to the "Caesar" line south of Rome where Tenth and Fourteenth Armies could join hands to form a connected front barring any further advance north. It was a faint hope now. Tenth Army was a beaten force and, on the day the "Hitler" line was breached, Fifth Army began its attack from Anzio which was soon to reduce Fourteenth Army to the same state. On the same day Kesselring ordered forward his last useful formation in Italy, the Hermann Goering Division from Leghorn. This was the first of the formations which the Italian offensive diverted from the western front; I commented at the time: "I cannot in all honesty say that I should welcome any more German divisions just at the moment but from the broader point of view no doubt it is for the common good."

Break-out from Anzio.

With the arrival of 36 Division there were now seven divisions at Anzio plus the Special Service Force and a Combat Engineer Regiment. The perimeter was held by four divisions and the Engineer Regiment and in reserve were I Armoured, 3 and 36 Infantry Divisions and the Special Service Force. I and 5 British Divisions, holding the left flank, were put directly under command of Fifth Army; they were to revert to command of my headquarters after the capture of Rome. I issued the orders for the operation on 2Ist May; this was not three days' warning but it did give General Truscott the two nights he had asked for and proved quite adequate. The plan of attack by VI Corps envisaged two phases: first a penetration of the enemy defences to seize a firm base on an arc of about a mile radius round Cisterna, and secondly an advance through Artena on Valmontone. The first phase was the task of I Armoured and 3 Infantry Divisions and the Special Service Force; when it was completed 36 Division, the freshest formation in the bridgehead, was to pass through and advance to a line running across the valley below Velletri, supported by I Armoured Division. Then, reinforced by 3 Division, it was to advance on Valmontone. The enemy force opposing numbered five divisions. Almost all the armour in Fourteenth Army had been sent to the main front[93] leaving only the assault guns of 3 Panzer Grenadier Division and a handful of Tigers and Panthers. The Hermann Goering Division was on its way but its leading elements had got no further than Viterbo the day the attack began. The last hope would have been 29 Panzer Grenadier Division but that, released at last from its fruitless guard over Civitavecchia, had been rushed down to Terracina where it went into action against II Corps on the 22nd. Once again Kesselring's mobile reserves had been misdirected.

VI Corps' attack began at 0630 hours on 23rd May, half an hour later than the attack on the "Hitler" line. For the last ten days the Corps artillery had fired heavy concentrations on the German lines and gun positions at widely differing times; this was to accustom the enemy to being fired on heavily without an infantry attack following, and to encourage him to reveal his defensive fire plans; it also showed us, as might have been expected, that he was particularly alert at dawn. General Truscott decided therefore to attack an hour after dawn, when vigilance had relaxed. The result was complete local surprise. The enemy defences, though they had been under development since early March, proved less formidable than those of the "Hitler" and "Gustav" lines; the minefields, however, were numerous and well laid and caused unusually high losses in tanks. The attack continued to gain ground on the 24th and by evening Cisterna was completely surrounded; it fell on the 25th. The German 715 and 362 Divisions were by these actions practically eliminated as effective units, particularly the former. On the same day as Cisterna fell II Corps advanced from Terracina and made contact with the bridgehead. Our forces were reunited at last; more important still was the advance of I Armoured Division which had broken out northwards from the salient driven into the German defences and was advancing towards Velletri and Artena.

Fall of Rome.

I had now got my Armies into the position I wanted. Now that VI Corps had made contact with the rest of Fifth Army it was no longer an isolated bridgehead, a threat in the enemy's rear, but the spearhead of the extended left flank of my group of Armies. To use old-fashioned military parlance, I was now employing the "oblique order" beloved by Frederick the Great, with my left advanced *en potence* and my right, 5 Corps, refused. In my centre I had a very strong and concentrated force, I Canadian and 13 Corps under Eighth Army, with which, while my left held the enemy by forcing him to fight for Rome, on whose retention he set much value, I intended to drive forward on an axis parallel to the extension of my left, break through the enemy's centre thus weakened and pursue up the centre of the peninsula, east of Rome. This would enable me to carry out the classical manoeuvre of parallel pursuit, for at the same time Fifth Army would continue to press hard against the extreme right of the enemy, continually forcing back his seaward flank. There were, therefore, topographically considered, two objectives; to capture Rome and to pass a force east of Rome up the axis of the Tiber where it flows southwards from the mountains of Umbria. These two objectives I allotted to the two Armies, the former to General Clark and the latter to General Leese. This allotment of tasks had, in fact, been made before the battle began and the operation had proceeded so closely in accordance with my original plan that there was no need to vary it.

General Leese issued orders to implement this part of the plan before the attack on the "Hitler" line went in. After the breach of the "Hitler" and "Caesar" lines his intention was to exploit to Rieti and Terni. This would mean that he would have to pass very close to Rome on the east, between the city and Tivoli, in order to get on to the two best routes to his objective, Routes 3 and 4, the ancient Via Flaminia and Via Salaria; if Fifth Army were already in or approaching the city it might be difficult to avoid traffic congestion, for the days when all roads from all parts of the civilised world converged on the Forum have left their mark still on the road-net of modern Italy. Fortunately the same reasons had provided plenty of bridges over the Tiber, but I foresaw that we should have to take forceful measures about road priorities.

The main advance up the valleys of the Liri and the Sacco was entrusted to 13 Corps, right, and I Canadian Corps, left. The Polish Corps, weakened by its high casualties and the shortage of replacements, was to be withdrawn as soon as it had completed the task of clearing Piedimonte and the slopes of Monte Cairo. I intended to use it later on the Adriatic sector, taking the place of 5 Corps, after it had had a little time for rest and reorganisation. 10 Corps, reduced by the withdrawal of two brigades for 6 South African Armoured Division, was to secure the right flank of the advance by blocking off the roads leading south from Sulmona, Opi and Atina. The New Zealand Division was on the southern flank of the Corps and advanced through San Biagio to Atina and Sora, on the road from Arce to Avezzano. For the advance in the valley the stages were to be, first the line Arce - Ceprano; secondly Ceccano and thirdly Valmontone, or near it, to link up with VI Corps. The two Corps would advance abreast, a great concentration of strength in so narrow a space.

The Germans were as well aware as we were of their position and of the danger of the centre of their line being rushed while their right was locked in a furious battle for Rome. At all events they must block the valley long enough to allow the withdrawal of their forces from the area to the south of it and ensure an orderly withdrawal into the "Caesar" line before Eighth Army joined hands with VI Corps. They also had to block the Sora and Subiaco roads to prevent a further envelopment by these routes, but this was a much simpler task for both roads run through narrow defiles on either side of the Simbruini mountains and can be held without much difficulty against any force which can advance up them. From a captured operation order it appears that they intended to hold the line of the Melfa river with 90 Panzer Grenadier and I Parachute Divisions but the order was issued too late; by the evening of the 24th the Canadians succeeded in forcing a crossing. This was a notable feat by 5 Canadian Armoured Division, which had advanced rapidly from the breach in the "Hitler" line with the right flank of its advance open since the enemy were still resisting 13 Corps in Aquino. The small bridgehead, only one company strong, resisted violent enemy counter-attacks all that night. Next morning, the enemy having withdrawn from Aquino and Piedimonte, 13 Corps was able to advance to the river line with 6 Armoured, 78 and 8 Indian Divisions, and the remainder of I Canadian Corps, which had been delayed by bad going and the inadequacy of routes forward, came up to the support of its advanced guard. There were now five divisions moving forward in the same general direction on a front of rather less than five miles and skilfully laid minefields and German delaying tactics added to the difficulty of bringing so large a force to bear in so restricted a space.

13 Corps' plan provided for an advance up the northern side of the valley. The

Corps axis was to run through Arce, exclusive of Ceprano, to Frosinone where it would swing right handed to run more or less parallel with Route 6 through Alatri to Genazzano. It was impossible to get started, however, until the enemy had been cleared from Aquino and an attempt to pass 6 Armoured Division south of Aquino involved it in confusion with 5 Canadian Armoured Division which was using the same axis; an undetected minefield caused further delay. They got across the Melfa on the 25th and advanced on the early morning of the 26th directed on Arce; the Canadians to the south advanced at the same time towards Ceprano. Shortly before Arce Route 6 runs through a defile formed by the main mass of Monte Cairo on the right and, on the left, by two prominent hills known as Monte Grande and Monte Piccolo, both rising about seven hundred feet above the general level of the valley. Monte Piccolo had been occupied by a small advanced detachment of I Guards Brigade late on the 26th but during the night I Parachute Division infiltrated back onto both hills and prepared for a stubborn defence. An attempt to force the defile on the 27th ran into heavy enfilade fire and we were obliged to desist from this attempt and withdraw the small force from Monte Piccolo. For the next two days attack and counter-attack continued and it was not until late on the 28th that the Germans evacuated Arce and fell back behind the upper Liri, which here cuts across Route 6 at right angles. Meanwhile the Canadians had made an assault boat crossing of the Liri south of Ceprano on 27th May. It was a difficult operation in face of heavy enemy artillery and small arms opposition but the town was captured by midday. Our bridgehead was still only supported by ferries and it was not until the afternoon of the 28th that a hundred and twenty foot bridge was completed over which the armoured brigade was to pass to advance to Frosinone. It had to be used instead, however, by 78 Division which I3 Corps had sent round to the south to outflank the enemy defenders of the Arce defile. This delayed the pursuit by the Canadian armour.

The first few days of the break-out by VI Corps had gone so well that the first object of the operations could be deemed to be secured; we were already threatening Route 6 and had destroyed or driven off all the enemy on the right flank of the original bridgehead. However the Hermann Goering Division had now begun to arrive in the Valmontone area where it had been joined by part of 92 Infantry Division from north of the Tiber and by units of 4 Parachute and 65 Infantry Divisions withdrawn from the left flank of the bridgehead. It had suffered heavy losses from air attacks, for its move from Leghorn had been so precipitate that it had mainly been made by day; but we knew its quality and that it was likely to put up a very stout defence. It was therefore decided to change the direction of VI Corps' attack and throw the main weight against the weakened left shoulder of the bridgehead in a drive to secure a line from Lanuvio to Campoleone station. Early on the 26th General Clark issued orders for the change, which he described as "a new attack along the most direct route to Rome". The intention was to continue the drive towards Valmontone with 3 Division, reinforced, and to employ for the new drive the 34th, 45th and I Armoured, supported by 36 Division, which had not been used for its original mission owing to the speedy success of the first attack. Within the very short space of twelve hours from the decision being taken the new attack was under way. Troops of 3 Division with their supporting tanks advanced with great dash to Artena, which they surrounded and captured next day. They were unable, however, in face of stiffening enemy resistance, to establish themselves across Route 6. 36 Division, which was to form the link between this drive and the main attack on the left, advanced towards Velletri, driving the enemy back into their prepared defensive line in its sector.

The new attack towards Lanuvio jumped off at II00 hours on the 26th simultaneously with 3 Division's attack; the successful shifting of the axis of the assault divisions was a notable feat of staff work. Progress on the first day was rapid, for the enemy was now falling back to the "Caesar" line, and though resistance stiffened on the 27th we were still not in contact with the main defences and were able to advance to within two miles of Lanuvio and Campoleone station. Next day we came up against the "Caesar" line proper and in three days of desperate fighting we were unable to breach it. The defences were not on a very elaborate scale but the country was difficult, broken and abrupt and the enemy had perfect observation from the summit of the Alban Hills. Gallant attacks by 34 Division against Villa Crocetta, between Lanuvio and Velletri, on the 28th, 29th and 30th, failed to make a breakthrough and were halted with heavy losses. Further to the left 45 and I Armoured Divisions, attacking at the same time, also came up against an impenetrable line of defences after they had captured Campoleone station.

Fifth Army regrouped again, intending once more to shift the main weight of the attack on the "Caesar" line. The troops were tired and one more offensive might exhaust them for a time; but it was evident that the enemy, too, was tired, and one more blow might drive him from his positions. It was decided to make another effort in the Valmontone direction. On 29th May II Corps took over the command of the right sector of VI Corps' front, with 3 and 85 Divisions; the latter came up on the 30th. Speed was essential to prevent the enemy from settling down in the "Caesar" line, for now that the right of the line was holding well Kesselring was bringing up every possible reinforcement to the danger point north of the Alban Hills, covering Valmontone. On our side 88 Division was moving up to II Corps and the French, who were approaching Carpineto on the 30th, would soon be ready to intervene. General Clark decided, however, not to wait for this additional strength, nor for Eighth Army to come up, and all preparations were in hand for a renewal of the attack, when a sudden turn of fortune, rapidly put to account, changed the whole aspect of the operations.

36 United States Division, the strongest and freshest in VI Corps, had been employed between the two thrusts on Lanuvio and Artena and had gradually advanced until by 30th May it had a firm hold on the Artena - Velletri road below the steep crest of Monte Artemisio, at the south-eastern extremity of the Alban Hills. Patrolling boldly forward it discovered that the Germans, drawn off by the fighting at Lanuvio and the threat to Valmontone, had left Monte Artemisio unguarded. The opportunity was instantly seized and on the night of the 30th one regiment of the division moved off silently in column of battalions through vineyards and thick woods up the mountain. The new moon cast a faint light, some dogs barked but no enemy were encountered. By dawn the summit, Hill 93I, and the high ground known as Maschio

di Lariano had been occupied. A second regiment followed and the third drove in behind Velletri and cut the escape route for the garrison of that town to Nemi. By the evening of 3Ist May the whole division was firmly established on the heights and had brushed aside hasty counter-attacks by the Hermann Goering Division. The "Caesar" line had been pierced at a vital point and the last defences of Rome broken.

The American success in the Alban Hills and the desperate position of Fourteenth Army did not alter Kesselring's determination to offer a continued and most stubborn resistence in the centre of his line where Eighth Army were fighting their way up the valley of the Sacco. Arce held out until the night of 28th May but to the south the Canadians were able to make better progress towards Frosinone. 5 Canadian Armoured Division, having got itself firmly established across the Liri at Ceprano, pushed forward on the 29th on two axes north and south of Pofi. Two rivers, the Fornelli and the Maringo, cut across this line of advance and both formed serious obstacles. Pofi was captured that night after a heavy dive-bombing attack. Next day the armoured division made contact with the French in Ceccano and on the right moved up to Route 6 at a point some five miles short of Frosinone. On the 30th I Canadian Infantry Division, which had relieved the armoured division, captured Frosinone, which stands on a steep escarpment commanding the junction with the road leading north through Subiaco. On the same day I0 Corps captured Alvito and were threatening Sora on the Arce - Avezzano road. I3 Corps, between the Canadians and I0 Corps, was advancing with difficulty on Alatri; in this sector also contested river crossings over the many tributaries of the Liri were the principal enemy delaying tactics.

It was during this period that the crisis of Fifth Army's attack in the Alban Hills was reached and on 3Ist May, in order to give them more freedom of action, I shifted the inter-Army boundary north to leave Route 6 to Fifth Army. Eighth Army were thereby directed further northwards in conformity with the movements of the enemy whose withdrawal was now much more northerly, up the Arce - Avezzano and Frosinone - Arsoli roads. I0 Corps was pursuing up the former, with the New Zealanders in the lead, and I3 Corps up the latter, with 8 Indian and 78 Divisions. The Canadian Corps was to move up Route 6 through Ferentino to the Army boundary and prepare to pass 6 South African Armoured Division through in pursuit through Rome. Should the enemy succeed in stabilizing on the "Caesar" line I3 Corps would join in a concentrated attack to the north of the Canadians. Ferentino fell on Ist June and the Canadians pushed on to Anagni, which was captured on the 3rd. By this time the fall of Rome was clearly imminent and Eighth Army turned its best efforts to get forward 6 South African and 6 British Armoured Divisions to lead the pursuit. It was not an easy task, for the South Africans had to pass through the whole Canadian Corps and then found Route 6 blocked by the French Expeditionary Corps and II Corps. In spite of these irksome difficulties it was inspiring to have these two fresh armoured divisions with which to press the pursuit of a fleeing enemy. As I signalled the night Rome fell "If only the country were more open we could make hay of the whole lot. However you may rest assured that both Armies will drive forward as fast as is physically possible."

Fifth Army was ready to exploit 36 United States Division's success and the final orders were issued on 31st May. VI Corps was to attack on 1st June to secure the Alban Hills in its sector and advance to cut the enemy's withdrawal routes through Rome. 5 British Division, under Army command, was to advance on the left of VI Corps to drive against the Tiber and destroy any forces which were turned southwards by this thrust. II Corps was to secure the high ground north of Valmontone, seize the northern part of the Alban Hills and pursue any enemy attempting to withdraw northwards across its front. The Germans were still resisting desperately and still apparently with the same orders, to keep us out of Rome at all costs. Even now, with Fifth Army on the Alban Hills and their centre disintegrating under Eighth Army's blows, they continued to hope that the situation might yet be stabilized; captured enemy documents show that as late as 2nd June von Mackensen was still ordering resistance to the last and making plans for the redisposition of his forces with apparent confidence in the possibility of success. It is a striking example of German reluctance to yield ground even in the most serious circumstances, carried this time to a disastrous extreme.

II Corps, once more with its old divisions, 85th and 88th, reinforced by the 3rd, made the greatest advance on 1st June. On that day they finally crossed Route 6 and on the 2nd they captured Valmontone and advanced almost up to Palestrina. VI Corps met very heavy resistance on the 1st but succeeded in capturing Velletri which had defied us so long. On the 2nd there was still no sign of weakening in the enemy determination to resist. That night, however, the Hermann Goering Division, though reinforced at last by 334 and part of 26 Panzer Divisions, had reached the limit of its endurance and turned to full retreat. It withdrew with all speed to the Aniene river, east of Rome, which it held with a light screen; 334 Division, whose losses had been particularly heavy, was taken out of the line entirely and sent north to re-form. It was now time for the Germans fighting south of the Alban Hills to pull out as well or risk destruction against the Tiber. By the afternoon of the 3rd both II and VI Corps were pressing forward on Rome by all the roads that lead to the city. 4 Parachute Division, from the extreme right, was left as a rearguard behind which the remainder slipped away through the city, over the Tiber bridges and precipitately north.[94] The parachutists were able to delay II Corps long enough, in an action at Centocelle, to frustrate the attempt to drive southwards towards the Tiber and link up with VI Corps. At 1915 hours on 4th June the first elements of 88 United States Division entered the Piazza Venezia below the Capitol.

So Rome fell to the Allied Armies in Italy two days before the Anglo-American invasion was launched against the shores of Normandy. It was but the latest of many captures of Rome in history but it was the first time since Belisarius captured it fourteen centuries ago that the Eternal City had been taken by an invading army from the south.

Influence of Operations in France on the Italian Campaign.

The fall of Rome preceded the invasion of France by two days. It was very gratifying to have provided a heartening piece of news so appositely, but before long the progress of operations in France began to exercise an influence which was most prejudicial to our exploitation of the victory in Italy. I must recapitulate a little to explain the connection. At the Quebec conference in August, 1943, it was decided that the forces in the Mediterranean were to contribute to the invasion of France by effecting a lodgement in Southern France, in the area of Toulon and Marseilles, as a diversion to the invasion of Normandy. This was confirmed after the Cairo conference in December of that year. The assault, given the codename ANVIL, was to be in the strength of at least two divisions, the date in May; it was an assumed prerequisite that our forces in Italy should have reached the Pisa - Rimini line. It will be remembered that OVERLORD was at that time planned for May. It was decided, however, at a conference held in Algiers in February, 1944, that there was no hope of getting enough craft to mount ANVIL in May and, at the beginning of March, the date was advanced to early June, thus making it once more simultaneous with OVERLORD whose date had also been postponed. Three divisions were now to be released from Italy for the assault. But the serious shortage of craft still continued and on 10th April the Combined Chiefs of Staff laid down that ANVIL would probably not take place before mid-July; it was intended to use craft released from OVERLORD.

I was not directly concerned in these plans, which were discussed between the Combined Chiefs of Staff and Allied Force Headquarters, except in so far as the troops for the Southern France operation would have to come from my command. It was, of course, distracting to have this uncertainty weighing over us but it was at least satisfactory, after April, to know that I should be able to plan my operations for the capture of Rome without having to lose three divisions at short notice. However I still had to look ahead and, since March, I had been pressing for guidance on what the long-term plan for Italy should be. I got this on 22nd May in the form of the following directive from General Wilson:

"Your task will continue to be the destruction of German forces in Italy.

(*a*) In carrying out this task you should bear in mind the importance of the capture of the Ancona area since its ports and airfields may be of considerable importance in any operations which may be taken across the Adriatic.

(*b*) It is also my intention, subject to conditions at the time, and further subject to the provisions that your operations will continue to have overriding priority in the allocation of resources until you have captured Rome, to prepare and mount an amphibious operation at the earliest opportunity, in any case not later than mid-September. This operation might take the form of an amphibious assault in close support of your ground advance or, alternatively, in areas outside your responsibility. For one operation in the latter category now being planned it is anticipated that three United States infantry divisions and all the French divisions at present in Allied Armies in Italy will be required. To make this possible it may be desirable for you to relieve formations to be concentrated under control of Allied Force Headquarters as early as follows: one United States division by 17th June; one French division by 24th June; one United States division by 27th June; thereafter the remaining formations at longer intervals. The dates given are the earliest you may have to meet, and then only if you have captured Rome. You should take this requirement into account in planning both immediate and subsequent operations.

In addition to the above an experienced United States Corps Headquarters should be relieved by 1st June, if you can do so without interfering with your present mission.

You will be notified from time to time regarding the assault lift and shipping which can be made available to you but it is unlikely that there will be sufficient resources (shore to shore) available this year to enable you to undertake an amphibious operation on a scale in excess of one division plus".

It will be noted that no decision had been taken, at the time this directive was issued, whether ANVIL should be mounted or not; on the other hand the forces to be provided for it from Italy had now risen to seven divisions. This uncertainty was a very great handicap to our planning, and its psychological effect on the troops expecting to be withdrawn, especially on the French, was undoubtedly serious. It is hard to expect troops to give of their best when they are continuously "looking over their shoulder" to a new objective, particularly when it is so attractive an objective as the liberation of their own country. This situation lasted throughout June. On the 14th I was instructed that VI Corps Headquarters was to be withdrawn at once, 3 Division on 17th June and the 36th on 27th June. On the 24th a French division was to be withdrawn to the Naples area, followed by a second in the first week of July. On the same day the Combined Chiefs of Staff signalled "the destruction of the German armed forces in Italy, south of the Pisa - Rimini line, must be completed. There should be no withdrawal from the battle of any Allied forces that are necessary for this purpose". Nevertheless I was informed on the 16th that, in order to preserve the possibility of mounting ANVIL, it was necessary to proceed with the programme of withdrawal of forces already laid down. We could still hope that we might get these troops back again later but this became more unlikely after it was known that General Eisenhower had strongly recommended the operation in a signal of 23rd June. The final decision in its favour was communicated to me on 5th July. ANVIL[95] was eventually launched on 15th August.

Whatever value the invasion of Southern France may have had as a contribution to operations in North-western Europe its effect on the Italian campaign was disastrous. The Allied Armies in full pursuit of a beaten enemy were called off from the chase, Kesselring was given a breathing space to reorganise his scattered forces and I was left with insufficient strength to break through the barrier of the Apennines. My Armies, which had just been built up into a strong, flexible and co-ordinated instrument, inspired by victory and conscious of their own superiority, were reduced once more to the shifts and improvisations which had marked the previous winter and faced again with the problems of overcoming not only the difficulties of the

Italian terrain and the stubbornness of the enemy's resistance, but also the lack of manpower on their own side.[96] I express no opinion on the correctness of the decision, but I was, to say the least, disappointed that our victory was not to be exploited as it deserved.

The Pursuit North of Rome.

The German flight north from Rome was, in the first few days, rapid and rather disorganised. The roads along which their flight had gone presented an amazing sight; mile after mile they were littered with the wrecks of armoured and other vehicles, destroyed either by our air forces or by our armoured pursuit or abandoned and wrecked by their drivers when fuel ran out. It was still Kesselring's intention, however, to delay us as far south as possible and retain as much territory as he could. He was, in fact, now back again in the same position as in September 1943, or rather in the position he then expected to find himself in, that is he was withdrawing up the leg of Italy pursued by a superior force. Now also, as then, his task was to fight a delaying action in front of a prepared position but this time his "winter position" was further back. The "Gothic" line, as it was called,[97] ran along the summit of the Northern Apennines; it was intended to be held to the last to preserve the rich lands of Northern Italy. When Rome fell it was far from completion and though for the immediate future the Germans would have to fall back quickly to avoid a complete rout, especially in the relatively open west coast sector, it would soon be necessary to bring this withdrawal to a halt and gain time for more work to be done. It was necessary, therefore, for Kesselring to weigh carefully the dangers involved in making a stand too soon, and thereby risking another defeat before he had had time to reorganise his forces, and, on the other hand, in delaying that stand too long and allowing the Allies to make contact too soon with the "Gothic" line. It was certainly essential to carry out as soon as possible some measure of reorganisation for at the moment divisions were not only severely weakened by casualties but also in most cases split up into small groups, often under various different commands. It shows the efficiency of the German leadership and staff work that they were successful in bringing order out of this chaos and rallying so quickly a defeated and, in part, dispersed army.

Since our offensive began on IIth May all the German divisions which were at that date in Tenth and Fourteenth Armies, including the two originally on the Adriatic coast, had been drawn into the battle south of Rome and west of the Apennines. Of the seventeen involved at that time three, the 7Ist, 94th and 7I5th, had temporarily ceased to exist as effective formations and the remainder had all been heavily mauled. Of the reinforcements brought in before the fall of Rome the Hermann Goering Division had suffered extremely heavy losses and 92 Infantry Division had been so battered that it was disbanded and never re-formed. However, in spite of the fact that the invasion of France had now begun, and the Russians were threatening East Prussia, Kesselring had been promised considerable reinforcements of new formations, quite apart from the normal replacement drafts. It is strikingly significant of the different value attached by the opposing sides to the Italian campaign that at the very same time as the Allies were withdrawing seven divisions from Italy to France the Germans were despatching to Italy the equivalent of eight divisions, some of them actually from the threatened West. I9 and 20 Luftwaffe Field Divisions came from Denmark and Holland respectively, I6 S.S. Panzer Grenadier and 42 Jaeger Divisions from the Balkans and 34 Infantry Division from Russia. Three other infantry divisions which were forming in Germany, one of which had already been equipped for the Russian front, were sent to Italy where they were given the numbers of divisions which had been destroyed in the battle for Rome and incorporated their survivors. In addition a battalion of Tiger tanks, 504 Heavy Tank Battalion, was taken from the G.H.Q. reserve in the great tank centre of Mailly-le-Camp in France. In view of the general German shortage of armour and the desperate need for heavy tanks to employ against General Eisenhower's gradually widening bridgehead, this transfer seems to me to be particularly significant.[98]

I reviewed the situation in a signal to General Wilson on 7th June. My object I defined as "to complete the destruction of the German armed forces in Italy and, in the process, to force the enemy to draw to the maximum on his reserves, whereby I shall be rendering the greatest assistance to the western invasion of which my Armies are capable". I calculated that the enemy, in spite of such reinforcements as we knew to have arrived, was not strong enough to hold the "Gothic" line against a really powerful attack. Of our own troops I wrote "I have now two highly organised and skilful Armies, capable of carrying out large scale attacks and mobile operations in the closest co-operation. Morale is irresistibly high as a result of recent successes and the whole forms one closely articulated machine, capable of carrying out assaults and rapid exploitation in the most difficult terrain. Neither the Apennines nor even the Alps should prove a serious obstacle to their enthusiasm and skill". I proposed, therefore, to give the enemy no breathing space but to continue to press the pursuit up the centre of the peninsula to the line Bibbiena - Florence - Pistoia - Pisa and then over the Apennines; if they were held in force I would mount a full-scale attack on Bologna not later than I5th August. I would then establish a firm base in the area of Bologna and Modena for the development of further operations either westwards into France or north-eastwards into Austria according to the requirements of Allied stategy at that time. At the same time I would secure and protect any airfield areas in the Po valley considered necessary for the operation of the Allied Air Forces. As I explained, this plan was only possible on the assumption that I retained the forces I then had in Italy; I had to work on this assumption as long as I could while the fate of ANVIL was being decided.

My tactical plans for the pursuit north of Rome envisaged two main lines of advance: along the west coast for Fifth Army and up the axis of the Tiber, both east and west of the river, for Eighth Army. Fifth Army's first objective was the port of Civitavecchia, which was now vital for our maintenance; Eighth Army was directed on the area of Terni and Rieti, the capture of which would disrupt any German plans for forming a continuous front across the peninsula and would threaten with envelopment the left wing of Tenth Army. From the point of view of terrain the former task was rather the easier, for the country is of an open, rolling nature while the route up the Tiber, though not difficult by comparison with the country between Naples and Rome, offered many opportunities for delaying actions, especially on the east bank of the river. Enemy opposition was also much weaker on our left, for most of Kesselring's divisions had withdrawn northward east of the Tiber and, having rashly destroyed all the bridges from Rome as far as Todi, sixty miles to the north, were having great difficulty in getting across to the west to come to the support of the weaker forces retreating up the west coast. VI Corps therefore set the pace, with 34 Division on the coast and the 36th inland, both supported by armour from I Armoured Division. At I030 hours on 7th June elements of 34 Division entered Civitavecchia. The speedy capture of this port, the most important between Naples and Leghorn, was a considerable gain and, although the Germans had carried out extensive demolitions, particularly fine efforts by the port reconstruction companies made it usable earlier than had been expected. The first Landing Ship, Tank berthed on I2th June and Liberty ships began unloading in the roads on the I4th.

The boundary between the German armies was now the Tiber, with Fourteenth west and Tenth east. General von Mackensen, the former commander of Fourteenth Army, had been relieved from his command after the fall of Rome and replaced on 6th June by General Lemelsen. To his assistance Kesselring directed all the newly arrived reinforcements, 356 Infantry Division from Genoa, 20 Luftwaffe Field Division from Holland, and the I62nd from Leghorn. The last named heralded its arrival with a charge of Cossack cavalry; this was the first we had seen of an arm of which we had heard such interesting reports but it proved ineffective against Fifth Army and the experiment was not repeated in Italy. In Tenth Army XIV Corps, retreating up the Rieti axis, had in the area of Carsoli and Orvinio a mixed group of 305 and 94 Infantry Divisions and, lined up north of the Aniene river from east of Tivoli to the Tiber, I Parachute, I5 Panzer Grenadier and Hermann Goering Divisions.

I3 Corps was the pursuit Corps for Eighth Army and the plan was to employ two armoured divisions in the lead, 6 South African up Route 3, the Via Flaminia, west of the Tiber, and 6 British up Route 4, the Via Salaria, east of the Tiber; 4 British Infantry Division with 25 Tank Brigade followed up the latter on the minor road leading due north from Tivoli through Palombara.[99] The French were already across the Aniene, east of Rome, which gave an initial advantage to the pursuit on the right but on the left the South Africans were hampered by having to pass through II Corps to use the Rome bridges across the Tiber. They were clear through, however, by the morning of the 6th and by that evening a dashing advance of thirty-three miles brought them to Civita Castellana. East of the Tiber our advance was more strongly opposed, in particular by the Hermann Goering Division which gave 6 British Armoured Division a stiff fight for Monterotondo; 4 Division also met resistance on the Palombara road from I5 Panzer Grenadier Division and I Parachute Division.

The situation was developing so favourably west of the Tiber that on the morning of 7th June I sent fresh orders to both Armies and to 5 Corps:

"I. The enemy has been greatly weakened by the fighting since IIth May and is now thoroughly disorganised. He is certainly in no position at present to launch a serious counter-attack. He will continue to suffer seriously during his retreat from attacks by our Air Forces and advancing columns.

2. To take full advantage of this situation Eighth Army will advance with all possible speed direct on the general area Florence - Bibbiena - Arezzo and Fifth Army on the general area Pisa - Lucca - Pistoia. Armies will maintain general contact on their inner flanks but will not wait on each other's advance. Enemy resistance will be by-passed wherever possible in order to reach the above vital areas quickly. Eighth Army will be responsible for any protection that may be necessary on its right flank.

3. To save transportation resources and bridging material 5 Corps will not follow up the enemy on their front. If the advance of Eighth Army fails to force the enemy to abandon Ancona, Polish Corps will be moved forward later on Eighth Army's eastern axis to take Ancona from the west.

4. The Commander-in-Chief authorizes Army Commanders to take extreme risks to secure the vital areas mentioned in paragraph 2 above before the enemy can reorganise or be reinforced."

On these orders the pursuit was pressed rapidly. The main difference was that 13 Corps was no longer directed on the Terni - Rieti area but farther afield; this meant that the South Africans were no longer to turn eastwards to cross the Tiber to seize Narni as originally planned, but to press on to Orvieto. Here again a difficult question of routeing was involved since both they and II Corps were in danger of arriving simultaneously at Viterbo. I decided to give precedence to the armour and II Corps was halted in place until the South Africans were through. Meanwhile VI Corps made rapid progress up the coast in spite of the arrival of two fresh German divisions. On the 9th it captured Tarquinia and a task force from I Armoured Division, operating on the inland flank, cut into II Corps' territory to capture the Viterbo airfield. On the IIth, however, VI Corps was relieved by IV Corps and moved to Naples, coming under command of Seventh Army for operation ANVIL. II Corps had pushed forward with 85 and 88 Divisions up the axis of Route 2 and consolidated the position between VI and 13 Corps. It was relieved by the French on 10th June. On the 9th Eighth Army had also carried out a regrouping; the Tiber was now to be the boundary between 13 and 10 Corps, with the latter commanding all the troops formerly in 13 Corps east of the river. The final result was to give 13 Corps 78 and 6 South African Divisions, with 4 Division in reserve, and 10 Corps 6 British Armoured and 8 Indian Infantry Divisions, with 10 Indian as reserve. The Canadians were grounded south of Rome. The Polish Corps, which had passed to Army Group reserve on 26th May after the capture of Piedimonte, assumed command of the Adriatic sector from 5 Corps on 17th June, remaining under direct command of my headquarters until 29th June when it passed to Eighth Army. The enemy had begun to fall back in the Adriatic sector on 8th June and on the 10th we occupied Pescara and Chieti.

For ten days after the regrouping the pursuit continued, though the enemy was now offering stronger resistance. Kesselring had at last managed to shift sufficient strength westwards to feel secure against a serious outflanking by Fifth Army up the west coast and he was beginning to feel the benefit of the fresh reinforcements he had received from elsewhere. He could now put twenty to twenty-one of his twenty-six divisions into the line. The revival of his strength was shown by the stiff action at Bagnoregio which delayed the fall of Orvieto to 78 Division until I4th June. IV Corps on the extreme left also had to fight hard for Orbetello and Grosseto; the latter fell on the I5th but little advance had been made beyond it by the 20th, for the Ombrone river was a difficult obstacle. During the same period of I0th-20th June the French, under a provisional "Pursuit Corps" Headquarters commanded by General de Larminat,[100] advanced up Route 2 on the right of Fifth Army with two divisions, I Motorised and 3 Algerian. On the IIth they seized Montefiascone and on the I8th stormed the strong position of Radicofani, the highest point on the road from Rome to Florence. By the 20th advanced elements were on the Orcia river, a tributary of the Ombrone. Our main forces had now reached the line on which the enemy had decided to stand but on the Adriatic they were not yet up with that line which in this sector was the River Chienti. On I6th June I had instructed the Poles to press on with all possible speed to secure the capture of Ancona. The Polish advance was indeed rapid and by the 20th they had crossed the River Aso and captured Fermo and Pedaso. On the 2Ist they even managed to secure a small bridgehead over the Chienti but next day this was destroyed by a heavy enemy counter-attack. It was clear that to force the Chienti would require a full Corps attack. General Anders[101] decided that in view of the time needed for concentration and for bringing up the necessary supplies and ammunition the probable date would be 4th July. I agreed to this plan and proposed to stage the attack in such a way as to be able to press directly on from the Chienti to Ancona, some twenty-two miles beyond the river.

On I4th June I divided my headquarters, and, leaving the bulk of the administrative branches and services in Caserta, to follow to Rome when space was available, I created a small Advanced Headquarters, consisting of my operational staff only. This was the system on which I had worked in Tunisia and Sicily and, now that the comparatively static period of the winter was over, I was anxious to be as close behind the Armies as possible. On I4th June I opened this advanced headquarters at Frascati, using for offices a small building which had previously been used for the same purpose by Field-Marshal Kesselring. This was soon left too far behind by the speed of our advance, and on 25th June I moved to a camp site on the eastern shores of Lake Bolsena.

The capture of Elba, early plans for which I have already mentioned, took place about this time. I originally wanted this operation to be launched if possible before the spring offensive opened but it had been postponed to a date between 20th and 25th May. On I6th May I was informed that it had been further postponed till mid-June. This removed almost all the value of the operation as by that time our troops, advancing overland, would be almost level with the island and on I2th June I asked whether the forces earmarked for Elba could not rather be used for a landing on the mainland in support of Fifth Army. However, this was considered unacceptable as the French would not consent to the use in Italy of 9 Colonial Infantry Division, which they wanted to keep for the landings in France. The operation therefore went in as planned in the early morning of 17th June; the occupation of the island was complete by the afternoon of the 19th. Steps were taken to emplace medium guns in the north-eastern corner of the island to command Piombino but the town fell on 25th June without the necessity for their use.

The Battle of the Trasimene Line.

It was clear that Kesselring had now decided not merely to stiffen his delaying resistance but to make a stand, although he was approaching the broadest part of the Italian peninsula. He calculated that the momentum of our pursuit, after the exhilaration of the chase north from Rome, now left a hundred and thirty miles behind, must be starting to flag and that he had his own troops well enough under control again to rally them for a defensive action on a coherent front; by thus imposing a pause on us he would gain time and space to prepare the "Gothic" line. His decision began to make itself felt about 20th June. The chosen line was based on the east coast on the River Chienti; west of the Apennines the key points were the high ground north of Perugia, Lake Trasimene and Chiusi, from where the line continued eastwards along the River Astrone to the Orcia and the upper Ombrone. By now the Germans were to a certain extent reorganised and regrouped and both armies were on the same line and fairly well balanced in strength. They had nineteen divisions, admittedly nearly all under strength, in the line and six in reserve; as against this we were maintaining the pursuit with nine only. The Army boundary ran through Montepulciano with Tenth Army east and Fourteenth west. On the Adriatic Tenth Army had LI Mountain Corps of four divisions, rather under strength. From the Tiber to the Army boundary was LXXVI Panzer Corps with seven divisions, including the good I5 Panzer Grenadier, I Parachute and Hermann Goering Divisions; it was this Corps which was given the task of delaying our I0 and I3 Corps either side of Lake Trasimene. In Fourteenth Army I Parachute Corps, between Montepulciano and Montalcino, had four divisions in the line, including 26 Panzer and 29 Panzer Grenadier. XIV Panzer Corps, on the west coast, was weaker; it had five divisions but only two, the 3rd and 90 Panzer Grenadiers, were of good quality and the other three were definitely poor. As the situation here deteriorated this Corps had to be reinforced with battle groups from two other divisions, I6 S.S. and 42 Jaeger. The general situation, however, was hopeful for the Germans; their best divisions were equally spaced at the vital points and had received heavy drafts of reinforcements and 34 Division was in process of arriving from the Russian front.

The line selected for a stand had been well chosen, in spite of its length.[102] There were no very obvious natural obstacles to our advance, except the river lines on the two coasts, and no prepared defences; but the country is hilly and in general thickly cultivated, especially in the vine-growing areas in the centre of the line. Our own lines of communication were severely stretched and these difficulties would not be eased before the capture of Leghorn and Ancona. The reconstruction of the railways was being pushed ahead with good speed but at the moment Eighth Army railhead was back at Roccasecca, two hundred miles from the battle front. The time had also been well chosen for two reasons, one of which was a most unusual spell of bad weather between 17th and 20th June. The more important reason was unknown to Kesselring: the uncertainty of the future on the Allied side which had reached its climax just at this time. I explained the situation on 28th June:

"The ghost of ANVIL hangs heavily over the battle front. For example the Americans have been ordered to send back 517 Regimental Combat Team and 117 Cavalry Reconnaissance Squadron which are actually engaged in contact with the enemy. They are also required to release now an engineer regiment and other service units required for the conduct of the battle. The French do not appear to be putting their hearts into the present operations and the reason is undoubtedly because they have their eyes turned in another direction. The air effort will shortly be curtailed owing to moves of fighting units to Corsica. Eighth Army are not directly concerned with ANVIL but as long as there is doubt and uncertainty about the future so long will there be a moral weakening. Armies have a very delicate sense and they are beginning to look over their shoulders. You will no doubt remember the Biblical quotation: 'If the trumpet give an uncertain sound who shall prepare himself for battle?'. If the momentum of my offensive is to be kept up to the maximum I must receive confirmation that the Italian campaign is to be backed. If on the other hand it is decided to go all out for ANVIL then I must know so that I can recast my present plan. In the event of the latter decision I have proposed that I should fly home and take certain proposals aimed at producing the best results my emasculated forces will be able to achieve in support of the war effort."

The battles for the Trasimene line may be considered as having lasted from 20th to 30th June. They were most severe in the centre where the Germans opposed 10 and 13 Corps; on the west coast, although the American advance was considerably slowed down, as compared with the first two weeks after the fall of Rome, the Germans were unable to prevent a steady gain of ground. IV Corps on the left, with 36 and 1 Armoured Divisions leading, captured Follonica on 24th June and Piombino on the 25th. Then stiffer resistance was met, particularly inland where 1 Armoured Division, opposed by a skilful enemy and difficult country, lost seventy-one tanks in the course of these ten days. The stiffest resistance was at Cecina, at the mouth of the river of the same name; the battle for the town lasted from 29th June to 1st July and cost 34 Division, which had relieved the 36th, fairly heavy casualties. 16 S.S. Division had been brought in here to strengthen the German defence and fought with skill and fanaticism. The French, directed on Siena, were held up from the 22nd to the 26th June on the River Orcia and were able only to make an advance of some two miles. On the night of the 27th, however, the Germans began to withdraw and only delaying actions were fought south of Siena, which was entered on 3rd July. By the 7th, with the capture of Colle di Val d'Elsa, the whole of Route 68, from its junction with Route 2 to the sea, had been secured.

The rolling hill country either side of Lake Trasimene, vine-clad and thickly cultivated, offered a wealth of alternative positions to the defenders and imposed a severe delay on 13 and 10 Corps. Eighth Army's task was to secure the general area of Florence, Bibbiena and Arezzo as quickly as possible as a base for operations against the Northern Apennines. For the attainment of this purpose the routes forward were limited: in the Army sector only one road appeared capable of carrying the weight of a highly mechanized Corps, Route 7I which skirts the western shore of Lake Trasimene and runs up the Chiana valley to Arezzo. There is a secondary road running up the west side of the valley through Sinalunga to Arezzo but east of the lake there is no route forward until the Tiber valley is reached and the road here, through Perugia and Umbertide to Sansepolcro, is narrowly confined in the river valley and unsuitable for a rapid pursuit. Looking further ahead Arezzo was likely to prove a bottleneck in the advance on both Bibbiena and Florence. The original Eighth Army plan was to send 10 Corps up Route 7I and 13 Corps by the Sinalunga road; but it was soon seen that the latter road would be quite inadequate for the task and the inter-Corps boundary was therefore altered to run through the centre of the lake. This meant that the two Corps could not give mutual support and, after the north end of the lake had been reached, their axes would again diverge.[103]

13 Corps had the more important task, the easier and more direct route, and met the stronger opposition. It had three divisions, 6 South African Armoured, 4 and 78 Infantry and two armoured brigades, 9 and I Canadian. 78 Division was due to be relieved at the end of June and leave the theatre for a short rest and reorganisation in the Middle East. It would be difficult to reinforce, should that be necessary, for all Army reserves had been left behind near railhead, for ease of administration; it was intended, however, to bring up gradually 10 Indian Division from 5 Corps. Facing 13 Corps were three German divisions, I Parachute, 334 Infantry (four regiments strong) and Hermann Goering, and part of a fourth to the west, 356 Infantry. Their chosen position was anchored on the east on the lake and on the west on a ridge of high ground extending north-west from Chiusi; the latter town, an ancient hilltop city of the Etruscans, was held as a strongpoint by the Hermann Goering Division. West of Chiusi the hills are steep and badly roaded and there was no chance of the French in Radicofani exercising any pressure to their right. Our attack would have to come between Lake Trasimene and Lake Chiusi and here the Germans had prepared a series of defences in depth based on small woods and farms on the north bank of the small River Pescia which proved a useful anti-tank obstacle. In front of the Pescia they held a line of outposts, the southernmost of which were the villages of Sanfatucchio and Vaiano.

We made contact with the forward positions on 20th June, when 78 Division attacked Sanfatucchio and Vaiano at the south-western corner of the lake and the South Africans began to work their way up the lower slopes of the hill crowned by Chiusi. By next day the nature of the enemy resistance became clear, and 13 Corps' Commander decided to commit his reserve division, 4 British. 78 Division succeeded, in very fierce hand-to-hand fighting, in clearing Sanfatucchio on the 21st but they had made no progress against Vaiano and the South Africans met most violent resistance in their attack on Chiusi. Only the Armoured Brigade was forward; they managed, after three days of heavy fighting, to get a company into the centre of the town early on the 23rd but the Germans counter-attacked and by the end of the day were again firmly in control. 78 Division now decided to put in a full-scale attack on the lower ground on their right, to carry the defences of the Pescia and exploit to Castiglione, in the centre of the west shore of the lake. The attack went in on the morning of the 24th and by the evening had secured a small bridgehead over the Pescia; but heavy rain delayed the armour which was to have supported the leading troops. As a result progress was slow on the 25th and by the 26th it was necessary to call a halt until 4 Division could close up on the left flank. They had had a hard struggle for Vaiano, which was not cleared until the 25th, and did not draw level until the 26th. In the meantime, however, the divisional reconnaissance regiment had pushed round the north shore of Lake Chiusi and in face of this threat the Germans withdrew from the town; the South Africans entered on the morning of the 26th but were held up by very extensive demolitions on all the exit roads.

The direct route up the west shore of the lake was still blocked by the strong defences of the line running west-south-west from Castiglione and 73 Division was unable to make any progress here. This meant that 4 Division would have to force the pace. It took a consolidated attack by four battalions to carry Frattavecchia in the centre of the line. By the end of 28th June the major part of the ridge north of the Pescia had been cleared and the Germans had been driven off the Trasimene Line. They had won a welcome respite, though at heavy cost in casualties which had severely depleted the I Parachute and 334 Divisions. They now had to fall back fairly rapidly on their next delaying position, covering Arezzo, but the flooded condition of the Val di Chiana would give them reasonable time for this and allow them to make firm dispositions. They could remain a little longer in the more broken ground immediately west of the lake and gave 4 Division a hard fight for Petrignano on the 30th. On 2nd July 78 Division cleared the northern shore of Lake Trasimene.

East of the lake I0 Corps could do little more than maintain pressure and keep level with I3 Corps' advance. The strong mountain positions north of Perugia, extending almost to the east shore of the lake, were unsuitable for operations by 6 British Armoured Division; the Germans rapidly appreciated this and were able to withdraw I5 Panzer Grenadier Division to the west side of the lake to oppose I3 Corps. They also pulled out 94 Infantry Division and sent it back to North Italy to re-form completely with fresh drafts. On 26th June I0 Corps regrouped; I0 Indian Division arrived and 6 Armoured was sent across to reinforce I3 Corps. The same day 8 Indian Division scored a gratifying success by the capture of Monte Pilonica, east of the Tiber. Between the river and the lake the Germans now began, on 27th June, to fall back as a result of their failure to hold I3 Corps. I0 Corps followed up, advancing as rapidly as their means permitted into the mountains either side of the Tiber. On their right the Poles, who came under command of Eighth Army on 29th June, continued to make preparations for the assault on the German position behind the Chienti but discovered that the general withdrawal on the night of the 29th applied to their front also; they therefore proceeded, although their concentration was by no means complete, to pursue across the river.

New Plans of Campaign.

So far I had been conducting operations on the assumption that the forces which had been withdrawn provisionally for ANVIL, or which were still to be withdrawn, might yet be returned to my command for the exploitation of the Italian campaign if the decision went against ANVIL. As the time lengthened during which that decision hung in the balance it became urgent to plan what could be done with the forces available on either hypothesis. I therefore called a conference of my Army Commanders on 23th June and explained what my plans would be if I were assured the same forces as at present. The object of operations in Italy must be to invade southern Germany by an overland advance through north-eastern Italy and the Ljubljana gap. By this means we should strike directly at territory which it was vital for the Germans to defend, even at the cost of diverting strength from other fronts, and have the possibility of joining hands with the southern wing of the Red Army and with Marshal Tito's partisan forces. The alternative, an advance into Southern France across the Maritime Alps, would be less profitable and more difficult. I appreciated that the enemy intended to hold the Northern Apennines until driven from that position in overwhelming force but, with the troops then available to him, he would be unable to do so and would be risking certain disaster, provided we could bring our whole strength against him. Coming down to tactical details, I considered that the "Gothic" line should be attacked in the centre both for topographical reasons, which I shall discuss later, and because that would lead most directly to the important objectives in Northern Italy. The conference agreed to the plan as outlined but took note that if ANVIL were launched it would not be practical. In particular the administrative organisation of the Allied Armies in Italy would be "hamstrung", in General Robertson's expression. General Clark also made the point about the bad effect of the present state of indecision on the morale and efficiency of the troops now engaged.

It is interesting to speculate what would have happened if I had been allowed to carry out this plan and had appeared with two strong armies on the southern frontier of Germany and at the gates of the Danube basin in the autumn of 1944. The effects would probably have been considerable, not only militarily but also politically. My plan was, however, fated to be stillborn though the final decision was not taken until the beginning of July and the discouraging feeling of uncertainty continued to hang over the battlefield. The demands of ANVIL had grown: the troops to be withdrawn included not only the whole French Corps and three United States divisions but also a considerable number of American Corps and Army troops.[104] I was informed that our air strength would also be reduced, probably by about seventy per cent. I expounded my views on what could be done with what was left in a letter to General Wilson on 23rd June. My forces would be much reduced, and unbalanced in infantry, but I came to the conclusion that an advance into north-eastern Italy would still be possible, though at a reduced tempo, and must be attempted.

Enemy strength was reckoned at the equivalent of about fourteen full-strength divisions; reinforcement from elsewhere might bring it up to the equivalent of between eighteen and twenty-one divisions. His intentions were correctly appreciated as to continue to withdraw fighting to the Apennines and to defend the, "Gothic" line. Our troops, assuming there were no further withdrawals than those already ordered, would amount to just over fourteen infantry and four armoured divisions, with seven independent armoured brigades. For a successful assault on the "Gothic" line, carried to the Po, a total of eighteen divisions would be required, of which not more than two or three should be armoured; to follow this up as far as the Piave would again require eighteen divisions and to force the Piave and exploit to the Ljubljana gap also eighteen divisions. It would obviously be impossible, however, although the Allied strength available just equalled eighteen divisions, to use the same divisions for all these assaults, even if the rôles of offence and defence were rotated; a reserve of at least a third, or six additional divisions, would be required. Various suggestions were made as to the source from which this additional strength could be derived. In the event all the major formations I asked for proved unobtainable though some of the minor ones were made available; but a more fruitful suggestion was there commendation that we should raise, arm and equip some Italian formations. For each phase of the attack a certain number of divisions had a purely defensive rôle, and for this the Italian "Gruppi di Combattimento" which we later raised proved most useful.

The decision to proceed with operation ANVIL was communicated by the Combined Chiefs of Staff to Allied Force Headquarters on 2nd July. As a result of the decision a new directive was issued by General Wilson on 5th July in the following terms:

1. My previous directive was cancelled and, from receipt of the telegram, operation ANVIL was to have priority of all Mediterranean resources. This priority was to hold good until the build-up of forces in the South of France reached ten divisions.

2. I was to be informed from time to time what resources were allotted to operation ANVIL and I was to take all necessary steps to have them available at the required place and time.

I was told, as a guide, that as the plan now stood not more than four French and three American divisions plus their appropriate Army, Corps and Service troops were to be taken from my command for this purpose. I was to be allotted 92 (Coloured) United States Infantry Division and also a Brazilian Infantry Division organised and equipped on the American basis. Firm dates would be notified later but for planning purposes approximate dates would be 15th September for 92 Division and 30th October for the Brazilians.

3. The destruction of the German forces in Italy continued to be my task. I was therefore-

(*a*) To advance over the Apennines and close to the line of the River Po securing the area Ravenna - Bologna - Modena to the coast north of Leghorn. If possible I was to seize Piacenza, an important road centre.

(*b*) Subsequently to cross the Po to the line Venice - Padua - Verona - Brescia. It was thought that with the advance of our forces in Southern

France up the Rhone Valley and my advances as outlined above all German formations would withdraw from north-west Italy thus making an offensive in that direction unnecessary.

4. I should receive further instructions after reaching the line defined in paragraph 3 (*b*) above.

5. All available resources in the Mediterranean less those required for operation ANVIL and for internal security would be made available to me for these operations.

6. Subject to the priority given to ANVIL the Air Commander-in-Chief was requested to give me maximum air support.

In order to be in a position to carry out this rather optimistic directive it was necessary to make contact, as quickly as possible, with the "Gothic" line. Now that we knew finally where we stood and what our resources would be we were at least free from the doubts and indecisions of the past month and could develop our strategy to suit our strength. The enemy was in no mood to accelerate his withdrawal, now that he was back "on balance" again; after being driven off the Trasimene line on 29th June he went back fairly steadily until 5th July but on that day he began once more to call a halt. The line selected ran from the west coast in the area of Rosignano, some six miles north of Cecina, to Volterra, thence across the Val di Chiana to the heights surrounding Arezzo; on the east coast Filottrano and Osimo were key points. The west coast was strongly defended by I6 S.S. Panzer Grenadier Division with 26 Panzer Division on its left. I9 Luftwaffe Field Division had been withdrawn from the line in this sector; it had suffered very heavy casualties and shortly afterwards it was disbanded and the survivors incorporated in its sister division, the 20th. Further east 90 Panzer Grenadier Division, with 20 Luftwaffe Field Division under command, defended the high ground around Volterra. From Poggibonsi to Arezzo, in the centre of the front, dispositions were much the same as they had been in the Trasimene line with, from west to east, I5 Panzer Grenadier, 334 Infantry, I Parachute, Hermann Goering and 4 Parachute Divisions. This was a formidable deployment and it was clear that we should have stiff fighting before we could drive these excellent troops from their positions. Their artillery support was better co-ordinated now, and a particular feature of the fighting here was the German use of their heavy artillery, especially the I7 centimetre gun, and of a reinforced strength in multi-barrelled rocket projectors. 305 and 44 Infantry Divisions, withdrawing from Perugia, had fallen back unhurriedly, the former closing in east of Arezzo. II4 Jaeger Division, moving up the centre of the peninsula, put in several counter-attacks to ease the pressure on its neighbours. On the Adriatic coast 278 Division, in its first major engagement, was fighting hard for Osimo and Filottrano and losing heavily.

IV Corps on the left had a very bitter struggle for Rosignano, which the S.S. Panzer Grenadiers defended against 34 United States Division with the same stubbornness as they had shown at Cecina. The town is situated on a hill top, very compactly built of large masonry houses with an ancient castle in the centre. In these circumstances street fighting was bound to be a long job; it lasted in fact from 3rd July until 9th July. Naturally only part of our force was directed into the town itself and the remainder endeavoured to outflank it to the east, but here too resistance from 26 Panzer Division was strong. Further east I United States Armoured Division was relieved by 88 United States Infantry Division which on the 8th captured the "far-famed hold" of Volterra.

Arezzo presented a more complicated problem. The town itself lies in a flat plain but it is surrounded by mountains on three sides. The broad and fertile Val di Chiana leads up to it from the west side of Lake Trasimene but some three miles short of it the plain ceases and the road turns north-eastwards to enter the town through a comparative defile. The advance on Arezzo from the Trasimene line was relatively rapid both by I3 Corps and I0 Corps, though the latter was employing only one infantry division and an armoured brigade. I3 Corps first met stiff resistance late on 5th July. The full strength of the German position was not immediately appreciated, for the exposed approaches and heavy shelling made reconnaissance difficult, and for the next three days the leading brigades continued to probe forward in the expectation that the Germans would turn once more to withdrawal under continued pressure without our having to mount a full-scale attack. 6 Armoured Division in the valley, having relieved 78 Division, attempted to press on by the direct route to Arezzo and succeeded in gaining a tenuous foothold on Monte Lignano, due south of the town on the right hand side of the defile. On the Corps' left 4 British Infantry and 6 South African Armoured Divisions tried to break through the enemy defences on the hills running parallel to the Arezzo - Siena road and thus break into the Arno valley west of Arezzo but though 4 Division succeeded in seizing one of the hills, Poggio all'Olmo, the main line held firm.

It was clear that further reinforcement would be needed before we could break through this line of defence. Our main weight must be developed in 13 Corps' sector, where the approach was easiest, but the three divisions which had fought their way through the Trasimene line were now stretched over a front of twenty-five miles and had no reserves.[105] In I0 Corps 8 Indian Division had been fighting with only four days break since the crossing of the Rapido; I0 Indian Division had arrived to reinforce and had taken over almost the whole Corps sector to allow the 8th a partial rest. 4 Indian Division, which had had three weeks mountain training, was coming forward and the first brigade reached the Umbertide area by 7th July. However, even when thus reinforced, I0 Corps could have little effect on the battle for Arezzo as the country east of the town is very broken and badly roaded and the Corps' main task was to press up the Tiber valley to Sansepolcro. It was necessary, therefore, to reinforce I3 Corps and strike at Arezzo by the natural route, from the southwest. The nearest reserves were in I Canadian Corps which had 2 New Zealand Division under command; they had not been needed for the pursuit so far and had been left in the Liri valley for ease of administration and in order to give them time to rest, reorganise and prepare for the attacks on the "Gothic" line. The most readily available formation was the New Zealand Division at Frosinone and I decided to bring this up; to give it time to arrive the attack would have to be postponed until the I5th.

This decision was reached on 9th July and for the next four days the enemy attempted, by a series of counter-attacks on different points of I3 Corps' front, to gain the initiative and re-establish his positions where they had been endangered. These were all repulsed with heavy losses and on our side an attempt to increase our hold on Monte Lignano, the main bulwark of the defence south of Arezzo, was also unsuccessful. In the meantime I0 Corps was able to make a gratifying and unexpected advance. 4 Indian Division was employed west of the Tiber, where a large mountain mass, culminating in the three thousand five hundred foot peak of Monte Favalto, blocks all access from the Tiber valley to Arezzo; there were no roads across this *massif* in either direction and shortage of bridging material meant that the divisional routes of access were severely restricted. Trusting in this inaccessibility the enemy held the ground here relatively lightly. But 4 Indian Division had already a fine reputation in mountains and recent training had polished up its knowledge; with I/9 Gurkhas in the lead it pushed resolutely into the tangled mass of ridges and peaks and by the I3th Monte Favalto was in our hands. The Army Commander, taking advantage of this, ordered the division to press on north across the Arezzo - Sansepolcro road, capture the Alpe di Poti and threaten Arezzo from the east. It was a difficult task, as the Indians had completely outstripped their road communications, and before this threat could be fully developed the Germans had been forced out of Arezzo; but the capture of Monte Favalto was undoubtedly a strong contributing factor in that success. I3 Corps' attack on Arezzo was launched at 0I00 hours on I5th July. The New Zealand Division attacked in the hills south of the town, Monte Lignano and Monte Gavino, and 6 Armoured Division on their left along the lower western slopes of Monte Lignano. Maximum artillery support was given from half an hour before midnight and at dawn the fighter-bombers joined in the battle. The enemy guns were for the most part silenced by the weight of this attack but the infantry in their strong positions still resisted firmly. The New Zealanders on the high ground made little progress in daylight and I Guards Brigade, lower down, were checked after an early advance. Nevertheless the balance of the day was in our favour; the New Zealanders were firm on Monte Lignano, which they captured before dawn, and 6 Armoured Division had driven a threatening wedge into the centre of the enemy's positions. That night the Germans broke contact everywhere. In the plain our armour went through and I6/5 Lancers entered Arezzo at 0945 hours on the I6th. On their left 2 Lothians, after a dashing advance at full speed, were rewarded by the capture of an intact bridge over the Arno.

Last light on the I6th saw the end of the battle for Arezzo; Florence was our next objective. The former was to be the administrative base and the latter the operational base for the attack on the "Gothic" line. I ought to mention here that we had been considerably hampered administratively by the stubborn German defence of Arezzo; it had been nominated as Eighth Army's main roadhead and eventual railhead and, in anticipation of its capture, the roadheads at Terni and Narni had been only lightly stocked. Railheads had been opened north of Rome in the general area of Orte and Civita Castellana at the end of the first week in July and we were pressing on with the construction of the line to Arezzo. We calculated that when that area was opened and developed we should be able to maintain a total of thirteen and a half divisions from Florence forwards. In the meanwhile the Germans, by delaying us for ten days in front of Arezzo, had gained that much more time for the completion of their "Gothic" line defences.

While Eighth Army was thus having to put forward its best efforts in the centre of the peninsula we were pressing attacks on both flanks to win the vital ports of Ancona and Leghorn. The Poles on the Adriatic captured Osimo on 6th July, inflicting severe losses on 278 Division; so severely was this division weakened that Kesselring began to move over I Parachute Division to its support.[106] General Anders then began preparations for the final attack on Ancona. IV Corps on the left was driving on Leghorn, which it planned to take by an enveloping movement from the east. The French, on Fifth Army's right, had celebrated I4th July by capturing Poggibonsi, on the direct route from Siena to Florence. The time for their relief was now, however, rapidly approaching; on 22nd July their sector was taken over by 8 Indian Division and in part by the New Zealanders, coming under command of I3 Corps. It was with very real regret that I saw the departure of the French Corps. They had most worthily upheld and reinforced the reputation of French arms in the country where Bayard and Gaston de Foix had first brought them fame. A marble tablet in the ancient city of San Gimignano, captured by 4 Mountain Division on I3th July, recalls their great advance from the Garigliano.

The Germans, having now made us deploy and fight hard for the two ports and Arezzo, initiated a programme of gradual withdrawal to the Arno based on a series of phase lines known by girls names in alphabetical order.[107] Their forces were now well balanced and there was little chance of seriously disrupting this programme. On I6th July Arezzo fell, on the I8th IV Corps reached the Arno east of Pisa, on the same day the Poles captured Ancona and on the I9th the Americans entered Leghorn. The Poles had had heavy fighting at Loretto and Filottrano; it took six days of fluctuating attack and counter-attack to clear the latter and the main attack was delayed thereby till the morning of the I7th. IV Coups had to beat off a final counter-attack on Rosignano on I0th July, and for the next two days progress to the east of the town was still slow. From the I3th to the I5th the advance was more rapid as the Germans fell back to their next delaying positions. 9I Division was the first unit in IV Corps to reach the Arno, capturing Pontedera on I8th July, but on the left 34 Division was held further south in the hills behind Leghorn and first entered the city at 0200 hours on the I9th. The Germans had devoted greater efforts than ever to render the port unusable. The dock area was heavily mined and booby-trapped, all the quays had been cratered and the harbour entrance was almost wholly blocked by sunken ships. By 23rd July 34 Division had captured the southern part of Pisa. All bridges over the Arno had been destroyed and the enemy was firmly posted on the north bank all along the Corps front. Leghorn harbour remained under fire from long-range artillery.

Fifth Army's sector was now reduced to a front of four divisions with IV Corps left and II Corps right; by the 23rd it ran along the Arno from the mouth to Empoli. The two Corps in the centre of Eighth Army's front meanwhile continued to press on up the mountainous centre of the peninsula to seize the bases for the attack on the

"Gothic" line. 13 Corps was now directed on Florence and 10 Corps therefore took over the area due north of Arezzo and advanced on Bibbiena by the parallel axes of the upper Arno and the upper Tiber. Between these two rivers is a great roadless *massif* known as the Alpe di Catenaia and west of the road from Arezzo to Bibbiena is the equally roadless, longer and slightly higher *massif* of the Pratomagno. 10 Corps now had two Indian infantry divisions, 4th and 10th, and an armoured brigade and on its extreme right two armoured car regiments, 12 Lancers and the Household Cavalry, operating in the tangled country between Gubbio and Fabriano. On 17th July 4 Indian Division captured the Alpe di Poti, north of the Arezzo - Sansepolcro road and on 18th July 4/10 Baluchis of 10 Indian Division cleared Monte Cedrone, west of Citta di Castello in the Tiber valley, a strong position which had delayed our advance here since the 13th. Citta di Castello fell on the 22nd. 4 Indian Division now took up the running on the heights of the Alpe di Catenaia and the weight of 10 Corps shifted to its left. On 5th August, after a swift advance across the trackless mountains, with the divisional engineers building a jeep track behind them at full speed, 3/5 Mahrattas captured the summit of Monte Il Castello. This was 10 Corps' high-water-mark. The plan for the attack on the "Gothic" line had now been changed and on 7th August, reduced in strength to 10 Indian Division only, the Corps went onto the defensive.

13 Corps in the meanwhile was operating north-westwards against Florence. It had five divisions under command, two of them armoured, but with the imminent disappearance of the French Corps it was about to take over a front of some forty miles. The original plan was to make the main effort on the right, up both sides of the valley of the Arno with 6 British Armoured Division, and along the west side of the Monti di Chianti, through Radda and Greve, with 4 British Infantry and 6 South African Armoured Divisions, the latter in the lead. 6 British Armoured Division had the advantage of the bridge over the Arno which they had captured intact the day Arezzo fell and were able to make some progress between the river and the heights of the Pratomagno. 4 Division paralleled this to the west of the river but by the 19th the Germans, now on their "Irmgard" delaying line, were able to impose a halt. The South Africans in the thickly cultivated Chianti hills had captured Radda in Chianti on the 18th. By the 20th, however, it became clear that the enemy intended to resist particularly strongly on our original line of advance, the Arno axis, with two and a half divisions east of the river and one, 715 Infantry, re-formed and brought up to strength after its disaster at Anzio, between the river and the crest of the Chianti mountains. The Corps Commander therefore decided to make his main effort on the left of his sector and employ both 8 Indian and 2 New Zealand Divisions to relieve the French Corps and press up the axis of Route 2.

By 22nd July the relief of the French was completed and the South Africans and New Zealanders were able to make good progress to the west of the Chianti chain. By the end of the 25th both were facing squarely up to the "Olga" line which ran roughly east and west through San Casciano, ten miles south of Florence. This advance loosened up the defence in the Arno valley and on the same day the right of the South Africans, and 4 British Division, were in contact with the enemy positions on Monte Scalari and Monte Moggio, the south-eastern bulwarks of the defence of

Florence. This was the "Lydia" line; "Olga", on Route 2, was held by 4 Parachute Division. Leaving "Lydia" to 4 Division, 13 Corps grouped the South Africans and New Zealanders for the attack on "Olga". There was stiff fighting on the 26th but the next day the New Zealanders captured San Casciano and the parachutists withdrew to "Paula", the last line covering Florence. 4 Division had very heavy fighting, lasting three days, for Monte Scalari, which was finally cleared on the 29th. On the left of the Corps front 8 Indian Division had reached the Arno east of Empoli.

We wanted Florence as quickly as possible, not for the sake of the name but because it is a centre of communications and the best operational base for the attack on the "Gothic" line. We planned, if possible, to capture the city by an outflanking movement on both sides of it, with our main strength on the west. The Germans were making promises to treat it as an open city but by this they appeared to mean that, while using its communication facilities themselves, they expected us to refrain from doing so when we should capture it; at any rate they had concentrated large forces immediately south of the city. From Figline on the upper Arno to Montelupo west of the city four and a half divisions, strong in artillery and heavy tanks, now confronted 13 Corps, with three and a half divisions forward. The German formations included 4 Parachute, 29 Panzer Grenadier and part of 3 Panzer Grenadier Divisions. 13 Corps decided to concentrate the New Zealanders on a narrow front west of Route 2 and breakthrough the "Paula" line by capturing the ridge of Pian' dei Cerri, which runs roughly east and west from the main road three miles south of Florence to the Arno opposite Signa, exploiting to the river west of Florence. East of the road the South Africans would make diversionary attacks and 4 Division would protect the Corps' right flank. The attack went in on 30th July and fierce fighting continued until the late evening of 2nd August, when the New Zealanders captured the crest of La Poggiona, at the eastern end of the enemy's ridge position. This was the turning point of the battle; the roads now led downhill into Florence and the enemy began to withdraw back across the Arno. They fought a stiff rearguard action on the River Ema which crosses Route 2 some two miles south of the Arno and on the night of 3rd August disengaged again over the Arno.

The local German commander had apparently been allowed discretion about demolishing the Arno bridges and exercised it by blowing up all but the Ponte Vecchio. The Ponte della Trinita, by many considered the most beautiful in the world, was a particularly severe loss; the Ponte Vecchio, though it has a certain charm of antiquity, is not so fine a work of art and in any case is too weak for all but the lightest traffic. It has been suggested that it was spared because it reminded the nostalgic parachutists of Nuremberg; but to ensure that military requirements were not unduly sacrificed to sentiment the ancient buildings at both ends were blown up in order to block the approaches. We were not, in fact, hampered militarily by all this destruction for we never intended to fight in Florence and, once the city was cleared, could build as many bridges as we wanted without loss of time or efficiency.

With the entry into the southern part of Florence on 4th August the campaign in central Italy came to an end,[108] and it was on the same day that the new plan for the attack on the "Gothic" line was decided on, a plan which involved a radical regrouping by Eighth Army. From the Garigliano to the Arno is two hundred and forty miles as the crow flies; by the shortest road it is two hundred and seventy miles. We had covered this distance in sixty-four days, breaking through three lines of prepared defences south of Rome and fighting two major battles, the Trasimene line and Arezzo, between Rome and Florence. I consider this a very satisfactory speed in Italian terrain, and the more so when it is remembered that, after the fall of Rome, I was being forced to make detachments to other fronts while Kesselring was being strenuously reinforced. I had admittedly the advantage of operating in a country whose inhabitants were well disposed. This was especially noticeable in Tuscany, where the local population frequently gave valuable information to our troops on matters of tactical importance, such as the location of enemy minefields. When we entered Florence some of the population engaged in skirmishes with supporters of the Fascist Republican Government and assisted our troops with information on German dispositions north of the river. I should also like to pay tribute to the courage and constancy of many hundreds of brave Italians, of all classes, who at the risk and sometimes forfeit of their lives, sheltered and protected Allied prisoners of war, crashed airmen and liaison officers operating behind the enemy lines. But it was a hard-fought struggle all the way, except for the first two weeks in June, and one which is infinitely to the credit of the troops of all nationalities under my command, for the German is a master in retreat and can seldom be hustled or panicked. I was determined to employ the minimum troops in the pursuit, to have the maximum strength for the attack on the Apennines. The result was that they were hard driven, and only the greatest enthusiasm and skill could have made the plan a success. I should like to mention particularly my three armoured divisions I United States, 6 British and 6 South African. Central Italy is not really cavalry country; it offers, on the contrary, innumerable opportunities for the anti-tank gun embuscade; but these three divisions gave a superb demonstration of that dash in the attack and tenacity in retention of captured objectives which have in this war distinguished the armoured descendants of the old mounted arm.

PART IV.
THE GOTHIC LINE BATTLES.

The "Gothic" Line.

In the region of the upper Tiber the Apennines, which have hitherto formed the backbone of Italy, turn north-west and run across the peninsula to join the Maritime Alps on the French border, thus cutting off Central Italy from the basin of the Po. This sudden bend has always interposed a sharp line of division, political and economic, between the thickly populated plains of Lombardy, intensively cultivated and at the same time highly industrialized, and the mountainous peninsula whose urban centres and industry are more widely dispersed on historically important river sites. From the military point of view the barrier is a first-class strategic obstacle. An army advancing from the south finds that what has hitherto been its best and broadest avenue of approach, the western coastal plain, comes suddenly to a dead end when it reaches the Magra river, just east of La Spezia. The eastern coastal belt, hitherto by far the less useful, now comes into its own for it continues round the angle of the bend and offers the only passage on the level into the plains of the Po valley. In spite of this great advantage, however, it retains the characteristics which have made it inferior hitherto, as a route for an army, to the western coastal route. It would be truer to say that the coast road, Route I6, offers the only passage on the level, for the spurs descending from the central chain run right down to the coast in the form of a continuous series of ridges, not high, at least near the sea, but not easy for the passage of troops. The soil, too, is heavy and movement is difficult after rain. The few roads which run parallel to Route I6, all of them narrow and badly surfaced, switchback up and down these ridges through small villages. More important still, the whole foothill region is intersected, at right angles to the direction of advance, by numerous water obstacles, some quite large rivers and some mere torrents but all liable to sudden flooding from the proximity of their mountain sources. They give a foretaste of the still more serious obstacles which face the attacker round the elbow of the mountains where broad embanked rivers flow north-eastwards across his path through the muddy plains of the Romagna.

   Between the two narrow coastal belts the mountains present an unbroken front about a hundred and forty miles long and fifty to sixty miles deep. There are no natural routes across them but the historical importance of the cities of the Arno valley on the one hand and the Po valley on the other has been such that no less than eleven roads, of all classes, have been constructed to link the two districts. Not all of these can be considered for military use. The two routes which lead from Viareggio through Aulla to Parma and Reggio, Routes 62 and 63, run through the wildest and deepest part of the Apennines; this disadvantage is not so serious as the fact that access to their starting point at Aulla is almost impossible, for the two mile coastal belt is commanded by a towering mountain wall on its right. Two roads lead from Lucca to

Modena, one up the Serchio and down the Secchia and the other, Route I2, over the Abetone Pass, four thousand three hundred feet high; the former is particularly bad but both are tortuous and difficult and the latter runs for eighty-five miles through the mountains which are here still very broad. From Pistoia Route 64 leads to Bologna, with a branch on the north side of the mountains to Modena. This is a reasonably good road, just over sixty miles long. Florence is the most important road centre with two roads leading to Bologna, one via Prato and the other over the Futa Pass - the latter with a branch to Imola *viâ* Firenzuola - a road to Faenza *viâ* Marradi and one to Forli *viâ* Dicomano. The most important is Route 65, the direct route to Bologna. The distance between the two cities is sixty-seven miles but the main chain of the Apennines begins at the Sieve river so that the actual distance through the mountains is only fifty miles. The highest point on the road is the Futa Pass, two thousand nine hundred feet, and the Pass of Il Giogo, on the lateral road to Firenzuola to the east, is a little lower. From the upper Arno valley, at Bibbiena Route 7I leads to Cesena; it is difficult of access and of inferior quality but is only fifty-five miles long. Its disadvantage is that, like Route 67 from Florence to Forli, it leads into a corner of the Romagna, well away from any important objective.

All these roads are artificial, cut into the sides of valleys to lift them over passes which in winter are snowbound and for a large part of the year are subjected to heavy rains. They are magnificent feats of engineering, recalling the fact that a genius for road building is one of the few undoubted inheritances of the Italians from the Romans, but for that very reason are peculiarly susceptible to demolition. The latter is a craft at which the Germans, after their experience in this war, can probably claim to be world masters; Kesselring himself had ordered his troops to carry out demolitions "with sadistic imaginativeness" and they had always proved themselves equal to this demand. The greater number of roads are in the western half of the area, between Florence and the Tyrrhenian Sea, and the shortest routes lead due north from Florence. In the eastern half there are only the two roads which lead to Forli and Cesena and both these run north-east instead of due north. Lateral communication is infinitely better on the northern side of the mountains than on the southern. On the latter movement from east to west is limited to a few poor roads across the mountains but on the Germans' side the Via Emilia, Route 9, runs along the whole length of the position. It is a broad, straight road on the flat, with numerous short roads leading off it into the mountains, for the crest line is nearer the southern than the northern edge and the secondary road system on the latter is therefore much more developed. This is an enormous advantage to the defender, for in the defence of a line it is vital to be able to move forces rapidly from one sector to another where the threat is greatest.

The original German plan for Italy, as Hitler told Mussolini at the Feltre conference in July, I943, was to hold nothing south of the line of the Northern Apennines so that the preliminary reconnaissances for the "Gothic" line were probably carried out about that time. Work appears to have begun in September, I943. The first work was done at the two ends, in the coastal plain south of La Spezia and behind the Foglia river on the Adriatic, and in the centre, where elaborate defences were constructed on the

Futa Pass. Italian forced labour and a Slovak Technical Brigade were used; but as the winter of 1943 progressed most of the labour force was diverted to work on the "Gustav", "Hitler" and "Caesar" lines, and it was not until the fall of Rome that priority was restored to the "Gothic" line and the work was pushed ahead at the highest pressure. It was principally to gain more time to allow for the "Gothic" line to be completed that Kesselring fought the battles of Lake Trasimene and Arezzo. At one time it was expected that it would be ready by 30th June but in fact our attack on the Adriatic on 25th August found many of the defences on the Foglia still unfinished while in some of the more inaccessible mountain sectors they were only in the early stages of development.

The total length of the line of defences was about two hundred miles. In the west the approaches to La Spezia and the valley of the Magra were barred by a system of anti-tank defences in depth with two artificial obstacles seven miles apart; this was the only example of defence in depth in the system. From the region of Carrara the line swung south-east through the Apuan Mountains to a strongpoint at Borgo a Mozzano, astride the two routes north from Lucca to Modena. This was the first of a series of strongpoints blocking all the routes north; they were connected with each other by a continuous line of positions running through the mountains, with subsidiary strongpoints at places of particular importance. The main blocking positions were at Porretta, north of Pistoia, the Vernio Pass north of Prato, and the Futa and Il Giogo Passes north of Florence. From here the line ran south-east, following the crest of the Alpe di San Benedetto, with strongpoints at the Casaglia and San Godenzo Passes on the Faenza and Forli roads, until it reached the Alpe di Serra where strongpoints at Serravalle and Valsavignone blocked the two roads to Cesena from the upper Arno and upper Tiber valleys. From here it turned roughly east again, following the course of the River Foglia, until it reached the sea at Pesaro. For the last thirteen miles, where the foothills are lower, the line was particularly strong, and the defences included anti-tank ditches, extensive minefields, bunkers and various types of built-in tank turrets. Attention had also been paid to the seaward flanks of the line to guard against an amphibious outflanking. This was scarcely a danger at the western end, but the defences of La Spezia were strengthened. On the Adriatic a line of cliffs runs from Pesaro to Cattolica and this was supplemented by defences extending as far north as Ravenna.

Early Plans for the Attack on the "Gothic" Line.

After the great victories of the spring offensive, with Rome in our hands and the Germans withdrawing rapidly through Latium and Tuscany, pursued with the utmost vigour by my two Armies, it seemed likely that the Northern Apennines would prove merely an incident in our pursuit, which would carry on almost unchecked across them into the plains of the Po valley. Even if this proved too optimistic a hope it was reasonable to expect that we should quickly be able to bring such forces to bear in a frontal attack as would ensure the piercing of the mountain barrier; the success of the French Corps in the Aurunci mountains had shown the way and proved that the Germans could no longer place such confidence for their defence as previously in the difficulties of the Italian terrain. But before the end of June these hopes were dashed by the withdrawal of seven divisions from our side and the arrival of eight reinforcing divisions for Kesselring. Encouraged by this the German troops, who in the early days of June were speaking gloomily of the Brenner as their next stop, were able to rally and convert our pursuit into a hard-fought advance. The withdrawal of forces for the operations in Southern France represented not merely a quantitative loss to my Armies of over twenty-five per cent. but also a qualitative loss, for the French Corps had the greatest experience and training in mountain warfare of all the troops under my command and included my only regular mountain division.

This considerable reduction in my strength did not at first alter my plans for dealing with the "Gothic" line, which were to attack it in the centre on a front from Dicomano to Pistoia and debouch into the Po plains at or near Bologna. From the topographical point of view the choice was narrowed down to two sectors, the centre and the extreme right, and there was little to choose between them. On the axis of Route 65 the mountains are higher but Bologna, the most important objective south of the Po, is nearer. On the east coast the ground is much lower but the ridges are at right angles to the direction of the advance and there are a number of serious water obstacles. It was, however, largely on considerations of timing that I rejected the idea of an attack up the east coast. It was vital not to allow the enemy a day more than was unavoidable to strengthen his defences and reorganise his formations. The bulk of my forces was advancing up the centre of the peninsula and the west coast by routes which would bring them to the Arno in the area of Florence and Pisa so that it would be both easier and quicker to concentrate for the attack round Florence than anywhere else. In the days when I still had my full forces I expected to be able to rush the Apennines almost without stopping; in my present situation some slight pause would be necessary but I was determined to reduce it to the minimum.

The plan involved a simultaneous attack by Fifth and Eighth Armies on parallel axes, each with their main strength on their contiguous wings. Eighth Army would be able to bring forward for the attack two fresh Corps, 5 and I Canadian, with five divisions between them, to be reinforced by I British Armoured Division which was arriving in the country. For the moment, until arrangements for forward maintenance could be perfected, these forces were to concentrate in the general area of Assisi with some elements to the west near Siena. On I7th July Eighth Army Headquarters produced a detailed appreciation. The conclusions were that the attack should be made by two Corps, each with two divisions forward, operating up the axes Florence - Firenzuola and Florence - Bologna. The Poles were to hold on the Adriatic coast and would be connected with the central front by a Corps with a defensive rôle. A cover-plan had already been put into force by my headquarters on 3rd July to suggest to the enemy that the main attack would come on the Adriatic coast.

It was more difficult to decide on the rôle and capabilities of Fifth Army which had now been reduced to one armoured and four infantry divisions, all of which had seen heavy and continuous fighting recently. On I9th July, in a letter to General Clark, I outlined the position as I saw it and my proposals for his actions preliminary to the main attack on the line. I suggested that it would almost certainly prove too costly to attempt to force a crossing of the Arno west of Pontedera, where the great Monte Pisano feature gave the enemy commanding observation, and proposed that he should hold the line from Pontedera to the sea with light forces and cross between there and Empoli, exploiting to capture Lucca and Pistoia. This would give us the desired start line for an attack from Pistoia arid the front from Pistoia to the sea could be held as a defensive flank with reduced forces. General Clark fully concurred with these plans and issued orders to that effect on 2Ist July; he estimated that D-day for the operation would be between 5th and I0th August and ordered measures to be taken in the meantime to ensure a thorough rest for all troops. At the same time Fifth Army took energetic steps to increase their potentiality by creating new defensive formations from the exiguous forces left by ANVIL. The most striking was the creation of "Task Force 45". This force, of roughly divisional strength, was made up from five American Light Anti-Aircraft battalions, a British Light Anti-Aircraft regiment, an American Tank battalion, part of two Tank Destroyer battalions, part of a divisional reconnaissance battalion and some miscellaneous service units; it was divided into three regiment-sized groups. Up to 24th July these units were still being employed in their original rôles, and had only a very short period of intensive training before taking over part of the line on the Arno from 34 Division. The success of this remarkable effort at conversion was very encouraging and "Task Force 45" remained for many months a valuable part of Fifth Army's order of battle, used for holding defensive fronts.

On 26th July I sent an appreciation on future operations to both Army Commanders. My general plan was divided into four phases and described as follows: "To penetrate the centre of the 'Gothic' line roughly between Dicomano and Pistoia; to thrust forward over the Apennines to secure the general line Imola - Bologna - Modena; to complete the destruction of the enemy forces south of the Po by rapid exploitation across the Po valley; to secure a bridgehead over the Po north of Ferrara and if possible at Ostiglia as well". Plans for Eighth Army's attack were unchanged and the main subject for decision was the task of Fifth Army, for the weakening of that Army was the chief new factor which had been introduced. General Clark would be unable to produce more than a Corps of two divisions plus for the attack. If Eighth Army was to attack up the main routes north from Florence on Bologna Fifth Army must clearly attack towards Modena, from either Lucca or Pistoia. On full consideration of topographical factors, which I need not detail here, the latter axis was clearly preferable. I calculated that Fifth Army would probably be strong enough to seize and secure Modena but that it could not be called on for any more than to exploit to a radius of some ten or fifteen miles from that objective. Eighth Army would therefore have to be responsible for the advance up to and across the Po. After bearing the brunt of the attack in the mountains it would probably only be able to exploit to the Po on one axis, to Ferrara, though it would be most desirable, if at all practicable, for it to seize a bridgehead also in the Ostiglia area.

From this appreciation it seemed clear that, after fighting our way through the mountains we should arrive in the plains too weak to exploit rapidly northwards. This conclusion I had reached some time before and I therefore decided to implement the plan which the Air Forces had already made for the destruction of the bridges over the Po. This operation, given the code-name MALLORY MAJOR, was first studied after the fall of Rome and an operational directive for it was issued on 17th June. The object given was "to disrupt the enemy's flow of supplies into northern Italy by the destruction of six rail bridges over the Po river and one across the Trebbia river, supplemented by the destruction of the Recco or Zoagli viaduct" (this was a long and vulnerable viaduct on the coastal line east of Genoa). The date of the operation was to be decided by me, to fit in with the situation on the ground. As originally conceived this was a part, but an especially important part, of the general plan then in force for disrupting the enemy's lines of communication; as I have already explained, it had been found by experience that the destruction of bridges caused very much more embarrassment to the enemy than the previous policy of attacking marshalling yards. This was, however, just that period in the first week of June when it seemed likely that we should be able to force our way rapidly through the Apennines and still have sufficient force to exploit into northern Italy on a large scale, and for this we wanted to have the chance of seizing a bridge over the Po. I was in fact planning an airborne operation for this very purpose using 2 Parachute Brigade which was shortly afterwards, unfortunately, withdrawn from me for use in the South of France. I therefore decided to cancel MALLORY MAJOR; but the decision to mount ANVIL put a very different complexion on the situation. The Po would now probably be the limit of our possible exploitation after we had broken through the mountains. The Air Force plan offered an opportunity of making a virtue of this necessity; I decided to pin my hopes on being able to bring the Germans to a decisive battle between the Apennines and the Po and drive them against the obstacle of a bridgeless river. In the meantime the enemy's maintenance would suffer from the interposition of this dramatic line of interdiction.

Orders for the operation went out on 11th July; its scope was extended and all bridges, both road and rail, were to be destroyed. During the first four days of the operation, 12th to 15th July, medium bombers concentrated on the nineteen bridges from Piacenza to the sea. Favourable weather contributed to the success of the attacks. In the first two days eleven bridges were rendered impassable and by the 15th the line of interdiction was complete. In some cases, however, the damage was not considered extensive enough and repeated attacks were made until, by the 27th all bridges over the Po east of and inclusive of the one at Torreberetti, north of Alessandria, were cut.

Change of Plan.

On 4th August I recast the plan for the attack on the "Gothic" line. The principal difference was in the rôle of Eighth Army; instead of exerting its main strength on its left and driving at the centre of the line side by side with Fifth Army it would now carry out a swift but secret transfer of strength to its right and strike at the extreme eastern end of the line in order to roll up the enemy's left at the point where he was least protected by the terrain. When this attack was well under way, and depending on the extent to which the enemy had weakened his centre to meet it, Fifth Army would launch a subsidiary attack up the axis Florence - Bologna. In order to strengthen this blow and make Fifth Army more nearly equivalent in strength to Eighth Army, and to what it had been before the recent withdrawals, I proposed to place under General Clark the British 13 Corps, of one armoured and two infantry divisions.[109] Thus Fifth Army once more regained its character of an Allied Army, which had distinguished it from the start.

The new plan, which was given the codename OLIVE was decided on at a short and informal conference on Orvieto airfield. There were only three of us present, General Leese, General Harding, my Chief of Staff, and myself and we sheltered from the sun under the wing of a Dakota while General Leese explained the reasons which led him to urge a reconsideration of our previous intentions. The proposal for a redirection of our attack was largely his idea and arose from his judgment of his Army's capabilities and the manner in which it could be best employed. I was already concerned at the prospect of extensive operations in mountains without my best mountain troops, the French. General Leese shared this concern and represented frankly that, although he was prepared to exert his utmost endeavours to carry out whatever strategy should seem best, he had not that confidence he would like to have in his ability to break through the centre of the Apennine position. With very small exceptions Eighth Army had no troops trained in mountain warfare and, of course, no organized mountain divisions; provision of pack transport trams and other vital necessities for this kind of operation was only improvised at present and the Army as a whole had had comparatively little experience of large-scale operations in mountains. On this line of attack, moreover, it would be unable to develop to the full extent its superiority in armour and artillery, the use of which in combination had been the mainstay of its successful African operations and which had recently given proof of its effectiveness in the Liri valley. The east coast route, on the other hand, appeared to provide much more the kind of battlefield to which Eighth Army was accustomed. It would have fewer mountains to contend with and the chance of employing its artillery in controlled and concentrated "set-piece" attacks, and the hope of flat country ahead beckoned to its desert-trained armour.

Eighth Army's preference for the east coast route of attack was based, it will be seen, on reasons both strictly military and also psychological. The latter reasons; as a well-known dictum of Napoleon's lays down, are as much military factors as the former and in a case where the courses available were fairly equally balanced it was obviously preferable to choose that course which inspired the greater confidence in those who were to carry it out. It was anything but certain that our heavy blow in the mountains of the centre would take us through to our objective and if the first attack there fell short of expectations the advantage would be all with the defenders. He had by far the easier lateral communications so that, once it was clear that all our strength was concentrated at one point, he could very rapidly build up a counter concentration. On the new plan we should be able to employ what I call the strategy of the "two-handed punch" or, more orthodoxly expressed, the strategy of attacking two points equally vital to the enemy (i.e., Ravenna and Bologna) either simultaneously or alternately in order to split the reserves available for the defence.

Plans to implement this decision were made in the greatest secrecy and only the minimum was committed to paper. In the order I issued to both Armies on 6th August, giving the preliminary operations to be carried out, I laid down "The scope and object of operation OLIVE have been settled in discussions between the Commander-in-Chief and Army Commanders and will not be referred to in writing at present." The greater part of the planning was left to Eighth Army who were faced with a tremendous task in transferring their strength to their right wing. The mounting of the operation involved complicated and difficult moves over an inadequate road-net, carried out in conditions of great secrecy, a large-scale cover plan (and the cancellation of the cover plan previously in force) and considerable preliminary engineer work. The plan of the attack, as given in orders issued on 13th August, provided for a simultaneous assault by three Corps in line. 2 Polish Corps, on the right, was to attack and seize the high ground north-west of Pesaro; this was all the Poles could do in their present weak state and after completion of this task they would revert to Army reserve. I Canadian Corps, in the centre, was to attack on the left of the Poles to capture the high ground west of Pesaro and from there, squeezing out the Poles, to reach the main road at Cattolica and drive up the road along the coast directed on Rimini. 5 Corps, on the left, was to advance on an axis to the west of Rimini, directed on Bologna and Ferrara. The movement across to the east coast began on 15th August on a heavy scale and was completed, by a triumph of organization, by 22nd August. 25th August was decided on as D-day. It was not expected that we should be in contact with the "Gothic" line on that date but this was no disadvantage as we intended to press up to and through the line in one motion. This would be of assistance in the matter of surprise. 13 Corps came under command of Fifth Army on 18th August. Between its right and the left of 5 Corps the mountainous central sector was the responsibility of 10 Corps, commanding only 10 Indian Division and a scratch brigade group, mainly of dismounted armoured car regiments.

There was little of interest in the preliminary operations before the offensive opened. On the left the Fifth Army front was quiet. II Corps had now taken over the right of the Army sector, with 91 Division; the 85th and 88th were in rear areas resting and training. West of Empoli there was no change along the line of the Arno. In Florence the Germans withdrew on the night of 10th August back from the north bank of the river to the line of the Mugnone canal, running through the northern outskirts of the city. Further to the right, however, on the Adriatic coast, there were considerable advances made as the Polish Corps pressed on to clear the high ground between the Cesano and Metauro rivers. By the 23rd the Poles were established on the right bank of the latter river from the sea to Fossornbrone, some fifteen miles inland, and with that the stage was set for the assault on Pesaro.

Orders for the Offensive.

The orders for the offensive were issued on 16th August. I defined my intention as "to drive the enemy out of the Apennine positions and to exploit to the general line of the lower Po, inflicting the maximum losses on the enemy in the process." Eighth

Army was to have the predominant rôle in the opening phases and to have priority in all requirements needed to obtain its object. Its task was to break through into the valley of the Po and exploit to seize Ferrara and Bologna. Fifth Army was to assist the first phases of the offensive by carrying out ostentatious preparations to simulate an imminent attack by both Armies on the front between Pontassieve and Pontedera, which was the sector originally chosen for the main attack. While these manoeuvres were in progress Fifth Army was to prepare an attack to break through the enemy's centre on the axis Florence - Bologna, using II and I3 Corps. This attack would be ordered by me as soon as it appeared that the enemy had weakened his centre sufficiently to meet Eighth Army's attack. It was naturally impossible to forecast when this would be, but General Clark was to be prepared to attack at twenty-four hours' notice, if possible, from D plus 5 of the Eighth Army attack, i.e., 30th August. The cover plan for the attack had to be radically altered and was now designed to persuade the enemy that our main blow was coming in the centre and that the Adriatic coast operations were a preliminary feint by our surplus armour.

The objectives for exploitation were given in summary form in this operation order. Eighth Army, on reaching the Ferrara area, was to secure a bridgehead over the Po in the general area north of Ferrara. Fifth Army was to secure Modena and exploit north and north-west of it as far as practicable with the resources available after returning I3 Corps to command of Eighth Army. It will be remembered that these were the eventual objectives foreseen in the original plan and the change in Eighth Army's plan made no difference to them. I dealt with further possibilities for exploitation more fully in a paper on future operations on 27th August, after the attack had begun. The new factor in the situation was the rapid advance of the invading armies in the South of France. The German resistance there had been so weak and had turned so quickly to a full withdrawal that by that date Toulon, Marseilles and Grenoble had all been captured and the Allies were pursuing at full speed up the Rhone valley. In these circumstances it seemed clear that if the Apennine line were pierced the enemy would be obliged to withdraw his forces from north-west Italy back to a line based on the Alps to Lake Garda, the Mincio and the Po, in order to avoid the risk of encirclement. This would mean that Fifth Army would be relieved of any threat to its left flank and could concentrate its weight on the right in a thrust across the Po at Ostiglia directed on Mantua and Verona. Eighth Army's main task on arriving in the plain must be to capture Venice, for until we could obtain the use of its port our lines of communication would be stretched to the limit and maintenance of any large force made most difficult. This would mean an advance on the axis Ferrara - Padua - Treviso, forcing in succession the Po, Adige and Brenta, and would certainly require the employment of all available formations, including I3 Corps. It is interesting to note that the axes of exploitation here given were those on which the Armies advanced after the great victory of Spring I945.

Disposition of Opposing Forces[110]

When the attack opened the forces under Kesselring's command totalled twenty-six German divisions and two Italian; they were fairly well up to strength, for drafts in

June, July and August amounted to some sixty thousand. There had been certain changes in the order of battle. At the end of July the Hermann Goering Panzer Division, which had been active in the Mediterranean theatre ever since it was formed, and first saw service in Tunisia, had been withdrawn to the East Prussian front. To replace it Kesselring received, in August, 98 Infantry Division which had been re-forming in the Zagreb area after its severe losses in the Crimea. In August two more mobile divisions, 3 and I5 Panzer Grenadier, were withdrawn for the western front; the two infantry divisions to replace them did not arrive until September. The Allied invasion of Southern France added two more German divisions to the order of battle in Italy, I48 Infantry and the I57 Mountain[III] Divisions. These were originally in Nineteenth Army but the rapid advance up the Rhone cut them off from their parent formation and they fell back on the Maritime Alps, coming under Kesselring's command. This invasion had, in its early stages, had the effect of weakening the forces opposing us. On getting wind of the preparations for the assault, which it was impossible to conceal, Kesselring decided that the blow was about to fall on the Ligurian coast. He therefore hastily moved 90 Panzer Grenadier Division to Genoa. It arrived there on I3th August, but when the real invasion came, two days later, it was re-directed to the Franco-Italian frontier.

In the two armies opposing us on the main battle front there were nineteen divisions. Tenth Army held the eastern half of the line, from the Adriatic to the inter-army boundary just west of Pontassieve, with LXXVI Panzer Corps left and LI Mountain Corps right; these Corps Headquarters had recently exchanged sectors. LXXVI Corps, from the sea to the area of Sansepolcro, had three divisions forward and two in reserve, all infantry and one, the 7Ist, at only half strength. 278 Infantry Division, on the seaward flank, after fighting a continuous withdrawal all the way up the Adriatic coast since June, had been badly shaken by the Poles in the heavy fighting from Ancona to the Metauro. Of the two divisions in reserve I62 (Turkoman) Infantry Division was not of high quality but the other was the famous I Parachute Division. This was resting in the rear of 278 Division on the coast and it was intended that the latter should withdraw through it for a badly needed rest in a quieter sector of the line. The mountainous sector of LI Corps, from Sansepolcro to Pontassieve, was held by five infantry divisions, mainly those which had suffered most in the retreat from Rome, such as the 44th, II4th and 334th. There was one infantry division, the recently arrived 98th, in Army reserve near Bologna. Fourteenth Army, from Pontassieve to the coast, had eight divisions, also divided between two Corps, I Parachute left and XIV Panzer right with the inter-Corps boundary at Empoli. The former had 4 Parachute and two infantry divisions, the latter 26 Panzer, I6 S.S. Panzer Grenadier and one infantry division. Army reserve consisted of 29 Panzer Grenadiers, north of Florence, and 20 Luftwaffe Field Division, which had now finally absorbed the remains of I9 Division, on the coast between the western end of the "Gothic" line and Viareggio.

It is more difficult to adduce these dispositions as a definite proof of the success of our cover plan than in the case of the spring offensive but they do show a tendency to concentrate on the defence of the central sector rather than the east coast.

Particularly significant is the fact that, of the three divisions in Army reserve, one was near Bologna and a second, the only mobile reserve, was between Florence and Bologna.[112] The enemy's order of battle on the east coast was not impressive except for the parachutists and the event soon showed that it would need heavy reinforcements if this sector of the front was to beheld. It also showed, unfortunately, the inevitable limitations of any cover plan: the two sectors which alone it was logical to threaten were, on the German side though not on our own, so closely connected by good lateral communications that reserves intended for the one could very rapidly be diverted to the other.

In northern Italy the Italians were now coming a little more into the picture. Marshal Graziani, Commander-in-Chief of the Fascist Republican Forces, was given command of a mixed Italo-Germany "Army of Liguria" of two Italian and two and a half German divisions. With these he was responsible for the coast from the French frontier to Spezia; the more important sectors, on the French border and covering Genoa and Spezia, were held by German troops. After the Allied invasion of France this command was increased by the addition of the two divisions from Nineteenth Army and 90 Panzer Grenadier Division, raising the Army of Liguria to a total of seven divisions. It played, however, a purely defensive rôle throughout. In the north-east, under Army Group command, the Germans had a reserve mountain division and one infantry division, the 94th, which was re-forming after its serious losses.

Against these forces we had twenty divisions and eight brigades. Eighth Army accounted for eleven divisions, all but two of which were in the three attacking Corps. On the right was the Polish Corps with 3 and 5 Divisions and an armoured brigade along the Metauro from the Adriatic on a front of about seven miles. Next, on a narrow front of just over two miles, covered by a screen of Polish units, was the Canadian Corps with I Infantry and 5 Armoured Divisions, supported by a British tank brigade. To the west, covering about twenty miles of front, was 5 Corps, the strongest of the attacking Corps, with two infantry divisions, 46 and 4 Indian, in the line and I Armoured and 4 and 56 Infantry Divisions, plus two armoured brigades, in reserve.I0 Corps covered lightly, with I0 Indian Division and a mixed brigade group, the area stretching from the upper Tiber valley to the Army boundary on the Pratomagno. In Army reserve was 2 New Zealand Division, to be reinforced by 3 Greek Mountain Brigade when the latter arrived from the Middle East. At the time the attack went in the New Zealanders were moving from the Siena area to concentrate between Falconara and Iesi.

Fifth Army had three Corps in line, accounting for the remaining nine divisions, four of them British. I3 Corps, on the right of the Army front, held the area from the Pratomagno range to about two miles west of Florence. In the line were I infantry, 6 Armoured and 8 Indian Divisions, supported by I Canadian Armoured Brigade. II Corps held a narrow sector of about four miles immediately on the left of I3 Corps; it had three infantry divisions under command, the 34th, 88th and 9Ist. All these were in reserve and the front was held by an independent Japanese-American Regimental Combat Team. On its left was IV Corps, responsible for the line of the Arno from due south of Prato to the sea; under command were the I Armoured and 85 Infantry

Divisions, a Regimental Combat Team of 92 (Negro) Infantry Division, which was in process of arriving, and "Task Force 45", the improvised formation I have already referred to. 6 South African Armoured Division was moving to come under command of IV Corps to relieve 85 Infantry Division, which was to pass to II Corps. Like Eighth Army, therefore, Fifth Army had its greatest strength on its right; IV Corps duplicated the rôle of I0 Corps in holding a long defensive sector with minimum forces.

As will be seen, we had all our goods in the shop window and it was impossible for me to create a central reserve with which to influence the battle. This was less important than it might seem, however, in view of the nature of the plan. The two Armies were fighting, in the opening stages, essentially separate battles and each of them had a strong striking Corps, 5 and II Corps, with plenty of reserves. In a sense, Fifth Army might be regarded as the Army Group reserve, for in the two-handed strategy which I planned its blow would be held back until the moment seemed right.

Opening of the Offensive.

Eighth Army's attack went in as planned an hour before midnight on 25th August. The opening stages were silent but a barrage was fired at midnight to cover the advance from the bridgeheads over the Metauro river. By dawn on the 26th all the five assaulting divisions were deep across the river, more or less without opposition. It soon became obvious that we had caught the Germans in the middle of a fairly complicated withdrawal and regrouping movement; their intention was to pass 278 Division back through I Parachute Division and bring it across to the western flank of LXXVI Corps where it would relieve 5 Mountain Division which was to move to the French frontier to relieve 90 Panzer Grenadier Division. The enemy was, therefore, prepared to yield ground and the fact that he was falling back voluntarily as we advanced made it difficult for him to detect the greater weight of our attacks on this occasion compared with the following-up attacks by which the Poles had up to now been pressing him back up the Adriatic coast. Eighth Army's secret concentration had completely escaped his notice; the presence of some new troops in the former Polish sector had indeed been established but, having overestimated the Polish casualties in the battle for Ancona, where his own losses had been heavy, he had in any case been expecting the Poles to be relieved. Moreover, there was still some twelve miles to go before the "Gothic" line was reached and the Germans probably expected us to delay our formal attack until we had actually reached it.

The effects of this German misappreciation lasted for some time and it was not until the 29th that the German Corps Commander issued a strong Order of the Day which showed that he had at last realized that a serious attempt at a break-through was intended. In spite of this on the 30th elements of both 5 Corps and the Canadians crossed the River Foglia and captured the advanced positions of the "Gothic" line before the enemy had time to man them. On 3Ist August and Ist September a further advance gave us a stretch of the main defences some twenty miles long, from the coast to Monte Calvo. The works were not manned, many of the minefields were still carefully marked and set at safe and in one case some recently arrived troops were actually captured while sweeping out the bunkers which they were to occupy. The parachutists, all of whom had acknowledged, by initialling, an order from Kesselring stating that the "Gothic" line was the last hope in Italy before the Brenner and that they were to hold their positions for three weeks, pulled out of Pesaro on the night of Ist September and raced back behind the Conca. In the fighting so far they had suffered very heavily, up to half the strength with which they went into action; it was only their hasty retreat which prevented them from being encircled by an outflanking move of the Polish Corps.

As always the Germans were quick to recover from their surprise. By 29th August a regiment from 26 Panzer Division, brought across from west of Empoli, had arrived and gone into action on the River Foglia; it was soon followed by the rest of the division. This was a standard manoeuvre; we had seen before, for instance in the Anzio crisis, the rapid transference of this division, now Kesselring's only armoured division, from one flank of the Army Group to the other, but this time it was committed so hastily and so unprepared that it suffered unduly heavy losses. At the same time 98 Division was committed from Army reserve. It fought with great vigour in this its first action in Italy and its casualties too were heavy. A regiment from I62 Turkoman Division was a less useful reinforcement. Finally, with that readiness to accept risks which had marked Kesselring's strategy throughout the campaign, and had gone far to retrieve the initial disasters to German arms which his invariable misreading of our intentions always incurred, the enemy Commander-in-Chief now removed his last reserve from the centre and left, 29 Panzer Grenadier Division, and despatched it in haste eastwards. The first elements of the division were in action by 4th September, but the bulk did not arrive until the 6th. On the latter day also a regiment of 5 Mountain Division, which had been taken out of the line on its way to the French frontier, was halted and brought back into the line.

It had been a great success for Eighth Army. By a combination of surprise in preparation and dash in the attack they had swept through a fortified line which had been twelve months in preparation almost as though it were not there. Only two assets now remained to Kesselring to retrieve the situation: the excellence of his lateral communications and the fact that the "Gothic" line had been built on the forward slopes of the range. The importance of the former factor in allowing a rapid reinforcement I have already emphasized; the latter meant that there was still one more ridge between the Allies and the plains, known from the village on its summit as the Coriano ridge. The Canadians were already over the Conca, on 2nd September, and 5 Corps were about to pass I Armoured Division through in a dash for the flat country beyond. Just in time Kesselring succeeded in manning the Coriano ridge with I Parachute, 26 Panzer and 29 Panzer Grenadier Divisions; these three excellent divisions, aided by very heavy rain from 5th to 7th September, resisted all attacks between the 4th and the I2th both on the ridge itself and on its southern flank at Gemmano.

As Eighth Army's offensive developed its full extent the enemy was forced to economize strength on the remainder of his front by withdrawing into the "Gothic" line. This was essential if he were to be able to make further reinforcements available for his left; it was also a natural measure of precaution in case a real break-through was achieved for, apart from LXXVI Corps, now engaged with Eighth Army, the rest of the German troops were still well south of the watershed of the Apennines. The withdrawal began on 30th August. LI Mountain Corps, between Urbino and Pontassieve, moved straight back into the line on a timed programme, releasing one division for the central sector, and I0 Corps, following up, made contact with the line on 3rd September. At the same time the enemy opposite Fifth Army began to pull back. On the extreme right they went back almost directly into the "Gothic" line. Opposite I3 Corps, however, the enemy stabilized on 3rd September on the line of hills north of Florence: Monte Morello, Monte Senario, Monte Calvana and Monte Giovi. IV Corps followed up across the Arno on 3Ist August and II Corps on Ist September. Little resistance was met and we were able to occupy the northern part of Pisa on the 2nd, Lucca on the 6th and Pistoia on the I2th.

This enemy withdrawal made it easier to concentrate forward the Fifth Army troops which were to launch the second punch of my two-handed attack on the "Gothic" line. Moreover, in the course of the withdrawal Kesselring still further weakened his centre, from which he had already removed 29 Panzer Grenadier Division, by relieving 356 Infantry Division and sending it over to the Adriatic. I decided, therefore, that the time was almost come for the Fifth Army attack to go in. I visited Eighth Army front on 8th September and it was clear to me from what I saw there that we could not continue our advance on to Rimini until we had driven the enemy off the Coriano ridge. This would need full preparation and would probably take two or three days more. I explained the situation in a signal next day, 9th September, and concluded by saying that for these reasons I had decided to unleash Fifth Army who would now go ahead with their offensive in the centre. The enemy's forces there were as weak as we could ever expect them to be and he was obligingly withdrawing from the high ground north of Florence without serious resistance, which saved us time and trouble. As soon as Fifth Army had forced the enemy back to the "Gothic" line they would launch a full-scale attack to break through and by that time I hoped Eighth Army would be just about ready for their attack on the Rimini positions and that we should be able to prevent Kesselring from shifting reserves from one Army front to another by keeping up a series of heavy blows by our two Armies in turn. The weather had improved and I hoped for a fine spell - another reason for launching Fifth Army then.

All preparations for Fifth Army's attack had been made by 8th September. The main blow was to be delivered by II Corps but, in order to gain surprise, its concentration was to be secret and it was to be launched into the attack through I3 Corps. The plan was that I3 Corps should attack first with 8 Indian Division to capture the line of hills from Monte Morello to Monte Giovi, already mentioned, then, in the second phase, II Corps would pass through the left of I3 Corps with its four divisions (34th, 85th, 88th and 9Ist) and advance up the axis Florence - Firenzuola. I3 Corps would shift its main thrust to the right and continue to advance up the two roads Dicomano to Forli and Borgo San Lorenzo to Faenza. IV Corps was to exert the maximum pressure in its area with 6 South African Armoured Division, a Negro

Regimental Combat Team and "Task Force 45" and release I Armoured Division for Army reserve to be used if a chance of exploitation arose.

This plan could not be carried out in its original form, for on 8th September the enemy withdrew voluntarily from the line of hills which was to have been 13 Corps' objective in the first phase. This was gratifying in itself and represented a further gain in that it gave us the chance of launching an attack on an enemy already engaged in withdrawing which, as Eighth Army's experience had shown, was one of the surest means of obtaining surprise. On 10th September, therefore, 91 and 34 Divisions of II Corps passed through I British Infantry Division on the left of 13 Corps, astride Route 65, and began an advance directed on the "Gothic" line north of the River Sieve. Considerable gains were made on the 10th and 11th as both Corps pressed on across the Sieve in face of little resistance, capturing Dicomano, Borgo San Lorenzo and Scarperia. The Germans offered only delaying resistance as they drew back into the "Gothic" line but the weight of the Allied attack surprised and disconcerted them and pushed them back quicker than they had expected or were prepared for. It was not until the strong position of Monte Calvi was captured on the 12th that it became clear that this was not merely an attack to gain contact with the line but to break through it.

Simultaneous Attacks by Fifth and Eighth Armies.

On the night of 12th September Eighth Army reopened its attack on the Coriano ridge and in the early morning of the 13th Fifth Army began the assault of the main "Gothic" line positions in the centre. This marked the beginning of a week of perhaps the heaviest fighting on both fronts that either Army had yet experienced. The Canadians on the right and 5 Corps on the left of Eighth Army succeeded in getting onto the Coriano ridge in their first attack, capturing over a thousand prisoners on the first day. The second phase was to exploit across the River Marano. The Germans, though shaken, were clearly determined to expend every effort to deny us Rimini and concentrated strong forces on a line running from the mountain on which is perched the small republic of San Marino to the sea in front of Rimini; on the coast the front was protected by the River Ausa and in the centre of the position by a strongpoint on the hill crowned by the village of San Fortunato, the last piece of high ground before the plains. Reinforcements continued to arrive. Before the battle for Coriano, Kesselring had brought over three divisions to the Adriatic sector from his centre and right; he now took another infantry division from the centre, the 356th, and another from the right, 20 Luftwaffe Field Division, and on the 19th added a regimental group from 90 Panzer Grenadier Division, brought from the French frontier. Kesselring had thus doubled the strength of his forces originally facing Eighth Army by the transfer of the equivalent of five divisions, but shortly after the attack on Rimini began he had to withdraw entirely two divisions to re-form. The importance which he attached to the Adriatic sector was based largely on the fact that, if he were driven off the Apennines, he would have to withdraw in a north-easterly direction to avoid being penned up against the Swiss and French frontiers, and this sector would be the vital hinge on which to swing back his exposed right. The transfer of 20 Luftwaffe Field

Division[113] was particularly significant for, as it passed behind the centre of the front, the first strongpoints of the "Gothic" line on the direct road to Bologna were already falling.

In spite of these reinforcements Eighth Army continued to make steady progress. They won a bridgehead over the Marano and by the I5th had advanced nearly three thousand yards north of it. The New Zealanders were now brought into the battle and a full-scale attack was launched on the I8th. After a desperate three day struggle San Fortunato was cleared on the 20th and the same night the Greeks, under command of I Canadian Division, entered Rimini. I was glad that this success had so early brightened the fortunes of that heroic country which had been the only ally to fight by our side in our darkest days and that a new victory in Italy should be added to the fame won in the mountains of Albania. More disheartening was a sudden fall of torrential rain, also on the night of the 20th, undercover of which the enemy withdrew across the broad and swollen Marecchia river. Only one bridge survived, the bridge built by Tiberius, nineteen hundred years ago, which had outlived the drums and tramplings of many conquests, and now carried troops from the Antipodes across the river onto the Via Emilia. As our patrols pushed forward on the 2Ist into the plains so long hoped for and so fiercely fought for the deluge foreboded a future of clogging mud and brimming watercourses.

II Corps' main offensive on the "Gothic" line began on the morning of I3th September when 85 Division moved forward to the attack through I British Infantry Division. The strongest enemy defences were at the Futa pass on the watershed crossed by the main road from Florence to Bologna, Route 65; General Clark had therefore decided to make his principal thrust to the east of this road up the Firenzuola road, using the Giogo pass. I3 Corps was to apply its main weight simultaneously to assist II Corps and to open the Marradi road. As I have already explained, the Germans had seriously weakened their force in this sector but the fanaticism and skill of 4 Parachute Division made up for this and initially little progress was made. On the centre of I3 Corps front, however, 8 Indian Division advanced across the trackless mountains, operating by night, and by the I5th had broken through the line in their sector and reached the watershed on the Alpe di Vitigliano, looking down on the Marradi road. This was the first breach of the "Gothic" line in the centre. On the I7th combined attacks by I British and 85 United States Divisions, directed against the junction of the enemy's Tenth and Fourteenth Armies, captured Monte Pratone, and on the same day the enemy resistance at last broke under the weight of our attack. Poggio Signorini, Monte Altuzzo, Monte Verruca and Monticelli were all occupied, and with these heights went possession of the Giogo Pass. Now it was time for Kesselring to scrape up reinforcements for yet another part of his front. He drew them from the right of the line and from the sector between the two Allied thrusts; from the former came 362 Division, which arrived on the I9th to cover Firenzuola, and from the latter 44 Division on the 2Ist to take over the sector of the Firenzuola - Imola road.

Fifth Army had now, by I8th September, got both its attacking Corps firmly on to the watershed. The terrain which there faced them presented a totally different picture from that in which they had been operating hitherto. So far they had been climbing up a steep ascent where the mountains offer a nearly continuous wall running east and west at right angles to the line of advance; once the line of the passes is reached the whole grain of the country is reversed and the mountains begin to trend north-eastwards in gradually descending spurs separated from each other by the valleys of swift rivers which drain into the plains of Lombardy. For the greater part of their course in the mountains these rivers run through deep gorges which offer no scope for deployment or manoeuvre but in a few places, as at Firenzuola on the upper Santerno, the valleys open out and it is possible for artillery and transport to deploy. The mountain spurs, as I said, descend gradually, and for nearly half their total length their height is very little less than that of the watershed, with isolated higher peaks offering good command of the surrounding terrain. There was little advantage, therefore, in the fact that we were now going, according to the map, "downhill"; the immense difficulties of supply to the forward troops and deployment of our strength in artillery still remained. So bad and so scanty were the forward routes that our lines of communication, the more we advanced, became more of a drag on our progress while the enemy, as his lines shortened, reaped proportionate advantages.

In spite of the enemy reinforcement Fifth Army still retained sufficient momentum from its capture of the Giogo pass to press down into the valley of the Santerno. On 21st September, 85 Infantry Division captured Firenzuola, and, pressing on north, stormed the strong position of Monte la Fine, west of the Imola road. On its right II Corps had put in, on the 21st, its last fresh division, 88 Infantry, with the task of clearing the east side of the Imola road. The 88th pressed on over desperately difficult country and on the 27th seized Monte La Battaglia, a great mountain mass dominating the Senio and Santerno valleys on either hand and only ten miles from Imola and the Emilian plain. The enemy now reacted with great vigour and began a series of most violent counter-attacks with elements of four divisions; these and the increasing difficulties of our communications brought a halt to our advance on Imola. I3 Corps during this time had had the task of protecting II Corps' right; it had still the same three divisions forward with which it had fought its way up from the Arno valley. Its sector of operations was dictated by the road-net and its main efforts must be down the roads to Faenza and Forli. On 24th September it captured Marradi on the former and San Benedetto on the latter. Meanwhile the left of II Corps had also been making good progress where 9I and 34 Divisions were advancing up the direct routes from Florence to Bologna. On the 21st the fate of the strong Futa Pass positions was sealed by the capture of Monte Gazzarro (or Guzzaso) on its eastern flank and by the 28th Route 65 was clear as far as the northern end of the Radicosa Pass, the second main pass on the Florence - Bologna road. On the Prato - Bologna road 34 Division had kept level until, on a change of corps boundaries at midnight 28th-29th September, they were relieved by the South Africans when just short of Castiglione dei Pepoli. Between them and the coast the task of IV Corps was to follow up the enemy; this had brought us by the 28th to a line some five miles north of Pistoia and running from there over the mountains north of Lucca to the coastal plain about three miles short of Massa where the western end of the "Gothic" line was secured by strong defences anchored on the sea. Viareggio was entered on 16th September by a British converted anti-aircraft battery of "Task Force 45". 6 Regimental Combat Team of the Brazilian Expeditionary Force took over a sector of the line on 16th September. This was the first contingent of an Allied South American state to see action in this war. While it was gaining battle experience it played a valuable rôle in holding an important part of the defensive front.

The "Gothic" line was now completely turned at its eastern end and pierced over a wide front in the centre. By the end of September the enemy had decided to abandon such of the prepared positions as still remained in his hands except for a small sector in the extreme west. In thus depriving the enemy of the permanent defences on which he had worked so long the Allied Armies in Italy had scored a great success, won at a great price, but it was difficult to exploit. The furthest advance had been made, as was intended, by the Eighth Army, which had advanced some thirty miles in twenty-six days. In a letter to me summing up the results of the action to date, written on 21st September, General Leese said he considered the fighting to have been as bitter as at Alamein and Cassino. The German artillery fire was very heavy and well-directed and the many counter-attacks were made in considerable strength; one village changed hands ten times. Eighth Army claimed to have "severely mauled" eleven German divisions and taken over eight thousand prisoners. The cost was over fourteen thousand casualties, of which over seven thousand in British infantry units, and two hundred and ten tanks lost. The tanks were easily replaceable, but the men were not and I was forced to take very unwelcome measures to keep up the strength of formations. 1 British Armoured Division, which had played a distinguished part in so many battles in Africa, was to be disbanded in less than three months after its arrival in Italy. A brigade of 56 Division was be reduced to a cadre basis. Finally, all United Kingdom infantry battalions were to be reorganised at once on the basis of three rifle companies.[114] Yet, although the price had been heavy, no one in Eighth Army doubted that a real victory had been gained, for it was confidently expected that, after breaking into the flat country of the Romagna, we should be able to exploit rapidly to the Po. It was not long, however, before, as the Eighth Army historian puts it, "the tactical implications of the local agricultural methods were realized" and the continuous water lines were found to be more serious obstacles than the mountains.

Not only the Eighth Army replacement situation but the general manpower situation of the Allied Armies in Italy was such as to give rise to anxiety. I explained the main features to the Chief of the Imperial General Staff on 21st September. After the loss of seven divisions to the invasion of Southern France the promised reinforcements to Italy, after deducting other subsequent decreases, had only amounted to one and a half divisions, including 78 Division, which would not be available until the first week in October. On that date, therefore, the net loss would be five and a half divisions. The enemy, on the other hand, had continued to reinforce Italy. Since May Kesselring had lost to other fronts three of his original twenty-three German divisions and had disbanded one other. In return he had received from elsewhere ten divisions and three divisions' worth of extra replacements; one of the new arrivals had now been likewise disbanded which left him with twenty-eight

German divisions all told.[115] To this should be added two Italian divisions which were at least useful for internal security duties. Even without counting the Italians the net German gains were five divisions, or eight if the three "shadow" divisions, incorporated as replacements in three of the original divisions, are counted. Summing up I said:

> "To put it briefly, we shall have to continue the battle of Italy with about twenty divisions, almost all of which have had long periods of heavy fighting this year, and some for several years, against the twenty German divisions committed to the battle front, with the prospect of four more German divisions, and probably two Italian divisions, joining in the battle at a later stage. We are inflicting very heavy losses on the enemy and are making slow but steady progress, but our losses are also heavy and we are fighting in country where, it is generally agreed, a superiority of at least three to one is required for successful offensive operations. It will be small wonder, therefore, if we fail to score a really decisive success when the opposing forces are so equally matched".

I was naturally fully conscious that by thus battling on against odds we were fulfilling our function in the grand strategy of the war, whatever the cost and even though we were to make no progress on the ground at all. I was repeatedly reminded that this was the crisis of the war and that now more than ever it was vital to hold down the maximum forces in Italy, away from the vital theatres in east and west.[116] From this point of view the balance of strength in Italy was definitely in our favour and I was determined to keep it so; but I could not help considering the question of how long I could keep up the pressure. With the present relationship between the opposing forces, even though enemy casualties exceeded ours, it would be impossible to continue hammering away at full stretch indefinitely, and to suspend operations, if the suspension were long extended, would be to renounce the whole object of the campaign. The first relief I could expect would be from the newly formed Italian Combat Groups; they were still an unknown quantity but would at least be useful in a defensive rôle. The first was expected to be ready by the end of October, the second by the middle of November; two more by the middle of December and two by January. In the event only five were formed; Cremona, Mantova, Folgore, Legnano and Friuli. Cremona was the first to see active service, in January 1945. The Brazilians were also an unknown quantity, though they were well equipped and in good strength. They gave a good account of themselves in the final offensive of the following spring. The coloured troops of the United States 92 Infantry Division proved unsuited for modern combat conditions; the division was eventually reorganized, and made into an effective formation by incorporating one Japanese-American and one white American Regimental Combat Team, the latter formed from converted anti-aircraft gunners.

Eighth Army enters the Romagna.

I have already alluded to the difficulties of operations in the Romagna and the fact that water was now the main obstacle to Eighth Army's advance rather than high ground. The whole area is nothing but a great reclaimed swamp - and not wholly reclaimed in some parts - formed by the lower courses of numerous rivers flowing down from the Apennines in their new north-easterly direction. The principal rivers are, in order from east to west, the Uso, the Savio, the Ronco, the Montone (these last two after their confluence take the name of Fiumi Uniti), the Lamone, the Senio, the Santerno, the Sillaro and the Idice; these are only the principal rivers and there are hundreds of smaller streams, canals and irrigation ditches in between them. By these, and by canalization of the main rivers, the primitive swamp had been drained after centuries of patient effort and, as the water flowed off, so the level of the ground sank; the river beds were thereby left higher than the surrounding ground and as soon as they descend into the plain all these rivers need high banks on either side to keep them in their course and to guard against the sudden rise of level which heavy rainfall in the mountains invariably causes. Even in the best drained areas the soil remembers its marshy origin and when rained on forms the richest mud known to the Italian theatre. It will be seen, therefore, that under autumn conditions we should have difficulty in making full use of our armoured superiority. Tanks were hampered also by the intensive cultivation, and in particular by the vineyards. The Germans had prepared fieldworks and well-studied plans for defence on all the main waterlines and were determined to offer the most stubborn resistance in this vital sector. To Kesselring his eastern flank was the pivot which, if a withdrawal was forced on him, he would have to hold firmly in order to swing back his right into a position blocking the approaches to Austria through north-eastern Italy, whether that position was based on the line of the Po and Ticino or the Adige. The pivot was not, however, in serious danger until he was forced back to a line between the Valli di Comacchio, a large lagoon on the Adriatic shore, south of the Po, and Bologna in the south-west. Before that position was reached he had reason to hope that the cumulative effect of so many opposed river crossings and the deterioration of the weather would bring Eighth Army's offensive to a standstill.

The Canadians crossed the Marecchia by Rimini on 21st September and the next day the New Zealanders passed through I Canadian Division to exploit up the coast. 5 Corps also reached the river on the 22nd, having mopped up the Coriano area, and on the 23rd exploited forward to make contact with the ridge between the Marecchia and the Uso. By the 25th the enemy was generally back behind the Uso but not in very good order and advances were made all along the Army front. In the plains we had cleared the whole eastern bank of the Fiumicino by 29th September but the enemy was still holding out in the foothills south of Route 9 when the rain descended with great violence for four successive days. All the fords over the Marecchia and Uso became impassable and the approaches to the bridges, necessarily more congested, were in very bad condition; the Fiumicino, normally a shallow trickle, swelled to a width of thirty feet and its speed and depth made it impossible for infantry patrols to cross. Going off the roads became quite impossible. The enemy took heart from this to maintain a steadfast resistance and it was not until 5th October that the Fiumicino was reached all along the 5 Corps front.[117]

During the period while Fifth and Eighth Armies were developing their main attacks I0 Corps, acting as the connecting link between the two forces (but under command of Eighth Army), had been following up and hastening the enemy's withdrawal on the axis of Route 7I; the Arezzo - Cesena road. Its frontage was very extensive for its small strength but the enemy also was weak in this sector. On 24th September the watershed was gained after a stiff fight for the Mandrioli Pass, for which the enemy put up a strong defence. After this heavy rains prevented further operations until 30th September; the division and the armoured brigade under command were transferred to the Adriatic sector and replaced by I Guards Brigade Group and 2 Anti-Aircraft Brigade from Fifth Army for use as infantry. With these forces, reinforced by three dismounted armoured car regiments and three independent infantry battalions, it was impossible to force the pace. The enemy, however, continued to withdraw and by 6th October I0 Corps had gained a position astride Route 7I on the upper reaches of the Savio, not much more than fifteen miles from Cesena.

Fifth Army resumes the Attack on Bologna.

The furthest point in Fifth Army's advance down the Imola road had been reached with the capture of Monte La Battaglia on 27th September. While the enemy was expending his strength in vain counter-attacks to recapture this vital position, attempts which continued until they died down from exhaustion on 6th October,[118] General Clark decided to take advantage of the progress made by the left wing of II Corps to concentrate the main weight of the Corps on the axis of Route 65, the direct road to Bologna. The factors which had militated against the choice of this axis for the original attack no longer applied, since we had now left well behind the strong defences and difficult terrain of the Futa Pass and were over the Radicosa Pass as well. Accordingly I3 Corps were to take over responsibility for the Imola axis and were to relieve 88 Division on Monte La Battaglia. I felt that this new drive would be the climax of our operations in the mountains; the season was already far advanced and the break in the weather had come earlier than usual;[119] unless we could get through now we were likely to be stuck in the mountains for the winter. In order, therefore, to give the maximum weight possible to the attack, and since all three divisions in I3 Corps were very tired after continuous fighting, I decided on 2nd October to reinforce it with 78 Division, my only fresh formation, just back from a restful tour of duty in the Middle East. Even with this addition, as I reported on the same date, I feared that "we may not be quite strong enough to carry it through". General Clark's plan was to continue to press forward with the troops already in the line, resting one regiment from 85, 88 and 9I Divisions and then to bring in these rested troops on I0th October in a concentrated attack. I3 Corps was to conform by attacking on the right of II Corps with its existing forces and then, relieving 88 Division with the 78th, to attack in concert with the Americans down the Santerno valley onto Route 9 northwest of Imola.

II Corps' new drive had started on Ist October with 85 Division advancing east of Route 65 and the 9Ist on the road itself, supported by diversionary attacks by 88 and

34 Divisions on the right and left flanks respectively. On 2nd October the relief of 88 Division on Monte La Battaglia began, in the first place by I Guards Brigade. The badness of the roads and tracks in rear of the position severely hampered the relief; the rain also continued remorselessly. On the left of II Corps good progress was made. On 2nd October 9I Division captured the village of Monghidoro, twenty-five miles by road from Bologna, and on the 3rd 34 Division captured Monte Venere, a commanding height to the west of the large village of Loiano. On the right 85 Division had reached the head waters of the River Idice. By the 4th II Corps had made good an advance of some four miles in two days against strong resistance and in abominable weather. Loiano, twenty-two miles from Bologna, fell to 9I Division on the 5th. On the same day 6 South African Armoured Division came under direct Fifth Army command with the task of operating on the left of II Corps up the Prato - Castiglione road; it had under it 24 Guards Brigade, an an independent Indian battalion (6/13 Frontier Force Rifles) and Combat Command "B" of I U.S. Armoured Division.

Slowly the advance on Bologna continued, with gains of the nature of two thousand yards in a day; for although we had now left the "Gothic" line defences far behind and were attacking, in a sense, downhill, the complexities of the mountain structure, the rain and the fanaticism of the defenders made every advance a hard fought struggle. The attack increased in intensity on 10th October when 88 Division, now completely relieved by 13 Corps, attacked simultaneously with 85 Division to the east of Route 65 and with 9I Division on the axis of the road itself. The enemy was now reinforcing fast.[120] 65 Division had already been brought round from the western sector and put in in a narrow sector on the Bologna road and, on the 13th, 44 Division, which had been taken out for a rest, was re-committed. The troops were encouraged by a personal order from Hitler, read out to all ranks on 6th October, that the Apennine position was to be held at all costs. On the 14th Vietinghoff decided to run risks in his vital left sector and began to bring across 29 Panzer Grenadier Division from the front opposite Eighth Army. In spite of this our advance continued. On the 12th 85 Division captured Monte delle Formiche, a two thousand foot peak to the east of the main road and level with Livergnano, a village only twelve miles by road from Bologna. Fighting continued for Livergnano itself from the 10th to the 15th. On the same day 34 Division, which had been relieved on the left of the Corps by I Armoured Division, took over a new sector between 9I and 85 Divisions, to strengthen the attack east of Route 65.

The climax of the assault was reached between 20th and 24th October. On the 20th 88 Division attacked and seized the great *massif* of Monte Grande and Monte Cerere. On the 22nd the same division captured La Costa, only four miles from Route 9 and on the 23rd 34 Division captured Monte Belmonte, about ten miles east of Route 65 and nine miles from the centre of Bologna. That same night 78 Division stormed Monte Spaduro for which the Irish Brigade had been struggling since the 20th. This was Fifth Army's finest effort of the winter campaign. For the Germans it was a real crisis, for a relatively small advance would put the Allies on Route 9, behind Tenth Army; the front would be split and even an immediate withdrawal might lead to disaster. The only course was to hope that we might be so exhausted by the struggle in the mountains as to be incapable of that supreme effort. As he had done at Cassino, Vietinghoff decided to hold on in that hope and to make the parallel still closer and strengthen the hope he brought across from opposite Eighth Army the two divisions famous for the defence of Cassino, 90 Panzer Grenadier and I Parachute Division. With the arrival of the remainder of 29 Panzer Grenadier Division the three best divisions in Italy barred the way to the plain. Assisted by torrential rains and winds of gale force, and by Fifth Army's exhaustion, the German line held firm. On 27th October I agreed to General Clark's assumption of the defensive.

To be robbed of a decisive success after so long and sanguinary a struggle was the more bitter in that the price already paid would have been heavy even if paid for victory. I cannot sufficiently express my admiration for the way in which the troops of Fifth Army, in spite of the most arduous and exhausting conditions, in mud and snow, returned again and again to the attack on one mountain position after another, regardless of the heavy and continuous losses which thinned their ranks. Casualties had been mounting steadily during the long drawn-out offensive, more particularly in II Corps, and, as with Eighth Army, a serious replacement crisis had arisen. On 9th October General Clark informed me that by Ist November, at the present rate of wastage, he would be eight thousand infantry short for his United States divisions which would mean a shortage of seventy-five men per rifle company. He had already asked General Devers,[12] Deputy Supreme Commander, if he could be allotted replacements from the pool scheduled for Seventh Army, which was in the theatre. General Devers did not feel able to comply with this request and on I5th October, as a last resort, I signalled personally to General Eisenhower to ask him if he could allot Fifth Army three thousand replacements from the resources of the European Theatre of Operations. This was rather a roundabout method, as replacements for Seventh Army, i.e. France, were then sailing from Naples and it would have been quicker to have diverted them northwards than to fetch fresh ones from France. General Eisenhower at once undertook to examine the matter urgently and replied on the 2Ist that he was proceeding to despatch our three thousand men immediately by air. It was a fine example of General Eisenhower's ready grasp of the big strategic picture and his willingness to cut through red tape to assist a friend in need. It also illustrates the advantage the Allies drew from our command of the facilities of air transport.

Eighth Army's Advance from the Fiumicino to the Ronco.

On Ist October General McCreery assumed command of Eighth Army in succession to General Leese, who had been appointed to command Allied Land Forces in South-eastern Asia. It was a well-deserved promotion for one who had worthily carried on the traditions established by General Montgomery and who had made his mark on the campaign in Italy by his handling of large forces in the Liri valley battles. General McCreery had commanded I0 Corps since the first landings at Salerno. That operation might be said to typify the kind of task in which he had ever since been engaged, the achievement of vital results with limited resources, by hard fighting in difficult terrain where a scientific adjustment of means to ends called for constant changes of tactics and all the craft of generalship. The first crossing of the Garigliano, and the operations east of Arezzo, are further examples of his successful use of the strategy of deception. I was well acquainted with General McCreery's qualities as a scientific soldier with a gift for the offensive from the time when he had been my Chief of Staff for the Alamein campaign and onward to final victory in Tunisia, and was therefore particularly pleased to have him as one of my Army Commanders.

The plan for the continuance of the advance on the Adriatic sector called for a full-scale offensive by 5 Corps and I Canadian Corps on an axis parallel to and north of the Rimini - Bologna road; weather permitting this was to be launched on the night of 6th/7th October. The weather did not permit; rain was continuous and of extraordinary violence, paralysing any movement in the plains. In the higher ground on the left the effect was not so serious and I0 Indian Division was able to exploit its bridgehead over the Fiumicino and to capture on 7th October Monte Farneto. This started a series of manoeuvres which were to characterize the next period: ground was gained on the left flank in order to turn from there the series of river lines. It was natural that this policy should commend itself to General McCreery, for he had recently been operating with very small forces in these mountains, while commanding I0 Corps, and had found them less of an obstacle to an advance than the continuous water lines of the deceptively attractive plains. The Germans were also surprised by our successes here and moved across 29 Panzer Grenadier Division to this sector from north of Route 9. It was not left there long, however, for on I4th October it began to transfer to the central front to meet Fifth Army's attack on Bologna. The result was that by the I6th both Corps had reached the line of the river Pisciatello.

On 17th October 2 Polish Corps, which had taken over the sector on the left of 5 Corps previously under I0 Corps (and commanded in the interim by the Headquarters of the disbanded I Armoured Division) opened an attack to improve our communications in the mountains. The principal object was to clear the minor road which leaves Route 7I at San Piero in Bagno and joins Route 67 at Rocca San Casciano, crossing the valleys of the Bidente and Rabbi. Possession of Route 67 would be of the greatest importance for improving communications between the two Armies. The Poles made good progress in the mountains. Galeata, commanding the upper Bidente valley, fell on I9th October and Strada, in the valley of the Rabbi, on the 2Ist; here the enemy showed signs of an intention to resist more strongly. Meanwhile in the plains Cesena had been entered on I9th October and on the 20th 4 Division seized a precarious but tenaciously defended bridgehead over the Savio in the neighbourhood of Route 9. Further to the south I0 Indian Division established two more bridgeheads and in the southernmost built up rapidly for an assault on Monte Cavallo, on the watershed between the Savio and the Ronco. By the2Ist there were no enemy forward of the Savio except in the coastal sector, where they still held Cervia.

Intentions now were for the Poles to press down the valley of the Rabbi towards Forli while 5 Corps advanced on the same objective on the axis of Route 9. The Polish attack began on 22nd October but made little progress until the 25th. 5 Corps also met heavy resistance to attempts to break out from its Cesena bridgehead over the

Savio. I0 Indian Division captured Monte Cavallo and began to thrust northwards. Resistance ceased on the 24th, however, when the enemy carried out his sole voluntary withdrawal on this front. The tactical situation, in particular the threat from Monte Cavallo, would indeed have forced a withdrawal in the near future but an even more pressing reason was the situation on the Fifth Army front where the crisis of the defence of Bologna had now been reached. Three first class divisions, 29 and 90 Panzer Grenadiers and I Parachute Division, had been withdrawn in succession to the central sector and it was vitally necessary to reduce the front of LXXVI Corps to allow for this reduction in strength. The line chosen was the river Ronco. By the 25th both the Canadians and 5 Corps had made contact with this line but the rain, which was at that very time foiling Fifth Army's attack on Bologna, now reached a new high pitch of intensity. On the 26th all bridges over the Savio, in our immediate rear, were swept away and our small bridgeheads over the Ronco were eliminated and destroyed. The Poles continued to advance and on the 27th captured Predappio Nuova. The situation remained more or less unchanged, like the weather, until the 3Ist when the enemy was forced back opposite 5 Corps to a switch line from the Ronco at Forli airfield to the Rabbi at Grisignano.

This was a most discouraging period for Eighth Army. The weather was abominable and the country difficult. Every river and canal was subject to sudden rises and floods which not merely made the seizing of a bridgehead in face of opposition desperately difficult but was liable also to interrupt at any moment maintenance and the movement of reinforcements. Some miles of waterlogged ground were gained but despite our best efforts it was impossible to prevent the enemy, making full use of these natural advantages, from withdrawing sufficient troops to block Fifth Army's advance. The capture of Cesena and Forlimpopoli, and even of Mussolini's birthplace at Predappio, were not sufficient recompense for the failure to capture Bologna. Eighth Army's strength was now also, declining, for early in October it had to release 4 Indian Division and the Greek Mountain Brigade Group to go to Greece. This was the beginning of a process which was to cost British troops in Italy eventually two more divisions.[122]

Plans for the Winter Campaign.

Operations in Italy in the winter of I944 to I945, the bitter and continuous fighting in the Apennines and in the waterlogged plains of the Romagna, can only be properly understood against the background of the general strategic picture of the war against Germany on all fronts. The main factor determining the situation was the decision by General Eisenhower, as Supreme Allied Commander in the West, that it would be necessary to fight a winter campaign on that front the effect of which would be either to bring about directly a German collapse or at least, by the attrition caused, to ensure that result next spring. The Italian campaign from its very inception had been designed to second and supplement the invasion of the west, even before that invasion was launched, and the Allied Armies in Italy were therefore now called on once more to make a direct contribution to the winter campaign on the Western front. I considered four possible courses to make that contribution: to transfer troops from

Italy to the west, to employ troops from Italy in Jugoslavia, to continue the offensive on the Italian front at full stretch to the limits set by exhaustion and material shortage or to halt the offensive now and build up for a renewal in greater strength at a later date. All these courses were judged solely by the criterion of which would have the greatest effect on operations in the west. The first was rejected because there was, on the current programme, no need for extra troops in France and the current maintenance situation would not allow any from Italy to be accepted as yet. To transfer troops to Jugoslavia was a project which I was then actively considering; it would have certain advantages, as I shall show, if we could first drive the enemy in Italy back to the Adige line, but it would have no effect on the Western front and would only begin to have one on the Eastern front next spring. Of the two courses which involved continuing to use our full resources in Italy the one which General Eisenhower considered more advantageous to him was the continuance of the offensive. I thoroughly appreciated this reading of the situation. It was for this reason that operations were pressed on in Italy despite all the difficulties of climate and terrain, of deficient manpower and material.

The consequences of this policy were expounded in a letter to both Army Commanders dated I0th October. For the reasons given the offensive must be continued, but it was already necessary to plan ahead and consider the question of when to call a halt; that it would be necessary to call a halt was deduced from the fact that there was no certainty of the war against Germany ending in I944 and that a major offensive in I945 would therefore be necessary. In order to meet that requirement it was vital, in view of the close approximation of the opposing strengths, to make a pause at some time to rest, reorganize and train our own troops. During this pause Eighth Army was to plan, and prepare to carry out, operations across the Adriatic. If northwest Italy were cleared it would be occupied by a British District Headquarters with one division under command (6 South African Armoured Division was tentatively nominated).The conclusions drawn were: that active operations with all available forces should continue as long as the state of our own troops and the weather permitted in the hope that by then we should have at least succeeded in driving the enemy back to the general line of the Adige and the Alps and in clearing up northwestern Italy. Secondly, when full-scale operations ceased, there should be a period of active defence during which the minimum forces would be committed against the enemy and the maximum attention paid to the rest, reorganisation and training of all formations in preparation for a renewal of the offensive as soon as the weather should permit.

This appreciation was brought up to date on 23rd October in a further letter to Fifth and Eighth Armies. In this, operations in Jugoslavia were brought more into the foreground for the major rôle in the proposed spring offensive and the question of when to halt the offensive in Italy was more closely studied. Between I0th and 23rd October the fiercest fighting on Fifth Army front had left us still short of Bologna, the exhaustion of our troops had increased and the lack of replacements, both British and American, had made itself felt. In this second paper, therefore, it was assumed that we were unlikely to have driven the enemy back to the line of the Adige by the time that it became necessary to halt the offensive; instead our immediate objectives were limited to the capture of Bologna and Ravenna. The plan proposed was that Eighth Army should continue their offensive with all available forces at least until I5th November in order to capture Ravenna and, to draw off the enemy from Fifth Army. The latter was to go on to the defensive forthwith (this was ordered on 27th October), withdraw forces from the line to rest and prepare them for one more offensive effort and then launch them as secretly as possible in a final attack on Bologna. If this plan was unsuccessful, then we should have to accept the best winter position that could be managed; Eighth Army must endeavour, however, to capture Forli and open Route 67 to improve lateral communications between the two Armies. I held a conference at my Headquarters to discuss this plan on 29th October. The principles of the plan were agreed to but I decided to advance the date at which the offensive efforts of both Armies must cease from I5th November to I5th December; Fifth Army's final attempt to capture Bologna was accordingly postponed until about 30th November. Eighth Army was to continue to attempt the capture of Ravenna and should be in a position to launch an attack with that object also by 30th November. I laid down, however, that the offensives were only to be launched if the weather was favourable and there appeared to be a good chance of success.

A critical shortage of artillery ammunition was among the other difficulties of this period. To a force which relied so much on artillery, the only effective superiority we possessed for a campaign in an Italian winter, this was a most serious matter, the more so as it was not an isolated phenomenon but a world-wide shortage both on the British and United States side. It had naturally been aggravated by our heavy expenditure during the "Gothic" line battles. The root cause, however, as I was informed by a signal from the War Office on I7th August, was a reduction in ammunition production all over the Allied-controlled world. This was a condition of affairs which could not hastily be unproved and, although I was on 20th October authorized to draw on the Supreme Allied Commander's reserve up to the full extent which the operational situation might necessitate, there was a serious danger that not only would current operations be severely limited but there might not be sufficient stocks on hand for the spring offensive. I drew this conclusion in a letter to General Wilson on I3th November:

> "As far as I am able to forecast I have just enough British ammunition for the current operations of Eighth Army and for an all-out offensive in December lasting about fifteen days. American ammunition is, however, only sufficient for about ten days intensive fighting between now and the end of the year. Deliveries in the first quarter of I945 in the case of both British and American types are so limited that it will be necessary to exercise the strictest economy for several months to build up large enough stocks to sustain a full-scale offensive in I945".

I have referred to plans for operations in Jugoslavia as part of our proposed spring offensive and although the necessity for such operations did not arise the plans themselves are of interest in illustrating the strategic problems which faced us in the autumn of 1944. If we were wholly successful in our attack on the Apennine positions we should be faced with a situation resembling that of September, 1943, before the German decision to stand south of Rome: that is the enemy would be withdrawing at his leisure to a prepared position in rear and we should be unable to make him stand in Italy. Just as in the preceding September, therefore, I turned my eyes to the other side of the Adriatic, where we could be certain of bringing the Germans to battle on ground of our choosing rather than theirs. From the point of view of containing the maximum number of German divisions, the line of the Apennines on which the Germans found themselves in October was the best suited to my purpose. Once driven off that, any other line they could stand on, or at least any other line north of and including the line of the Po, would require less troops to hold. It was considered that, once Bologna fell, the enemy would withdraw to a line based on the rivers Po and Ticino, abandoning north-west Italy, and that he was not likely to delay long on that river line but, under pressure, when and if we could apply it, he would withdraw to the Adige. [123] Once back on the Adige he would be able to spare divisions from Italy and instead of our containing him, he would be containing us.

Looking ahead to such a possibility, at a time when we seemed likely to break through the Apennines, I thought it advisable to consider other employment for the forces which would become surplus on our side as well as on the German, for if the Germans, on our calculations, would only need the equivalent of eleven divisions to hold the Adige line soon the Allied side we could probably only use one Army against that position. The Balkans once more offered an obvious and attractive field. The Russians were advancing in eastern Hungary and approaching Jugoslavia (Belgrade fell on 20th October) and the Partisans were clearing the ports of southern and central Dalmatia. Ever since the fall of Rome I had borne in mind the possibility of forcing an entry into Austria through the Ljubljana gap, a stroke which might even lead us to Vienna. Before the withdrawal of troops for the invasion of Southern France it had seemed likely that this could be achieved by an overland advance through north-eastern Italy, possibly assisted by an amphibious operation against Istria or Trieste. With our present reduced strength, and especially after the losses and exhaustion incurred in the battles for the Apennines, it would be impossible, after breaking through into the Po valley, to be certain of destroying the enemy south of the river and I should have to face a succession of hard fought frontal attacks against a still powerful enemy on the many river lines of Venetia: the Adige, the Brenta, the Piave, the Tagliamento and the Isonzo. [124] Rather than accept this it would be better to make a two-handed attack up the two opposite coasts, designed to meet at the head of the Adriatic. This would undoubtedly tie down more German forces than a frontal attack on the Adige and would give more scope for a flexible strategy and a greater chance for a decisive success.

I first brought forward the plan on 2nd October, at a conference attended by General Wilson, and it was elaborated at several subsequent conferences. In its final form it proposed that, after the Germans had been driven back to their Adige line. Fifth Army should become wholly responsible for operations in Italy, taking under command the Polish Corps, whose employment in Jugoslavia might have been politically embarrassing. Eighth Army should prepare a base in the area of the ports of Split, Sibenik and Zadar, occupying them with light forces, and then, in early spring, bring in their main forces, in the strength of at least six divisions, for a rapid advance on Ljubljana and Fiume. I would retain a Corps of two Indian divisions in Army Group reserve, ready to support either Army. A good deal of detailed planning was done to prepare for this but in the event the plan turned out to be unneccesary and was cancelled on 4th February, 1945. The main reason was the failure to capture Bologna, which meant that we continued to keep the enemy in Italy still stretched to the maximum extent. A further reason was the withdrawal, in early 1945, of the whole of the Canadian Corps to join the Canadians on the Western front and the diversion to the West of 5 Division which was intended to return to my command from the Middle East. It is interesting to speculate on what the results might have been if the plan had been carried into effect. The terrain of Dalmatia is rugged and unpromising for operations and the maintenance of the force would have met serious difficulties. On the other hand the relatively weak and inexperienced German troops would probably have offered only an ineffectual resistance to six veteran divisions of Eighth Army, assisted by strongly reinforced Partisan formations, and an entry into Austria might have been possible before the general capitulation. But the conditions which would have rendered operations in Jugoslavia possible and profitable failed to eventuate; the Germans continued to hold their extended line in the mountains and it was neither necessary nor practical for us to open a new front on which to contain them.

Final Winter Operations.

On 31st October Eighth Army crossed the Ronco near Forli but the weather again intervened and the town did not fall until 9th November. We then had a week's fine weather and were able to drive the enemy back to the line of the Montone and Cosina by the 16th. Route 67 was now open at last but the collapse of a vital bridge prevented our using it until 21st November. A further offensive by 5 Corps and 2 Polish Corps between 20 and 25 November brought us to the line of the river Lamone but another break in the weather prevented exploitation into Faenza. In the meantime Fifth Army had been resting and regrouping its troops according to plan, I Division of 13 Corps relieved 88 Division on Monte Grande and II Corps took advantage of this to pull out for a rest as many troops as could be spared. Unfortunately the line we were holding was so extended that periods spent out of the line could only be very short although the discomforts of the mountainous terrain and the severe Italian winter were very great. During this period, the remainder of 92 Division and a second regiment of the Brazilian Expeditionary Force arrived; it was not practicable, however, to employ these troops in the important II Corps sector.

Plans for the resumption of the offensive were studied in an appreciation produced by my Headquarters on 19th November, to serve as a basis for an Army Commanders' conference on 26th November. It was calculated that Eighth Army had enough artillery ammunition for about three weeks' offensive. They had one armoured and three infantry divisions resting and training in preparation for this; one infantry division at present engaged, however, (the 4th) was due to be withdrawn shortly to go to the Middle East and its relieving division (the 5th) was not due to arrive until January.[125] This strength should be sufficient to reach the Santerno river and, possibly, secure bridgeheads across it. An offensive with this object in view was to be launched on 21st November, as already provided for, and it was estimated that it would hardly have reached its objective before the first week in December.[126] This determined the timing for Fifth Army. By 5th December it would have completed its programme for the relief, rest and training of the four American infantry divisions in II Corps; 13 Corps had only been able to rotate their forces so that only a limited offensive effort could be called for from them. American artillery ammunition was sufficient for not more than about fifteen days' full-scale offensive operations. In view of that fact and the other considerations which made it inevitable that this should be the last major offensive before the spring of 1945 it was essential that every chance should be calculated to ensure its success and I directed that the actual timing of the offensive, which would be some date after 7th December, must be dependent on the weather and, if necessary, it must be postponed until the weather was propitious.

The outline plan was as follows. Eighth Army was to develop its present operations so as to reach the line of the Santerno, and, if possible, secure bridgeheads across it, as early as enemy resistance and the weather permitted. Fifth Army was to prepare to carry out an offensive with all available resources up Route 65 and to co-operate with Eighth Army by an attack from the Monte Grande position against Castel San Pietro, on Route 9 south-east of Bologna. The plan and proposed timings were agreed at an Army Commanders' conference in Florence on 26th November. Orders for the operation were issued on 28th November. The second paragraph showed the reasons for the offensive as I have already described them; my intention was "To afford the greatest possible support to the Allied winter offensive on the Western and Eastern fronts by bringing the enemy to battle, thereby compelling him to employ in Italy manpower and resources which might otherwise be available for use on the other fronts."

Before these plans could be carried into operation I was appointed, on 12th December, Supreme Allied Commander in the Mediterranean Theatre. General Mark Clark took over from me the tactical direction of the two Armies with a small operational staff under the name, revived for the purpose, of Fifteenth Army Group. Headquarters, Allied Armies in Italy, was disbanded; part came with me to Allied Force Headquarters and part, in particular the operations and intelligence staff, went to General Clark's headquarters. I should like to express here my appreciation of the work of my staff throughout the campaign. This narrative will have made it clear that our successes were never won by force of numbers, never by a simple marshalling of overwhelming resources, but always by stratagems, secret concentrations and surprise moves. It is the task of the Commander-in-Chief to think out the broad lines of such a strategy but it is for his staff to evolve the detailed orders and arrangements which will carry his conception into effect. In this my staff, headed by General Harding and his American deputy, General Lemnitzer,[127] thoroughly fulfilled all demands made on them and ensured the smooth working of a complicated and intricate machine. This achievement was the more remarkable as the staff was composed in almost equal proportions of representatives of two different nationalities. This is an extraordinary fact to which, in my opinion, too little attention has been paid. It might have been expected, on a "realistic" view of human nature, that a mixed headquarters of this nature commanding a mixed group of Armies would tend to split in its approach to day to day operational problems on national lines, a British staff officer favouring, even if only subconsciously, the Eighth Army and an American staff officer, similarly, the Fifth Army. Nothing of this kind occurred. All branches and all individuals worked as parts of one integrated machine, loyal to the common cause and, I take justified pride in claiming, to their Commander-in-Chief.

My administrative staff was headed by General Robertson whose experience in this vitally important branch of the military art reached back to the early days of Abyssinia and the Western Desert. I have referred from time to time in the earlier parts of my Despatch to various particular difficulties which faced us in the supply of our troops in Italy and if I have not referred to these problems since then it is because so firm a foundation had been laid down that subsequent problems were solved almost automatically by the existing organisation. The proverb calls that land happy which has no history and certainly an administrative machine can be known to be working at its best when nothing is heard of it either for good or evil. It must not be imagined that the basic and permanent difficulties of the Italian scene were abolished; the blocked and mined ports, the demolished roads and bridges, the railway lines torn up by special machines, all these remained and presented a yet more difficult appearance as the Germans grew more experienced at the work of destruction. The merit of the administrative staff is that they took them in their stride and the proof is that, instead of recounting a series of achievements, it is only necessary to record that operations were never hamstrung and operational plans never radically altered because of any administrative considerations.

For the faultless working of the operational and administrative machinery the achievements already recorded will provide sufficient evidence. The successes of military intelligence have appeared less frequently and from their very nature they are much more difficult to record; there is also the difficulty that that nature is very widely misunderstood by a public whose mind, especially in wartime, is occupied by stories true or false of spies and secret agents. In actual fact espionage can never play anything but the most minor rôle in military intelligence and certainly in Italy it produced no information of any importance. Military Intelligence is a more prosaic affair, dependent on an efficient machine for the collection and evaluation of every sort of item of information, a machine which extends from the front line troops right up to the Army Group staff in which hundreds of individuals all play a vital part. But if its methods of working are humdrum its achievements have been dramatic. For me in Italy the result was that the "fog of war" was dispersed and the enemy's strength and dispositions were always clear and obvious. It will be apparent how useful this knowledge was in enabling me to economize forces and achieve important results with the minimum effort and avoiding casualties and losses.

My relations with the Naval and Air Forces grew closer and more intimate as the campaign progressed. Admiral Sir Andrew Cunningham, whose name had been associated with the hardest and most glorious days of naval warfare in the Mediterranean, was succeeded on 23rd October, 1943, by Admiral Sir John Cunningham.[128] The latter's period of command, in the absence of any enemy fleet to contest our supremacy on the open sea, was devoted almost exclusively to the support and assistance of land operations. In this task I always received from him the fullest and most understanding co-operation. If I should single out any one incident it would be to recall the Anzio operation where the Allied Navies uncomplainingly accepted a burden both greater in degree and of longer duration than had been expected and maintained a force which by May had grown to over seven divisions through a harbour no bigger than a fishing port and under continuous fire.[129] I must mention also the rôle of the Allied Air Forces in support of the Army. Air Marshal Coningham,[130] to whom I owe so much and to whom I have referred in my Despatch on the Conquest of Sicily, returned to the United Kingdom as part of the OVERLORD team and was succeeded, as Commander of the Tactical Air Force, by General Cannon[131] of the United States Army Air Force. General Cannon showed from the start a thorough acquaintance with the problems of co-operation between ground and air. Our headquarters were always together and relations between us were so close and constant that I could be certain that the operations of our respective forces would blend into a perfect three-dimensional whole. I cannot speak too highly of General Cannon's gifts as a leader or of the encouragement which his assistance and support always gave me. The measure of his achievement can be seen in the complete immunity we enjoyed from enemy air attacks, the close and effective support enjoyed by the ground forces, and the long lines of destroyed enemy vehicles, the smashed bridges and useless railways found by my Armies wherever they advanced into enemy territory.

General Clark was the obvious choice to succeed me at Army Group Headquarters; he was the senior of my two Army Commanders and General McCreery, now commanding Eighth Army, had previously served under him when he commanded 10 Corps. This is a good opportunity to record my gratitude and appreciation of General Clark's achievements in Italy since the landing in the Gulf of Salerno in September, 1943. Although his operational experience up to that time had been slight I had the greatest confidence in his capacity and as the campaign developed was glad to see that judgment fully confirmed. He was quick to learn the difficult art of warfare in a mountainous region, keen to profit by every experience of his own or of other commanders and resourceful in the conduct of complex battle situations both in good and evil days. To all the mental resources of a trained soldier he united great gifts of leadership. Just as he had had under his command both American and British troops, and other nationalities also, to whom he stood in a mutual and reciprocal relationship of confidence and loyalty so I found him a most loyal subordinate, unquestioning in obedience and eager to give the utmost co-operation to the common design. It is strange for me to think, and gratifying to recollect with hopes for the future of co-operation between our two nations, that just as I had myself taken orders from an American commander so I could give orders to an American subordinate, involving the lives of thousands of American soldiers, in the certainty that they would be implicitly executed. It was something new in the history of war and the fact that custom soon made it matter of course should not be allowed to obscure its value.

It proved impossible to launch the offensive in December. The requisite precondition on which I insisted, an adequate spell of good weather, was never fulfilled. Had we undertaken an offensive in the weather that prevailed it would almost certainly have fallen short of success and the resulting expenditure of ammunition would have meant the postponement of the offensive of next spring. Eighth Army took advantage of some fitful spells of clear weather to improve its positions; Ravenna fell on 4th December and Faenza on the l6th and by 6th January our line was on the river Senio and touching the southern shore of the Valli di Comacchio. Here the advance was halted and both sides settled down to an uneasy lull. It is surprising to note that, up to this time, the Germans had shown clearly their intention to maintain their strength in Italy. Two infantry divisions were hastily despatched in November to meet a crisis in Hungary but were immediately replaced; one of the new formations was a division from Norway which had travelled all the way through western Germany at the time when Rundstedt's Ardennes offensive was raging without being drawn into it. At the end of the year, therefore, Kesselring still had twenty-seven[131] German divisions, four Italian divisions and a Cossack cavalry division. Though we had failed to break through the Apennines we had succeeded in our mission. The Germans found themselves obliged by the very measure of their success in the winter fighting to await our attack in the following spring on an extended and uneconomical line and I was able to accomplish what I had feared impossible the previous autumn, the effective destruction of the enemy armies south of the Po.

The Final Victory.

The full story of the battles which brought us complete victory in the spring of 1945 is given in my Despatch as Supreme Allied Commander, forwarded to the Combined Chiefs of Staff. Before proceeding, however, to my concluding evaluation of the Italian campaign it will be as well to complete the picture of the over-running of Italy from Cape Passero to the Brenner by giving in broad outline the events which led up to the final capitulation. It is unnecessary to be detailed, for the stage had been set by the events of the winter and the action proceeded according to the plans laid down then. The problem was to disrupt the enemy's defences in the valley of the Po by attacks at two separate points, to surround as much as possible of the forces disposed between the two points of rupture and to exploit with the utmost speed to the Po both in order to forestall any attempt to reorganize the defences of the river line and to cut off and destroy the maximum number of enemy south of the river. There were two axes on which to operate, each of them capable of serving for the advance of an army: Route I2 (Modena - Ostiglia - Verona) for Fifth Army and Route I6 (Ferrara - Rovigo - Padua) for Eighth Army. On the former route the problem for Fifth Army was to break out of the mountains where they had been locked up since the previous winter; once in the plains their advance would go with the grain of the country. The obstacles facing Eighth Army were, as in the previous winter, a series of water barriers, especially the fortified lines of the rivers Senio, Santerno, Sillaro and Idice. Above all the road to Ferrara was narrowed to a heavily defended defile by extensive artificial flooding in the area of the town of Argenta. This defile, known to us as the Argenta Gap, loomed large in all our appreciations; in order to advance rapidly to the necessary crossing sites on the Po we must either force it or outflank it and the latter looked the more difficult, and certainly the more time-wasting, of the two possible courses. North of the Po the enemy had constructed defence lines based on the rivers Adige, Tagliamento and Isonzo, and behind them was the final line of the Alps. I was less concerned with these, as if we were successful in our battle south of the Po the enemy would have no troops left to man them.

It will be seen that the Germans had made most elaborate preparations for a protracted defence in Italy and it may well be asked why, when the Thousand Year Reich was clearly crumbling to ruin nine hundred and eighty-eight years short of its proposed span, great masses of slave labourers should still be toiling to throw up defences in the plains of Venetia. The answer must probably be connected with the Nazi plan for a "National Redoubt". For the sake of the example for the future, and because the armies were still firm in the hand of a man who was determined never to surrender, it was still necessary to plan as if there were some hope left. The only prospect which appeared to offer any chance for protracting resistance was to abandon the defence of the open country of North Germany and concentrate on holding for as long as possible the mountains of the south in the area of Tyrol, Salzburg and Western Carinthia. It was questionable how long, if at all, this fortress could be held and there must have been many commanders who doubted but, such as it was, this represented the only future plan which could be contemplated. To carry it out the forces fighting in Italy were absolutely essential; they represented the only large coherent body of men left in the spring of 1945. They were in a position to withdraw straight into the southern face of the redoubt; they might, moreover, retain for at least a time the food-producing and industrial areas of Northern Italy. Undoubtedly if they had been able to withdraw across the Po in good order they would have given a very good account of themselves in the defence of the Alps; it was more than ever necessary, therefore, to ensure their destruction south of the river.

The armies facing us were still strong[132] well equipped and in good heart. Four divisions, by no means the best, had been transferred to the Eastern front between January and March to balance the transference of the Canadian Corps and 5 British Division from my command but General von Vietinghoff, who succeeded Field-Marshal Kesselring on 23rd March, on the latter's transfer to the Western front, commanded on that date a force of twenty-three German and four Italian (German-equipped) divisions. [133] Furthermore, by contrast with other fronts, the divisions which faced us in Italy were real divisions and not the scratch battle-groups which usurped the name elsewhere. Reinforcements had continued to arrive and a vigorous comb-out of rear areas and a considerable reduction in all but essential services had maintained fighting strength. The parachutists, for example, were particularly strong - I and 4 Parachute Divisions went into action with sixteen thousand and nearly fourteen thousand men respectively - and so were the mobile divisions; in fact the average strength for German divisions was eleven thousand five hundred, slightly over the standard war establishment strength for infantry divisions at that period of the war.[134] The troops were well rested and had spent the period of the lull in intensive training. Morale was astonishingly good. In spite of the desperate situation of German arms in the homeland itself the Germans in Italy continued to show the same resolute spirit of resistance and dash in counter-attack which had distinguished them hitherto. It was not until they had been driven against the Po, and had lost all their heavy weapons in the vain attempt to cross it, that any large-scale surrenders were recorded.[135] To oppose this force I had in Italy seventeen divisions, four Italian Combat Groups and six armoured and four infantry brigades.[136]

The spring offensive began with Eighth Army's attack on 9th April on the enemy's left. It was a resumption of the battle of the previous winter, for the enemy were still on the same defence line and had been forbidden, by Hitler, to make even the smallest withdrawal. But the weather was now dry and favourable and our troops, though diminished in numbers, were thoroughly rested; the speed and weight of their blows were such that the enemy was unable to occupy any of his prepared alternative positions. The Senio and Santerno lines were breached and by the 17th Argenta had been captured and we were about to debouch through the Gap on to Ferrara. Meanwhile on the 14th Fifth Army had begun its drive on Bologna, after a two day postponement due to weather. By contrast with Eighth Army, which in the plain had been able to maintain a steady rate of progress, Fifth Army had first to burst out of the mountains. For a week the German defenders contested every height with the greatest stubbornness until the battered survivors were pushed off the last ridge of the Apennines down into the plain. Then the cost of this stubborn resistance was seen; unable to form any coherent line of defence the troops of Fourteenth Army were swept back to the Po in full flight and Fifth Army, after its slow and painful struggle in the mountains, was able to race ahead in sweeping thrusts. Bologna fell on the 21st, entered simultaneously by the Poles of Eighth Army and II Corps of Fifth Army. On the evening of the 22nd 10 United States Mountain Division reached the Po at San Benedetto and next day 5 Corps reached the river in strength either side of Ferrara. Between them these two thrusts had trapped and immobilized thousands of German troops and the number of prisoners was mounting to embarrassing proportions. From the Po northwards it was a pursuit, pressed with the utmost vigour against an enemy who had received a mortal blow and lost almost all his heavy weapons, but who still resisted, where he could, with the same determination and skill.

Indeed the last battle in Italy was as hard fought as the first. I was not faced with a broken and disintegrating army, nor was the outcome influenced in any degree by demoralization or lack of supplies on the German side.[137] It was a straightforward military operation which, by first enveloping the enemy's left wing in a classical outflanking manoeuvre and then breaking through with a sudden blow his weakened centre, drove him against the Po and annihilated him there. The capitulation of 2nd May only sealed a fate which had already been decided. An army of half a million men had been destroyed and all forces remaining in Italy and Austria laid down their arms in unconditional surrender.

For just under two years, since the invasion of Sicily in 1943, Allied troops had been fighting on Italian soil. In this period of twenty-two months the troops under my command had four times carried out an assault landing, the most difficult operation in war. Three great offensives with the full force of an Army Group had been launched, in May and August, 1944, and in April, 1945. From Cape Passero to the Brenner is eleven hundred and forty miles by road; except for the plains of Lombardy, reached only at the end of the long struggle, that road led almost everywhere through mountains. In the course of the fighting we inflicted on the enemy casualties in killed, wounded and missing which have been estimated, largely from German figures, at five hundred and thirty-six thousand;[138] Allied casualties were three hundred and twelve thousand. But statistics, however striking,[139] are barren materials for an evaluation of the results of a campaign which must rather be considered against the background of the whole strategy of the war. In an attempt to set the campaign against that background I feel it would be least invidious to change the point of view and to consider the importance of the struggle in Italy from the German side.

From the beginning both Germans and Allies regarded Italy as a secondary theatre and looked for the main decision to be given on either the Eastern or the Western front. Both sides were therefore bound above all to consider whether this admitted "side-show" was making a positive contribution to the main object of strategy and whether it was making it at the cheapest possible cost. The Allies' avowed intention, laid down in May, 1943, and never varied, was not to occupy any particular territory but to bring to battle the maximum number of German troops; it was also the main German object (but not their only object) to contain as many Allied troops as possible and weaken by that amount the strength which could be brought to the assault of the West Wall and the Rhine. At every minute of the campaign, therefore, I had to pose to myself the question, who was containing whom in Italy? This was the vital question for the Germans also, and to them the answer can never have been satisfactory.[140] In all forty-five German divisions were employed in Italy, together with four Italian regular divisions, one Cossack division and miscellaneous formations of Czechs, Slovaks and Russians. The Allies employed in Italy a total of forty divisions of which eight were transferred to Western front in 1943 and ten in 1944 and followed by three diverted to the Balkans. Like us the Germans never employed this whole force at once but the details of opposing strength at each stage of the campaign show the same advantage on the Allied side. In October, 1943, there were nineteen German to fifteen Allied divisions, and in December twenty-one to fifteen and a half. Next May the numerical balance shifted slightly in our favour with twenty-seven to twenty-three but with this minor superiority we were able to inflict such losses on the enemy that by August they had been obliged to reinforce to a total of twenty-five (and two Italian) against our twenty. When the final attack begin in April, 1945, we had seventeen divisions to their twenty-three German and four Italian. Nor should we restrict our survey solely to the divisions contained in Italy, for our forces in that country represented such a threat to the whole of the southern coastline of Europe that strong garrisons had to be maintained in Southern France, and the Balkans; in the summer of 1944 for example, the most critical moment of the war when the main effort of Great Britain and the United States was launched against the beaches of Normandy, the presence of our forces in Italy tied down fifty-five divisions in the Mediterranean area.[141]

It was the Germans therefore, who were contained in Italy and not the Allies; the Italian campaign drained their strength more than ours. The reasons why the Germans decided to fight in Italy rather than withdraw to the Alps I have already discussed; they were not, or at least the more important were not, military reasons but political. Perhaps the future German historian, if he is as eager as his predecessors have always been to extol the virtues of Prussian military science, will admit the folly of protracted resistance in Italy and, throwing the blame on a megalomaniac Fuehrer, will seek consolation by pointing to the bravery and stubbornness in defence of the German soldier. He will be justified in so doing; but a still finer theme will be that of the historian who describes how that stubborn defence and the barrier of so many mountains and rivers were triumphantly overcome by the Allies.

APPENDIX "A"

NATIONALITIES IN ITALY

Troops representing the following nationalities served in the Allied Armies in Italy:

Allied

American[142], French[143], Polish, Nepalese, Belgian, Greek, Brazilian, Syro-Lebanese, Jewish, Jugoslav.

Imperial

British, Canadian, New Zealand, South African, Newfoundland, Indian, Ceylonese, Basuto, Swazi, Bechuana, Seychellois, Mauritian, Rodriguez Islanders, Caribbean, Cypriot.

Co-Belligerent

Italian.

APPENDIX "B"

ORDER OF BATTLE OF GERMAN FORCES IN ITALY AND SLOVENIA

As at 3rd September, 1943

I. MAIN BATTLE FRONT (Kesselring's Command)

C.-in-C. South
(Field-Marshal Kesselring)

Tenth Army
(Colonel-General Vietinghoff)

XIV Panzer Corps (General Hube)
I6 Panzer Division
Hermann Goering Panzer Division
I5 Panzer Grenadier Division

LXXVI Panzer Corps (General Herr)
29 Panzer Grenadier Division
26 Panzer Division
I Parachute Division

XI Flieger Corps (General Student)
3 Panzer Grenadier Division
2 Parachute Division

2. SARDINIA AND CORSICA
90 Panzer Grenadier Division
SS Assault Brigade "Reichfuehrer SS"

3. NORTHERN ITALY (Rommel's Command)

Army Group "B"
(Field-Marshal Rommel)

LXXXVII Corps (General Lemelsen)
76 Infantry Division
94 Infantry Division
305 Infantry Division
24 Panzer Division

LI Mountain Corps (General Feuerstein)
SS Panzer Division "Adolf Hitler"
65 Infantry Division
44 "Hoch und Deutschmeister" Infantry Division
Mountain Brigade Doehla

"Corps Witthoeft"
L. of C. Units

Adriatic Coast Command
71 Infantry Division

APPENDIX "C"

ORDER OF BATTLE OF ALLIED ARMIES IN ITALY[144]

As at 22nd January, 1944

FIFTEENTH ARMY GROUP	**REMARKS**
2 N.Z. Div.	Concentrated Termoli area. Passed from under command Eighth Army I9th January.
FIFTH (U.S.) ARMY	
I (U.S.) Armd. Div. (less C.C.B.)	Reverted to Army control I2th January.
45 (U.S.) Inf. Div.	Relieved by 3 (Alg.) Inf. Div. I0th January.
I S.S.F.	Relieved I7th January and moved to Caserta area.
I Italian Mot. Gp.	
2 S.S. Bde.	Sorrento area.
II (U.S.) Corps	
34 (U.S.) Inf. Div.	Diversionary attack Cassino area 20th January.
36 (U.S.) Inf. Div.	Attack across R. Rapido started night 20th January.
C.C.B., I (U.S.) Armd. Div.	Mignano area.
VI (U.S.) Corps	
3 (U.S.) Inf. Div.	Landing in Anzio area during early hours of 22nd January.
I (Br.) Inf. Div.	
French Expeditionary Corps	Took over VI Corps' sector 3rd January.
2 Moroccan Inf. Div.	Attacked 0630 hours 22nd January and captured S. Croce and other points.

3 Algerian Inf. Div.	Took over 45 Div. sector l0th January.
3 & 4 Gp. Tabors	
2 Tk. Gp.	
l0 (*Br.*) *Corps*	Assault on R. Garigliano started 2l00 hours l7th January.
5 (Br.) Inf. Div.	From Eighth Army to Fifth Army 6 January, on left of line in Minturno area.
46 (Br.) Inf. Div.	Attacking across R. Garigliano.
56 (Br.) Inf. Div.	Castelforte and Damiano areas.
23 Armd. Bde.	On R. Garigliano.

EIGHTH ARMY

3 Carpathian Inf. Div.	Not in Army area.
5 (Cdn.) Armd. Div.	Moving to Army area - came under command l3 Corps 25th January.
I (*Cdn.*) *Corps*	Not in Army area.
5 (*Br.*) *Corps*	
I (Cdn.) Inf. Div.	Approaching Tollo.
8 (Ind.) Inf. Div.	East of Orsogna.
2 Para. Bde.	Under command 8 Ind. Div. l6th January.
I (Cdn.) Armd. Bde.	
l3 (*Br.*) *Corps*	
4 (Ind.) Inf. Div.	Relieved 2 N.Z. Div. l6th January.
78 (Br.) Inf. Div.	North of Agnone.
II (Cdn.) Inf. Bde. Gp.	Under command 4th Ind. Div. 20th
January.	
4 Armd. Bde.	Moving to U.K.

APPENDIX "D"

ORDER OF BATTLE OF ARMY GROUP "C"

As at 22nd January, 1944

TENTH ARMY   REMARKS

LXXVI Panzer Corps
   I Parachute Division

   26 Panzer Division

   334 Infantry Division
     Infantry Division
   3 Panzer Grenadier Division
     (less one regiment).

Gruppe Hauck
   305 Infantry Division

XIV Panzer Corps
   5 Mountain Division

   44 (Hoch und Deutschmeister)
     Infantry Division.
   I5 Panzer Grenadier Division

   94 Infantry Division
   Hermann Goering Panzer Division
   29 Panzer Grenadier Division
   90 Panzer Grenadier Division

REMARKS:

Hermann Goering Armoured Reconnaissance Battalion was acting as link between I Parachute and 26 Panzer Divisions. Regimental Group from 65

  Moving into Corps Reserve.

A G.H.Q. High Mountain Battalion under command.

Supported by a regiment of 3 Panzer Grenadier Division, two battalions of I5 Panzer Grenadier Division and a G.H.Q, High Mountain Battalion. Two regiments of 7I Infantry Division under command. Less two battalions detached to 5 Mountain Division.

Less elements.

I Parachute Corps

4 Parachute Division	Still incomplete. Assault Regiment (Sturm. Regiment) still forming at Perugia.
92 Infantry Division	Cadre only.
Miscellaneous G.A.F. Units.	

Remainder 90 Panzer Grenadier Division moving in from Adriatic Sector.

FOURTEENTH ARMY

LXXXVII Corps	Liguria and N. Tuscany.
65 Infantry Division	Genoa.
356 Infantry Division	Spezia - Leghorn.
I6 SS Division	Elements Leghorn; remainder, still forming, Ljubljana.
LI Mountain Corps	Romagna and Marches.
278 Infantry Division	Forming at Bologna.
362 Infantry Division	Rimini area.
Army Reserve	
I88 Reserve Mountain Division	Trentino.
I62 (Turkoman) Infantry Division	North of Fiume.

Build-up of enemy forces in the Anzio bridgehead (22nd January - I6th February)

FOURTEENTH ARMY (Arrived about 29th January)

I Parachute Corps

4 Parachute Division	Elements arrived 23rd/24th January.
65 Infantry Division	Arrived from Genoa before 30th January.
7I5 Infantry Division (mot.)	Arrived from Southern France by 4th February.
II4 Jaeger Division	Arrived from Jugoslavia by I0th February.

LXXVI Panzer Corps.

(Arrived from Adriatic sector by Ist February.)

3 Panzer Grenadier Division	Elements arrived with a Regiment of I5 Panzer Grenadier Division by 23rd January.
26 Panzer Division	Almost complete in line before 30th January.

Hermann Goering Parachute Panzer Division	Complete in line before 30th January, with elements of I Parachute Division.
Battle Group I6 S.S. Panzer Grenadier Divsion	Placed under command of Hermann Goering Division in early February.
362 Infantry Division	In Army reserve by 30th January, elements committed on I6th February.

In addition the following Independent Regiments arrived before I6th February:
    Infantry Lehr Regiment (three battalions)
    I027 Reinforced Panzer Grenadier Regiment (two battalions)
    I028 Reinforced Panzer Grenadier Regiment (two battalions).

Total German Divisions in Fourteenth Army before I6th February, I944

Armoured Divisions	2
Motorised Divisions	I
Parachute Divisions	I
Infantry Divisions	4
(of which two semi-motorised)	
Total nominal Divisions	8

With three Independent Regiments, an S.S. Battle Group and miscellaneous Luftwaffe ground troops, the total of German forces in the Anzio bridgehead area by I6th February was equivalent to nine divisions.

APPENDIX "E"

ORDER OF BATTLE OF ALLIED ARMIES IN ITALY

As at IIth May, 1944

HEADQUARTERS, ALLIED ARMIES IN ITALY	REMARKS
5 (*Br.*) *Corps*	Adriatic Coast sector.
4 (Ind.) Inf. Div.	
"D" Force (H.C.R., C.I.H., II K.R.R.C., 9 Manch.)	
I0 (Ind.) Inf. Div.	
23 Armd. Bde.	
7 Armd. Bde. Gp.	Not yet in Corps area.
FIFTH (U.S.) ARMY	
H.Q. IV (U.S.) Corps	
36 (U.S.) Inf. Div.	Army reserve, later moved to Anzio beachhead.
909 Para. Bn.	
II (*U.S.*) *Corps*	Garigliano sector.
85 (U.S.) Div.	
88 (U.S.) Div.	
I Armd. Gp.	
VI (*U.S.*) *Corps*	Anzio beachhead.
3 (U.S.) Inf. Div.	
34 (U.S.) Inf. Div.	
45 (U.S.) Inf. Div.	
I (U.S.) Armd. Div.	
I S.S.F.	

I (Br.) Inf. Div.
5 (Br.) Inf. Div.

French Expeditionary Corps   Aurunci Mountains sector.
I Mot. Inf. Div.
2 (Mor.) Inf. Div.
3 (Alg.) Inf. Div.
4 (Mor.) Mtn. Div.
I Gp. Tabor
3 Gp. Tabor
4 Gp. Tabor
2 Armd. Gp.

EIGHTH ARMY
6 (S.A.) Amid. Div.   Came under command Ist May -
  (less I2 S.A. Mot. Bde.)   under command I Cdn. Corps
                                            3Ist May.

I0 *(Br.) Corps*   Apennine sector.
2 N.Z. Div.
I2 (S.A.) Mot. Bde.   Under comd. 5th - 23rd May,
24 (Br.) Gds. Bde.   To 6 S.A. Armd. Div. 3Ist May.
2 (Br.) Para. Bde.
Hermon Force (K.D.G., I2 L.)
Italian Mot. Gp.
II Cdn. Inf. Bde. Gp.   Relieved by I2 (S.A.) Mot. Bde. and
                                            moved to under comd. 5 Cdn. Armd.
                                            Div. 5th/6th May.

I3 *(Br.) Corps*   Cassino and R. Rapido sector.
6 (Br.) Armd. Div.
4 (Br.) Inf. Div.
I (Br.) Gds. Bde.
78 (Br.) Inf. Div.
8 (Ind.) Inf. Div.
I Cdn. Armd. Bde.

I *Cdn. Corps*   Moved to south of Mignano 9th May;
                                            assumed command of 8 Ind. Div. sector
                                            2230 hrs. I6th May.

5 Cdn. Armd. Div.   North of Capua - concentrated west of
                                            R. Garigliano 20th May - passed
                                            through 3 Cdn. Inf. Bde. 24th May.

I Cdn. Inf. Div.

Moved to S. Agata area 5th May - started to relieve 8 Ind. Div. night I5th/I6th May; under comd. I3 Corps till 2230 hrs. I6th May.

25 Tk. Bde.

2 *Polish Corps*
  3 Carp. Inf. Div.
  5 Kres. Inf. Div.
  2 Polish Armd. Bde.

Took over Monte Cassino sector 27th April.

APPENDIX "F"

ORDER OF BATTLE OF ARMY GROUP "C"

As at 11th May, 1944

TENTH ARMY	REMARKS.
"Gruppe Hauck"	
305 Infantry Division	
334 Infantry Division	
114 Jaeger Division	
LI Mountain Corps	
5 Mountain Division	Two G.H.Q. High Mountain Battalions under command.
44 (Hoch und Deutschmeister) Infantry Division	
I Parachute Division	
XIV Panzer Corps	
Bode Blocking Group	Regimental Group from 305 Division.
15 Panzer Grenadier Division	Elements in Liri valley, bulk in reserve.
71 Infantry Division	Three battalions of 44 Division under command.
94 Infantry Division	
Army Reserve	
90 Panzer Grenadier Division	
FOURTEENTH ARMY	
LXXVI Panzer Corps	
362 Infantry Division	
715 Infantry Division	
26 Panzer Division	In Corps reserve.
I Parachute Corps	

3 Panzer Grenadier Division
65 Infantry Division
4 Parachute Division

Army Reserve
29 Panzer Grenadier Division
92 Infantry Division

ARMEEGRUPPE VON ZANGEN

LXXV Corps
Hermann Goering Division
I62 (Turkoman) Infantry Division
356 Infantry Division
I35 Fortress Brigade

Corps Witthoeft
Elements 278 Infantry Division
L. of C. Units

Adriatic Coast Command
(Adriatisches Kuestenland)
Bulk of 278 Infantry Division
I88 Reserve Mountain Division

Alpenvorland and Nordwest Alpen
L. of C. Units only

Total German Divisions in Army Group "C"

Armoured Divisions	2
Motorised Divisions	4
Parachute Divisions	2
Mountain, Jaeger and	
Infantry Divisions	I4
Training Divisions	I
Total	23 Divisions

ORDER OF BATTLE OF ALLIED ARMIES IN ITALY

As at 25th August, 1944

	REMARKS
A.A.I.	
FIFTH (U.S.) ARMY	
H.Q. Brazilian Expeditionary Force	
6 Brazilian Inf. Regt.	
II (U.S.) Corps	West of Florence.
34 (U.S.) Inf. Div.	In reserve.
88 (U.S.) Inf. Div.	In reserve.
9I (U.S.) Inf. Div.	In reserve.
752 (U.S.) Tk. Bn.	
755 (U.S.) Tk. Bn.	
760 (U.S.) Tk. Bn.	
442 (U.S.) R.C.T.	
IV (U.S.) Corps	West coast Pisa sector.
I (U.S.) Armd. Div.	In reserve.
6 (S.A.) Armd. Div.	
85 (U.S.) Inf. Div.	
370 R.C.T. (92 (U.S.)	In reserve.
Negro Inf. Div.)	
I Armd. Gp.	
2 Armd. Gp.	
I3 *(Br.) Corps*	East of Florence.
I (Br.) Inf. Div.	
6 (Br.) Araid. Div.	
8 (Ind.) Inf. Div.	
I Cdn. Armd. Bde.	

EIGHTH ARMY

2 N.Z. Div.	Still west of Apennines near Siena.
3 Greek Mtn. Bde.	
C.I.L.	Italian force of about divisional strength.
I *Cdn. Corps*	Adriatic coastal plain.
I Cdn. Inf. Div.	
5 Cdn. Armd. Div.	
2I (Br.) Tk. Bde.	
H.C.R.	
2 *Polish Corps*	Adriatic coast
3 Carp. Div.	
5 Kres. Div.	
2 Polish Armd. Bde.	
7 Hussars	
2 Italian Bde. (ex-C.I.L.)	
5 *(Br.) Corps*	Apennine foothills on Adriatic sector
I (Br.) Armd. Div.	
4 (Br.) Inf. Div.	
4 (Ind.) Inf. Div.	
46 (Br.) Inf. Div.	
56 (Br.) Inf. Div.	
7 (Br.) Armd. Bde	
25 (Br.) Tk. Bde.	
I0 *(Br.) Corps*	Central Apennines.
I0 (Ind.) Inf. Div.	
9 (Br.) Armd. Bde.	
K.D.G.	
I2 L.	
27 L.	
Lovat Scouts	

APPENDIX "H"

ORDER OF BATTLE OF ARMY GROUP "C"

As at 25th August, 1944

TENTH ARMY	REMARKS
LXXVI Panzer Corps	Adriatic to area Sansepolcro.
278 Infantry Division	
7I Infantry Division	
5 Mountain Division	Being withdrawn to N.W. Italy.
I Parachute Division	In Corps reserve on Adriatic coast.
I62 (Turkoman) Infantry Division	In Corps reserve on Adriatic coast.
LI Mountain Corps Area	Sansepolcro to Pontassieve.
II4 Jaeger Division	
44 Infantry Division	
305 Infantry Division	
334 Infantry Division	
7I5 Infantry Division	
Army Reserve	
98 Infantry Division	*Bologna area.*
FOURTEENTH ARMY	
I Parachute Corps	Pontassieve to Empoli.
356 Infantry Division	
4 Parachute Division	
362 Infantry Division	
XIV Panzer Corps	
26 Panzer Division	
65 Infantry Division	
I6 S.S. Panzer Grenadier Division	
Army Reserve	
29 Panzer Grenadier	Division North of Florence.

20 Luftwaffe Field Division   Area Viareggio.

ARMY LIGURIA
Corps Lombardy   Savona to La Spezia.
   I35 Fortress Brigade   La Spezia.
   Monte Rosa (Italian)   La Spezia to Genoa (excl.).
      Mountain Division
   42 Jaeger Division   Genoa.
   San Marco (Italian)   Savona area.
      Infantry Division
   34 Infantry Division   Italo-French frontier.

LXXV Corps
   I48 Infantry Division   Italo-French frontier, south.
   90 Panzer Grenadier Division   Italo-French frontier, centre.
   I57 Mountain Division   Italo-French frontier, north.

Directly under Army Group "C"
Adriatic Coast Command
   94 Infantry Division   Area Udine.
   I88 Reserve Mountain Division   Istria.

Total Divisions in Army Group "C"

German		*Italian*	
Armoured Divisions	I	Mountain Divisions	I
Motorised Divisions	3	Infantry Divisions	I
Parachute Divisions	2		
Mountain, Jaeger and		**Total**	**2**
Infantry DivisionsI9			
Training Divisions	I		
Total	**26**		

Advance elements of a further Infantry Division arriving.

APPENDIX "I"

ORDER OF BATTLE OF FIFTEENTH ARMY GROUP

As at 9th April, 1945

	REMARKS
FIFTH (U.S.) ARMY	
92 (U.S.) Inf. Div.	West coast sector.
85 (U.S.) Inf. Div.	Army Reserve, Porretta area.
II (U.S.) Corps	Monte Grande to Route 64.
Legnano Combat Gp.	
34 (U.S.) Inf. Div.	
9I (U.S.) Inf. Div.	
88 (U.S.) Inf. Div.	
6 South.African Armd. Div.	
IV (U.S.)Corps	Route 64 to east of Bagni di Lucca.
I (U.S.) Armd. Div.	
I0 (U.S.) Mtn. Div.	
Brazilian Expeditionary Force	
37I R.C.T.	Detached from 92 (U.S.) Inf. Div.
365 R.C.T.	Detached from 92 (U.S.) Inf. Div.
EIGHTH ARMY	
5 *(Br.) Corps*	Adriatic to south of Lugo.
56 (Br.) Inf. Div.	
Cremona Combat Gp.	
8 (Ind.) Inf. Div.	
78 (Br.) Inf. Div.	
2 N.Z. Div.	
2 Armd. Bde.	
9 Armd. Bde.	
2I Tk. Bde.	
2 Commando Bde.	

2 *Polish Corps*   Astride Via Emilia.
   3 Carp. Div.
   5 Kres. Div.
   2 Polish Armd. Bde.
   7 Armd. Bde.
   43 (Ind.) Lor. Inf. Bde.

I0 *(Br.) Corps*   Excl. Route 9 to south of Imola.
   Jewish Inf. Bde. Gp.
   Friuli Combat Gp.

I3 *(Br.) Corps*   South of Imola to Monte Grande.
   Folgore Combat Gp.
   I0 (Ind.) Inf. Div.

Army Reserve
   6 (Br.) Armd. Div.
   2 Para. Bde.

APPENDIX "J"

ORDER OF BATTLE OF ARMY GROUP "C"

As at 9th April, 1945

TENTH ARMY	REMARKS
LXXVI Panzer Corps	Adriatic to north of Route 9.
I62 (Turkoman) Infantry Division	
42 Jaeger Division	
362 Infantry Division	
98 Infantry Division	
I Parachute Corps	Route 9 to Monte Grande.
26 Panzer Division	
4 Parachute Division	
278 Infantry Division	
I Parachute Division	
305 Infantry Division	
LXXIII Corps	Venice area.
Minor defensive units only	
XCVII Corps[145]	North-eastern Italy.
I88 Mountain Division	
237 Infantry Division	
Army Reserve	
29 Panzer Grenadier Division	Area Venice - Treviso.
I55 Infantry Division	
FOURTEENTH ARMY	
XIV Panzer Corps	Monte Grande to Route 64.
65 Infantry Division	
8 Mountain Division	
94 Infantry Division	
LI Mountain Corps	Route 64 to coast.

334 Infantry Division
II4 Jaeger Division
232 Infantry Division
Italia Infantry Division
I48 Infantry Division

Army Group Reserve   S.W. of Modena.
  90 Panzer Grenadier Division

ARMY LIGURIA
Corps Lombardy   Coast of the Gulf of Genoa.
  San Marco Infantry Division
  Battle Group Meinhold   Genoa.

LXXV Corps   Franco-Italian frontier.
  34 Infantry Division
  Littorio Infantry Division
  5 Mountain Division
  Monte Rosa Mountain Division

Total Divisions in Army Group "C"

German		Italian	
Armoured Divisions	I	Infantry Divisions	3
Motorised Divisions	2	Mountain Divisions	I
Parachute Divisions	2		
Mountain, Jaeger and Infantry		**Total**	**4**
Divisions	I8		
Total	**23**		

APPENDIX "K"

ADMINISTRATION IN THE ITALIAN CAMPAIGN

Planning

Administrative planning for the invasion of Italy was made unusually difficult by two factors; the flexibility of the operational plans and the remoteness of the base. The decision between the various plans for invasion which had been prepared was of necessity postponed until very shortly, comparatively speaking, before the dates on which they were due to be put into action. As a result it was impossible to prepare well in advance an overall plan for the administrative side of the campaign and the arrangements eventually come to had to be hastily made and advisedly provisional in character.

There were three major headquarters in the Mediterranean theatre, concerned with operations against Europe. Allied Force Headquarters at Algiers, Anglo-American in composition but working on the American staff system, was in general responsible for all directives and policy; for operations against Europe; it met all administrative demands for the forces operating in Italy either from its own resources in the Mediterranean or by demand on Washington and London. It was also responsible for mounting formations and units proceeding overseas from the area under its command, viz., North Africa west of Tripoiitania. General Headquarters, Middle East Forces, was a British headquarters located in Cairo. It was responsible for mounting all formations and units which came from its command i.e., the bulk of Eighth Army and I0 Corps, and assisting A.F.H.Q. with such resources as it could make available. Fifthteenth Army Group Headquarters, though originally intended to assume responsibility for administrative policy and co-ordination of general administration of the fighting forces, ground and air, did not in fact assume that responsibility for the campaign in Sicily and the early stages in Italy. This came about more by circumstance than by design. On the American side its responsibilities would inevitably have been small, since on the American system the Services of Supply, North African Theatre of Operations, worked direct to Army. On the British side there was already a headquarters administering the bulk of the forces, Tripoli Base under General Robertson,[146] and Eighth Army planned to bring this over to Sicily as "Fortbase." This had the advantage that the headquarters was already well acquainted with the formations to be administered and the existing channels of supply to the

Middle East and had a close and confident relationship with the Commander and staff of Eighth Army. Both Armies thus had their own administrative organisations, and the function of Fifteenth Army Group was limited to general supervision and co-ordination and the rendering of advice to the Army Group Commander.

No base depots holding large buffer stocks were established in Sicily, nor was Sicily ever considered as a base for future operations. We did, however, dump fairly large stocks at Syracuse, Catania, Messina and Milazzo which were used to provide initial maintenance of the forces to be mounted from the island. After 25th August, 1943, supply convoys, which hitherto had come from North Africa and Middle East, began to arrive direct from the United Kingdom and United States. This shifting of the base back to the producer countries meant that it was necessary to submit long-term forecasts of requirements sometimes weeks before arrival. The effect was a loss of flexibility with a consequent waste of shipping and congestion of ports, due to convoys arriving with stores which were not immediately needed, or in excess of current requirements.

Initial Maintenance

After much study the administrative plans for the initial major landings were settled. Troops landing in the Reggio area would be supplied by coasters carrying standard loads from North Africa and Sicily, petrol and stores ships sailing direct from the Middle East and the United Kingdom, and landing craft ferrying stores from Sicily to the mainland. Up to D plus 14 detailed requirement demands were made by 13 Corps Headquarters, and after that date responsibility rested with Eighth Army; Army demands in turn were submitted by Fortbase to A.F.H.Q. thirty days before they would be delivered. The arrangements for SLAPSTICK, the landing by I Airborne Division at Taranto, were necessarily of a more improvised nature. It was agreed that the force should be maintained initially through Taranto itself, but that subsequently the ports of Brindisi and Bari would be opened and used. A programme was worked out based on the shipping available and an arbitrary calculation of requirements for six weeks' maintenance and fifteen days reserve. After the initial pre-loaded shipments had been exhausted demands would be made via Fortbase to A.F.H.Q. The landings at Salerno were to be maintained initially over the beaches, but it was planned to develop Naples and the adjacent ports as soon as possible after their capture. Fifth Army retained a line of communication that went back through NATOUSA[147] and was exclusively American; while, to deal with British administrative matters, a British Increment was added to its headquarters.

The system of command and supply that had been thus hastily evolved showed certain practical difficulties when applied to operations. The absence of any large stocks close at hand and the congestion in the North African ports meant that the situation was bound to be delicate until considerable supplies had been built up on the mainland; and, until this was so, the situation there was ripe for a serious breakdown if an emergency arose before a satisfactory system of overall working had been evolved by trial and error. Such an emergency did occur very soon.

The initial Eighth Army landings went according to plan and rapid progress was everywhere made, troops in the Toe being maintained easily through the several small undamaged ports there. In the Heel matters were not so satisfactory, since there had been insufficient time to make adequate arrangements, and troops there had to be placed on short rations for a few days, but their capture intact of the major ports of Taranto and Brindisi was of the utmost importance and was shortly be to the means of averting the complete breakdown which otherwise might well have occurred. For, when it was apparent that the Fifth Army at Salerno was meeting heavy opposition, Eighth Army was ordered to move to its aid with all speed; and its subsequent advance across a country with poor communications - although justified by the operational results - yet inevitably caused a breakdown in the supply system. The decision was therefore taken to switch the Army's supply line to the Heel, where the existence of railways, better roads and far better ports offered security for the future. This decision, involving the transference of stocks from Calabria to the Taranto area at the same time as the Army had to be supplied in its continual advance, placed a very great strain on the services involved, but its advantages were considered to outweigh its drawbacks. By the end of September there were signs of improvement. The ammunition position was satisfactory but petrol - particularly cased petrol - remained in poor supply owing to the shipping situation, and there was a grave shortage of transport.

Fifth Army meanwhile had been experiencing difficulties of a different kind. The landings at Salerno had met stiff opposition, and the accumulation of supplies had to be made under enemy fire; but the administrative planning had been very thorough, and the arrangements made proved very satisfactory until bad weather on D plus I2 stopped all unloading for three days. Salerno port, though soon captured, was initially rendered unusable by enemy shellfire, and the harbour at Castellamare was found to have been so damaged as to be useless; but the small port of Torre Annunziata was captured in good repair by the end of September and this, with the use of Salerno and of various beaches, sufficed thereafter until the opening of the port of Naples. When this city was entered on Ist October it was found that the port had been most systematically obstructed and the facilities there destroyed. The resuscitation of the port was immediately put under way, with such ingenuity and to such good effect that by the second week of October it was already discharging 5,000 tons per day. This was sufficient to keep Fifth Army supplied with essential commodities but owing to the accelerated arrival of new formations and the partly unforeseen demands of the civilian population reserve stocks were not built up according to schedule.

Reorganisation of Administrative Command

The necessity for some new organisation of administrative command was obvious. An actual breakdown seemed now to have been averted, but the margin of safety had been a very narrow one and Eighth Army was forced to halt on the Termoli line to allow its supplies to be built up. The solution decided upon was the establishment at Naples of an Advanced Administrative Echelon of A.F.H.Q., which on 24th October took over the functions of administration formerly exercised by Fortbase. Major-General Robertson, who had commanded Fortbase, was appointed to the command of the Echelon; he was instructed to co-ordinate all administration on the mainland of Italy, to make the necessary arrangements to support the operations of Fifteenth Army Group and the North-West African Tactical Air

Forces, and to act as personal administrative adviser to the Army Group Commander.

The primary task of the new headquarters was to undertake the reorganisation of our lines of communication. From the disposition of the forces at the time, it followed that Eighth Army should be supplied by the Heel ports and the east coast roads, while Fifth Army used Naples and roads on the west coast, each Army taking over additional ports as it moved north. It was not, however, possible to keep British and American lines of supply separate, as they had been in Sicily; for the Heel ports were not capable of supporting the whole British force and furthermore there was - and would be for a long time yet - at least one British Corps under American command near the west coast. Naples, with its large though damaged port, was clearly capable of being developed to accept a great tonnage; and so it was decided to establish a full complement of British depots there and in the Heel, resources being split equally between the two areas. At first sight this might appear wasteful in administrative resources; but it did allow a flexibility that was invaluable later when it came to switching large forces rapidly from one coast to the other.

By the end of the year the new headquarters had succeeded in its major reorganisation and there was a great change from the uncomfortable position of October. Although the build-up had not gone as fast as had at one time been hoped - due mainly to lack of transport facilities - the main commodities were, with the exception of ammunition[148], in good supply. Port development was sound and Naples was unloading some I5,000 tons daily; on the east coast the position had weakened to some extent as a result of the German air raid of Ist December which had destroyed I7 ships and 40,000 tons of cargo at Bari, but there was still a daily turnover of from I0,000 to II,000 tons per day. We could at last say that our base in Italy was now quite firm.

A further reorganisation took place when General Eisenhower left the Mediterranean theatre. It was decided then that all responsibility for Italy should devolve as much as possible on Fifteenth Army Group. The obvious step then was to transfer the A.F.H.Q. Administrative Echelon entire to that Headquarters, renamed "Headquarters Allied Armies in Italy." This transfer involved no change in the administrative system, and took place on 24th February, 1944. After this reorganisation the administrative side of the campaign presented no problems out of the ordinary.[149] So successful was the basis which had been laid that the great regrouping of the spring of I944 was carried out without a hitch and the pursuit from the Garigliano to the Arno proceeded without ever being embarrassed by shortage of supplies.

ANNEX I

to Appendix "K"

THE AMMUNITION SHORTAGE IN ITALY

On two occasions during the fighting in Italy - in the winter of 1943-44 and again a year later - operations were prejudiced by a shortage of gun ammunition. The first shortage was, initially, an artificial one and there were always enough rounds in the gun pits; but the fact that fighting was heavier than had been expected, that the arrival of the Strategic Air Force in Italy delayed the build-up of reserves, and that there was a general shortage of transport and harbour facilities meant that reserves at Army level were inadequate. To meet this local shortage, considerably aggravated by our commitment at Anzio early in 1944, it was necessary to ship to Italy all available surplus stocks from the Middle East, North Africa and Sicily and the result was a shortage of ammunition throughout the Mediterranean theatre so serious that in early February I flew home to the War Office in an attempt to obtain immediate shipments of ammunition and an increase in the general allotment. I managed to obtain a certain increase, after I had fully explained our difficulties, but I was forced to issue stringent orders that the expenditure of ammunition should be drastically rationed and, except when they were repelling an attack or supporting an offensive, 25 pounders would be limited to 15 and medium guns to 10 rounds per gun per day.

The ammunition crisis again came to a head in the late autumn of 1944, and this time it was not only a theatre shortage but was, in fact, world-wide and affected American as well as British stocks. The first notification we had of it came in a message from the War Office in August which said that a shortfall in production meant that future supplies would have to be cut down. This news, coming at a time when we were engaged in the "Gothic" line battles with their heavy expenditure of ammunition, caused grave concern. The immediate shortage was overcome by the use of A.F.H.Q.'s reserve but this unfortunately could be no widow's cruse and by mid-November the position was so acute that no large scale offensive could be considered for another four months. Again it was necessary to impose a strict system of rationing which was to remain in force until the final offensive began in the spring of 1945.

ANNEX II

to Appendix "K"

THE ADMINISTRATION OF THE ANZIO BRIDGEHEAD

My administrative staff regarded the commitment entailed by the Anzio bridgehead as very heavy. The plan relied on the continuous maintenance of a mixed force, requiring both British and American supplies, over open beaches for an indefinite time at a season when the weather was likely to be at its worst. It is very much to their credit that these serious difficulties were overcome.

Fifth Army was in charge of the detailed planning for the administration, which they considered to fall into four phases. Initially supplies had to be built up in the area of Naples, and a loading programme and convoy schedules had to be organised. Then, in the assault, the force would have to be maintained over the beaches and beach dumps built up. In the next phase maintenance would continue in the same way, but it was hoped that the port of Anzio could be used. Finally, when the bridgehead force linked up with the main front, maintenance would obviously be discontinued over the beaches and would be resumed through the normal channels.

The planning and the accumulation of supplies worked according to plan and when on 22nd January fine weather and calm seas enabled the unloading to be done without difficulty it was found that the dumps could be built up well inland and not just on the beaches as originally considered.[150] Bad weather on D plus 2 prevented use of one beach, supplies for which were thereafter diverted to another. Anzio harbour had not been demolished at all; it was found to be usable in all weathers and its capacity was rapidly increased by our harbour engineers.[151] Despite the bad weather that on two occasions caused hold-up and dislocation in the unloading, until the end of January a daily average of 7,400 tons was discharged.

When, in early February, it became apparent that the maintenance of a force at Anzio would have to continue for a much longer time than had originally been considered, new steps had to be taken. Thereafter special Liberty ships were loaded in North Africa and sailed to Naples; there they were top-loaded with any special items needed in the bridgehead to which they sailed when called forward by the authorities there. These ships, however, were too large to be berthed in Anzio harbour, and had instead to discharge into smaller craft; and this fact, coupled with bad weather, lack of craft and the constant enemy fire entailed a very considerable drop in the rate of unloading and caused a serious backlog of Liberty ships waiting at

Naples to be called forward. Under these circumstances severe economy was exercised by the troops in the bridgehead in order to cut down their requirements, and more stores than hitherto were carried there on loaded cargo trucks in Landing Ships, Tank; at the same time A.F.H.Q. was able to lay its hands on some more craft for us and these factors enabled us to build up supplies to so satisfactory a position that, in May, we were able to cut down on shipping requirements. When the troops at Anzio broke out of their bridgehead there were ample reserves of supplies to support them.

APPENDIX "L"

NOTES ON THE AIR IMPLICATION OF AN ASSAULT ON THE ITALIAN MAINLAND - NAPLES AREA

To AIR COMMANDER-IN-CHIEF

I. *Distance from Fighter Bases*

For the purpose of these notes it is assumed that the assault will be made in the Salerno area which is the nearest point that an assault can be made to our air bases.

Distances to Salerno

Milo (Trapani)	226 miles
Gerbini	224 "
Reggio	184 "
N.E. Sicily	178 "
Vibo Valentia	152 "

3. *Fighter Performance* (including 10 minutes combat)

P-38 with one long range tank	350 miles
A-36 with one long range tank	200 "
Spitfire with one long range tank (90 gal.)	180 "
P-39 and P-40F with long range tanks (75 gal.)	150 "
Beaufighter	300 "

4. *Probable Location of Axis Air Forces*

Fighter bombers and L.R. bombers	Airfields in the "Heel".
	Airfields in the Foggia area.
	Airfields in Sardinia.
Fighters	Airfields in the Naples area.
L.R. Bombers	Airfields in Lombardy.

REMARKS

5. *Available Airfield Accommodation within Range of Assault*

(*a*) Gerbini	Sufficient airfield space (backed by port facilities) to accommodate such fighters as are capable of reaching Salerno. (Distance 224 miles.)
(*b*) Reggio	4 to 6 S.E.F. Sqns. can be augmented by strip farther north if ground in our possession. (Distance 184 miles.)
(*c*) N.E. corner of Sicily	One small strip only reported. Probable that others can be constructed quickly. Estimate 4 to 6 S.E.F. Sqns. (Distance 178 miles.)
(*d*) Milo (Trapani)	2 good airfields would take 2 gps. T.E.F. (Distance 226 miles.)

6. *Availability of Aircraft Carrier Support*

(*a*) Mediterranean	1 carrier.
N.W. Scotland	1 carrier.
Pacific	2 carriers.

(*b*) Auxiliary carriers are still considered unsuitable for air operations of this nature as they are still incapable of operating modern fighters of the Seafire class.

7. *Availability of Fighters*

3 Groups T.E.F. (day)	P-38's (augmented).
2 Groups F.B.	A-36's.
18 Squadrons S.E.F.	Spits.
4 Squadrons T.E.F. (night)	Beaufighters.

8. *Airborne Operations*

It will be necessary to capture the airfield at Salerno at an early moment, and it may therefore be found essential to employ airborne forces for the purpose. If airborne forces are employed by day, or require part daylight fighter cover, the commitment will compete with long range fighter resources required for the assault.

9. *Bomber Operations*

(*a*) A-20's (Bostons, range 280 miles) with Doolittle tanks are the only light bombers capable of reaching enemy airfields in the "Heel", Naples and Sardinia.

(*b*) While heavy bombers (B-I7's) can reach all airfields, including those in Northern Italy, from which the enemy are likely to operate air forces, the mediums are capable of operating against the majority of airfields in the Rome/Naples area, including the "Heel" - also Sardinia.

I0. *General*

(*a*) Problem primarily one of producing long range shore based fighter cover to cover an assault in either the Naples or Salerno area. Assault in the Salerno area offers more attractive proposition from air point of view for following reasons:-
   (i)   Spitfires with 90 gal. L.R.T. can reach it.
   (ii) A good airfield capable of taking 4 S.E.F. Squadrons is within 3 miles of assault beach and might therefore be brought into very early use.
   (iii) Is close to a good port which should fall into our hands quickly.

(*b*) The Salerno assault suffers however from the bottleneck of Salerno town and harbour which must be kept free for land advance to Naples.

(*c*) Long range tanks (90 gal.) may place a limitation on number of Spitfires employed, but suitable airfield accommodation within Spitfire range is more likely to be the bottleneck. Total stocks of long range (90 gal.) tanks at present within the theatre are estimated at 840.

(*d*) Beaufighters would be able to provide night protection operating from airfields in Sicily (Gerbini).

II. *Conclusion*

(*a*) P-38 (Lightning) and A-36 (Mustang), and Beaufighters (night) can be used for cover of any of the projected assaults in the Naples area.

(*b*) Spitfires with long range tanks can be used for an assault in the Salerno area only.

(*c*) P-39 (Aircobra), P-40 (Kittyhawk and Warhawk) are unusable except for short range convoy cover.

(*d*) All enemy airfields, including those in Northern Italy, can be reached by our heavy bombers, while the airfields in the "Heel", Naples area and Sardinia can be covered by the heavies and mediums, and a proportion of the light bombers.

(*e*) Bombers would have to operate unescorted.

(*f*) Employment of Spitfires will depend upon adequate landing strips for 18 Squadrons in N.E. corner of Sicily or the use of Reggio. About 10 days will be available in which to construct these landing strips and move up supplies.

Air Plans   (Sgd.) A.C.
25/7/43   G./Capt.

NOTE I. - DAY FIGHTER SORTIE ANALYSIS

   (i) P-38 (Lightning) 3 Gps.   9 x 18 = 162

       A-36 (Mustang) 2 Gps.   6 x 18 = 108

       Spitfires 18 Sqns.   18 x 12 = 210 *(Sic)*

                                          480

  (ii) 480 aircraft.   2 sorties per day. 960 sorties.

 (iii) $\frac{960}{12}$ = 80 - 12 aircraft sorties daily.

 (iv) Estimated time over patrol :

       P-38   1 hour

       A-36   30 mins.

       Spits   20 mins.

  (v) Providing airfields can be produced in the N.E. corner of Sicily in time for these operations fighter cover will probably be adequate.

GLOSSARY OF ABBREVIATIONS USED IN THE APPENDICES

A.F.H.Q. = Allied Force Headquarters.

Alg. = Algerian.

Armd. = Armoured.

Br. = British.

Carp. = Carpathian.

C.C.B. = Combat Command "B" (Armoured Brigade Group of about divisional strength).

Cdn. = Canadian.

C.I.H. = Central India Horse.

C.I.L. = Corpo Italiano della Liberazione (Italian formation).

F.B. = Fighter/Bomber.

G.A.F. = German Air Force.

Gp. = Group.

H.C.R. = Household Cavalry Regiment.

Ind. = Indian.

Kres. = Kresowa.

K.R.R.C. = King's Royal Rifle Corps.

L. of C. = Lines of Communication.

L.R. = Long range.

Manch. = Manchester Regiment.

Mor. = Moroccan.

Mot. = Motorised.

Mtn. = Mountain.

N.Z. = New Zealand.

Para. = Parachute.

Pol. = Polish.

R.C.T. = Regimental Combat Team (Infantry Brigade Group).

S.A. = South African.

S.E.F. = Single-engined fighter(s).

S.S.F. = Special Service Force.

T.E.F. = Twin-engined fighter(s).

Tk. = Tank.

U.S. = United States.

Footnotes

1   General of the Army Dwight D. Eisenhower. (The title of his appointment was
    "Commander-in-Chief, Allied Force." Another title frequently used was "Allied
    Commander-in-Chief, Mediterranean Theatre". On 9th March, 1944, when General
    (now Field-Marshal Lord) Wilson held the appointment, the title was altered to
    "Supreme Allied Commander, Mediterranean Theatre". For the sake of clarity the later
    title is used throughout the Despatch).

2   Figures as of May 1943; the Italian Army remained at a round figure of some sixty
    divisions until it capitulated.

3   The formations eventually selected were: British 50 and 51 Infantry and 1 Airborne
    Divisions; United States 2 Armoured, 1 and 9 Infantry and 82 Airborne Divisions; 7
    British Armoured Division was later added to this list.

4   War Office footnote:- Strategic attacks by the Air Forces which were later based on
    Italy, and other strategic aspects of the campaign, are described in the Supreme Allied
    Commander's Reports on the Italian Campaign (Part I - 8th January, 1944 to 10th May
    1944; Parts II and III - 10th May, 1944 to 12th December, 1944) by Field-Marshal Lord
    Wilson.

5   The best alternative available was an invasion of the Balkans. To do this it would first
    have been necessary, for the sake of air cover, to break into the "outer ring" of islands
    from Crete to Rhodes, a difficult operation in autumn. Balkan terrain is even worse
    suited for offensive operations than Italian, and it must be remembered that our
    amphibious resources were destined to dwindle to the advantage of the Western
    Theatre. A final argument against this course was that the United States Government
    was most reluctant to become involved in a Balkan campaign.

6   Admiral Sir Andrew Cunningham; now Admiral of the Fleet The Viscount Cunningham
    of Hyndhope, K.T., G.C.B., O.M., D.S.O.

7   Also known as Crotone, which, as nearer to the classical form, was favoured by
    Mussolini.

8   1 and 4 British Infantry Divisions for 5 Corps, to be supplemented later by part of 82
    (United States) Airborne Division and 78 Division from Sicily; 7 Armoured, 46 and 56
    Infantry Divisions for 10 Corps.

9   Général d'Armée Henri H. Giraud - Commander-in-Chief French Forces in North
    Africa and Joint President of the French Committee of National Liberation.

10 This was a correct reading of popular feeling, which was marked by complete apathy
    and inertia, but had failed to allow for a "palace revolution".

11 Now Marshal of the Royal Air Force The Lord Tedder, G.C.B.

12 Throughout this Despatch, Corps printed with Roman numerals (e.g. VI Corps) are
    American Corps and those with Arabic numerals (e.g 10 Corps) are British Corps.

13 Enemy air strength within 110 miles of Salerno was calculated at 380 German and 225
    Italian day fighters and 50 night fighters (German); reinforcement within two days at
    140 Italian fighters from North Italy and up to 60 German from Sardinia; bomber
    strength at 270 German and 275 Italian aircraft plus 120 German bombers based in
    Sardinia. For factors governing our own air strategy see Appendix "L" - a
    memorandum by Air Plans, Allied Force Headquarters.

14 By contrast some of the Anzio beaches, for example, had gradients of worse than one in
    a hundred.

15 Now Field-Marshal The Viscount Montgomery of Alamein, K.G., G.C.B., D.S.O.

16 Lieutenant-General (later Sir Brian) Horrocks, K.C.B., K.B.E., D.S.O., M.C., had been
    wounded in an enemy air raid on Bizerta on 19 August. I requested the War Office to

despatch Lieutenant-General (now General Sir Richard) McCreery, G.C.B., K.B.E., D.S.O., M.C. by air to replace him; he had been my Chief of Staff in Middle East and at Eighteenth Army Group.

17   Major-General Ernest J. Dawley, United States Army, later replaced by Major-General John P. Lucas, United States Army.

18   The additional fighters provided in this way by the Fleet Air Arm made a most valuable contribution to our air cover but they could not have been relied upon to the exclusion of land-based fighters for they could only guarantee eighty sorties on the first day, the number dropping rapidly thereafter, and the effort could only be sustained for a little over three days. It is clear therefore that carrier-borne aircraft alone would have been inadequate to support a landing further north.

19   Provided the weather remained fine. Rain would have rendered unserviceable the hastily constructed strips in the Milazzo area and precluded the use of the land-based short-range fighters which were to provide the greater part of the fighter protection over the assault area. It was one more risk involved in the operation.

20   Before the assault naval forces, including battleships, heavily bombarded the coast defences. The assault was supported by three cruisers, three monitors, two gunboats and six destroyers. The naval operations were directed by Rear-Admiral (now Admiral Sir Rhoderick) McGrigor, K.C.B., D.S.O.

21   The Supreme Headquarters of the Armed Forces equivalent to our Chiefs of Staff or the German O.K.W.

22   Major-General (now Lieutenant-General) Walter B. Smith, United States Army and Major-General K.W.D. Strong, C.B., O.B.E. (G-2 = Intelligence branch.)

23   There was, of course, the insurrection of 25 April 1945; but this was after the German armies had been destroyed in battle south of the Po, after they had opened negotiations for surrender and only a week before their final capitulation. I do not wish to disparage in any way the gallant efforts of the Italian Partisans but it is a fact that, up to this date, they did not present a serious military problem to the Germans and were kept in check mainly by second quality troops such as Czechs, Slovaks, Cossacks, etc.

24   For instance the time which elapsed between 18 August, our first contact with the Italians, 3 September, the signing of the armistice and 9 September, the Salerno landing, has been ascribed to our intransigent insistence on, and Italian reluctance to accept, the principle of unconditional surrender. In fact the Italians never, raised any difficulties on this; their delay was caused possibly by natural hesitation and certainly by their desire to discover our plans before committing themselves finally. The date of 9 September, of course, was determined by the availability of landing craft and the phases of the moon.

25   General Castellano has published an account of these negotiations under the title "Come Firmai l'Armistizio di Cassibile". It is strikingly factual and sober.

26   The former was sent, apparently on his own initiative, by General Roatta, Chief of the Army General Staff; Lieutenant-General (now Sir Adrian) Carton de Wiart, V.C., K.B.E., C.B., C.M.G., D.S.O., a prisoner of war in Italy, was released as a pledge of good faith.

27   Marshal Badoglio wanted us to land also at Ancona. Amphibious operations are difficult for the non-expert to understand, as has been clearly demonstrated by the published works on the Italian campaign. It may give a better sense of proportion to point out that the seaborne assault force for the Normandy landings, the supreme effort of the United Kingdom and the United States, was five divisions.

28   *One motorised and three infantry divisions and an armoured division in process of re-formation which was being equipped with German tanks.*

29   *An alternative plan for Fifth Army had been prepared for study on 24 August, in case the increase in enemy strength should make AVALANCHE impracticable. It was suggested that Fifth Army should substitute a direct assault on the Heel of Italy for the landing at Salerno; this operation could not have been carried out before 21 September.*

30   *German losses only. Total Axis prisoners in the final capitulation amounted to 248,000.*

31   *The minutes of the meeting were found among the Mussolini papers.*

32   *This was, roughly, the Trasimene line on which they offered delaying resistance in June 1944 on their withdrawal from Rome to the "Gothic" line.*

33   *It formed the basis for the German "Winter" line of 1943-1944.*

34   *The German order of battle at this date is given at Appendix "B".*

35   *Less its armour. I Battalion of its tank regiment, equipped with Panther tanks, never came to Italy. II Battalion, with Mark III's and IV's, was at this time north of Rome with 3 Panzer Grenadier Division.*

36   *The fact that we gained strategic surprise is sometimes obscured by the fact that we did not gain, nor had hoped for, tactical surprise. To sail, so large a fleet into the Gulf of Salerno without attracting the attention of somebody on shore would have been too much to expect.*

37   *The late Major-General G.F. Hopkinson.*

38   *Lieutenant-General (now Sir Charles) Allfrey, K.B.E., C.B., D.S.O., M.C.*

39   *Brigadier-General (now Major-General) Maxwell D. Taylor, United States Army.*

40   *The Germans had three pre-arranged "states of alarm" (Alarmzustände) for troops on coast defence. Alarmzustand I meant merely that the possibility of an invasion existed and appropriate measures were to be taken; II meant that an invasion fleet was at sea, destination unknown, and all units were to make preparations to be able to move at short notice; III meant that a landing on the unit or formation's actual sector was imminent. State of Alarm II was nothing new for the German coastal troops; it had often been ordered in the past weeks, particularly by units in the Gulf of Gaeta. It is not known when, if ever, State of Alarm III was ordered at Salerno.*

41   *The late Major-General A.A. Richardson.*

42   *The arrival of the craft bringing these reinforcements apparently suggested to the Germans that we were re-embarking; their broadcast propaganda claimed a "Second Dunkirk".*

43   *See Appendix "K".*

44   *Up to 14 September the total transport of I Airborne Division amounted to seven jeeps and two trailers, two requisitioned cars, one motorcycle and two bicycles.*

45   *General Sir Alan Brooke (now Field-Marshal The Viscount Alanbrooke, K.G., G.C.B., O.M., D.S.O.*

46   *In addition on 13 October I was promised 5 Canadian Armoured Division and I Canadian Corps Headquarters with its complement of Corps troops.*

47   *We were at the time pressing hard to get Turkey to declare war and two armoured divisions were standing by in the Middle East for her defence.*

48   *German sources show that the definite order to stand on the line Gaeta - Ortona was given on 10 October but this apparently confirmed an order which had been given slightly earlier.*

49   *German "Winterstellung" which means more properly winter position; it was not a line but a series of defended positions in depth.*

50   *Field-Marshal Albert Kesselring, a regular artillery officer who transferred to the*

Luftwaffe when it was recreated, first came to the Mediterranean in late 1941 as commander of Luftflotte 2. In April 1942 he became "Commander-in-Chief South" with authority over all the shores of the Mediterranean and all arms; he was particularly responsible for the campaign in Africa. He now took the title of Commander-in-Chief Southwest (Oberbefehlshaber Südwest or OBSW); the Army ground forces under his command were known as Army Group "C".

51   *I have here dealt with the proposed operations in the Balkans from the purely military point of view. There were, of course, political reasons both for and against such a course.*

52   *For those to whom such statistics mean little, the mean annual rainfall of London is 23 inches. The Italian winter climate came as a great disappointment to all those who were only acquainted with it from tourist propaganda*

53   *Known as the "Barbara" line.*

54   *Not all these were in fact available to Kesselring whose actual strength available for Italy was nineteen divisions and one brigade group. There was a good deal of movement going on in North Italy at the time: one infantry and three armoured divisions were in process of moving to Russia and three infantry divisions were moving into the country to take their place. There was also some doubt whether the two divisions in the Alps on the Franco - Italian border, which actually came under C-in-C West, were not to be considered as available for Italy and a motorized division which had moved down into the area between Nice and Modane was also regarded as a likely arrival. A certain amount of over-estimation was in the circumstances not unnatural and in any event the disparity of strength was striking enough.*

55   *Actually the Germans were over-estimating our strength, as usual; captured German sources show that they credited me in November with three more divisions than I in fact had.*

56   *Also known as the Colli Laziali or Latin Hills.*

57   *56 Division had been fighting continuously since the landing at Salerno on 9 September. It was understrength then and its subsequent losses had been heavy, particularly in officers and N.C.O.s.*

58   *I Italian Motorised Group, in about brigade strength, which came under command on 31 October, was used once in an offensive role, but was subsequently employed on less active sectors for which its state of armament and training made it more suitable.*

59   *General Sir Henry Maitland Wilson: now Field-Marshal The Lord Wilson of Libya, G.C.B., G.B.E., D.S.O.*

60   *Lieutenant-General Sir Oliver Leese, Bt., K.C.B., C.B.E., D.S.O.*

61   *For a short time it was known as "Allied Central Mediterranean Forces".*

62   *Rear-Admiral F.J. Lowry, United States Navy.*

63   *3 United States Division was nominated on 13 December.*

64   *At that time the target date for the invasion was in May and it was agreed that this readjustment would not affect that date.*

65   *Major-General (now General) Sir Brian Robertson, Bt., K.C.M.G., K.C.V.O., C.B., C.B.E., D.S.O., M.C.*

66   *Lieutenant-General (now Sir John) Harding, K.C.B., C.B.E., D.S.O., M.C.*

67   *Appendices "C" and "D".*

68   *Ten British, five American, two French and one Polish.*

69   *In addition there were dispersed on the seventy-three miles of coast from the Tiber to Terracina three engineer companies and part of the 29 Reconnaissance Battalion.*

70 *His Excellency Lieutenant-General Sir Bernard Freyberg, V.C., G.C.M.G., K.C.B., K.B.E., D.S.O.*

71 *One of our most serious handicaps in Italy was the lack of formations trained and organized for mountain fighting. I had 4 Moroccan Mountain Division for just over three months and eventually got the American 10 Mountain Division, in February 1945, for the last three months. I had frequently asked for the only British Mountain Division, the 52nd. This division was held in reserve in the United Kingdom, presumably for projected operations elsewhere. In fact it was never employed in mountain warfare but was retrained and eventually deployed in Holland in the autumn of 1944.*

72 *Major-General (now Lieutenant-General) Lucien K. Truscott Jr., United States Army - subsequently Commanding General, Fifth Army.*

73 *German sources give their casualties from 16 to 20 February as 5,389 in killed, wounded and missing.*

74 *Major-General (now Lieutenant-General) John K. Cannon, United States Army Air Force.*

75 *The technical experience we gained from this experiment was subsequently of great use on the Western front.*

76 *I was not then aware of the proposed date for OVERLORD.*

77 *As far as Italy was concerned, the fallacy of the policy of attacks on marshalling yards, lay in the fact that these are usually on level ground and always contain a large number of parallel tracks so that any damage can be rapidly repaired and a through line established in a very brief time. A reduction in rolling stock and facilities was of little importance as for their military purposes the Germans only needed about sixteen per cent. of the total available. A broken bridge, on the other hand, meant a long delay and stores had to be ferried round the break by road, thus wasting as much fuel as would be lost from the destruction of a good-sized dump.*

78 *As I have already explained, it was well below strength when it went to the bridgehead, and had been fighting continuously since 9 September.*

79 *Kesselring ordered at 1840 hours 1 March all concentrated attacks to be halted; Mackensen had already called off the offensive. German losses in the two days amounted to 2,215 (excluding 362 Division's losses for 29 February).*

80 *The first elements of the Parachutists had arrived for the second battle, in February, when they held the heights, including Monastery Hill. For the March assault they were responsible for the town as well.*

81 *Captured enemy documents show that they were aware of the move of Eighth Army Headquarters though they placed it some twelve miles from its true location, presumably by an error in Direction Finding.*

82 *A good example is 15 Panzer Grenadier Division. This was one of the hardest worked formations in Tenth Army and only came out of the line at the beginning of May but its strength on 6 May was 13,984 plus 915 Italians employed mainly in the divisional services.*

83 *Appendix "F".*

84 *Appendix "E".*

85 *A Goum equals roughly a company and a Tabor a battalion, both on the large side. The total of goumiers was about 12,000. They are native Moroccan troops under French officers and N.C.O.s and are particularly skilled in mountain warfare.*

86 *The Polish divisions were only two brigades strong, however, so that the Corps amounted to one armoured and four infantry brigades.*

87 *The name of my headquarters had been changed on 9 March from "Allied Central*

Mediterranean Forces" to "Allied Armies in Italy" and this was the first operation order issued since the change of title.

88   The Hermann Goering Division was at Leghorn, and responsible for guarding the coast in that area but for this we cannot claim the credit; the division was still earmarked for France.

89   The date of the attack was also well concealed. Captured documents show that General von Vietinghoff, commanding Tenth Army, proposed to return to Germany on leave on II May. One of his Corps Commanders picked on 24 May as our D-day

90   As an example of the losses in ferries, in I0 Brigade sector on the right of 4 Division, all but five boats out of forty had been lost by 0800 hours on I2May and by I600 hours there were none left.

9I   Général de Corps d'Armée (now Général d'Armée) A.P. Juin, K.C.B., Commander of the French Expeditionary Corps.

92   305 and 334 Infantry Divisions; they were replaced by 278 Infantry Division from Istria.

93   The last detachment of 26 Panzer Division had left for the main front just before VI Corps attacked; it was consequently of no use to either sector at the moment it was most needed.

94   The German offer to declare Rome an open city belongs rather to a history of propaganda than to a military history. The offer was broadcast at a time when Allied troops were already in the outskirts of the city following hard on the heels of the enemy retreating through it. In the circumstances the enemy undertaking "to carry out no troop movements in Rome" was both belated and insincere. The most significant point about this announcement is that it showed the Germans had not expected Rome to fall so soon.

95   Shortly before the operation the codename was changed to DRAGOON.

96   The loss of the French was particularly severely felt as they were expected to repeat in the Apennines their feats in the Aurunci mountains. 4 Moroccan Mountain Division was, as I have explained, my only mountain division.

97   We took this name from a map captured in Kesselring's Headquarters at Monte Soratte and it was the name we always used for the line. This name "Gotenstellung" appears to have been given to the whole Apennine position in the planning stage but on I6 June it was changed to the "Green" Line (Grüne Linie), which was what the Germans called the actual line on the ground. There is no special connection between the Northern Apennines and the Goths but the Germans often showed themselves conscious, not only by their behaviour, that in Italy they were treading in the footsteps of their barbarous forefathers; for instance two minor defensive positions in Campania were called after Totila and Alboin.

98   Other reinforcements were of less value. Two German equipped Italian divisions arrived towards the end of July and were employed at first on coastal defence and internal security. The Czech Army had arrived in Northern Italy about the time of the fall of Rome. It was twelve battalions strong and was used mainly for guarding railways and dumps in Northern Italy and keeping order among the Italian population. I Slovak Infantry Division, reorganised as a "Technical Brigade" for work on fortifications, had been in Italy since January I944. There were also various Russian formations and units but, except for I62 Division and certain battalions, these were also normally employed only in rear areas. The indirect contribution of all these non-German formations in releasing German troops for active service was, of course, considerable.

99   I intended to employ only the minimum force necessary in the pursuit; among other

reasons maintenance ruled out a large force, as railhead was still back in the Cassino area. The remaining divisions were grounded in areas where they could be easily maintained.

100   *Général de Corps d'Armée E.R.M. de Larminat.*

101   *General Wladyslaw Anders, C.B.E., D.S.O.*

102   *The position was apparently reconnoitred in August 1943 when the Germans considered holding a line Grosseto - Monte - Amiata - Perugia - Ancona.*

103   *I warned General Leese not to fall into the same trap as the Romans on this spot; he assured me that he had carefully studied the records of the earlier battle and would avoid the errors of Flaminius.*

104   *These included: a mechanized Cavalry Reconnaissance Squadron, three tank battalions, three tank destroyer battalions, eleven batteries of artillery, two engineer combat regiments and a combat battalion, and a large number of anti-aircraft units. Between 1 June and 1 August the strength of Fifth Army fell by almost forty per cent., from 249,000 to 153,000.*

105   *78 Division, which had been engaged almost continuously since Sicily, was due to leave for the Middle East in the normal programme of rotation; 46 and 56 Divisions were returning from the Middle East to replace it.*

106   *He may also have been influenced in this by our deception plan which indicated the Adriatic sector as the area of our intended attack on the "Gothic" line.*

107   *The ones with which we were most concerned were, from south to north, "Irmgard", "Karin", "Lydia", "Maedchen", "Olga" and "Paula".*

108   *The clearing of the Pontassieve loop of the Arno, east of Florence, lasted until 9 August.*

109   *6 South African Armoured, 1 British and 8 Indian Infantry Divisions. The South Africans were later put under command of IV Corps and replaced by 6 British Armoured Division. 78 Division was added in October.*

110   *Appendices "G" and "H".*

111   *Later renumbered 8 Mountain Division.*

112   *20 Luftwaffe Field Division was not a very important reserve and its location is irrelevant to the problem. 90 Panzer Grenadier Division, before its move to the north-west, had been resting west of Bologna.*

113   *Relieved by 42 Jaeger Division from Genoa.*

114   *I had received 13,000 infantry replacements from the United Kingdom in April 1944 and was told that I should have no more. Realizing that this quota would not last beyond the end of July I set on foot a plan for creating more reinforcements from theatre resources. By disbanding Light Anti-Aircraft and some Royal Armoured Corps units I got together 17,000 reinforcements, 9,000 of which went to infantry units. In August I converted a further 5,000 gunners into infantry but even this was insufficient to make up for our losses in the "Gothic" line battles.*

115   *232 and 237 Infantry Divisions had now arrived to replace 3 and 15 Panzer Grenadier Divisions; the former went, in the first place, to Liguria and the latter to Istria. It will be remembered that August and September, the period when this reinforcement of Italy was set in train, were months of very severe crisis on the Western Front.*

116   *General Eisenhower's forces first crossed the German frontier on 11 September.*

117   *I am unable to say definitely when I crossed the Rubicon until historians decide which river it is; the Uso, Fiumicino and Pisciatello are the candidates in that order of preference.*

118 There was a further unsuccessful counter-attack on Monte La Battaglia on the night of 10/11 October.

119 Although the Italian weather is regular only in its extreme variability and although heavy rainfall is a feature of every month in the calendar the rain in September and October 1944 was both heavier and earlier in its incidence than the general average of past years seemed to prognosticate.

120 At the beginning of October Field-Marshal Kesselring was seriously injured in a car accident on Route 9 and did not return until the end of December. He was succeeded in the interim by General von Vietinghoff of Tenth Army.

121 Lieutenant-General (now General) Jacob L. Devers, United States Army.

122 One brigade of 46 Division in November; 4 British Infantry Division during December; remainder of 46 Division during January and February.

123 Since the end of July the Germans had been at work on a line of permanent defences based on the Adige and the Euganean and Berici hills, running from the Adriatic at Chioggia to Lake Garda; it was known as the "Venetian" line and by October was already formidable. Defences were also prepared on the line of the Po - Ticino and, south of the Po, on the Santerno, Sillaro and Idice, the last-named known as the "Genghis Khan" position.

124 The Germans were known to be constructing defences on the two last, in rear of the "Venetian" line.

125 In the event 4 Division went to Greece and the 5th to Twenty-first Army Group in Germany.

126 General McCreery considered that by 7 December he would probably only be on the Senio; a fresh break in the weather was the main factor which helped to prove him right.

127 Major-General Lyman L. Lemnitzer, United States Army.

128 Now Admiral of the Fleet Sir John Cunningham, G.C.B., M.V.O.

129 Besides providing gun support, the Allied Navies, up to the breakout from the beachhead on 23rd May, landed no less than 478,407 tons of ammunition and supplies, in the face of air attack.

130 The late Air Marshal Sir Arthur Coningham.

131 Lieutenant-General John K. Cannon, United States Army Air Force.

131 20 Luftwaffe Field Division had by then been absorbed into 26 Panzer Division.

132 The German Order of Battle on 9th April, 1945 is given at Appendix "J".

133 On 10th April XCVII Corps in north-eastern Italy, with two divisions, was transferred to the Commander-in-Chief South-east. There were also in Italy various foreign levies, a Cossack division, 29 S.S. Grenadier Division (Italian troops with German officers) and other Italian formations to a strength of 126,000.

134 These figures are from an official German document from Headquarters Army Group "C".

135 This was a disheartening result for the large organization engaged in propaganda and "Psychological Warfare" to the German troops. In general the verdict must be that this had no military effect whatsoever; the enemy continued to resist beyond the limits of what could have been thought possible. Such deserters as gave themselves up during the campaign were naturally claimed as successes of our psychological warfare but it would be difficult to prove that they would not have deserted in any case, especially as the great majority of them were persons of non-German origin, forcibly conscripted. There will always be deserters in a war fought in such unpleasant conditions; the surprising thing is that their numbers were so entirely insignificant.

136 *The Allied Order of Battle at 9th April, 1945, is given at Appendix "I".*

137 *We did, however, achieve our usual success in deceiving the enemy as to our plans. By simulating an intention to make an amphibious landing on the Venetian coast (which my naval advisers assured me was in fact quite impossible) we persuaded him to divert 29 Panzer Grenadier Division, his principal mobile reserve, north of the Po. Not only did this reduce his ability to resist Eighth Army's attack but also it was a great strain on enemy resources to carry out this lengthy move, eating into the meagre fuel stocks available, and then to bring the division, when the deception was discovered, back again over the Po crossings under the hammering of our air attack to be thrown too late into a losing battle.*

138 *This does not include casualties inflicted on the Italians, when they were still at war with us, or the Germans who surrendered after the capitulation. The German figures referred to cover the period from 3 September 1943 to 20 April 1945.*

139 *Another interesting figure is the total of nationalities under my command - twenty-six. A full list is given in Appendix "A."*

140 *That is to say, the real answer had they known it, since their faulty Intelligence continually overrated our strength they undoubtedly believed themselves to be containing forces superior to their own almost all the time. The chief advantage of our own Intelligence was that it enabled us to achieve our object with the greatest economy of force.*

141 *Twenty-five in Italy, nineteen in the Balkans and eleven in the South of France.*

142 *Including a Negro division and a Japanese-American Regimental Combat Team.*

143 *Including Algerian, Moroccan, Tunisian and Senegalese.*

144 *The title in use at this date was "Allied Central Mediterranean Force" (See footnote on Page 43).*

145 *Transferred to Army Group "E" on 10th April, 1945.*

146 *Major-General (now General) Sir Brian Robertson, Bt., K.C.M.G., K.C.V.O., C.B., C.B.E., D.S.O., M.C.*

147 *North African Theatre of Operations, United States Army.*

148 *Annex I.*

149 *I add a note, at Annex II, on the maintenance of the Anzio bridgehead, which presented certain original features.*

150 *One novel expedient was tried in the administration of the Anzio bridgehead and, contrary to the Navy's expectations, fully justified itself. Everyday a number of American 2 ton cargo trucks were loaded with 5 tons of supplies at Naples and were driven on board Landing Ships, Tank which then sailed for Anzio. On arrival there the trucks were driven direct to dumps and unloaded. Empty trucks were loaded with salvage and then taken back to Naples in the returning ships. Great flexibility was achieved in this way, and large quantities of supplies needed in an emergency could be provided within 72 hours of the emergency arising.*

151 *Its initial capacity was for four Landing Ships, Tank, and three Landing Craft, Tank. Ten days later it could berth eight Landing Ships, Tank, eight Landing Craft, Tank and five Landing Craft, Infantry at the same time.*

ABBREVIATIONS

A/S	Anti-Submarine
AA	Anti-Aircraft
AFHQ	Allied Force Headquarters
Alg.	Algerian
AMGOT	Allied Military Government of Occupied Territories
Armd.	Armoured
ASV	Aircraft to Surface Vessel (radar)
Br.	British
Bt, Btn	Battalion
BYMS	British Yacht Minesweeper
Carp.	Carpathian
CB	Companion of The Most Honourable Order of the Bath
CBE	Commander of the Order of the British Empire
CCB	Combat Command "B" (Armoured Brigade Group of about divisional strength)
Cdn.	Canadian
CG NATOUSA	Commanding General, North African Theatre of Operations, United States Army
C-in-C	Commander-in-Chief
C-in-CFF	Commander-in-Chief French Forces
CIH	Central India Horse
CIL	*Corpo Italiano della Liberazione* (an Italian formation)
CSI	Companion of the Order of the Star of India
DSO	Distinguished Service Order
F/B	Fighter/Bomber
FOSY	Flag Officer Sicily
GAF	German Air Force
GCB	Knight Grand Cross of The Most Honourable Order of the Bath
GCIE	Knight Grand Commander of The Most Eminent Order of the Indian Empire
GCSI	Knight Grand Commander of The Most Exalted Order of the Star of India

GCVO	Knight Grand Cross of The Royal Victorian Order
GHQ	General Headquarters
GOC	General Officer Commanding
GOC in C	General Officer Commanding-in-Chief
Gp.	Group
GSOI	General Staff Officer I
HCR	Household Cavalry Regiment
HDML	Harbour Defence Motor Launch
HMS	His Majesty's Ship
HNMS	His Norwegian Majesty's Ship
HQ	Headquarters
Hrs.	Hours
Ind.	Indian
KBE	Knight Commander of the Most Excellent Order of the British Empire
KCB	Knight Commander of the Most Honourable Order of the Bath
KCIE	Knight Commander of The Most Eminent Order of the Indian Empire
KCMG	Knight Commander of The Most Distinguished Order of Saint Michael and Saint George
KCSI	Knight Commander of The Most Exalted Order of the Star of India
KCVO	Knight Commander of The Royal Victorian Order
KG	Knight of the Most Noble Order of the Garter
KMF	UK to North Africa Fast (a convoy designation)
KMS	UK to North Africa Slow (a convoy designation)
Kres.	Kresowa
KRRC	King's Royal Rifle Corps
KT	Knight Companion of The Most Ancient and Most Noble Order of the Thistle
L of C	Line(s) of Communication
LCA	Landing Craft, Assault
LCF	Landing Craft, Flak
LCG	Landing Craft, Gun
LCM	Landing Craft, Mechanized
LCP	Landing Craft, Personnel
LCP(L)	Landing Craft, Personnel (Large)
LCR	Landing Craft, Rocket
LCS	Landing Craft, Support
LCT	Landing Craft, Tank
LR	Long Range
LSI	Landing Ship, Infantry

LSP	Landing Ship, Personnel
LST	Landing Ship, Tank
Lt-Gen	Lieutenant Colonel
M/S	Mine Sweeping
Manch.	Manchester Regiment
MC	Military Cross
MKF	Mediterranean–UK Fast (a convoy designation)
MKS	Mediterranean–UK Slow (a convoy designation)
ML	Motor Launch
MMS	Motor Minesweeper
Mor.	Moroccan
Mot.	Motorised
MT	Motor Transport
Mtn.	Mountain
NATOUSA	North African Theatre of Operations, United States Army
NCETF	Naval Commander Eastern Task Force
NCFA	Naval Commander Force "A"
NCFB	Naval Commander Force "B"
NCFV	Naval Commander Force "V"
NOIC	Naval Officer In Charge
NZ	New Zealand
OBE	Most Excellent Order of the British Empire
OM	Order of Merit
Para.	Parachute
Pol.	Polish
PT	Patrol Torpedo (boat)
RCT	Regimental Combat Team
RDF	Radio Direction Finding (radar)
SA	South African
SAS	Special Air Service
SB (Squadron)	Special Boat (Squadron)
SE	Single-engined [*sic*]
SEF	Single-engined [*sic*] fighter(s)
SNOL	Senior Naval Officer Landing
SS	Steam Ship
SSF	Special Service Force
TEF	Twin-engined [*sic*] fighter(s)
Tk.	Tank
US	United States
USN	United States Navy
V/S	Visual Sighting
VC	Victoria Cross

INDEX OF NAVAL, MILITARY AND AIR FORCE UNITS

Orders of Battle are detailed in the various appendices and the entries for these do not feature in this index.

INDEX OF PERSONS